The Right to Development in International Law

The Case of Pakistan

The Right to Development in International Law rigorously explores the right to development (RTD) from the perspectives of international as well as the constitutionally guaranteed fundamental rights and the Islamic concept of social justice in Pakistan. The volume draws on a wide range of relevant sources to analyse the legal status of international cooperation in contemporary international law, before exploring the domestic application of the right to development looking at the example of Pakistan, a country that is undergoing radical transformation in terms of its internal governance structures and the challenges it faces for enforcing the rule of law. Of particular importance is the examination of the RTD and *Shari'ah* law in Pakistan which adds a new perspective to the RTD debate and enriches the discussion about human rights and *Shari'ah* across the world.

Through focusing on Pakistan the book links international perspectives and the international human rights framework with the domestic constitutional apparatus for enforcing the RTD within that jurisdiction. In doing so, Khurshid Iqbal argues that the RTD may be promoted through existing constitutional mechanisms if fundamental rights are widely interpreted by the superior courts, effectively implemented by the lower courts and if *Shari'ah* law is progressively interpreted in the public interest.

Iqbal's work will appeal to researchers, professionals and students in the fields of law, human rights, development, international law, South Asian Studies, Islamic law and international development studies.

Dr Khurshid Iqbal researches and teaches Constitutional Law, International Human Rights Law and International Trade Law. Iqbal is an Additional District and Sessions Judge in Pakistan. He holds an MA in Politics and LLB from Peshawar (Pakistan), an LLM from Hull (UK) and a PhD from Ulster, N. Ireland.

Routledge Research in Human Rights Law

Forthcoming titles in this series include:

Children and International Human Rights Law: The Right of the Child to be Heard
Aisling Parkes

The European Convention on Human Rights and its new Contracting Parties
Democratic transition and consolidation in the European Jurisprudence
James A. Sweeney

The Right to Religious Freedom in International Law
Between group rights and individual rights
Anat Scolnicov

The Right to Health
Global Health and Human Rights
John Harrington and Maria Stuttaford

The Right to Development in International Law

The Case of Pakistan

Khurshid Iqbal

Routledge
Taylor & Francis Group
LONDON AND NEW YORK

First published 2010
by Routledge
2 Park Square, Milton Park, Abingdon, Oxon, OX14 4RN

Simultaneously published in the USA and Canada
by Routledge
270 Madison Avenue, New York, NY 10016

Routledge is an imprint of the Taylor & Francis Group, an informa business

Typeset in Garamond by RefineCatch Limited, Bungay, Suffolk
Printed and bound in Great Britain by
CPI Antony Rowe, Chippenham, Wiltshire

British Library Cataloguing in Publication Data
A catalogue record for this book is available from the British Library

Library of Congress Cataloging-in-Publication Data
Iqbal, Khurshid.
The right to development in international law : the case of Pakistan / Khurshid Iqbal.
p. cm.
Simultaneously published in the USA and Canada.
Includes bibliographical references.
1. Human rights—Pakistan. 2. Rule of law—Pakistan. 3. Islamic law—Pakistan. 4. Law and economic development. 5. Economic development—Religious aspects—Islam. 6. Social justice—Pakistan. I. Title.
KPL2095.I63 2009
342.549108'5—dc22

2009000265

ISBN 10: 0–415–47941–X (hbk)
ISBN 10: 0–203–87497–8 (ebk)

ISBN 13: 978–0–415–47941–7 (hbk)
ISBN 13: 978–0–203–87497–4 (ebk)

To my (late) father, who inculcated in me a spirit of lifelong learning and to my mother (may she live long), who taught me patience and tolerance

Contents

Acknowledgements xiii
List of Abbreviations xv
Table of Cases xix
Table of Statutory Material xxiii

1 Introduction 1

Background and research thesis 1
International dimension of the RTD 3
Why Pakistan as a case study? 4
Human rights and development 8
Pakistan: towards a rights-based approach to development? 12
Approach of the book 12
Structure of the book 14

PART I
The RTD: Concept and challenges 17

2 History, politics and concept of the RTD 19

Introduction 19
Historical overview 19
From economic sovereignty to the RTD 19
The Declaration (1986) 22
The Vienna Declaration (1993) 22
The current status of the RTD (2004–2007) 23
Regional and national perspectives 24
The politics of the RTD 26
The North–South divide 26
The political positions of states/groups of states 27
The voting trends in the General Assembly 29

The Commission on Human Rights 32
Human rights in development programmes 34
Conceptual basis 35
The capability approach 35
Capability and human rights 37
List of capabilities 39
Realizing capabilities through the RTD 39
Islamic perspective vis-à-vis capability and human rights 40
Conclusion 41

3 The jurisprudence of the RTD 43

Introduction 43
Sources 44
The right to self-determination 44
Article 28 of the UDHR 48
Articles 55 and 56 of the UN Charter 49
Other international instruments 51
Subjects 52
State as a subject 52
State as a duty-holder 53
Peoples as a subject 54
Individual as a subject 55
Content 56
Individual right 57
Collective right 58
The right to a process of development 59
Justiciability 62
Rights and duties in analytical jurisprudence 64
Rights as goals: ethical jurisprudence 66
The Maastricht Guidelines 68
The pluralistic foundations of human rights 70
Justiciability at the national level 71
Justiciability at the international level 73
Rights and duties in Islamic jurisprudence 74
Conclusion 74

4 The declaration and the working groups 77

Introduction 77
The first working group and the drafting of the Declaration 79
The working group report 79

An analysis of the working group report 80
The drafting of the Declaration 81
The main features of the Declaration 83
Unity of human rights 83
Participation 84
International cooperation 86
The concept of development 87
Sustainable development 90
Weaknesses of the Declaration 92
Vague and imprecise 92
A compromise document 93
Reference to the NIEO 94
Women's rights 95
Realization of the RTD 96
The global consultation 96
The second and third working groups 98
The current status of the realization 100
The independent expert and the task force 100
The Development Compact 101
Debate in the working group 103
A critical appraisal of the Development Compact 104
The high-level task force 105
Evaluation of the task force reports 107
Conclusion 108

PART II
The RTD in international law 111

5 The legal status of the RTD in public international law 113

Introduction 113
Sources of international law 114
Custom 115
What is meant by 'recommendation'? 116
Opinio juris 119
State practice 122
Is the USA a 'persistent objector'? 126
General principles of law 128
Is the Declaration a soft law? 130
The RTD and 'new sources' 132
The value of the Declaration: determining factors 135

Competency of General Assembly 135
'The nature and content' 136
'Time and circumstances' 136
'Terms and intent' or language 136
'Voting pattern' 137
'International organization practice' 137
Implementation or follow-up mechanism 138
'Community values, needs and expectations' 138
Conclusion 140

PART III
The RTD at the national level: Pakistan as a case study 143

6 The nature and extent of the realization of the RTD in Pakistan 145

Introduction 145
The political economy of Pakistan 146
Economy: far from distributive justice 146
Constitution-making: still a dilemma 147
The national dimension of the RTD 152
The Declaration 152
Pakistan's role in the mainstream RTD debate 153
Constitutional mechanisms versus the features of the RTD 154
The nature of the constitutional obligations 155
Public Interest Litigation: prospects for the RTD 156
Conceptual basis 156
An analysis of case law 157
Right to life (Article 9) 158
Prohibition of forced labour (Article 11) 159
Freedom of association (Article 25): political participation 161
Equality of citizens (Article 25) 162
Women's rights 162
Protection of the environment 163
The Principles of Policy 165
Problems and prospects of PIL 166
Impact of the current judicial crisis 167
Conclusion 169

7 Reconceptualizing the RTD in Islamic law 171

Introduction 171

Shari'ah: meaning, sources and purpose 171
Meaning of the *Shari'ah* 171
Primary sources: the Qur'an and the Sunnah 173
Juristic techniques 175
The purpose of the *Shari'ah*: the doctrine of *maslahah* 176
Maslahah and the RTD 178
General relevance of *maslahah* to the RTD 178
Human rights and Islamic law 181
The challenge of cultural relativism 181
How to achieve compatibility 184
Islamization and the RTD in Pakistan 186
Jinnah's vision of Pakistan 186
The Objectives Resolution 188
The Islamic provisions of the 1973 constitution 189
The Islamic concept of social justice 190
Zia's Islamization movement and the RTD 191
The judicial system 191
Economic reform 193
Implications for the RTD 194
The role of the judiciary 197
Implications for other Muslim countries 200
Conclusion 201

8 **Pakistan's Poverty-Reduction Strategy and the RTD** 203

Introduction 203
The PRSP framework 204
Introduction and background 204
The guidelines 205
Principles of the PRSP and the RTD 207
Country ownership 207
Participation 209
Other principles 211
Pakistan's PRSP and the RTD 212
National ownership and participation 212
AJP in the PRSP 216
Governance 217
The rule of law 218
The judiciary in the RTD debate 219
The guidelines and judicial reforms 220
Guideline 8 and the AJP 220

(A) *Importance of the right of equal access to justice* 220
(A.1) *The rationale of the AJP* 221
(B) *The scope of the right of equal access to justice (the guideline)* 222
(B.1) *Objectives and scope of the AJP* 222
(C) *Key targets and indicators* 224
(C.1) *The AJP* 224
(D) *Key features of a strategy for realizing the right of equal access to justice* 224
(D.1) *The AJP framework* 225
(D.2) *A comparison of the two strategies* 225
Evaluation of the AJP 230
Conclusion 231

9 **Conclusion** 233

Glossary of Islamic words 239
Bibliography 241
Index 261

Acknowledgements

Two institutions deserve my gratitude in the first instance: the Peshawar High Court (Pakistan) and the University of Ulster (UK). Mr Justice Mian Shakirullah Jan, the former Chief Justice of the Peshawar High Court (now an Honourable Judge of the Supreme Court of Pakistan) generously allowed me three years' leave for my PhD studies in the UK. The University of Ulster provided me with full financial support through the Vice Chancellor Research Studentship. Next, credit must go to Professor Javaid Rehman and Dermot Feenan, School of Law and Professor Siddiq-ur-Rehman Osmani, Department of Economics, University of Ulster, who supervised my PhD studies. Professor Rehman deserves special thanks because he continued to support me informally even after he moved to undertake an assignment at Brunel University, London.

I am highly grateful to my personal friend, Dr Niaz A. Shah, lecturer, Hull University. Throughout my studies, Dr Shah always helped me to keep myself on the right track. Without his moral support, it would have been impossible to make this book ready for publication. Thanks are also due to Professor Muhammad Munir, Department of Law, International Islamic University, Islamabad, for his valuable comments on Chapter 7 of this book. I must express my thanks to Dr Francis Bolchway, Hull University and Prof. Joshua Castellino, Ulster University for their appreciable suggestions.

The staff of the library of Queen's University, Belfast assisted me greatly in obtaining some of the most relevant reading material. My special thanks are due to them. I also appreciate the help of the staff of the library of the United Nations Office at Geneva who, at the request of Professor Osmani, sent me relevant documents.

The support of some of my friends and colleagues from Pakistan may also be mentioned here. Mr Niaz Muhammad Khan, Additional District and Sessions Judge, and Mr Bashirullah Khan, Advocate of the High Court, took the trouble to send me up-to-date and relevant judicial cases for some parts of my studies. Throughout this long journey, my wife always stood by me in all circumstances and shared all my stress and strain. Our trips to some of the most attractive seasides of Northern Ireland and our frequent roaming in the Belfast Botanic Gardens in the beautiful Irish summers will always remain alive in our memories.

List of Abbreviations

ACP	African Caribbean and Pacific Countries
ADB	Asian Development Bank
ADR	Alternative Dispute Resolution
AJDF	Access to Justice Development Fund
AJK	Azad Jammu and Kashmir
AJP	Access to Justice Programme
APRM	African Peer Review Mechanism
AU	African Union (formerly Organization of African Unity)
CCA	Common Country Assessment
CDA	Capital Development Authority
CDF	Comprehensive Development Framework
CEDR	Centre for Effective Dispute Resolution
CHR	(UN) Commission (now Council) on Human Rights
CPAG	Child Poverty Action Group
CRC	Conventions on the Rights of the Child
CSOs	Civil Society Organisations
DAC	Development Assistance Committee
DRD	Declaration on the Right to Development
DSU	Dispute Settlement Understanding
ECA	Economic Commission for Africa
ECOSOC	Economic and Social Council
EIROP	Essential Institutional Reforms Operationalization Programme
EU	European Union
FAO	Food and Agriculture Organization
FIDH	International Federation for Human Rights
FRG	Federal Republic of Germany
FSC	Federal Shariat Court
GATT	General Agreement on Tariffs and Trade
GDP	Gross Domestic Product
GNI	Gross National Income
GNP	Gross National Product
HDR	Human Development Report
HIPC	Heavily Indebted Poor Countries

HPI	Human Poverty Index
HRCP	Human Rights Commission of Pakistan
ICCPR	International Covenant on Civil and Political Rights
ICESCR	International Covenant on Economic, Social and Cultural Rights
ICJ	International Court of Justice
IFC	International Finance Corporation
IFIs	International Financial Institutions
ILO	International Labour Organization
IMF	International Monetary Fund
IT	Information Technology
KDCs	Key Donor Countries
LMG	Like-Minded Group
MCA	Millennium Challenge Account
MDGs	Millennium Development Goals
MMA	Muttahida Majlis-e-Amal
NAM	Non-Alignment Movement
NEAP	National Environmental Action Plan
NEPAD	New Partnership for Africa's Development
NGO	Non-Governmental Organisation
NIEO	New International Economic Order
NJPMC	National Judicial Policy Making Committee
NRB	National Reconstruction Bureau
NWFP	North West Frontier Province
ODA	Official Development Assistance
ODI	Overseas Development Institute
OECD	Organisation of Economic Cooperation and Development
OEWG	Open-Ended Working Group
OHCHR	Office of the High Commissioner for Human Rights
OIC	Organization of Islamic Conference
PCr.LJ	Pakistan Criminal Law Journal
PEPI-MENA	Private Enterprise Partnership–Middle East and North Africa
PIL	Public Interest Litigation
PILER	Pakistan Institute of Labour Education and Research
PLD	Pakistan Legal Decisions
PLJ	Pakistan Law Journal
PRSC	Poverty Reduction Strategy Credit
PRSP	Poverty Reduction Strategy Paper
RTD	Right to Development
SAARC	South Asian Association for Regional Cooperation
SDC	Swiss Development Cooperation
TCT	Technical Consolidated Text
UDHR	Universal Declaration of Human Rights
UIDHR	Universal Islamic Declaration of Human Rights

UK	United Kingdom
UN	United Nations
UNCTAD	United Nations Conference on Trade and Development
UNDAF	United Nations Development Assistance Framework
UNDG	United Nations Development Group
UNDP	United Nations Development Programme
UNESCO	United Nations Educational, Scientific and Cultural Organisation
UNGA	United Nations General Assembly
UNHCHR	United Nations High Commissioner for Human Rights
UNICEF	United Nations Children's Fund (formerly United Nations International Children's Emergency Fund)
UNITAR	United Nations Institute for Training and Research
USA	United States of America
WAPDA	Water and Power Development Authority
WHO	World Health Organization
WSSD	World Summit on Sustainable Development
WTO	World Trade Organization

Table of Cases

Bangladesh
Hefzur Rahman Case 47 (1995) Dhaka Law Reports 54 (Bangladesh) 13

Human Rights Committee
Hertzberg v Finland, Communication No. R.14/61 (7 August 1979), U.N. Doc. Supp. No. 40 (A/37/40) 185

India
Almitra H. Patel v Union of India, 2000, 3 SCC 166. 167
Mehta (M. C.) v Union of India and Others, AIR 1996 SC 2231 167
Municipal Council, Ratlam v Shri Vardichand and Others, 1980. 166
Pattanayak (Kishen) v State of Orissa, AIR 1989 SC 677 166
Shah Bano Case, AIR 1986 SC 945 13

International Court of Justice (ICJ)
Case Concerning Military and Paramilitary Activities in and against Nicaragua (Nicaragua v United States of America) 1986 WL 522 (I.C.J.), 1986 I.C.J. 14 . . . 117, 121
Case Concerning the Barcelona Traction, Light and Power Company, Limited (New Application: 1962) (Belgium v Spain) 1970 WL 1 (I.C.J.), 1970 I.C.J. 3 50
Case Concerning the Gabcikovo-Nagymaros Project, (Hungary/Slovakia), 1997 WL 1168556 (I.C.J.), 1997 I.C.J. 7 . . . . 25, 91, 117–18
Fisheries Case, United Kingdom v Norway 1951 WL 12 (I.C.J.), 1951 I.C.J. 116. 117
North Sea Continental Shelf Case ICJ Reports [1969]. 119
Reservation to the Convention on the Prevention and Punishment of the Crime of Genocide 1951 WL 3 (I.C.J.), 1951 I.C.J. 15 117
Voting Procedure on Questions Relating to Reports and Petitions Concerning the Territory of South-West Africa 1955 WL 2 (I.C.J.), 1955 I.C.J. 67 116

Pakistan
Abbas (Akhtar) v Nayyar Hussain, 1982 SCMR 549 158
Akram (Muhammad) v Mst. Farman Bi, PLD 1990 SC 28. 198
Ali (Ghulam) v Mst. Ghulam Sarwar Naqvi, PLD 1990 SC 1 163
Al-Jehad Trust 1999 SCMR 1379 162
Begum (Zohra) v Sh. Latif Ahmad Munawwar, PLD 1965 (West Pakistan) Lahore 695 . . . 197
Bhutto (Begum Nusrat) v Chief of Army Staff, PLD 1977 SC 657 149
Bhutto (Benazir) and another v Federation of Pakistan and another, PLD 1989 SC 66 161
Bhutto (Benazir) v Federation of Pakistan, PLD 1988 SC 416. . . . . 6, 158, 165
Bibi (Khurshid) v Muhammad Amin PLD 1967 SC 97 197

Bibi (Sajida) v Incharge, Chouki No. 2 Police Station Saddar, Sahiwal, PLD 1997 Lah. 666 163
Botta (Muhammad) v Commissioner Sargodha, PLD 1973 Lah. 580 157
Bukhsh (Huzoor) v Federation of Pakistan, Federal Shariat Court 1981, 145 13
Burney (Ansar) v Federation of Pakistan, PLD 1983 Federal Shariat Court 73 198–9
Chowdhry (Fazlul Quader) v Muhammad Abdul Haq, PLD 1963 SC 486 197
Cowasjee (Ardeshir) v Multiline Associates, Karachi, PLD 1993 Kar. 237 158
Haider (Moulvi Iqbal) v Capital Development Authority, PLD 2006 SC 394. . . . . 12, 164
Human Rights Case (Environmental Pollution in Baluchistan), PLD 1994 SC 102 163–4
Human Rights Case No 5091 160
Jan (Fazal) v Roshan Din, PLD 1992 SC 811 163
Jan (Mian Fazal) v Lahore Development Trust, PLD 1969 SC 223. 157
Jilani (Miss Asma) v Government of Pakistan, PLD 1972 S.C. 139. 148
Khan (Haji Nizam) v Additional District Judge, Lyallpur, PLD 1976 Lah. 930 197
Khan (Maulvi Tamiz-ud-Din) v Governor-General of Pakistan, PLD 1955 Federal Court 240. 147
Khan (Tika Iqbal Muhammad) v General Pervez, PLD 2008 SC 615 . . . . . 150, 167, 168
Masih (Darshan) v The State, PLD1990 SC 513 . . . . . 158, 159
Mehmood (Humaira) v State, PLD 1999 Lahore 494 198
Mina (Jehan) v The State, PLJ 1983 FSC 134 199
Munir (Shirin) v Government of Punjab, PLD 1990 SC 295 . . . . . 12, 163, 165
Nasreen v Fayyaz Khan, PLD 1991 SC 412. 165
Nawaz (Muhammad) v The State, 1990 SCMR 886 199
Pakistan and others v Public-at-Large and others, PLD 1987 SC 304 198
Pakistan and others v Public-at-Large and others, PLD 1988 SC 202 198
Pakistan Chest Foundation v Government of Pakistan, 1997 CLC 1379. 158
Pakistan through Secretary, Ministry of Defence v The General Public PLD 1989 SC 6. 198
Pakistan v Hazoor Bakhsh PLD 1988 FSC 283. 199
Pakistan v Muhammad Ishaq, PLD 1983 SC 273 198
Patel (Begum Rashida) v Federation of Pakistan, PLD 1989 FSC 95 199
Province of East Pakistan v M.D. Mehdi Ali Khan, PLD 1959 SC 387 157
Qasim (Muhammad) v The State, 1997 PCr. LJ 10965 FSC. 199
Rakha (Allah) and others v Federation of Pakistan, PLD 2000 FSC 1 191
Reference by the President of Pakistan under Article 186 of the Constitution of the Islamic Republic of Pakistan, 1973 200
Sadiq (Muhammad) v The State, 1997 PCr. LJ 546 (FSC) 199
Saeed (Tariq) v Director, Anti-Corruption Establishment, 1996 MLD 1864 166
Saima v The State PLD 2003 Lah. 747 165
Sajjad (Wasim) and others v Federation of Pakistan, PLD 2001 SC 233 149
Shah (Syed Ghayyur Hussain) and another v Gharib Alam, PLD 1990 Lah. 432. 198
Shah (Zafar Ali) and others v General Pervez Musharraf, Chief Executive of Pakistan PLD 2000 SC 869. 149
Sharif (Muhammad Nawaz) v President of Pakistan, PLD 1993 SC 473. . . . . 149, 161, 165
Sheikh (Aziz) v The Commissioner of Income-Tax Investigation, Lahore, PLD 1989 SC 613. 165
Siani v The State, PLD 1984 FSC 121 199
State v Dosso and others, PLD 1958 SC 533 148
State v Senior Superintendent of Police, PLD1991 Lah. 224 . . . . . 158, 163
State v Zia-ur-Rehman, PLD 1973 SC 49. . . . . 148, 188
Tariq Transport Company, Lahore v Sargodha-Bhera Bus Service, PLD 1958 SC 437 . . . . . 157, 158
Taslem v The State, PLJ 1996, FSC 138 199
United Bank v M/s Farooq Brothers etc 2002 193

Wahid (Abdul) v Asma Jehangir, PLD 1997 Lahore 301 198
Wattan Party v Federation of Pakistan, PLD 2006 SC 697. . . . . .6, 158
Zaheerudin v The State, 1993 SCMR 1718. 198
Zaib-un-Nisa v Government of the Punjab, Education Department,
1995 CLC 1281 165–6
Zia (Shehla) v WAPDA, PLD 1994 SC 693 . . . . .158, 163–4

Table of Statutory Material

International Treaties and Declarations
African Charter on Human and Peoples' Rights 1981 ....24, 55, 97, 137
Art 22..........................137
Protocol
Art 24.........................137

Cairo Declaration on Human Rights....198
Convention on the Elimination of All Forms of Discrimination against Women 1979 ....162, 181, 184
Art 11..........................184
Art 16..........................198

Convention on the Prevention and Punishment of the Crime of Genocide 50
Convention on the Rights of the Child 1989.....................159, 181
Art 4...........................130
Art 24(4) 130
Art 32..........................159

Convention to Prevent and Punish the Acts of Terrorism Taking the Form of Crimes against Persons and Related Extortion that are of International Significance 1971 ...139
Cotonou Agreement 2000 97
European Convention on Human Rights.........................56
ILO Convention No. 29 concerning Forced Labour 1930.............159
ILO Convention No. 105 concerning the Abolition of Forced Labour 1957.........................159
International Bill of Rights 27
International Covenant on Civil and Political Rights 1966.......1, 22, 45, 46, 56, 181, 184, 196
Art 1(1) 44, 45, 46
Art 14 ....162, 217
Art 19..........................185

International Covenant on Economic Social and Cultural Rights 1966 ....1, 22, 45, 46, 51, 139, 181, 184, 196
Art 1(1) 44, 45, 46
Art 2............................51
Art 2(1) 130
Art 6...........................184
Art 11(1) 139
Art 11(2)................51, 130, 139

Lomé Conventions
Convention I 1975.................97
Convention II 1980................97
Convention III 1985 97
Art 121........................97
Convention IV 1990 97

Maastricht Guidelines on Violation of Economic Social and Cultural Rights 1997..................68–9
Rio Declaration on Environment and Development...........90, 139, 164
Principle 3 90
Principle 15 164

Social Charter of the South Asian Association for Regional Cooperation 2004....24, 25, 137, 154
Art II 24

Statute of the International Court of Justice 1945
Art 38..........................132
Art 38(1) 114
Art 38(1)(b) 115
Art 38(1)(c) 128

Art 59 . . . 114

Tehran Declaration 1968 . . . 20, 49, 139
UN Supplementary Convention on the Abolition of Slavery, the Slave Trade and Institutions and Practices similar to Slavery 1956 . . . 159
United Nations Charter 1945 . . . 22, 28, 75, 79, 235
Art 2(2) . . . 130
Art 10-Art 14 . . . 116
Art 17 . . . 116
Art 21 . . . 116
Art 22 . . . 116, 130
Art 28 . . . 130
Art 55 . . . 49–50, 93, 122, 129, 139
Art 56 . . . 49–50, 83, 93, 122, 129, 130, 139

Universal Declaration of Human Rights 1948 . . . 27, 29, 32, 34, 40, 41, 70, 71, 86, 129, 139, 162, 179, 181, 234
Art 3 . . . 40, 179
Art 10 . . . 162
Art 16 . . . 40, 179
Art 17 . . . 179
Art 18 . . . 40, 179
Art 28 . . . 40, 48–9, 50, 51, 74

Universal Islamic Declaration of Human Rights 1981 . . . 180
Vienna Convention on the Law of Treaties
Art 31(3)(c) . . . 115
Art 53 . . . 50

Vienna Declaration and Programme of Action 1993 . . . 22–3, 28, 53, 55, 127, 130, 139
Art 1(10) . . . 24
Art 2(1) . . . 127
Art 10 . . . 2, 28, 127

World Trade Organization Treaty 1995 . 115
Dispute Settlement Understanding
Art 3(2) . . . 115

National Constitutions and Laws
Austrian Federal Law of 10 July 1974 . . . 125
Constitution of the Federal Democratic Republic of Ethiopia 1994
Art 43 . . . 25

Constitution of the Republic of Benin 1990
Art 9 . . . 25

Constitution of the Republic of Malawi 1994
Art 30 . . . 25

Constitution of the Republic of Uganda 1995
Art IX . . . 25

Government of India Act 1935 . . . 147
Indian Independence Act 1947 . . . 147
Restatement of the Foreign Relations Law of the United States (Revised) . . . 126
Swiss Federal Law of 19 March 1976 . . . 125

Pakistan: Constitutions and Laws
Baluchistan (Criminal Law) (Special Provisions) Ordinance II of 1968 . . . 162
Bonded Labour System (Abolition) Act 1992 . . . 159, 161
s 5 . . . 159, 160

Bonded Labour System (Abolition) Rules 1995 . . . 159
Constitution of 1956 . . . 147
Constitution of 1962 . . . 147, 148
Art 7-Art 8 . . . 148

Constitution of 1973 . . . 4, 147, 148, 149, 154–5, 156–7, 165, 169, 171, 189, 191, 203
Art 1 . . . 189
Art 2 . . . 189
Art 2A . . . 147, 156, 188, 192, 198
Art 9 . . . 158–9
Art 11 . . . 159–61
Art 14 . . . 158
Art 17 . . . 158, 161
Art 17(2) . . . 161
Art 25 . . . 158, 162–3, 184
Art 29 . . . 155
Art 29(1) . . . 156
Art 30 . . . 155
Art 30(2) . . . 156
Art 34 . . . 4, 155
Art 37 . . . 161
Art 37(f) . . . 155
Art 38 . . . 154, 161
Art 184(3) . . . 157, 168
Art 199(1)(a)(i)-(ii) . . . 157
Art 199(1)(c) . . . 157
Art 203B(c) . . . 191
Art 203C . . . 191
Art 203D . . . 191
Art 203DD . . . 192

Art 227-Art 228 189
Preamble 4, 148
para 4-para 5 4
para 8 4
Principles of Policy 4, 163, 165–6, 203, 233
Art 31 165
Art 34 165
Art 37 . . . . 160, 165
Art 38 165

Enforcement of Shari'ah Act 1991 . . . . 192, 197
s 4 197

Environmental Protection Act 1997 . . . . 163, 165
Environmental Protection Ordinance 1983 163
Evidence Act 1872 192
Interim Constitution of 1972 . . . . . 147, 148
Law (Continuous in Force) Order 1958 147
Law (Continuous in Force) Order 1977 147
Legal Framework Order 2002 149
Mudaraba Ordinance 1981 193
Muslim Family Law 191
NWFP Provincial Assembly (Powers, Immunities and Privileges) Act 1988 199
Objectives Resolution 1948 . . . . . . 147, 148, 149, 155, 156, 171, 188, 189, 192, 233
Pakistan (Provisional Constitution) Order 1947 147
Political Parties Act 1962 158
Protection of Women (Criminal Laws Amendment) Act 2006 . . . . 150, 162, 192
Provisional Constitutional Order 1969 147
Provisional Constitutional Order 1981 147
Provisional Constitutional Order 1999 147
Qanun-e-Shahadat Order [the law of evidence] 1984 192
Art 17(2) 192

Representation of People Act 1962 161
Shariat Ordinance 192
Small Claims and Minor Offences Ordinance 2002 227

Zakat and Ushr Ordinance 1980 193

United Nations General Assembly Resolutions

Agenda for Development (A/Res/47/181) 77
Charter of Economic Rights and Duties of States (A/Res/3281) 20
Declaration on Principles of International Law Concerning Friendly Relations and Cooperation among States in accordance with the Charter of the United Nations (A/Res/2625(XXV)) 79, 86, 117
Declaration on Social Progress and Development 1969 (A/Res/2542(XXIV)) 20, 51, 83–4
Art 12 51

Declaration on the Establishment of a New International Economic Order (A/Res/3201(S-VI)) 20, 79
Declaration on the Right to Development (A/Res/41/128) 1–2, 4, 5, 7, 10, 22, 28, 43, 53, 54, 56, 62, 63, 72, 73, 81–96, 89, 115, 116, 118, 121, 129, 130–2, 135–41, 145, 152, 154, 178, 181, 196, 203, 233, 236
Art 1 . . . . 83, 152
Art 1(1) 1, 9, 43, 54, 55, 57, 58, 59, 60, 61, 85, 155, 178
Art 1(2) 54, 57, 59
Art 2 . . . . 57, 152
Art 2(1) 53, 55, 57, 136, 155, 211
Art 2(2) 43, 63
Art 2(3) 4, 5, 53, 55, 57, 59, 63, 85, 90, 92, 136, 147, 152, 155, 178, 196, 207
Art 2(4) 123
Art 3 90
Art 3(1) 53, 57, 58, 59, 71, 73, 145, 207
Art 3(2) 57, 72, 73, 86, 92, 180
Art 3(3) 54, 58, 63, 73, 86, 93, 94, 131
Art 3(8) 203
Art 4(1) 4, 54, 58, 63, 92, 93, 131
Art 4(2) 54, 57, 58, 73, 86, 92, 136
Art 5 . . . . 54, 57, 95
Art 6 . . . . 57, 59, 83, 93, 153
Art 6(1) 63, 73, 93, 95, 131
Art 6(2) 4, 9, 63, 136, 155

Art 6(3) 28, 53, 58, 145, 155
Art 7 . . . . 57, 59, 63, 83
Art 8 . . . . 53, 54, 57, 58, 59, 85, 89, 90, 95, 136, 152, 153, 163, 196
Art 8(1) 4, 5, 39, 57, 63, 132, 145, 152, 155, 207, 210, 211
Art 8(2) 57, 63, 85, 155
Art 9 153
Art 10 . . . . 55, 132
Preamble 153
para 2 . . . . 4, 57, 88, 155
para 3 48
para 6 44
para 10 . . . . 28, 53
para 15 94

First United Nations Decade for the Eradication of Poverty (A/Res/51/178) 11
Art 4 11

International Development Strategy for the Second United Nations Development Decade 1970 (A/Res/2626 (XXV)) 3, 50, 123
International Development Strategy for the Third United Nations Development Decade (A/Res/35/56) 50, 123
Programme of Action on the Establishment of a New International Economic Order (A/Res/3202(S-IV)) 20, 26, 50
Resolution 1514 (XV) 139
Resolution 1522 (XV) 1960 . . . . 3, 123
Resolution 1803 (XVII) 45
Resolution A/32/130 140
Resolution A/34/46 . . . . 21, 140
Resolution A/41/133 . . . . 82, 95, 153
Resolution A/45/97 98
Resolution A/45/199 98
Resolution A/48/141 23
Resolution A/50/214 23
Resolution A/52/136 27
Resolution A/53/155 23
Resolution A/54/175 121
Resolution A/55/2 (Millennium Declaration) 24, 130, 154
Resolution A/1161(XII) 84
Resolution A/1710 (United Nations Development Decade) 50

United Nations Human Rights Commission (Council) Resolutions

Resolution 1/4 33
Resolution 4 (XXXV) 140
Resolution 4 (XXXIII)/1977 21
Resolution 4/4 24
Resolution 5 (XXXV)/1979 21
Resolution 6 (XXXVI) 140
Resolution 36 (XXXVII/1981) 2, 21, 79
Resolution 1989/45 22
Resolution 1993/22 . . . . 23, 98
Resolution 1996/15 . . . . 23, 98
Resolution 1998/72 . . . . 23, 27, 32, 100
Resolution 1999/22 32
Resolution 1999/79 32
Resolution 2000/5 32
Resolution 2003/83 33
Resolution 2004/7 . . . . 23, 33
Resolution 2005/4 33

1 Introduction

BACKGROUND AND RESEARCH THESIS

The Right to Development (RTD) is a notable, but highly controversial, third-generation human right.[1] It was first articulated in the 1970s and formally pronounced in 1986 in the Declaration on the Right to Development (Declaration) passed by the United Nations (UN) General Assembly. Article 1(1) of the Declaration defines the RTD as:

> an inalienable human right by virtue of which every human person and all peoples are entitled to participate in, contribute to, and enjoy economic, social, cultural and political development, in which all human rights and fundamental freedoms can be fully realized.

The Declaration proclaims that the RTD has both international and national dimensions.[2] The RTD emerged in the post-colonial era of the 1960s, in the context of the developing countries' demand for reforms in the international economic rules and policies. Developing countries attributed the causes of

1 See Karel Vasak, 'A 30-year struggle, the sustained efforts to give force of law to the Universal Declaration of Human Rights', *UNESCO Courier*, 1977, 29. Karel Vasak argues that the third-generation rights 'reflect a certain conception of community life'. Other third-generation rights include the rights to development, peace, environment and the common heritage of mankind. These rights are also called collective rights or peoples' rights. The first-generation rights are those contained in the International Covenant on Civil and Political Rights (ICCPR). The second-generation rights are laid down in the International Covenant on Economic, Social and Cultural Rights (ICESCR). Both were adopted in 1966. The ICCPR along with an optional protocol came into force on 23 March 1976; the ICESCR came into force on 3 Jan. 1976.

2 See the Declaration on the Right to Development (hereinafter referred to as DRD), United Nations General Assembly (UNGA) Resolution (Res.) A/41/128, adopted at the 97th Plenary Meeting, 4 Dec. 1986, by 146 votes in favour, 1 against (the USA), with 8 abstentions (Denmark, Finland, Federal Republic of Germany (as it then was), Iceland, Israel, Japan, Sweden and the United Kingdom). Article 3 says: 'States have the prime responsibility for the creation of national and international development policies.'

their economic under-development to the developed counties, most of which were the former colonial powers. For these historic and political reasons, the developed countries of the North were opposed to the concept of the RTD from the very beginning. Academic controversies also surround the concept of the RTD. For example, can it be legitimately argued that, being a collective right, the RTD cannot be a human right? Similarly, the legal position of the right-holders and the duty-bearers is also not clear. The juridical definition of the word 'development' is another question that needs to be settled. As a General Assembly resolution, the Declaration is a mere recommendation and as such its legal status is contentious. The adoption of the Declaration by the General Assembly was not done smoothly because of the opposition of the developed countries and lack of consensus over the content and scope of the RTD in the first working group.[3] The United States of America (USA) cast a negative vote and most developed countries abstained from voting. The Declaration is a compromise document, which, consequently, has some vague and uncertain parts.

At the Vienna Conference on Human Rights in 1993, a consensus over the RTD emerged between the developing and the developed countries.[4] But the legal value of that consensus is not clear. However, continuous efforts are made in the United Nations (UN) forums through various working groups to clarify the concept of the RTD and to search for ways to realize this right at the national and international levels. The RTD is a core element in the current human rights and development discourse. Hence, there is considerable scope for research and analysis of the concept of the RTD. The promotion of the RTD depends on the legal status of the RTD in international law vis-à-vis state practice. This book focuses on the legal status of the RTD in international law and on the fundamental rights in the constitution of Pakistan. It examines the status of the Declaration in customary international law and the role of Pakistan's judiciary in the development of the RTD through the protection of fundamental rights guaranteed in the constitution of Pakistan.

The book argues that the RTD may become an established right if international cooperation is recognized as a legal obligation at the international level and human rights are widely interpreted at the national level. It focuses on the legal status of foreign development aid as a tool of international cooperation[5] and the state practice of Pakistan through its judicial experience.

3 E/CN.4/1489. The first working group was formed in the light of the United Nations Human Rights Commission (now Council) Resolution 36 of 11 Feb. 1982 (hereinafter the Commission's (now the Council's) resolutions to be cited as CHR Res.).

4 At the Vienna Conference, as many as 171 countries (including the USA, a staunch opponent of the RTD) unanimously agreed that the RTD as established in the DRD 'is a universal and inalienable right and an integral part of fundamental human rights'. See A/Conf.157/23, Vienna Declaration and Program of Action, 12 July 1993, Article 10; see also A/Conf.157/24 (Part I), 13 Oct. 1993, Report of the Secretary-General.

5 Foreign development aid was launched by the USA in 1949 and by Western European countries in 1951. Since the 1960s, foreign development aid by developed countries has

It is argued that the judiciary – the superior as well as the lower Courts[6] – in protecting fundamental rights, may promote the RTD in the following three ways: firstly, a wider interpretation of fundamental rights through Public Interest Litigation (PIL); secondly, a progressive interpretation of the *Shari'ah* (Islamic law) through *istihsan* (juristic preference) to serve *maslahah* (public interest)[7]; thirdly, an effective and efficient judicial service at the grassroots level.

An in-depth analysis of the legal and political challenges is, however, necessary before proceeding to probe the legal position of the RTD in international law from the perspective of state practice.

INTERNATIONAL DIMENSION OF THE RTD

The study of the international dimension of the RTD is necessary because, firstly, the RTD emerged as a notion in the realm of international law. However, as noted above, the legal position of the RTD in international law is highly controversial because the Declaration, being a resolution of the General Assembly, does not enjoy a legally binding effect. Secondly, the international dimension of the RTD faces significant challenges, such as its collective dimension as a human right and lack of consensus between developing and developed countries in the UN working group over its implementation. The critics of the RTD argue that a collective right cannot be a human right because for a human right one needs

become an important international issue. The UN General Assembly has passed many resolutions in which aid targets were set initially at 0.7 per cent and, subsequently, at 1.0 per cent. See UNGA Res. 1522 (XV) 15 Dec. 1960 and 2626 (XXV) 24 Oct. 1970.

6 The superior judiciary here means those courts which are created under the constitution; they are the Supreme Court of Pakistan, the High Court of a province and the Federal Shariat Court. The lower judiciary means those courts which are established by the statutory laws and which are normally subordinate to the High Court.

7 *Istihsan* is a technique of juristic deduction. It is applied by a court/jurist to disregard a rule of law, the application of which may cause hardship and inconvenience, and to rely on the rule which is beneficial. *Maslahah* aims at securing public interest and preventing harm. *Maslahah* is the objective of the Lawgiver (God). *Istihsan* seeks to expound the law from the existing sources of law; *maslahah*, having wider scope, may bring about independent legislation in areas not explicitly covered by primary sources – the Qur'an and Sunnah – of Islamic law. *Maslahah* has been recognized since the early days of the development of Islamic jurisprudence. It was, however, extensively developed by Imam Shatibi (d.790 A.H. (After Hijra)/1388 C.E. (Christian Era)), a scholar of Muslim Spain. In modern times, it was revived in the second half of the nineteenth century by a prominent Egyptian scholar, Muhammad Abduh (d.1905). *Maslahah* is the end goal of juristic deduction to meet the exigencies of the day. For a recent work on *maslahah*, see Ahmad Al-Raysuni, *Imam Al-Shatibi's Theory of the Higher Objectives and Intents of Islamic Law* (translated by Nancy Robert), London/Washington, The International Institute of Islamic Thought, 2005.

to be a human being.[8] Thirdly, the Declaration emphasizes the duty of international cooperation:

> states have *the duty to co-operate* with each other in ensuring development and eliminating obstacles to development . . . States have *the duty* to take steps, individually and collectively, to formulate international development policies with a view to facilitate the full realisation of the [RTD].[9]

The main focus of this book is on the judicial practice of Pakistan.

WHY PAKISTAN AS A CASE STUDY?

The case study of Pakistan is chosen for a number of important reasons. Firstly, Pakistan favoured the 1986 Declaration and subsequent resolutions on the RTD in the General Assembly. Pakistan's 1973 constitution (hereafter constitution) recognizes many civil and political rights as fundamental rights. But the constitution does not recognize the RTD as a fundamental right. However, some features of the RTD – equality of opportunity in access to basic resources, respect for human rights, development as a comprehensive process and participation of women in the process of development – have similarities with the Preamble and the Principles of Policy, the guiding principles of a national development policy, mentioned in the constitution of Pakistan.[10]

Secondly, the constitution of Pakistan also makes it obligatory that political and socio-economic development are pursued in accordance with the commands of the religion of Islam:

> The principles of democracy, freedom, equality, tolerance and social justice, as enunciated by Islam, shall be fully observed . . . Wherein the Muslims shall be enabled to order their lives in the individual and

8 See, e.g., Jack Donnelly, 'In Search of a Unicorn: the Jurisprudence and Politics of the Right to Development', *California Western International Law Journal* 15, 1985, 473–509.

9 DRD, Articles 2(3) and 4(1).

10 The preambular paragraphs 4, 5 and 8 of the constitution are comparable with Articles 8(1), 6(2) of and preambular paragraph 2 of DRD, respectively. Article 34 of the constitution and Article 8(1) of the DRD both stress the role of women in the process of development.

collective spheres in accordance with the teachings and requirements of Islam as set out in the Holy Qur'an[11] and Sunnah.[12]

In the context of Islamic law, this book will argue that despite some conceptual differences, the Islamic law doctrine of *maslahah* is generally compatible with the features of the RTD. The Declaration provides that the state must ensure fairness, justice and equity in the distribution of development gains.[13] On the other hand, *maslahah*, as observed above, is the main guideline for economic and social legislation and policy to help achieve social justice in a Muslim society. The Qur'an proclaims that the institution of Prophethood was created in order to establish justice.[14] Moreover, *maslahah* aims at the preservation of five objectives of the *Shari'ah*: life, religion, property, family and reason.[15] These objectives generally overlap with some basic human rights such as the right to life, religion and property and may help enhance basic human capabilities such as health and education. Furthermore, in case of incompatibility between international human rights and the *Shari'ah*, the doctrine of *maslahah* may greatly contribute to resolving it.[16] This book deals with two kinds of *maslahah*. Firstly, *maslahah mu'tabarah* (recognized) is that which is validated by the primary sources of law. Secondly, *maslahah mursalah* (conveyed or independent) is that which is neither supported nor opposed by the primary sources of law.[17]

Thirdly, there is evidence that when the executive and legislative branches of the state fail to discharge their constitutional obligations in the area of social and economic development, Pakistan's superior judiciary sometimes play an interventionist role by interpreting, through PIL jurisprudence, the fundamental rights provisions in the context of social and economic

11 'Qur'an is the name of the collection of those revelations which were made to Prophet Muhammad (May God's Blessings be upon him) when he was vested with the office of the Prophet and Messenger of God. The revelations were made in God's own words as containing His wishes and command.' See Abdur Rahim, *The Principles of Muhammadan Jurisprudence*, Lahore, PLD Publishers (first published 1911), p 17.

12 The Sunnah are the traditions of the Prophet Muhammad (May God's Blessings be upon him) that include both his sayings and practices.

13 DRD, Arts. 2(3) and 8(1).

14 'We sent aforetime Our messengers with clear Signs and sent down with them the Book and the Balance (of Right and Wrong) that men may stand forth in justice' (57:25).

15 Al-Raysuni, op. cit., p 122.

16 See, e.g., Mashood A. Baderin, *International Human Rights and Islamic Law*, Oxford, Oxford University Press, 2003. For a discussion on the concept of human rights in Islam, see, e.g., J. Paul Martin, 'The Three Monotheistic World Religions and International Human Rights', *Journal of Social Sciences* 61(4), 2005, 827–45.

17 For a detailed jurisprudential discussion on *maslahah*, see Imran Ahsan Khan Nyazee, *Islamic Jurisprudence*, Islamabad, International Institute of Islamic Thought and Islamic Research Institute, 2000, p 195.

justice.[18] Such contextual interpretation, extending the scope of the fundamental rights to the Principles of Policy, has positive implications for the promotion of the RTD.[19] Therefore, an analysis of judicial activism in the implementation of social justice is considered necessary.

Fourthly, Pakistan enjoyed a central position in global politics during the Cold War, which ended in the fall of communism. Currently, Pakistan is a key ally in the 'war on terror'. The international community, particularly the Western countries, has high expectations from Pakistan to help fight terrorism. Contrary to this, there is popular discontent among the masses, who believe that the US-led war against terrorism has an anti-Islam agenda and that Pakistan's support for this war is a threat to their Islamic values.[20] Moreover, the diversion of limited resources to the 'war on terror' creates a deficit in socio-economic development, which may prove counter-productive. A meaningful implementation of the RTD seems crucial in responding to these challenges because it will ensure socio-economic development as well as the promotion and protection of all human rights and fundamental freedoms.

Fifthly, in general, Pakistan's current development programmes, supported by some bilateral and multilateral donors, are pursuing a rights-based approach to development.[21] Of particular interest to this book is Pakistan's reform of its judicial institutions to improve their efficiency and enhance

18 On the occasion of its 50th anniversary in August 2006, the Supreme Court proclaimed in a Declaration that the PIL is a technique of speedy justice. The Declaration stressed the role of the Supreme Court in the rule of law and good governance. The text of the Declaration appeared in *The News International*, 16 Aug. 2006. The disagreement between the executive and the judiciary over the suspension of the Chief Justice of Pakistan by the President of Pakistan on 9 March 2007 led to unprecedented opposition from lawyers and political parties. The Chief Justice was reinstated by a larger bench of the Supreme Court on 20 July 2007. Since then, a number of high-profile cases have been decided by the Supreme Court against the government. Notable cases, which are traditionally dealt with by the executive, include the prices of medicines, missing persons, traffic congestion and the transplantation of human organs. See Dr Noman Ahmad, 'What our Courts cannot do', *The Dawn* newspaper, 27 Aug. 2007. On 3 Nov. 2007, emergency rule was imposed by President Musharraf, as a result of which more than 40 judges of the superior courts were removed from service. The restoration of those judges became an important political issue, which proved one of the main causes of the defeat of the pro-Musharraf party in the 18 Feb. 2008 general elections.

19 See, e.g., *Benazir Bhutto v Federation of Pakistan*, PLD 1988 SC 416. For a later PIL case, see *Wattan Party v Federation of Pakistan*, PLD 2006 SC 697. In this case, the privatization of Pakistan's Steel Mill was set aside. This case is a good example of the Court's intervention.

20 A US-based independent poll organization – Terror Free Tomorrow – conducted a survey in August 2007 in Pakistan, which showed that 66 per cent of Pakistanis think the 'war against terror' is against Islam and Muslims. The survey's report is available at: <http://www.terrorfreetomorrow.org/upimagestft/Pakistan%20Poll%20Report.pdf> (accessed 27 Feb. 2009).

21 For example, the United Nations Development Program (UNDP)'s commitment to a human rights-based approach: see 'Applying a Human Rights-Based Approach to Development Cooperation and Programming: A UNDP Capacity Development Resource',

accessibility in the justice service for all, particularly the poor.[22] Such reforms may prove helpful in promoting human rights, including the RTD.[23] A rights-based approach has the potential to help promote human rights and enhance basic capabilities. This book will argue that Amartya Sen's 'capabilities' approach[24] significantly influences the normative basis of the RTD.

It may be necessary to see whether the focus on one country (such as Pakistan) imposes any limitations on understanding the RTD. One limitation, for example, may be that the Declaration itself gives the option to adopt such development policies as are considered suitable by the states according to their own specific conditions.[25] The specific social, economic and political conditions vary from country to country. What then are the implications of the experience of one country for the national and international RTD? Regarding the RTD at the national level, it may be argued that despite differences in their social, economic and political conditions, most developing countries have some similarities. For example, historically, most of these countries were former colonies. Moreover, they are facing similar problems, such as bad governance, weak institutions, corruption and lack of the rule of law, in achieving social and economic justice.[26] Thus in such similar conditions, the states can draw lessons from one another. Pakistan's experience in the Islamization of law and society has some implications also for other

Capacity Development Group, Bureau for Development Policy, UNDP, Sept. 2006. Online. Available at: <http://www.hurilink.org/tools/Applying_a_HR_approach_to_UNDP_Technical_Cooperation_unr-revision.pdf> (accessed 27 Feb. 2009). Swiss Development Cooperation (SDC) says it applies a human rights-based approach in Pakistan. Available at: <http://www.sdcpakistan.org/index.php?navID=61891&langID=1&.> (accessed 28 June 2008).

22 The reforms are in the Access to Justice Programme (AJP), was launched in 2001 with the financial and technical assistance of the Asian Development Bank (ADB).

23 Elaborating national actions for implementation of the RTD, the Independent Expert observed: 'A right to development approach in a development programme will be concerned with . . . changes in the institutions and social arrangements to realize a set of targeted objectives as [a] human right, identified as expansion of capabilities and freedoms.' See E/CN.4/2002/WG.18/2, Fourth Report of the Independent Expert on the RTD, para. 20.

24 The 'capabilities' approach sees development as the enhancement of human capabilities. Capability is the ability to achieve something which one has reason to value. Capability reflects 'the person's freedom to lead one type of life or another . . . freedom to choose from possible livings.' See Amartya Sen, *Inequality Re-examined*, Oxford, Clarendon Press, 1992, p 39.

25 DRD does not adopt a universal model of development. 'The states should be encouraged to adopt their own benchmarks, as setting universal benchmarks has proven to be impossible.' This was suggested by Philip Alston, the Chairman of the Committee on Economic, Social and Cultural Rights in his statement before the fourth session of the Working Group on the RTD. See E/CN.4/1996/10.

26 See, e.g., Richard Sannerholm, 'Legal, Judicial and Administrative Reforms in Post-Conflict Societies: Beyond the Rule of Law Template', *Journal of Conflict & Security Law* 12(1), 2007, 65–94.

Muslim countries which follow Sunni Islamic law. So far as the international RTD is concerned, developing countries mainly support the RTD because the national dimension of the RTD depends on international cooperation.[27] As part of international cooperation, development aid policies are now focusing on country ownership of development programmes, such as the Poverty Reduction Strategy Papers (PRSP).[28] It seems necessary to briefly discuss the influence of the RTD on the current human rights and development discourse.

HUMAN RIGHTS AND DEVELOPMENT

'Development as a concept first entered the human rights edifice through the debate on the [RTD].'[29] The integration of human rights into the framework of development policies is a paradigm shift in the thinking about development. This shift characterizes the recognition of the fact that the human rights system and development policy are interdependent. The development community now uses the language of human rights.[30]

While the human rights community was, and even still is, to some extent, debating the justiciable nature of the second generation of human rights, the third generation has brought about a significant change in the human rights philosophy. Firstly, the concept of third-generation rights has stretched human rights to groups and peoples, in sharp contrast to the traditional view that the individual is the sole and exclusive subject of human right.[31] Secondly, the implementation of third-generation rights involves the 'combined efforts of every one: individual, states and other bodies, as well as public and private institutions'.[32] Since the Cold War ended in 1990s, the schism between the first two sets of human rights also appears to be fading away. At the Vienna Conference, a global consensus developed over the unity and interdependence of all human rights. Since then the RTD has become part of the mandate of the UN High Commissioner for Human Rights (UNHCHR).

27 See Chapter 2 for detailed discussion.

28 One of the principles of the World Bank/IMF's Comprehensive Development Framework (CDF) is that an aid recipient country will own and direct the development agenda. See also the Second Report of the Independent Expert on the RTD. The experience of different countries, including Pakistan, in the formulation of their PRSP will be examined in Chapter 8.

29 Peter Uvin, *Human Rights and Development*, Bloomfield, Connecticut, Kumarian Press, Inc., 2004, p 40.

30 See James D. Wolfensohn, 'Some Reflections on Human Rights and Development' and Mary Robinson, 'What Rights Can Add to Good Development Practice' in Philip Alston and Mary Robinson (eds), *Human Rights and Development: Towards Mutual Reinforcement*, Oxford, Oxford University Press, 2005, pp 19–24 and pp 25–41, respectively.

31 Vasak, op. cit., p 29.

32 Ibid.

The RTD can potentially change the way development is understood and achieved, both nationally and in international cooperative efforts. However, the current human rights and development discourse suggests that a pure RTD model is problematic for two reasons. Firstly, the RTD is not binding in customary international law. This weakness is being used as a pretext by the developed countries to avoid their obligations of international cooperation. Secondly, with the exception of a few African states, most of the developing countries, including Pakistan, have not legally recognized the RTD as a human right at the domestic level. This fact is also an obstacle to the recognition of the RTD of the individual. While the civil and political rights of the individual are justiciable, the economic, social and cultural rights of the individual are not. The latter categories of rights are to be realized progressively. The added value of the RTD is that the human rights are indivisible, interrelated and interdependent. Thus a development policy should promote human rights in such a way that the promotion of one kind of human right encourages the promotion of other kinds of human right. In this way the state will be able to respect, protect and fulfil the human rights of all, particularly the vulnerable poor.

The rights-based approach to development is currently much talked about in both the development and human rights communities. This approach requires that the human rights norms and values laid down in all international human rights instruments, shall form the basis of all development policies and the guidelines for the institutions implementing such policies. The strength of this approach lies in the fact that it considers human rights as legal claims and human beings as right-holders of such claims. The state is under the obligation to respect, protect and fulfil such legal claims through various institutions, including courts.

Article 1(1) of the Declaration, cited above, pronounces this approach in two parts. Firstly, development is a comprehensive concept, which creates an enabling environment for the realization of all human rights and fundamental freedoms. Secondly, 'every human person and all peoples are entitled to participate in, contribute to, and enjoy' such a broad-based development. Thus by referring to all human rights and fundamental freedoms, the said article of the Declaration (and Article 6(2) expressly) recognizes the indivisibility, interdependence and interrelatedness of these human rights. This, as Osmani notes, 'paves the way for finally bridging the schism that led to the adoption of two separate covenants in 1966'.[33] The value added of the rights-based approach to development is that it recognizes the obligation of the state and grants legitimacy to peoples' claims/rights; equality and non-discrimination; participation; and accountability.[34]

33 S.R. Osmani, 'An Essay on Human Rights Approach to Development' in Arjun Sengupta, et al. (eds), *Reflections of the Right to Development*, New Delhi, Sage, 2006, pp 110–26 at p 112.

34 Ibid. p 121.

Some commentators argue that 'the [RTD] cannot function as a substitute for a human rights approach to development because of its vagueness, lack of obligation laid down in an international treaty, and lack of consensus'.[35] The advocates of the RTD, however, argue that the rights-based approach is not sufficient in itself because it relies on the realization of individual rights.

> There are important *interactions* and *inter-relations* among different parts that might be missed if the focus is exclusively on individual rights. By adopting a holistic approach, the [RTD] forces us to take cognisance of . . . *(a)* the complementarities of rights, *(b)* trade-offs among rights, and *(c)* international co-operation as a human rights obligation.[36]

The UN Independent Expert on the RTD has described the RTD as a 'vector' of different human rights together with different elements of economic growth. The Independent Expert observes the close connection between the two as follows:[37]

> There are two basic characteristics of that vector. Firstly, each of the elements of the right have to be realised according to the rights-based approach spelled out above. This means that the [RTD] as a whole will also have to be realized in a rights-based manner that is transparent, accountable, participatory and non-discriminatory, as well as equitable and just. Secondly, all the elements are interdependent in the sense that the level of realization of a right, say, the right to health, depends on the levels of realization of other rights, such as the right to food, the right to housing, the right to liberty and security of person or the right to freedom of expression, including freedom of information. Similarly, the realization of all these rights in a sustainable manner over time depends upon the rates of growth in per capita consumption, output, and employment.

The argument that the RTD is vague, lacks international obligation and lacks consensus seems to be valid. But the argument that the RTD cannot be a substitute for a rights-based approach has no force. One basic problem with this argument is that it ignores the fact that a rights-based approach is derived from the Declaration. Hence, it is a part of the RTD. Moreover, an exclusive focus on a rights-based approach ignores the principles of indivisibility and interdependence of human rights.

The human rights and development discourse also holistically informs

35 Brigitte I. Hamm, 'A Human Rights Approach to Development', *Human Rights Quarterly* 23(4), 2001, 1005–31 at 1010.

36 Osmani, 'Rights Approach' in Sengupta et al. (eds), op. cit., p 123.

37 The Independent Expert Second Report, paras 24 and 23. See also the Independent Expert First Report, para. 67.

efforts to eradicate poverty. The Vienna Conference, 1993, confirmed that extreme poverty is linked to human rights violations. It is difficult to define poverty in precise terms.[38] According to the World Bank, poverty is 'the inability to attain a minimal standard of living'.[39] In Townsend's view, poverty is the lack or denial of certain basic necessities and resources, which deprive people 'in any or all of the spheres of life'.[40] According to Sen, 'poverty must be seen as the deprivation of basic capabilities rather than mere lowness of income, which is the standard criterion of identification of poverty'.[41] Capability entails opportunity to have different patterns and the freedom to prefer a pattern of one's choice. Arguably, Sen's thoughts are echoed in the definition of poverty offered by the UN's World Summit for Social Development that looks at poverty as lack of basic amenities such as food, basic health, adequate housing, education; social discrimination and exclusion and a secure environment; 'lack of participation in decision making and in civil, social and cultural life'.[42] In this book, poverty will be seen in such a multidimensional perspective. The relevance of poverty to human rights, including the RTD, has been acknowledged by the General Assembly resolution that 1997–2006 should be the First UN Decade for Eradication of Poverty.[43] The Independent Expert on the RTD has suggested that while implementing the RTD, 'a State might concentrate on a programme for the eradication of poverty'.[44]

38 See, generally, Martin Rein, 'Problems in the Definition and Measurement of Poverty' in Peter Townsend (ed.), *The Concept of Poverty, Working Papers on Methods of Investigation and Life-Styles of the Poor in Different Countries*, London, Heinemann, 1971, pp 46–63. For various definitions of poverty, see Wilfred Beckerman and S. Clark, *Poverty and Social Security in Britain Since 1961*, Oxford, Oxford University Press, 1982, p 20; B. Seebohm Rowntree and G.R. Lavers, *Poverty and the Welfare State, A third study of York dealing only with economic questions*, London, Longman, 1951, p 40; S.M. Miller and P. Roby, 'Poverty: Changing Social Stratification' in P. Townsend, op. cit., pp 124–45.

39 Marilyn Howard, et al., *Poverty: the Facts*, London, CPAG, 4th edition, 2001, p 18.

40 Townsend (ed.), op. cit., pp 46–63.

41 Amartya Sen, *Development as Freedom*, Oxford, Oxford University Press, 1999, p 87. See also Amartya Sen, *Poor, Relatively Speaking*, Dublin, Economic and Social Research Institute, Fifteenth Geary Lecture, 1983, pp 11–12.

42 Report of the World Summit for Social Development, Copenhagen, Denmark, 6–12 March, 1995, Annex II, p 41. Online. Available at: <http://www.un.org.documents/ga/conf166/aconf166-9.htm> (accessed 27 Feb. 2009).

43 UNGA A/Res/51/178, 11 Feb. 1997. Article 4 'recommends that, within the context of overall action for the eradication of poverty, special attention should be given to the multidimensional nature of poverty and to the national and international framework conditions and policies that are conducive to its eradication, which should aim at *the social and economic integration of people living in poverty and the promotion and protection of all human rights and fundamental freedoms for all, including the [RTD]*' (emphasis added).

44 See the Independent Expert, Second Report, para. 36. The Council has carried out some specific studies on extreme poverty and human rights. They are: E/CN.4/Sub.2/1996/13, Report of Independent Expert (Leonardo Despouy) and E/CN.4/1999/48, Report of Independent Expert (Ms A.-M. Lizin).

PAKISTAN: TOWARDS A RIGHTS-BASED APPROACH TO DEVELOPMENT?

As noted above, the constitution of Pakistan does not expressly recognize the RTD as a fundamental right. However, there is evidence that the courts have interpreted the existing fundamental rights in a way that can strongly influence the realization of the RTD.[45] Various economic and social rights are enforced by the superior courts through PIL.[46] The judicial interpretation of the Islamic provisions of the constitution could be seen as another influencing factor in the realization of the RTD. This trend of the courts is significant because not only does the constitution provide that the state is obliged to promote the Islamic way of life, unity and the observance of Islamic moral standards, but there is also popular activism among the masses for the promotion of an Islamic way of life through the enforcement of the *Shari'ah* in all spheres of life.

Pakistan's key institutions, such as the judiciary and the police, have a record of poor performance in the delivery of basic services to the common people, particularly the vulnerable sections of society. The inefficiency of these key governing institutions thus creates obstacles in the promotion and protection of human rights and the realization of the RTD. However, during the past few years there have been efforts to improve the structure of governance, notably the judiciary. These reforms are important for the RTD because firstly, they share common features with a rights-based approach to development. Secondly, these reforms will improve the delivery of basic services to the people at the local level. Thirdly, the aid for these reforms is being provided by donor countries/agencies. As will be seen later in this book, the granting of aid reflects the moral obligation of the international community. Two such aid programmes, the Access to Justice Programme (AJP) and the Essential Institutional Reforms Operationalization Programme (EIROP) are worth mentioning here.

APPROACH OF THE BOOK

This book takes an analytical approach, drawing on an examination of the current work of the UN Human Rights Commission (now Council), particularly the reports of the Independent Expert and the Task Force and the sources of international law. Moreover, Pakistan's human rights jurisprudence, the constitutional status of the Islamic concept of social justice and judicial reform are also analysed.

45 See, e.g., on the right to public participation in the decision-making process of a development project, *Moulvi Iqbal Haider v Capital Development Authority*, PLD 2006 SC 394.

46 See, e.g., on the right to education, *Shirin Munir v Government of Punjab*, PLD 1990 SC 295.

The book utilizes primary sources such as the Holy Qur'an,[47] international legal instruments, the constitution of Pakistan and international and national laws and official documents; and secondary sources including books, academic literature, journals, case law of Pakistani courts, international tribunals and newspapers. The book also analyses the doctrine of *maslahah* to explore the status of the RTD in the *Shari'ah*. When quoting verses from the Holy Qur'an, Abdullah Yousaf Ali's translation will be reproduced because the superior courts in South Asia have cited it in a number of cases.[48] In citing the Qur'an, the first number denotes the chapter (*sura*), the second denotes the number of the verse, for example, 26:192. There are four Sunni schools of Islamic jurisprudence: they are Hanafi, Maliki, Shafi and Hanbali. 'The principles of these four schools are substantially the same, and they differ from each other merely in matters of details.'[49] However, the judicial interpretation of Islamic laws adopted mainly by the Hanafi scholars will be used as this school of Islamic jurisprudence is followed by the majority Sunni Muslim population in Pakistan. Muslims are divided into two sects, viz., Sunnis and Shias; in Pakistan, Sunnis make up over 90 per cent of the population, Shias 9 per cent. The views of scholars of other schools of thought may also be referred to and relied upon where the general principles of social justice are discussed. In this book, the Islamic concept of social justice is understood as a concept that broadly includes a just role for the social, economic and political institutions for the common good (*maslahah*) in accordance with the *Shari'ah*.[50]

47 According to Islamic jurisprudence, the Holy Qur'an is the primary source of Islamic law (Rahim, op. cit., p 17). The Qur'an itself says, 'Verily this is a Revelation from the Lord of the Worlds' (26:192); 'The revelation of the Book is from Allah the Exalted in Power, Full of Wisdom' (45:2).

48 *Hazoor Bukhsh* Case (Federal Shariat Court, 1981, p 145) (Pakistan); *Shah Bano* Case, AIR 1986, p 945 (India); *Hefzur Rahman* Case 47 (1995) Dhaka Law Reports 54 (Bangladesh); see, generally, Niaz A. Shah, *Women, the Koran and International Human Rights Law: the Experience of Pakistan*, Leiden, Martinus Nijhoff Publishers, 2006.

49 Rahim, op. cit., p 23.

50 In the West, the concept of social justice was first coined by an Italian thinker, Luigi Taparelli in 1840. Luigi, a Catholic priest and philosopher, advocated the revival of moral Christian teachings and values to respond to the advent of the Industrial Revolution that endangered pious platitudes. See Thomas Behr, 'Luigi Taparelli and Social Justice: Rediscovering the Origin of a "Hallowed Concept" ', *Social Justice in Context* 1, 2005, 3–16. Online. Available at: <http://www.ecu.edu/che/cfbi/socialjustice2005vol1.pdf> (accessed 27 Feb. 2009). John Rawls defines social justice as 'the basic structure of society, or more exactly the way, in which the major social institutions . . . determine the division, advantage and social cooperation'. See John Rawls, *A Theory of Justice*, Oxford, Oxford University Press, 1972, p 7. For a critical view of the concept of social justice, see Friedrich Hayek, *Law, Legislation and Liberty, A new statement of the liberal principles of justice and political economy: Volume 2 The Mirage of Social Justice*, London and Henley, Routledge & Kegan Paul, 1976, p 96. See also Stephen Marks, 'The Human Rights Framework for Development: Seven Approaches' in Sengupta, et al. (eds), op. cit., pp 23–60 at p 29. The writer argues that the social justice approach is one of seven approaches. For the relevance of social justice to human rights, see Thomas Pogge, *World Poverty and Human Rights*, Cambridge, Polity Press, 2002.

> The main objective of the [*Shari'ah*] is to establish social justice through the process of managing and allocating physical and human resources in a way that harmonises the objective goals of distributive equity and economic efficiency.[51]

In recent years, there have been few studies on the RTD. In 2002, two studies were carried out: one by J.M.M. Ansah and another by I.D. Bunn. Focusing on the Malawian constitution that recognizes the RTD as a right, Ansah argues that the RTD aims at equitable policies and programmes to bring equality of opportunity for all.[52] Bunn argues that a meaningful realization of the RTD requires a critical examination of international economic law and policy. Bunn's study looks at the moral and legal dimensions of the RTD from the perspective of Christian social ethics.[53] Another study was carried out by M.E. Salomon in 2003.[54] The main argument of Salomon is that interdependence conditions human rights obligations. Using the RTD as a case study, Salomon focuses on minorities and indigenous peoples as among the beneficiaries of the RTD.

The present book argues that the promotion of the RTD depends on the recognition of international cooperation as a source of obligation in international law. It further argues that although the practice of international development aid, a tool of international cooperation, is general and consistent, it is not accepted as a legal obligation by developed countries. The main focus of this book is the promotion of the RTD at the national level in Pakistan, a state which has not recognized the RTD in its constitution. It is argued that the protection of the constitutionally guaranteed fundamental rights through a strong and independent judiciary may help promote the RTD in Pakistan. Of particular interest to this book is the struggle for the implementation of the *Shari'ah*, a pressing issue of constitution-making in Pakistan. This book explores the implications of the *Shari'ah* for the promotion of the RTD in Pakistan and other Muslim countries which follow Sunni Islamic law.

STRUCTURE OF THE BOOK

The book is divided into three parts. Part I addresses the conceptual issues and the legal and political challenges to the RTD, which are necessary to put

51 See Masudul Alam Choudhury and Uzir Abdul Malik, *The Foundations of Islamic Political Economy*, London, Macmillan, 1992, p 1.

52 J.M.M. Ansah, 'The Right to Development and the Malawian Law: A Critical Study', PhD Dissertation, University of Nottingham, 2002, p 2.

53 Isabella D. Bunn, 'Legal and Moral Implications of the Right to Development: Implications for International Economic Law', PhD Dissertation, University of Bristol, 2002, p 1.

54 Margot E. Salomon, 'Globalization of Responsibility: Interdependence and Cooperation in the Protection of Human Rights in International Law', PhD Dissertation, London School of Economics, 2003, p 1.

the discussion on the RTD in proper perspective. Chapter 2 briefly traces the origin and evolution of the RTD. It also looks at the politics of the RTD by examining voting patterns in the General Assembly and the Human Rights Council. The discussion on the politics of the RTD will help explore the legal implications of the voting pattern. Chapter 3 focuses on the jurisprudential controversies, such as the sources, the subjects, content and justiciability of the RTD. The main purpose of Chapter 3 is to find out where do the jurisprudential controversies presently stand and how they could be resolved. Chapter 4 carries out a textual analysis of the Declaration by bringing out its main features and weaknesses. It also critically scrutinizes the deliberations of the various UN Working Groups on the RTD and focuses on the reports of the Independent Expert and the Task Force.

Parts II and III proceed to the core issues of the legal status of the RTD in international law and in the practice of Pakistan. Part II consists of Chapter 5, which explores the legal status of the RTD in public international law. While focusing on the role of the Declaration in the area of customary international law, the chapter examines the contributions of General Assembly resolutions towards custom as one of the sources of international law. The two elements of custom, viz. *opinio juris* and state practice, particularly practice in the area of foreign development assistance, are analysed. The chapter also examines the legal status of the Declaration in relation to consensus, cooperation and interdependence as 'new sources' of international law.

Part III uses the practice of Pakistan's judiciary as a case study to investigate whether the judicial interpretation and application of fundamental rights in the perspective of Islamic jurisprudence complement or contradict the guiding principles of the Declaration. The focus is on the role of the judiciary for the reason that the rule of law is a crucial element of a rights-based approach to development. This part is divided into three chapters. Chapter 6 looks at the nature and extent of an RTD in the perspective of fundamental rights and the Principle of Policy. It examines the nature of constitutional obligations and PIL case law. Chapter 7 reconceptualizes the RTD with reference to the Islamic concept of social justice, drawing on the doctrine of *maslahah*. Chapter 8 discusses the implementation of the Declaration in the perspective of Pakistan's PRSP. It compares the principles of the Declaration and the PRSP and focuses on the current judicial reform in the lower judiciary to see whether such reform promotes a human-rights approach to development. Chapter 9 sums up and draws a conclusion from the arguments.

Part I

The RTD

Concept and challenges

2 History, politics and concept of the RTD

INTRODUCTION

Part I examines the evolution, jurisprudential and political challenges and the debate over the implementation of the RTD in the UN Working Groups. In order to gain a basic understanding of the RTD, it is necessary to discuss when, why and how the concept of the RTD emerged and what is its moral basis. An analysis of the voting patterns in the UN General Assembly and the Commission on Human Rights (Commission) will highlight the political positions of different groups of countries. As the book focuses on the legal status of the RTD, therefore an analysis of the jurisprudential controversies is important (Chapter 3). An examination of the current Working Group is required to explore the implications of the efforts to forge a consensus for international cooperation for the realization of the RTD (Chapter 4).

This chapter focuses on the history, politics and conceptual underpinnings of the RTD. It briefly traces the background in which the RTD emerged as a concept and was soon placed on the Commission's agenda. The Declaration and the current status of efforts for its realization are also examined. The discussion then turns to the politics of the RTD and analyses the political positions of different groups of countries as reflected in the voting patterns on RTD resolutions in the General Assembly and the Commission. The analysis of the voting patterns, particularly in the General Assembly, is helpful in exploring the legal status of the RTD, because of the important role of the General Assembly in the progressive development of international law. Finally, the chapter examines the conceptual foundations of the RTD in the context of Amartya Sen's capability approach.

HISTORICAL OVERVIEW

From economic sovereignty to the RTD

With the advent of decolonization in the 1960s, many former colonies of the Western imperial powers emerged as new countries on the international scene. The economies of the newly independent countries remained largely dependent on the economic muscle of developed countries,[1] mostly their former colonial masters. In international law, these countries are referred to as third world countries and/or developing countries, with both terms being used interchangeably[2] (in this book the term 'developing countries' is used).[3] The economic activity of developing countries was confined to primary products only. Thus they were unable to compete with the developed nations in global trade on an equal footing. Developing countries believed that their economic underdevelopment was due to the unjust rules of international economic relations, mainly promoted by developed countries. They wanted such changes in the basic principles governing international economic relations that could guarantee not only their economic progress, but also their economic independence. Hence, they called for a New International Economic Order (NIEO)[4] to achieve economic sovereignty. It may be mentioned here that an international Conference on Human Rights, held in Tehran in 1968, asserted that economic development was profoundly connected with the realization of human rights. In 1969, the General Assembly adopted a resolution which stressed the need for social progress and development to raise the standard of living within the realm of human rights.[5]

Developed countries rejected the call for an NIEO. They argued that economic activities are regulated by free markets in an environment of perfect competition. Thus the NIEO emerged as a hot political issue between developing and developed countries. It was in such a situation that, in 1972, the RTD was first raised by Keba M'Baye, a Senegalese jurist.[6] In 1974, the General Assembly passed a resolution on the NIEO,[7] followed by another resolution, called the Programme of Action on the Establishment of an NIEO.[8]

1 A.W. Lewis, *The Evolution of the International Economic Order*, Princeton, NJ, Princeton University Press, 1978, p 3.

2 See Antonio Cassese, *International Law in a Divided World*, Oxford, Clarendon Press, 1986, para. 68.

3 Here 'developing countries' also include the least developed countries.

4 See, generally, Mohammed Bedjaoui, *Towards a New International Economic Order*, Paris, UNESCO, 1979; Ervin Laszalo, et al., *The Obstacles to the New International Economic Order*, Oxford, Pergamon Press, 1980; Upendra Baxi, 'The New International Economic Order, Basic Needs and Rights: Noted Towards Development of the Right of Development', *Indian Journal of International Law* 23, 1983, 225–45.

5 UNGA Res. A/Res/2542 (XXIV) of 11 Dec. 1969.

6 Keba M'Baye, 'Le droit de développement comme un droit de l'homme', *Revue des Droits de l'homme* 5, 1972, 505–34. Some jurists claim that Cardinal Duval was the first to use the words 'right to development' in 1969; see Mohammed Bedjaoui, 'The Right to Development' in Mohammed Bedjaoui (ed.), *International Law: Achievements and Prospects*, Paris, UNESCO, 1991, p 1178; Roland Y. Rich, 'The Right to Development an Emerging Human Right', *Virginia Journal of International Law* 23(2), 1983, 287–327 at 290.

7 UNGA Res. A/Res/3201 (S-VI), 1974.

8 UNGA Res. A/Res/3202 (S-VI), 1974. See also UNGA Res. A/Res/3281. Through this resolution the Charter of Economic Rights and Duties was adopted.

The former resolution spelt out in detail the principles of an NIEO. Those principles included the right of self-determination of all people, cooperation of all countries based on equity, full and effective participation in solving the world economic problems, permanent sovereignty over natural resources, the right of every country to adopt economic policies suitable for its own people and active assistance to developing countries, without any political and military conditions. The latter resolution stressed the need for addressing 'continuing severe economic imbalance in relations between developed and developing countries . . . [and that] urgent and effective measures need to be taken by the international community to assist the developing countries'.[9]

The NIEO resolutions did not make any reference to the RTD. However, developing countries tried to supplement the agenda of the NIEO with the RTD.[10] Thus in a 1977 resolution, the Commission declared the RTD as a human right and linked its international dimension to the NIEO. The Commission requested the Secretary-General to undertake a study of 'the international dimension of the [RTD] as a human right in relation with other human rights based on international co-operation including the right to peace, taking into account the requirements of the [NIEO] and fundamental human needs'.[11]

The Commission also declared the RTD a human right in a resolution passed in 1979[12] and invited the Secretary-General to conduct a further study on the regional and national dimensions of the RTD as a human right, paying particular attention to the obstacles encountered by developing countries in their efforts to secure the enjoyment of that right. The same year, the General Assembly, in a resolution, emphasized 'that the [RTD] is a human right and that equality of opportunity is as much a prerogative of nations as of individuals within nations'.[13] As some commentators argued, the NIEO provided 'the only blue-print of the [RTD]'.[14] The concept of the RTD significantly brought into focus a link between human rights and international development cooperation.

The Hague Academy of International Law arranged a workshop on the RTD in which eminent jurists presented their papers on the subject. This workshop also gave international prominence to the RTD. In 1981, a working group (see Chapter 4) was established by the Commission.[15] Its principal

9 Ibid. Introduction.

10 See, generally, Cassese, op. cit., para. 214.

11 CHR Res. 4 (XXXIII) 1977.

12 CHR Res. 4 (XXXIII) 1977 and 5 (XXXV) 1979.

13 UNGA Res. A/34/46.

14 George Abi-Saab, 'The Legal Formulation of a Right to Development' in R.-J. Dupuy (ed.), *The Right to Development at the International Level, the Hague Academy of International Law Worskhop*, The Hague, Sijhoff & Noordhoff, 1980, pp 159–75, at p 167.

15 CHR Res. 36 (XXXVII), 1981. The report of the working group is discussed in Chapter 3.

task was to study the scope and content of the RTD and to prepare a draft international instrument on the RTD.

The Declaration (1986)

The Declaration was adopted in 1986 as General Assembly Resolution 41/128, by 146 votes in favour, 1 against (cast by the USA) and 8 abstentions (Denmark, Finland, Federal Republic of Germany (as it then was), Iceland, Israel, Japan, Sweden and the UK). The Declaration contains 16 preambular paragraphs and 10 Articles. In the former part, it draws inspiration from the UN Charter, the two International Covenants on civil, political and economic, social and cultural rights, self-determination, sovereignty over natural wealth and resources, the link between disarmament and development, the new international economic order, the central position of the human person in the process of development and the indivisibility and interdependence of human rights. In the latter part, the Declaration calls the RTD a collective as well as an individual right, declares that the states have the right and duty to formulate appropriate national development policies, and provides that the states have the duty to cooperate with each other in ensuring development and further declares that the states should implement the RTD at the national level. In 1989, a Global Consultation was organized by the Secretary-General in response to the request made by the Commission.[16] A brief drafting history along with the features and weaknesses of the Declaration and the results of the consultation will be discussed in Chapter 4.

The Vienna Declaration (1993)

At the Vienna Conference in 1993, a Declaration and Programme of Action was adopted with a consensus. The Declaration reaffirmed the RTD as a part of fundamental human rights. Its relevant text reads:[17]

> The World Conference on Human Rights reaffirms the [RTD], as established in the [Declaration], as a universal and inalienable right and an integral part of fundamental human rights. As stated in the [Declaration], the human person is the central subject of development. States should cooperate with each other in ensuring development and eliminating obstacles to development. The international community should promote an effective international cooperation for the realization of the [RTD] and the elimination of obstacles to development.

16 CHR Res. 1989/45.

17 A/CONF.157/23. Online. Available at: <http://www.unhchr.ch/huridocda/huridoca.nsf/(Symbol)/A.CONF.157.23.En?OpenDocument> 12 July 1993 (accessed 27 Feb. 2009).

> Lasting progress towards the implementation of the [RTD] requires effective development policies at the national level, as well as equitable economic relations and a favourable economic environment at the international level.

The supporters of the RTD claimed the reaffirmation of the RTD as a victory.[18] The Commission organized a second working group in order to identify obstacles to the RTD and to recommend ways and means towards the realization of the RTD by all states.[19] After the Vienna Declaration, through a General Assembly resolution, the RTD became a part of the mandate of the Commission.[20] In 1993, a working group, initially for a period of three years, was established by the Commission. In 1995, the General Assembly required the Commission to establish a new branch on the RTD.[21] In its resolution 1996/15, the Commission reaffirmed the implementation of the RTD and set up another intergovernmental working group of experts for a period of two years.[22] Another important step was taken by the Commission in April 1998 through a consensus resolution that recommended to the Economic and Social Council (Council) the establishment of a follow-up mechanism through an Open-Ended Working Group (OEWG) and the appointment of an Independent Expert.[23] The Independent Expert was obliged to support the working group by submitting a study on the current state of progress in the implementation of the RTD as a basis for a focused discussion. The General Assembly passed a resolution in 1999 and invited the follow-up mechanism 'to consider the question of elaborating a convention on the [RTD]'.[24]

The current status of the RTD (2004–2007)

By the year 2007, the OEWG had held eight sessions, whereas the Independent Expert had submitted six reports. The Commission arranged a two-day seminar on 9 and 10 February 2004, in Geneva. The seminar included panel discussions on contributions of the UN agencies and programmes, partnership for development and national perspectives on the RTD.[25] The Commission, through resolution 2004/7, established a high-level task force on the implementation of the RTD.[26] The high-level task force held three meetings

18 Uvin, op. cit., p 42.
19 CHR Res. 1993/22.
20 UNGA Res. A/48/141 (1993).
21 UNGA Res. A/50/214 (1995).
22 CHR Res. 1996/15.
23 CHR Res. 1998/72.
24 UNGA Res. A/53/155 (1999), para. 21(b).
25 E/CN.4/2004/23 Add.1, 23 March 2004.
26 CHR Res. 2004/7, adopted on 13 April 2004 by a recorded vote of 49 votes to 3.

up to 2007. Its reports were considered by the working group in its sixth–eighth sessions.[27]

A review of the current status of the work would show that through a resolution, the Human Rights Council (previously the Commission) welcomed the report of the eighth session of the working group.[28] The Council decided to ensure that its agenda promotes sustainable development and the achievement of Millennium Development Goals (MDGs).[29] The Council also endorsed the working group's recommendation regarding the periodic evaluation of global partnerships for development. The work of the OEWG and the reports of the Independent Expert will be discussed in Chapter 4 in order to critically examine the efforts made towards realization of the RTD. The RTD has been reiterated and further elaborated upon – by consensus – at various UN conferences and meetings.[30]

Regional and national perspectives

At the regional level, the African (Banjul) Charter on Human Rights incorporated the RTD.[31] Most recently, the Social Charter adopted by the South Asian Association for Regional Cooperation (SAARC) has set out goals for the promotion and protection of all human rights, particularly the RTD. It relevant paragraph reads:[32]

> States parties agree . . . to promote universal respect for and observance and protection of human rights and fundamental freedoms for all, in particular the [RTD]; promote the effective exercise of rights and the discharge of responsibilities in a balanced manner at all levels of society; promote gender equity; promote the welfare and interest of children and youth; promote social integration and strengthen civil society.

27 See reports of sixth session, E/CN.4/2005/25; seventh session, E/CN.4/2006/26; eighth session, A/HRC/4/47.

28 CHR, Res. 4/4.

29 UNGA Res. A/55/2. The MDGs are: Eradicate extreme poverty and hunger; achieve universal primary education; promote gender equality and empower women; reduce child mortality; improve maternal health; combat HIV/AIDS, malaria and other diseases; ensure environmental sustainability; develop a global partnership for development.

30 They are the UN World Conference on Human Rights (Vienna), the International Conference on Population and Development (Cairo), the World Summit on Social Development (Copenhagen) and the Fourth World Conference on Women (Beijing). (Article I(10) of the Vienna Declaration, Principle 3 of the Cairo Programme of Action, Commitment 1(n) of the Copenhagen Declaration and Article 213 of the Beijing Platform of Action).

31 Text available at: <http://www1.umn.edu/humanrts/instree/z1afchar.htm> (accessed 27 Feb. 2009).

32 Article II of the SAARC Social Charter adopted in Dec. 2004. Text available at: <http://saarc-sdmc.nic.in/pdf/social_charter.pdf> (accessed 14 March 2009).

At the national level, some developing countries in Africa have recognized the RTD as a human right in their respective constitutions. They are Benin, Burundi, the Central African Republic, the Democratic Republic of Congo, Eritrea, Ethiopia, the Republic of Côte d'Ivoire (Ivory Coast), Malawi, Senegal and Uganda.[33] Malawi has recognized the RTD in Article 30 of its constitution as a human right. Thus, some case law specific to Malawi is available.[34] No other developing country has, so far, adopted it in its constitution. However, most of these countries have voted in favour of the Declaration and still continue to actively support it in the UN. Pakistan also has not recognized the RTD in its constitution but in 2005 adopted a plan of action to implement the SAARC Social Charter.[35] This Charter has specifically recognized the RTD as one of its goals and objectives. Pakistan's plan of action does not, however, mention the RTD. Pakistan's judiciary has been widely interpreting the constitutionally mandated fundamental rights and the Principles of State Policy so as to address the issue of social justice. This judicial practice has some implications for the RTD in Pakistan. Some judicial cases with elements of social and economic justice litigated through PIL in Pakistan will be examined in detail in Chapter 6. The RTD was cited by the International Court of Justice (ICJ) in the *Gabcikovo-Nagymaros Case*.[36] No specific case law on the RTD is available from an international judicial forum. According to the Lizin report, Portugal, Bulgaria and Yemen have promulgated social welfare legislation for combating poverty, which can serve as a rights-based approach to development.[37] Hence, poverty reduction strategies at the national level, too, can help in the realization of the RTD. Pakistan's PRSP, with particular reference to good governance and the rule of law vis-à-vis the RTD, will be critically examined in Chapter 8.

At the national level, countries have yet to pursue specific RTD-based development policies. The discussion on the RTD in the UN is guided by political considerations. As Stephen Marks has observed: 'the first obstacle to

33 See, generally, the constitutions of Benin, Article 9. Available at: <http://www.chr.up.ac.za/hr_docs/constitutions/docs/BeninC(englishsummary)(rev).doc>; Ethiopia, Article 43. Available at: <http://www.africa.upenn.edu/Hornet/Ethiopian_Constitution.html>; Malawi, Article 30. Available at: <http://www.sdnp.org.mw/ constitut/chapter4.html#30>; Uganda, Article IX, available at <http://www. trybunal.gov.pl/constit/constitu/constit/uganda/uganda-e.htm> (all accessed 27 Feb. 2009). See, generally, Ansah, op. cit.

34 Ibid.

35 Pakistan, 'Plan of Action to Implement SAARC Social Charter'. Available at: <http://www.pakistan.gov.pk/ministries/planninganddevelopment-ministry/usefull%20links/Economics/SAARC%20SOCIAL%20CHARTER.pdf> (accessed 27 Feb. 2009).

36 *Case Concerning the Gabcikovo-Nagymaros Project*, (Hungary/Slovakia), 1997 WL 1168556 (I.C.J.), 1997 I.C.J. 7. This case will be examined in Chapter 5.

37 See E/CN.4/1999/48, Report of Independent Expert (Ms. A.-M. Lizin), op. cit., paras 96–107.

the realisation of RTD is a political one.'[38] The nature of this political obstacle is that delegates in the UN forums vote for the RTD merely as a goal of foreign policy rather than to pursue a practical approach of mainstreaming the RTD in national and international development policies and practice.[39]

THE POLITICS OF THE RTD

The North–South divide

As discussed above, from its inception, the RTD has been one of the political issues between the North and the South. Since the 1960s, the newly independent developing countries wanted their economic self-determination as they were not satisfied with the international financial and trade institutions.[40] For instance, they wanted recognition of their economic inequality and exemption from the existing legal rules as well as the adoption of new ones in the international trade regime.[41] Similarly, through the NIEO Programme of Action, they demanded full and effective participation in the decision-making process of the International Monetary Fund (IMF).[42] The developing countries struggled hard for a change in the international economic order, using various forums, such as the Council, the United Nations Conference on Trade and Development (UNCTAD), the International Labour Organization (ILO), the Food and Agriculture Organization (FAO), and the World Health Organization (WHO), but with no success.[43] While North–South political relations were already tense, the two oil prices shocks of 1973 and 1979 further deepened the chasm between the two.[44] Although the Carter Administration in the USA 'was open to many of the goals and even some of the means contained in the demand for the establishment of a [NIEO]', the Reagan Administration, in the mid-1980s, adopted a tough stance on the issue, rejecting the notion of economic and social human rights.[45] Orford

38 Stephen Marks, 'Obstacles to the Right to Development', 2003. Online. Available at: <http://harvardfxbcenter.org/resources/working-papers/FXBC_WP17_Marks.pdf> (accessed 7 May 2009).

39 Ibid. p 13.

40 Chakravarthy Raghavan, *Recolonization: GATT, the Uruguay Round and the Third World*, London, Zed Books, 1990, p 83.

41 Kabir-Ur-Rahman Khan, 'The International Right to Development and the Law of G.A.T.T.', *Third World Legal Studies*, 1984, 160–74, at 162. See, generally, Abdulqawi A. Yusuf, 'Differential Treatment as a Dimension of the Right to Development' in R.-J. Dupuy (ed.), op. cit., 1980, pp 233–45.

42 UNGA Res. 3202 (S.VI), Article II.1(d).

43 Raghavan, op. cit., pp. 45–52.

44 Anne Orford, 'Globalization and the Right to Development' in Philip Alston (ed.) *The Rights of Peoples*, Oxford, Oxford University Press, 2001, pp 127–84, at p 130.

45 Ibid.; Philip Alston, 'Revitalising United Nations Work on Human Rights and Development', *Melbourne University Law Review* 18, 1991, 216–57, at 219–20 [hereinafter Alston, 'Revitalising UN Work'].

argues that the Reagan Administration's harsh posture had a deep and long-standing impact on the policies of international trade and financial institutions: the World Bank, from 1986 onwards, started making its loans conditional on structural adjustment policies, such as privatization and trade and investment liberalization; and the General Agreement on Tariffs and Trade (GATT) Uruguay round of talks, which concluded in the establishment of the World Trade Organization (WTO), further negatively influenced the RTD in the form of globalization.[46]

The debate over the RTD, inside the UN, is also highly politically charged between the North and the South, and as such does not seem to move from a 'predictable' political position to a 'practical dialogue on the implementation of the RTD'.[47] For example, the General Assembly, in its resolution 52/136, adopted in 1997, affirmed that the inclusion of the Declaration in the International Bill of Rights would be an appropriate means of celebrating the fiftieth anniversary of the Universal Declaration of Human Rights (UDHR).[48] A resolution submitted by Colombia on behalf of the Non-Aligned Movement (NAM) to the Commission, in its 1998 session, would have given effect to the said resolution of the General Assembly, but was withdrawn because of lack of support.[49] However, the Commission passed a different resolution on the RTD, which recognized that the fiftieth anniversary of the UDHR provided an important opportunity to place all human rights – and, in this context, the RTD in particular – at the top of the global agenda.[50] The politics of the RTD are vigorously played out by the states during the meetings of the General Assembly, the Commission and the working groups. Different countries and/or groups of countries have adopted different political positions, which are examined here.

The political positions of states/groups of states

The political positions of the states could be roughly seen along three groups.[51] First are the hard-liner developing countries (also called the Like-Minded Group (LMG)).[52] The hard-liners comprise Algeria, Bangladesh, Bhutan, China, Cuba, Egypt, India, Indonesia, Iran, Malaysia, Myanmar,

46 Orford, op. cit., p 130.
47 Stephen Marks, 'The Human Right to Development: Between Rhetoric and Reality', *Harvard Human Rights Law Journal* 17, 2004, 137–68, at 141.
48 UNGA Res. A/52/136 (1997).
49 Orford, op. cit., p 133.
50 CHR Res. 1998/72.
51 Marks, op. cit., p 141. Since 2004, the LMG has ceased to exist and the group speaks through Malaysia as the representative of the Non-Alignment Movement (NAM). Marks has divided the states into four groups. One group, he believes, genuinely wants to incorporate human rights into their national development policies and wants good relations with the donor community. Marks, however, does not specify which countries these are.
52 Ibid.

Nepal, Pakistan, the Philippines, Sri Lanka, Sudan and Vietnam. The main goal of this group is pursuance of the international dimension of the RTD, which addresses, amongst other things, inequalities in global trade, adverse effects of globalization, differential access to technology and debt relief.[53] The group also believes that the national dimension of the RTD could not be realized without international cooperation. Their main argument in support of their position is that the RTD is a claim of developing countries against developed countries for assistance in achieving economic development. In other words, they believe that the duty of cooperation as envisaged in the UN Charter is the foundation of the RTD.[54] This group continues to stress the importance of economic and social rights in connection with the RTD. It has also proposed the preparation of a binding instrument on the RTD. The position of this group has been the same throughout this period.

Another group of states is mainly led by the USA and includes smaller countries under its influence such as Israel, the Marshall Islands and Palau.[55] Since the USA is the main opponent of the RTD, therefore its main arguments, as put forward by its delegates in the UN forums, may be discussed here. The USA argues that development can be achieved through a free market economy as well as protection of civil and political rights, not through an RTD.[56] It is not clear from the USA position how the Declaration and the concept of a free market economy are incompatible with each other.[57] The USA also argues that developing countries support the RTD on the pretext of justifying violation of civil and political rights. This argument has no force because the Declaration emphasizes equal and urgent consideration for all human rights, including elimination of obstacles to development, which may be caused by failure to observe civil and political rights and economic, social and cultural rights.[58] The Vienna Declaration and Programme of Action further strengthens this exhortation because it proclaims that the pursuance of development may not be used as an excuse for the violation of internationally recognized human rights.[59] It may be mentioned that in a 1999 address to the Commission, the USA delegate supported this reaffirmation by the Vienna Declaration.[60] Another area of concern for the USA is the linkage of economic and social rights to the RTD. The USA sees these rights as mere aspirations and argues that these rights do not involve legal obligations.[61] Developing countries, on the other hand, argue that economic and

53 Ibid.

54 Rich, op. cit., 302.

55 Marks, op. cit., 'The other members of this group vary according to circumstances and have included Japan, Denmark, and Australia', p 142.

56 Ibid.

57 Ibid. p 146.

58 DRD, Preamble, para.10 and Article 6(3).

59 Vienna Declaration, Article 10.

60 E/CN.4/1999/SR.10, Commission on Human Rights, fifty-sixth session, Summary Record of the 10th Meeting, 30 March 1999.

61 Marks, op. cit., p 147.

social rights are equally important for development. The nature of economic and social rights was also a matter of dispute between capitalist and communist countries during the drafting process of the UDHR (see Chapter 3). The Declaration makes it clear that human rights are indivisible and interdependent; it treats the economic and social rights as being on a par with civil and political rights. The USA holds the view that the issues pertaining to the international political economy cannot be discussed in the human rights forums of the UN. Developing countries are using 'the Commission and the treaty bodies as the principal sources of pressure on states to ensure that human rights are not forgotten in the economic and financial negotiations'.[62] The USA is also actively opposing the creation of any legally binding instrument on the RTD.[63] Like the first group, the US position on the RTD has also remained unchanged. The status of the legal position of the USA in international law will be examined in Chapter 5.

A third group of states, comprising developed countries, appears to be inclined towards a dialogue between the developing and the developed world.[64] In this group, the European Union (EU) sometimes votes in favour of the RTD and sometimes prefers to abstain from voting.[65] Initially, almost all Western European states opposed the RTD outright (see Chapter 4). However, as will be seen below, they have changed their position with the passage of time.

The voting trends in the General Assembly

Of significant importance is the changing position of the third group, mostly comprising the principal donor countries, namely: Australia, Austria, Belgium, Canada, Denmark, France, Germany, Norway, Sweden and the UK.[66] It is interesting to note that from 1997 to 2006, the position of some of these countries (particularly those in Europe) has moved from outright opposition to abstention during the voting proceedings in 2002 and 2003 and shifted to support of the RTD resolutions in 2004 and 2005. Since the meaningful support of these countries for the RTD can bring about significant changes in the RTD debate, therefore it is deemed necessary to critically analyse its political position.

Table 2.1 illustrates the voting pattern. Although, since 2004, the LMG has ceased to exist and the group speaks through Malaysia as the representative of the NAM, for the sake of analysis, the categorization of the hard-liners as LMG is retained here, while the term Key Donor Countries (KDCs) is

62 Ibid. p 150.
63 Ibid.
64 Ibid. p 142.
65 Ibid.
66 Ibid.

Table 2.1

Year	*Resolution*	*Votes in favour*	*Votes against*	*Abstentions*	*Total*
1997	A/Res/52/136	LMG + 1 KDC + Others	5 KDC + USA + Japan + others	4 KDC + others	129 votes to 12, with 32 abstentions
1998	A/Res/53/155	LMG + others	USA	10 KDC + Japan + others	125 votes to 1, with 42 abstentions
1999	A/Res/54/175	LMG + other	5 KDC + USA + Japan + others	6 KDC + others	119 votes to 10, with 38 abstentions
	(The Resolution as whole)				
Separate voting	Eighth Preambular paragraph	LMG + others	10 KDC + USA + Japan + others	1	113 votes to 44, with 1 abstention
	Thirteenth Preambular paragraph	LMG + others	10 KDC + USA + Japan + others	1	111 votes to 44, with 1 abstention
	Operative para. 3(c)	LMG + others	10 KDC + USA + Japan + others	3	113 votes to 42, with 3 abstentions
	Operative para. 3(e)	LMG + others	10 KDC + Japan + others	0	121 votes to 30, with no abstentions
	Operative para. 13	LMG + others	10 KDC + USA + Japan + others	1	114 votes to 43, with 1 abstention
	Operative para. 21	LMG + others	10 KDC + USA + Japan + others	2	112 votes to 43, with 2 abstentions
	Operative para. 22	LMG + others	10 KDC + USA + Japan + others	0	115 votes to 42, with no abstentions
	Draft Resolution as a whole	LMG + others	4 KDC + USA + Japan + others	6 KDC + others	119 votes to 10, with 38 abstentions
2000	A/Res/55/108		Adopted without a vote		
2001	A/Res/56/150	LMG + others	1 KDC + USA + Japan + others	9 KDC + others	123 votes to 4, with 44 abstentions
2002	A/Res/57/223	LMG + others	1 KDC + USA + others	9 KDC + Japan + others	133 votes to 4, with 47 abstentions
2003	A/Res/58/172	LMG + 7 KDC + others	USA + others	3 KDC + Japan + others	173 votes to 3, with 5 abstentions
2004	A/Res/59/185	LMG + 7 KDC + others	USA + others	3 KDC + Japan + others	181 votes to 2, with 4 abstentions
2005	A/Res/60/157	LMG + 8 KDC + others	USA + others	2 KDC + Japan + others	172 votes to 2, with 5 abstentions
2006	A/Res/61/169	LMG + others	10 KDC + USA + Japan + others	0	134 votes to 53, with no abstentions

Source: Data collected from the Official Documents System of the UN. Available at <http://daccessdds.un.org/doc/UNDOC/GEN/N01/705/38/PDF/N0170538.pdf?Open Element> (accessed 9 May 2006).

used for the donor countries. The positions of the USA and Japan, being the main adversaries of the RTD, are shown separately.

The eight KDCs that have supported the RTD resolutions in the period 2003–2004 are: Austria, Belgium, Denmark, France, Germany, Norway and the UK. In the 2005 session, Sweden, which abstained in the earlier two sessions, favoured the RTD resolution; hence the total number of KDCs was eight. The separate voting on different parts of the 1999 resolution suggests the degree of conflict between the developed and developing countries over some key issues underlying the RTD in the international context. They are the negative impacts of sanctions, the existence and preservation of human rights as a condition for assistance, the participation of developing countries in the international economic decision-making process through its democratization, the humanitarian effects of sanctions, in particular on women and children, the impact of poverty, structural adjustment, globalization, financial and trade liberalization, and deregulation. Most countries from the EU joined the USA and Japan in voting against the above-mentioned aspects of the international dimension of the RTD. The representative of the EU explained the EU's negative vote on this resolution, but showed the willingness of the EU to work on the RTD:

> The [EU] stands prepared to work for the realization of the [RTD] in constructive partnership with all interested countries. For that purpose, we have great expectations and hopes, for the follow-up mechanism, which was established with the support of all Member States . . . the implementation of the [RTD] deserves active support from the international community. The European Union reiterates its willingness to continue, in a true partnership, its cooperation in implementing the [RTD]. Such partnership should, in our view, be reflected in a joint commitment to each consensus in multilateral forums. We therefore hope that the open-ended working group on the [RTD] will be able to lay the foundations for a return to consensus on the important subject of the [RTD].[67]

This statement and the 2004–2005 voting pattern show a radical shift in the political position of major European countries. The figures also indicate that the USA and small countries under its influence have remained the only countries that still oppose the RTD resolutions. The official records of the resolutions show that two other major donor countries, Australia and Canada, abstained from 2003 to 2005. Japan voted against the RTD resolutions in 1997 and 2001, while abstaining in 1998 and 2002–2005. The legal implications of these trends for customary international law will be further discussed in Chapter 5. A recent study of the UK's Overseas Development

67 UN, 'Official Records of the GA 54th session, 83rd Plenary Meeting', 17 Dec. 1999, A/54//PV.83, pp 25–26 Available at: <http://daccessdds.un.org/doc/UNDOC/GEN/N00/277/29/PDF/N0027729.pdf?OpenElement> (accessed 28 Feb. 2009).

Institute (ODI) shows that the change in the policy of the EU countries could be attributed to an overall shift in the policy of some of the key donor countries to make aid more effective by linking it to poverty reduction programmes and human rights.[68]

The Commission on Human Rights

The political positions of states and/or groups of states, discussed above, also reflect in the debate on the RTD at the Commission. For example, during the fifty-seventh session of the Commission in March 2001, the USA delegate reiterated that a free market economy and a focus on civil and political rights were necessary for development.[69] In a 2005 session of the Commission, the USA representative repeated this position with a hint about individual RTD in the context of the UDHR: 'we can talk about an individual's [RTD]. However, we cannot talk about a nation's [RTD], at least in these precincts, for the simple reason that nations do not have human rights.'[70] The EU has maintained its conciliatory approach in the Commission, but has put more emphasis on the national dimension of the RTD. This is clear from the statement of its representative delivered to the fifty-eighth session in 2002.[71] The position of developing countries in the Commission has remained unchanged.

A look at the fifty-fourth to fifty-sixth sessions (1998–2000)[72] of the

68 See Laure-Helene Piron (ODI), 'Integrating Human Rights into Development, A Synthesis of Donor Approaches and Experiences', prepared for the OECD DAC Network on Governance (GOVNET), Sept. 2005. The study aims at 'assisting an action-oriented policy in 2006'. See Executive Summary at: <http://www.odi.org.uk/rights/Publications/humanrights_into_development_execsumm.pdf> (accessed 28 Feb. 2009).

69 See Ambassador George Moose, US Delegation and US Permanent Representative to the UN Offices in Geneva, Remarks to the 57th Session of the UN Commission on Human Rights, Geneva, Switzerland, 27 March 2001. Available at: <http://www.usmission.ch/humanrights/2002/statements/0327development.html> (accessed 28 Feb. 2009).

70 Statement by Lino J. Piedra, Public Member of the US delegation before the Commission on 22 March 2005. Available at: <http://geneva.usmission.gov/humanrights/2005/0322Item7.htm> (accessed 28 Feb. 2009).

71 EU Presidency Statement: 'Commission on Human Rights – Right to Development'. Available at: <http://www.europa-eu-un.org/articles/en/article_1296_en.htm>. See also statement of the EU Presidency delivered to the Commission in 2005, which says that the EU is firmly committed to the realization of the RTD. Available at: <http://www.europa-eu-un.org/articles/en/article_5414_en.htm> (accessed 28 Feb. 2009).

72 CHR Res. 1998/72; 1999/79; 2000/5. All these resolutions were adopted without a vote. However, the same session adopted another resolution (1999/22) by 30 votes to 15, with 8 abstentions. This resolution pertained to 'Effects of the full enjoyment of human rights of the economic adjustment policies arising from foreign debt and, in particular, on the implementation of the Declaration on the Right to Development'. See Commission on Human Rights, Reports of the Fifty-Fourth session (16 March–24 April 1998), ECOSOC, Chapter VI, pp 116–28; Fifty-Fifth session (22 March–30 April 1999), Chapter VII, pp 103–10; Fifty-Sixth session, (20 March–28 April 2000), Official Record 2000, Supplement No. 3, Chapter VII, p 399.

Commission reveals that the RTD resolutions were adopted without a vote. Interestingly, most of the KDC countries co-sponsored these resolutions. The UK, Canada and Japan supported the proposal during all the separate votes. In the 2001 session,[73] an RTD resolution was adopted by the Commission by 48 votes to 2, with 3 abstentions. Belgium, France and Germany favoured the resolution, Canada and the UK abstained and Japan and the USA opposed it. In the 2002 session,[74] the KDC preferred to abstain from the voting when the resolution urged them to make concrete efforts towards meeting the target of 0.7 per cent of their Gross Domestic Product (GDP) for official development assistance to developing countries and 0.15 to 0.2 per cent of their Gross National Product (GNP) to least developed countries for development purposes, market access for developing countries to agricultural and non-agricultural products, etc. The record of the fifty-ninth to sixty-first sessions (2003–2005)[75] show that Austria, Belgium, France, Germany and the UK have favoured the RTD resolutions, Australia has voted against all these resolutions, while Canada has abstained from the voting in 2003 and 2005. Japan voted against the RTD resolutions in 2003 and 2004 and abstained in 2005. The USA has maintained its negative posture throughout. On 30 June 2006, the newly established Human Rights Council, which replaced the Commission, adopted a resolution on the RTD without a vote.[76] It may be pointed out that the USA is not a member of the current Human Rights Council. If it were, it would have probably opposed the RTD resolution.

What are the implications of the above voting patterns for the legal position of the RTD? It appears that there is no consensus between developing and developed countries over the international dimension of the RTD. Despite changes in its position, the EU does not seem willing to support certain international economic issues, such as trade liberalization, particularly market access in agriculture, the transfer of technology, development aid, debt-burden relief and the participation of developing countries in the decision-making processes of international trade and financial rules and policies. This suggests that developed countries are not willing to support a resolution of the General Assembly and/or the Commission that may create an international convention on the RTD.

73 E/CN.4/2001/167 (2001). See Report of the Fifty-Seventh session (19 March–27 April 2001), ECOSOC, Official Record, Supplement No. 3, Chapter VII, pp 374–6.

74 E/CN.4/2002/69. See Report of the Fifty-Eighth session, (18 March–26 April 2002), ECOSOC, Official Record, Supplement No. 3, Chapter VII, pp 428–9.

75 CHR Res. 2003/83; 2004/7; 2005/4. See ECOSOC Official Records, Supplement No.3 of Reports of the Fifty-Ninth session (17 March–25 April 2003), Chapter VII, pp 355–356, Sixtieth session (15 March–23 April 2004), Chapter VII, pp 367–8, Sixty-First session (14 March–22 April 2005), Chapter VII, pp 1–3.

76 HRC, Res. 1/4.

Human rights in development programmes

Despite all the political wrangling, since its early days, the RTD has been the focus of various seminars, conferences and colloquia sponsored by the International Commission of Jurists, United Nations Educational, Scientific and Cultural Organisation (UNESCO) and the Division of Human Rights.[77] The aftermath of the Cold War has brought significant changes in the development-human rights debate.[78] Irrespective of the voting patterns analysed above, many developed countries such as Australia, Denmark, Germany, Norway, Sweden and the UK[79] are willing to integrate human rights into their respective development assistance programmes. This can prove helpful in promoting the RTD.

All the UN development-related programmes have similarities with the features of the RTD. The United Nations Development Group (UNDG) is an instrument for UN reform, created by the Secretary-General in 1997, in order to improve the effectiveness of UN development activities at the country level to help them achieve the MDGs, which link development to human rights. The United Nations Development Assistance Framework (UNDAF) has also been established, which 'provides a collective, coherent and integrated United Nations' response to the national priorities and needs within the framework of the MDGs'.[80] The World Bank has also started using the language of human rights in its policy documents. In 1998, the World Bank issued a report on the occasion of the fiftieth anniversary of the UDHR in which it recognized the promotion of human rights as a challenge.[81] Very recently, the World Bank has stated that 'human rights are an intrinsic part of the Bank's mission'.[82] All these international frameworks for development cooperation have been discussed by the Independent Expert in his reports submitted to the OEWG on the RTD. While all these changes are still only at the level of rhetoric, they are, apart from a long political and historical background, also underpinned by a paradigm shift in the conceptualization of development itself.

77 Donnelly, 'In Search of a Unicorn', 475.

78 Alston, 'Revitalising UN Work', 221.

79 Hamm, op. cit., 1011.

80 Available at: <http://www.un.org/special-rep/ohrlls/ohrlls/cca_undaf_prsp.htm> (accessed 28 Feb. 2009). The 'UNDAF process in each country is based on a Common Country Assessment (CCA), an overview of national development prepared in the light of a common set of indicators'.

81 World Bank, *Development and Human Rights: The Role of the World Bank*, Washington, 1998. Available at: <www.worldbank.org/html/extdr/rights/hrtext.pdf> (accessed 28 Feb. 2009).

82 Ana Palacio, 'The Way Forward: Human Rights and the World Bank', *The World Bank Development Outreach*, Jan. 2007. Online. Available at: <http://www1.worldbank.org/devoutreach/article.asp?id=388> (accessed 28 Feb. 2009).

CONCEPTUAL BASIS

In some of his reports, the Independent Expert on the RTD has elaborated the concept of the RTD in the perspective of Sen's capability approach, a philosophical notion of development. The Independent Expert on the RTD sees the connection between the RTD and the capabilities approach thus:

> In order to . . . have much more useful categorization of the variables in making development policy, Sen . . . *approached this problem almost entirely from the point of view of the* [RTD]. According to [. . .] Sen, development is best seen as a process of expanding substantive freedoms that people enjoy.[83]

The Independent Expert also observes that 'the implications of treating the [RTD] as a human right have been fairly well explored in the literature, including Sen's *Development as Freedom*'.[84] It is necessary to examine the capabilities approach, particularly its relation with human rights.

The capability approach

In precise terms, this approach sees development as enhancement of human capabilities. As Sen has put it, this is: 'the capacity to lead the kind of life that he or she has reason to value'.[85] In order to achieve development that can lead to meaningful freedom, a mere increase in the GNP is not the only instrument, so 'we must look well beyond it'.[86] It is due to looking at functionings and capabilities with particular reference to economic inequality that development is seen as a means of real freedom. As 'the primary end', expansion of freedom plays a 'constitutive role', while as 'the principal means, it plays an "instrumental role" ' in development.[87] In his 1985 Tanner Lectures at Cambridge, Sen precisely defined functioning and capability thus:

> A functioning is an achievement, whereas a capability is the ability to achieve. Functioning are different aspects of living conditions. Capabilities, in contrast, are notions of freedom in the positive sense: what real opportunities you have regarding the life you may lead.[88]

83 First Report of the Independent Expert, para. 55 (emphasis added).

84 Third Report of the Independent Expert, para. 20.

85 Sen, *Development as Freedom*, p 87.

86 Ibid. p 14.

87 Ibid. p 35.

88 Sen, 'Lives and Capabilities', in Geoffrey Hawthorn (ed.) *The Standard of Living*, Cambridge, Cambridge University Press, 1987, pp 20–38, at p 36 [hereinafter Sen, 'Lives and Capabilities']. For a more elaborate definition of functioning and capability, see Sen, *Inequality Re-examined*, op. cit., p 39.

Sen begins with simple questions such as: 'Is he well off? Does she have much freedom? Can he get what he wants? Can she do what she would like to do?'[89] Sen argues that the answers to these questions lie in 'well-being' and 'advantage'. The former is a matter related to 'a person's achievement' and the latter is connected with 'opportunities that the person has, especially compared to others'.[90]

The actual achievement ('what we *manage* to accomplish') must be different from the freedom to achieve ('with *real opportunity* that we have to accomplish what we value').[91] The freedom to achieve is ultimately possible by means of capability. Diverging from the traditional economic perspective of well-being and advantage, the capability approach concentrates on 'functionings' rather than commodities, for example, bicycling and possessing a bike.[92] It further advocates that there must be freedom to choose a variety of 'functionings'. It follows that firstly, bicycling should not be the only functioning. Secondly, the individual should have the freedom to choose whichever she/he likes from the stock of other available alternatives. The capability approach thus provides absolutely different benchmarks to measure the standard of living. It follows that capability implies opportunity to have a variety of alternative patterns and the freedom to choose a pattern of one's choice.

The capability approach rejects the traditional utilitarian method of GNP for measuring human welfare. Utilitarianism is confined to sufficiency of total goods. This method of valuation of welfare ignores individual welfare. It ignores distributional effects. It lacks substance because of diversities and variations among human beings.[93] For example, between the utilities of a 'pleasure-wizard person' and 'a crippled person', utilitarianism would not go beyond utility of the former, leaving the latter 'doubly worse off'.[94] Sen asserts that utilitarianism looks at total utility and total utility alone, overlooking all other things.[95] While considering a person's happiness, utilitarianism does not extend to such questions as how it occurs, what are its causes and whether it is confined to a few persons or enjoyed by a lot of people.[96]

The capability approach further divulges that utilitarianism considers that the mere feeling of an individual being happy is enough. A person cannot be called happy if s/he is simply saying that s/he is happy and satisfied. As Sen puts it: 'I still value x, but I haven't got it, and *have learnt to be happy and*

89 Sen, *Commodities and Capabilities*, London, North-Holland, 1985, p 1.

90 Ibid. p 5.

91 Sen, *Inequality Re-examined*, op. cit., pp 20–31.

92 Sen, *Commodities and Capabilities*, op. cit., p 10.

93 Sen, 'Equality of What?' in Sen, *Choice, Welfare and Measurement*, Oxford, Basil Blackwell, 1982, pp 353–69, p 355.

94 Ibid. p 367.

95 Sen, 'Rights and Capabilities' in Ted Honderich (ed.) *Morality and Objectivity – A Tribute to J.L. Mackie*, Routledge & Kegan Paul, 1985, pp 130–48.

96 Ibid. p 131.

satisfied without it.'[97] Where people have become used to their bad conditions of life, they usually feel satisfied in their extreme poverty; they are unable to recognize the level of their deprivation, which they quietly accept as a consequence of their fate.[98] It is generally observed that this way of thinking is common in those parts of the world where poverty has long been a condition of life.

Capability and human rights

Capability and human rights are closely related to each other. Human rights are those rights which are inherent to human beings. A right is a claim, the opposite of which is an obligation. There is a dispute over the nature of the claim and the nature of the obligation of human rights, which is discussed in the next chapter. It may be mentioned here that the debate is significantly informed by the notions of positive freedom and negative freedom, a well-known distinction drawn by Isaiah Berlin. The former implies the freedom 'of the individual to be his [/her] own master'.[99] The latter denotes the liberty of an individual to act 'unobstructed by others'. Sen argues that 'concern with positive freedom leads directly to valuing people's capabilities and instrumentally to valuing things that enhance these capabilities'.[100] The capability approach claims an improvement over the constraint-based view of rights. This view, advanced by Nozick, argues that rights or entitlements obtained through legitimate rules of 'ownership, transfer and rectification' should not be compromised for the sake of greater social good.[101] In other words, the obligation to respect a right is in the form of a constraint on others. This view is closely related to negative freedom. While the merit of the constraint-based view of rights cannot be underestimated, it champions the cause of negative freedom in a piecemeal fashion and does not concern positive freedom at all.[102] Moreover, this view cannot do justice to human rights, because, for the promotion of human rights, the scope of the obligation of the principle duty-bearer, i.e. the state, extends much further than the mere constraint of non-interference. The state has various levels of obligations, such as not to violate human rights (i.e. to respect), to protect others from violation (i.e. to protect) and to take positive action for the realization of human rights (i.e. to fulfil).

Sen has argued that opportunities and processes, being important aspects

97 Sen, 'Concepts and Critiques' in Hawthorn, *The Standard of Living*, op. cit., pp 1–19 at p 8 (emphasis added).

98 Sen, 'Rights and Capabilities', op. cit., p 132; Martha Nussbaum, 'Capabilities and Human Rights', *Fordham Law Review* 66, 1997, 273–300, at 282.

99 Isaiah Berlin, *Four Essays on Liberty*, Oxford, Oxford University Press, 1969, p 131.

100 Sen, 'Rights and Capabilities', op. cit., p 148.

101 See Robert Nozick, *Anarchy, State and Utopia*, Oxford, Basil Blackwell, 1974, pp 151–2.

102 Sen, 'Rights and Agency', *Philosophy and Public Affairs* 11(1), 1982, 3–39.

of freedom, are crucial parts of the contents of human rights.[103] The opportunity aspect of freedom implies that a person must have various options that should include valuing free choice, for example 'choosing freely to go out'.[104] When one is forced to do something without freedom of choice, for example 'being forced to go out', it is a violation of process freedom. Forcing one to do something one would not choose to do, if one had had plausible alternatives, amounts to violation of opportunity freedom. The capability approach thus significantly contributes to the opportunity aspect of freedom.[105] Sen has, however, clarified that the capability approach cannot go adequately with the process aspect of human rights. The reason Sen advances is that capability is a characteristic of individual advantages, while processes of freedom (human rights) need to be fair and equitable. The capabilities, Sen argues, 'fall short of telling us enough about the fairness or equity of the processes involved, or about the freedom of citizens to invoke and utilise procedures that are equitable'.[106] Thus capability can be realized, in this limited perspective, through a system of rights.

The reason that rights are understood in the language of capabilities is that capabilities provide functioning to realize rights; the mere guarantee of a right is not enough unless the state creates a conducive atmosphere for its practical realization,[107] a system based on a wider scope of obligation of the state, as discussed above. From the perspective of positive freedom, the capability approach also sees rights as goals of social and economic development. The realization of goal rights can enhance capabilities. Hence, goal rights, Sen argues, are best called capability rights.[108] What substantive rights are to be included in capability rights?[109] Sen answers that goal rights can be formulated in terms of peoples' rights to capabilities,[110] which include both negative and positive rights.

The capability approach also links poverty with human rights. Poverty is not merely a low level of income but a very low level of well-being and can be defined as a failure to realize basic capabilities, such as to be free from hunger, to be able to lead a life free from avoidable morbidity and mortality, to be able to take part in the life of the community, to be able to appear in public with dignity.[111] There is a growing view that poverty should be seen as denial of a number of human rights in the perspective of the capability approach.

103 Sen, 'Human Rights and Capabilities', *Journal of Human Development* 6(2), 2005, 151–66.
104 Ibid. p 155.
105 Ibid. p 163.
106 Sen, 'Human Rights and Capabilities', op. cit., p 156.
107 Nussbaum, op. cit., p 295.
108 Sen, 'Rights and Agency', p 16.
109 Ibid. p 15.
110 Ibid. See also S.R. Osmani, 'Poverty and Human Rights: Building on the Capability Approach', *Journal of Human Development* 6(2), 2005, 205–19.
111 Osmani, op. cit., 207.

However, it is necessary to clarify that denial of a human right would amount to poverty only when firstly, the human right in question is related to some notion of basic capabilities and secondly, 'lack of command over economic resources should play some mediating role in the causal mechanism leading to the denial of right'.[112] The implications of a human rights-capability combination for policy options in the poverty reduction programme of Pakistan will be explored in Chapter 8.

List of capabilities

Is the listing of capabilities necessary to elucidate human rights?[113] Sen argues that while capabilities may be listed by theorists, they should, in the ultimate analysis, be subjected to public discussion.[114] There could be a list of minimally basic capabilities, such as education, health services, food, housing and employment (for example, mentioned in Article 8(1) of the Declaration). A list of capabilities shall not, however, be fixed and exhaustive; it shall be open-ended in order to be attuned to the changing needs of people. Moreover, the capabilities should be prioritized according to the circumstances.[115] For example, during a famine, the right to food will be at the top of the agenda.[116] In a society with mass illiteracy, the right to education may be given priority. Nussbaum's list of capabilities, which she calls a list of opportunities for functioning, contains life, bodily health, bodily integrity, senses, imagination and thought, emotions, practical reason, affiliations, such as friendship and respect; play and recreation and control over environment.[117]

Realizing capabilities through the RTD

How, then, could capabilities be achieved? The capability approach may be incorporated in national as well as international development policies as a political goal.[118] The United Nations Development Programme (UNDP) has adopted this approach for measurement of quality of life: 'development *of* the people means investing in human capabilities'.[119] The *Human Development Report*, 1996, recognizes human development as an end, and economic growth as a means.[120]

112 Ibid. 218.
113 Sen, 'Human Rights and Capabilities', p 152.
114 Ibid. pp 157–58.
115 Ibid.
116 Ibid.
117 Nussbaum, op. cit., pp 286–8; the author discloses that she has revised the list in the light of her visit to India.
118 Ibid. pp 276, 89.
119 UNDP, *Human Development Report*, New York/Oxford, Oxford University Press, 1993, p 3 (emphasis in original); see also ibid. p 275.
120 UNDP *Human Development Report*, New York/Oxford, Oxford University Press, 1996, p 1.

According to Nussbaum, capabilities must be provided to an individual as rights, while functioning should be left to individual choice.[121] Expressing capabilities in the language of rights is advantageous because the language of rights conveys the sense that peoples' claims are justified as well as urgent; the language of rights contains an element of agreement; the language of rights carries force; and, the force adds a value.[122] Referring to her proposed list of capabilities discussed above, Nussbaum concludes that 'we are doing wrong to people when we do not secure to them capabilities'.[123]

At the international level, the capability approach may prove very helpful to the formulation and implementation of international development policies. The bilateral and multilateral aid agencies may learn much from this approach to ensure that development aid is spent on enhancing basic capabilities of the poor, particularly the vulnerable among them. The international community can do a lot to enable the state in implementing a capability-based human development programme for its people. The capability approach has, thus, a key role in the promotion of solidarity rights, notably the RTD. In this respect, the pursuance of ideals based on cooperation may ensure international distributive justice,[124] and may promote the RTD.

Islamic perspective vis-à-vis capability and human rights

In Chapter 7, capability and human rights will be seen in the perspective of the *Shari̔ah* (Islamic law). A few words seem necessary here. In the *Shari̔ah*, the principal objective of the Lawgiver (God) is the promotion of human welfare (*maslahah*). The higher objectives of law (*Maqasid al-Shari̔ah*) comprise five essentials, viz. religion, life, intellect, lineage and property. Some of the key human rights as laid down in the UDHR, such as the right to life, religion, property and family life[125] appear to overlap with these broad purposes of the *Shari̔ah*. This list of purposes of the *Shari̔ah* is also comparable with Nussbaum's list of capabilities, mentioned above. The doctrine of *maslahah* and the capability-human rights combination may help each other. Moreover, *maslahah* is also supported by contemporary Muslim scholars to allow a progressive interpretation of Islamic law to address the broader issues of social and economic development in the Muslim world.[126]

121 Nussbaum, op. cit., p 293.
122 Ibid. pp 295–6.
123 Ibid. p 300.
124 Janna Thompson, *Justice and World Order A Philosophical Inquiry*, Routledge, London, 1992, p 37.
125 Articles 3, 18, 28 and 16.
126 Al-Raysuni, op. cit.

CONCLUSION

While all human rights in general are the products of the post-Second World War era, the RTD as a third-generation human right is deeply rooted in the colonial past. Some commentators have argued that the term 'third world' itself flouts the definition of freedom and equality.[127] Hence, it is a continuation of the hate and dejection felt by the people of the developing world towards the developed world that existed in the era of colonialism. In the post-colonial era, the struggle shifted from political independence to economic self-determination under the auspices of the UN. The RTD emerged as a buzzword of that struggle. Although the movement of the developing countries for an NIEO ended in the mid-1970s, the RTD survived. The developing countries have successfully managed to keep it alive in the General Assembly and the Commission. As a political issue, it found expression in the Vienna Declaration, 1993, which is claimed as a victory by the developing countries. In the General Assembly, it is receiving support from some major Western donor countries. This indicates a visible change in the political will of these countries. However, it appears that these countries are not willing to support the international dimension of the RTD, which stresses international solidarity that is based on cooperation for a comprehensive development policy, aimed at enhancing the capability of the world's poor population. Conceptually, the RTD could be linked with Sen's capability approach, which has been adopted by the UNDP and other major bilateral and multilateral development organizations. In a limited sense, the capability approach can facilitate the realization of human rights. The capability-human rights combination can also inform the Islamic concept of social justice through the lens of the *Shari'ah* doctrine of *maslahah*. A major theoretical issue of the RTD, however, relates to jurisprudential controversies, which are taken up in the next chapter.

127 C.G. Clayton Weeramantry, 'Fundamental Perspective on Equality and Freedom: some Third World Aspects' in Carl Wellman, Saint Louis (ed.), *Equality And Freedom: Past, Present and Future*, Wiesbaden, Germany, Franz Steiner Verlag, 1977, p 17.

3 The jurisprudence of the RTD

INTRODUCTION

The legal status of the RTD as a human right is the most important issue that needs to be addressed while examining its legal status in international law. According to the Declaration, the RTD is a human right. But this assertion is contentious and controversial. The Declaration envisages that every human person and all peoples are at the same time the right-bearers as well as duty-holders of the RTD.[1] It also declares: 'states have the primary responsibility', 'the duty to cooperate with each other', 'the duty to take steps, individually and collectively' to facilitate the realization of the RTD. All these appear to be vague phrases. While the vagueness in the content of the language is common to all human rights instruments,[2] given the controversial position of the RTD, this problem needs to be addressed to resolve the issue of justiciability. Thus when the discussion comes to the actual realization of the RTD, it is found that the rights and duties assumed thereunder are not totally simple and clear. Hence, the RTD faces a challenge. The debate surrounds many issues, for example what is the source of this right? Who should be the right-holder and who should be the duty-bearer? What should be the content of such a right? How can such a right be enforced? The controversy becomes more complicated when the RTD of people, or a group or a state is talked about. This leads to what may be called the heart of the debate: the implementation (justiciability) of the RTD. This chapter addresses all these issues: the sources, the subjects, the content and the justiciability of the RTD.

1 DRD, Articles 1(1) and 2(2).

2 See Philip Alston, 'Making Space for New Human Rights: The Case of the Right to Development', *Harvard Human Rights Year Book of International Law* 1, 1988, 3–40, at 31 (hereinafter Alston, 'Making Space for New Human Rights').

SOURCES

The bulk of the current literature shows that the RTD has two sources, viz. the right to self-determination and Article 28 of the UDHR. It is pertinent to examine the brief drafting history of these two sources in order to seek the foundations of the RTD in the current human rights discourse.

The right to self-determination

The drafters of the Declaration realized that the right to self-determination is an important aspect of the RTD. Thus the sixth preambular paragraph of the Declaration draws inspiration from the right to self-determination in the following words:

> Recalling the right of peoples to self-determination, by virtue of which they have the right freely to determine their political status and to pursue their economic, social and cultural development.

Almost all of these words are borrowed from paragraph 1 of Article 1 of the two covenants, viz. ICCPR and ICESCR.[3] This common article of the two covenants emphasizes the importance of the right to self-determination for human rights. The UN Human Rights Committee has observed: 'The right to self-determination is of particular importance because its realization is an essential condition for the effective guarantee and observance of individual human rights and for the promotion and strengthening of those rights.'[4] It appears from this statement that the right to self-determination, which is basically a collective right, is closely related to individual human rights. It seems necessary to explain the distinction and relationship between the two. Collective

3 It reads:

1. All peoples have the right of self-determination. By virtue of that right they freely determine their political status and freely pursue their economic, social and cultural development.
2. All peoples may, for their own ends, freely dispose of their natural wealth and resources without prejudice to any obligations arising out of international economic co-operation, based upon the principle of mutual benefit, and international law. In no case may a people be deprived of its own means of subsistence.
3. The States Parties to the present Covenant, including those having responsibility for the administration of Non-Self-Governing and Trust Territories, shall promote the realization of the right of self-determination, and shall respect that right, in conformity with the provisions of the Charter of the United Nations.

4 General Comment 12 on the Right of Self-determination of Peoples, The UN Committee on Human Rights, Twenty-first session, 1984. See also Allan Rosas, 'The Right of Self-determination' in Asbjorn Eide, Catarina Kraus and Allan Rosas (eds) *Economic, Social and Cultural Rights, A Text Book*, The Hague, Martinus Nijhoff Publishers, 1995, pp 79–86 at p 79.

rights are those which are exercised by individuals together.[5] 'The fundamental element in collective rights . . . is the protection of the rights of individuals exercised collectively.'[6] Individual human rights are those which are derived from inherent human dignity, which one has merely as a human being. It will be argued that the RTD is both a collective and an individual right.

Is the right to self-determination a source of the RTD? According to Bedjaoui, the right to self-determination is the undoubted source of the RTD.[7] In support of his view, Bedjaoui argues that the present international community, the vast majority of which comprises developing countries, owes its existence to the right to self-determination. He further argues that the self-determination is *jus cogens* because other principles governing the international community are derived from it.[8] This view is also supported by Keba M'baye, who argues that the right to self-determination is recognized in international law as provided by the International Covenants on Human Rights and the General Assembly resolution (1803 (XVII)) on permanent sovereignty over natural resources.[9] Most developing countries achieved their independence by exercising their right of self-determination. It is on the basis of this right that they can claim an RTD to pursue their economic and social development. While the right to self-determination and the RTD are not one and the same, they are so closely related in the sense that the former would be of no use if the latter were not recognized.[10] Thus the right to self-determination is seen as the source of a collective RTD, i.e. of people or state. A question arises: could the right to self-determination also be a source of an individual RTD? This question will be answered later in this section.

Donnelly, a known critic of the RTD, argues that the right of self-determination, as laid down in common Article 1(1) of the two Covenants[11] may be an implicit source, but 'it is explicitly only a right to pursue development . . . neither does it imply [that] an *individual* [RTD] . . . is a right of peoples only'.[12] He further argues that considering the right of

5 Margot E. Salomon with Arjun Sengupta, *The Right to Development: Obligations of States and the Rights of Minorities and Indigenous Peoples*, London, Minority Group International, 2003, pp 9–10.

6 Ibid.

7 Bedjaoui, 'The Right to Development' in Bedjaoui, (ed.) op. cit., pp 1177–203, at p 1178.

8 Ibid.

9 Keba M'baye, 'Human Rights and Peoples' Rights' in Bedjaoui (ed.), op. cit., pp 1041–58 at p 1049.

10 Bedjaoui, op. cit., p 1184.

11 Article 1(1): 'All peoples have the right of self-determination. By virtue of that right they freely determine their political status and freely pursue their economic, social and cultural development.'

12 Donnelly, 'In Search of a Unicorn', op. cit., 484. For a response to Donnelly, see Philip Alston, 'The Shortcomings of a "Garfield the Cat" Approach to the Right to Development', *California Western International Law Journal*, 15, 1985, 510–18 [hereinafter Alston, 'Garfield').

self-determination as the simple source of the RTD amounts to a misunderstanding of the Covenants.[13] Crawford also believes that Article 1(1) of the two Covenants guarantees the rights of peoples.[14] Cassese, another critic of the RTD, asserts that the content of the right of self-determination cannot be used for the protection of peoples' rights because in international law, the states act on behalf of the peoples.[15] He cites the example of the dispute between the UK and Argentina over the Falkland Islands, in which the Western countries supported the contention of the UK and the developing countries supported the contention of Argentina.[16]

Whether it is a people's right (Donnelly) or a state's right on behalf of peoples (Cassese), there appears to be a consensus of opinion over its being a collective right. In the case of the former, people can assert it. In the case of the latter, the state can assert it on behalf of the people. If the right to self-determination is a collective right (a solidarity right) – the right of people and/or state – the question arises as to whether it could be a human right. In this respect, a reference may be made to the drafting history of this right. During the drafting process, there was a considerable debate over the issue whether self-determination was a 'political principle' or a 'right'.[17] One group of delegates viewed it as a collective 'right' as well as a 'political principle'.[18] The other group argued that it cannot be a 'right' because of lack of its precise definition, particularly of some key relevant words, for example 'peoples' and 'nation'. Hence, this group favoured it as a 'political principle'.

Regarding the question of whether the right of self-determination is a source of an individual RTD, it is argued that the inclusion of this right in the two covenants (i.e. ICCPR and ICESCR) was proposed for the reason that this right was indispensable for the enjoyment of all other human rights.[19] However, it was pointed out that the right was to be promoted immediately in relation to civil and political rights and progressively in relation to economic, social and cultural rights.[20] Western countries opposed its status as a human right, but it was finally agreed to be a human right.[21]

The right of self-determination, as a collective right, is crucial for the

13 Donnelly, 'In Search of a Unicorn', 484.

14 James Crawford, (ed.) *The Rights of Peoples*, Oxford, Oxford University Press, 1988, pp 58–9.

15 Cassese, *International Law in a Divided World*, paras 92, 13 and 214.

16 Ibid.

17 M.J. Bossuyt, *Guide to the 'Trauvax Preparatoires' of the International Covenant on Civil and Political Rights*, Dordrecht/Lancaster, Martinus Nijhoff Publishers, 1987, pp 19–48, at p 20.

18 Ibid.

19 Ibid. p 25.

20 Ibid. p 35.

21 Ibid. p 36. See George Abi-Saab, 'The Legal Formulation of a Right to Development' in R.-J. Dupuy (ed.) op. cit., pp 159–75, at p 163. See also Bedjaoui, op. cit., pp 1184–8.

realization of individual human rights because the individual is the ultimate beneficiary of human rights. Moreover, self-determination has economic, social and cultural aspects, and as such is a necessary source of the RTD. The right to 'freely determine their political status and to pursue their economic, social and cultural development' points to the RTD in two respects. Firstly, the free pursuit of economic, social and cultural development is not possible without international cooperation. The demand of developing countries for greater participation in the decision-making process of the rules and policies of the International Financial Institutions (IFIs) and the WTO illustrates this point. Secondly, the states have the right to devise suitable development policies for the well-being of the population as a whole and of all individuals by allowing them true and meaningful participation, which is a key feature of the RTD (see Chapter 4).

According to Abi-Saab, the RTD is a collective right as well as an individual right.[22] Bedjaoui[23] and Brownlie[24] also support this view. While discussing the conflict between human rights and peoples' rights, Keba M'baye also explains that peoples' rights, though collective, are individual as well, for the reason that an individual is the ultimate beneficiary of rights.[25] Quoting from J. Rivero, Espiel contends that some existing rights (such as the right to meet, to strike, to unionize) do qualify for both individual and collective rights.[26] Espiel maintains that the RTD 'would be an individual right in its beginning and its end, and a collective right in its implementation'.[27] Searching for the foundations of this right in international law, Alston is of the opinion that firstly, new problems and perceptions of the global community have necessitated the creation of new rights (obviously the RTD being one of them).[28] Secondly, Alston rebuts the argument that this right is a synthesis of existing rights, or superfluous and useless in the presence of the social and economic rights, arguing that this right aims at creating such an environment for social, cultural and economic development at the international level as can improve respect for human rights.[29] Alston seems to subscribe to the view expressed by the UN Committee on Human Rights, referred to above. In other words, the international aspect of the RTD may help create a new international economic order. Moreover, acknowledgement of this means that

22 Abi-Saab, op. cit.

23 Bedjaoui, op. cit., p 1182.

24 Ian Brownlie, *The Human Right to Development*, London, Commonwealth Secretariat, 1989, para. 34.

25 M'baye, in Bedjaoui (ed.), op. cit., p 1053.

26 H.G. Espiel, 'The Right to Development as a Human Right', *Texas International Law Journal* 16, 1981, pp 189–205, at p 196. See also Stephen Marks, 'Emerging Human Rights: A New Generation for the 1980s?' *Rutgers Law Review* 33, 1981, 435–52.

27 Espiel, op. cit.

28 Philip Alston, 'The Right to Development at the International Level', in F.E. Snyder and S. Sathirathai (eds), *Third World Attitudes Towards International Law*, Dordrecht/Lancaster, Martinus Nijhoff Publishers, 1987, pp 812–13, at p 813.

29 Ibid. p 819.

existing rights are not sufficient and adequate. But conversely, it may also be argued that the RTD may act as a means to strengthen the existing rights.[30] Another possibility is that in future social and economic rights may merge into the RTD. Some would also argue that the RTD is based on economic self-determination.[31] Realization of individual rights is necessary for collective rights. Conversely, collective rights pave the way for the fulfilment of individual rights.

Article 28 of the UDHR

Article 28 of the UDHR is said to be another source of the RTD.[32] Being the principal human rights document, the UDHR was substantively considered by the founding fathers of the Declaration. Article 28 of the UDHR was reproduced verbatim in the third preambular paragraph of the Declaration. It reads:

> Considering that under the provisions of the Universal Declaration of Human Rights *everyone is entitled to a social and international order in which the rights and freedoms set forth in this Declaration can be fully realized.*[33]

This Article provides that a social and international order is essential for the realization of the human rights laid down in the UDHR. It is made clear that the Article refers to an international order for the realization of human rights. However, the Article does not make an explicit reference to the RTD. It may be seen as an implicit source of the RTD. Firstly, the existence and maintenance of an international order require a duty of cooperation on the part of the states. Secondly, a reference to the rights in the UDHR includes all rights, i.e. civil and political and economic, social and cultural rights – implying the indivisibility of all human rights. But then the question is, as Donnelly argues, whether it includes 'development'. It means 'prohibiting *structures* that deny opportunities or resources for the realization of civil and political, economic, social and cultural human rights'.[34] Donnelly's argument comes very close to the notion of the RTD when he admits the importance of economic development for the realization of human rights, which is a central issue of the RTD. Developing countries claim the RTD to correct the international economic structure, which they say denies them the opportunities or resources for the realization of human rights. As argued in Chapter 2, the linkage of development and human rights was a demand of developing

30 Ibid. p 818.
31 Rich, 'The Right to Development an Emerging Human Right', 319.
32 Ibid. 301.
33 Italics used for the words of Article 28 UDHR.
34 Donnelly, op. cit., 486.

countries for a long time. The 1968 Tehran Declaration and a 1969 General Assembly resolution are the earliest examples. Thus Article 28 could be seen as creating an entitlement of everyone to such an international order as leads to the realization of all human rights, which is the ultimate goal of the RTD. An effective and efficient international order is, however, possible when there is recognition of the duty of cooperation, which the international community has pledged in Articles 55 and 56 of the Charter.

Articles 55 and 56 of UN Charter

The international community has recognized the principle of international economic and social cooperation in Articles 55 and 56 of the Charter of the UN.[35] In these Articles, the international community recognizes the principle of international cooperation (i.e. solidarity) for the realization of human rights and promotion of economic, social and cultural development and self-determination of peoples. The principle of cooperation pronounced in these two Articles is one of the main features of the RTD. Referring to Keba M'Baye, Mestdagh considers these two Articles as sources of the RTD.[36] However, Bedjaoui, another proponent of the RTD, calls it a doubtful source of the RTD.[37] The concept of the solidarity rights is perceived as the principle of *fraternity* envisaged by the French Revolution.[38] The word cooperation used

35 UDHR

> Article 55: With a view to the creation of conditions of stability and well-being which are necessary for peaceful and friendly relations among nations based on respect for the principle of equal rights and self-determination of peoples, the United Nations shall promote:
>
> a. higher standards of living, full employment, and conditions of economic and social progress development;
> b. solutions of international economic, social, health, and related problems; and international cultural and educational co-operation; and
> c. universal respect for, and observance of, human rights and fundamental freedoms for all without distinction as to race, sex, language, or religion.
>
> Article 56: All Members pledge themselves to take joint and separate action in co-operation with the Organisation for the achievement of the purposes set forth in Article 55.

36 See Karel de Vey Mestdagh, 'The Right to Development', *Netherlands International Law Review* 3, 1981, pp 30–53 at 33.

37 Bedjaoui, op. cit., p 1183.

38 The other two principles are liberty and egalitarianism. Liberty is attributed to the French Revolution – civil and political rights; egalitarianism to the Russian Revolution – social, cultural and economic rights; and solidarity to international cooperation of the twentieth century. This approach, known as generational theory, is attributed to Karel Vasak. For this see Rich, op. cit., 322. According to T.H. Marshall, a British sociologist, the eighteenth century was the century of civil rights, the nineteenth century that of political rights and the twentieth century that of social rights; quoted in Henry Steiner and Philip Alston, *International Human Rights in Context: Texts and Materials: Law, Politics and Morals*, Oxford, Oxford University Press, 2000, p 1319.

in the Charter can be most plausibly taken as conveying the meaning of solidarity. Cooperation as a source of obligation in international law will be discussed in Chapter 5.

Donnelly argues that solidarity cannot give rise to a human right because 'to have a human right, one needs be nothing other than a human being, nor do anything other than be born human'.[39] He also argues that the economic and moral interdependence of states does not create any right, much less a human right, because interdependence 'implies a cooperative joint undertaking . . . likely to involve contractual or quasi-contractual rights'.[40] In support of the RTD as a solidarity right, Bedjaoui says that (1) the 'international community of States as a whole' is recognized as *jus cogens* in Article 53 of the Vienna Convention on the Law of Treaties, (2) which has also been articulated by the ICJ in *the Barcelona Traction Case*, 1970.[41] Moreover, in the context of international law, particularly international economic law, international solidarity means interdependence of states. While Donnelly does not agree that Article 28 is a source of the RTD, he agrees that the said Article 'would seem to imply only a right to the removal of such impediments to development – at most a right to a [NIEO]'.[42] It has been argued in Chapter 2 that the NIEO is seen as the root cause of the RTD. Moreover, many resolutions of the General Assembly spelling out a state's obligation to support international economic development, for example the Declaration and Programme of Action on the Establishment of an NIEO, have been passed with consensus.[43] Some others are mentioned below.

39 Donnelly, op. cit., 493.

40 Ibid.

41 Bedjaoui, 'The Right to Development', pp 1184–1185; For the *Barcelona Traction* case see 1970 WL 1 (I.C.J.), 1970 I.C.J. 3 *Case Concerning the Barcelona Traction, Light and Power Company, Limited (New Application: 1962) (Belgium v. Spain)*, In this case, the Court held: 'In view of the importance of the rights involved, all States can be held to have a legal interest in their protection; they are obligations *erga omnes*. Such obligations derive, for example, in contemporary international law, from the outlawing of acts of aggression, and of genocide, as also from *the principles and rules concerning the basic rights of the human person*, including protection from slavery and racial discrimination. Some of the corresponding rights of protection have entered into the body of general international law (Reservations to the Convention on the Prevention and Punishment of the Crime of Genocide, Advisory Opinion, I.C.J. Reports 1951, p 23); others are conferred by international instruments of a universal or quasi-universal character' (emphasis added).

42 Donnelly, op. cit., 487.

43 Rich, op. cit., 299; they are UNGA Res. A/Res//1710, 1960, quoted in Rich, op. cit., p 299, and A/Res/2626 (XXV), 1970 and A/Res/35/56.

Other international instruments[44]

Article 28 has been followed up in various international instruments of significant importance. The ICESCR, for instance, in its preamble, recognizes that 'freedom from fear and want can only be achieved if conditions are created whereby every one may enjoy his[/her] economic, social and cultural rights as well as civil and political rights'. The emphasis on the principle of cooperation in Articles 2 and 11(2) of the ICESCR further lends support to the ideals of a social and international order laid down in Article 28 of the UDHR.

The General Assembly Declaration on Social Progress and Development is also 'seen as a significant step in the follow up of the UDHR'.[45] According to Article 12 of the Declaration, one of the main objectives of social progress and development is:

> The creation of conditions for rapid and sustained social and economic development, particularly in the developing countries; change in international economic relations; new and effective methods of international co-operation in which equality of opportunity should be as much a prerogative of nations as of individuals within a nation.

It is clear from the above discussion that in the immediate aftermath of the Second World War, the international community, particularly in the West, was willing to include social and economic development in the international human rights law. But very soon this commitment gave way to the ideological division of the two blocs.

This situation created a challenge for both the human rights academics and development practitioners.[46] Arguably, the rights-based approach to development, as a means of the RTD, is but a part of the effort to meet this challenge. The rights-based approach is instrumental in realizing the RTD. However, care must be taken that these are not the same. (The distinction between the two was explained in Chapter 1.) It may be mentioned here that the RTD has an added value because it must take note of complementarities, trade-offs among rights and international cooperation as a human rights obligation.

The Declaration specifically refers to the right to self-determination and Article 28 (including the UN Charter, the two covenants and other norms of international law) in both its preamble and its operative parts. But all these are simply aspirations and ideals only. The challenges to the RTD are the

44 Asbjorn Eide, 'Article 28' in Asbjorn Eide, et al (eds), *The Universal Declaration of Human Rights: A Commentary*, Oslo, Scandinavian University Press, 1992, pp 433–47, at pp 440–7. The discussion here is mainly drawn from Eide.

45 Ibid.

46 B.-A. Andreassen, 'Article 22' in Asbjorn Eide et al. (eds), op. cit., p 352.

legal recognition of the right to a social and international order (Article 28) and the national efforts and international cooperation (Article 22) together with the right to self-determination.

SUBJECTS

Who are the subjects of the RTD? The state (or peoples) or the individual or both are the subjects of the RTD. The argument that the state is a duty-holder at the national level and a subject at the international level constitutes a debate that goes to the roots of the concept of rights. A question also arises as to whether individuals are the subjects or the beneficiaries of the RTD.[47] This is the most debated issue of the jurisprudence of the RTD, which is examined below.

State as a subject

Donnelly argues that considering the state as a subject of the RTD is highly problematic for the reason that 'the right-holder [the state] is not a physical person, and thus an institutional "person" must exercise [the right]'.[48] Donnelly further argues that states or peoples do have rights and that collective rights do exist, but they are not human rights. The crux of his arguments is that a collective right cannot be a human right. This view appears to be based on what Alston calls an 'excessively individualistic approach to human rights'. The disadvantage of this approach is that it does not take stock of the social and economic conditions of the communities in which the individuals live.[49] The view that for human rights one needs to be nothing other than a human being may not be an unjust one. However, it is not a sufficient criterion for human rights if the living conditions of people are not considered.[50] Moreover, human rights are demanded from the community at large through the intervention of the state.[51] In fact, the privilege of a human right is available to a human being as a member of the community. A human right thus cannot be seen in the strict sense as a separate notion from the community. The human rights of individuals assume much more importance when as members of a group or a community they 'suffer disadvantage, oppression or exploitation as a result of membership of that group or community'.[52] The protection of the human rights of those individuals is possible

47 Anja Lindroos, *The Right to Development*, Helsinki, The Erik Castren Institute of International Law and Human Rights Research Report 2/1999, pp 30–31.

48 Donnelly, op. cit., 498.

49 Alston, 'Garfield', op. cit., 516.

50 Orford, op. cit., p 137.

51 Alston, 'Garfield', op. cit., 512.

52 Orford, op. cit., p 138.

through the collective rights of the group or community. In other words, an individual right could not be exercised without the realization of the collective right.

The RTD does not simply mean development of an individual by guaranteeing him/her human rights; if it did, it would stop the argument on existing human rights, rendering the RTD of the individual unnecessary.[53] A separate RTD should not be considered as the aggregate of all the existing human rights of each individual 'but of all the individuals constituting a collectivity'. Secondly, it is necessary to look at the RTD directly from the perspective of the collective right by considering it either as the economic dimension of the right of self-determination or as parallel to self-determination.[54]

Critics of the RTD also assert that the notion of the state being a beneficiary of the RTD is a dangerous one. The reason they advance this view is that the state can violate the human rights of the individual while still claiming *its* own human right.[55] Yash Ghai shares this view and argues that Asian states support the RTD in order to give greater importance to economic development than to human rights.[56] The opposition of the USA towards the RTD is also based on this argument, among others. This argument was examined in the previous chapter, where it was argued that preambular paragraph 10 and Article 6(3) of the Declaration and the Vienna Declaration and Programme of Action prohibit violation of human rights for the sake of development. It may be added here that Article 2(1) of the Declaration puts the human person as the central subject of development, an objective also reiterated by the Vienna Declaration.

State as a duty-holder

According to the Declaration, the state is the duty-holder at the national level as well as at the international level.[57] It appears to be generally accepted that the primary duty for the RTD lies with the state. Some commentators, however, believe that 'the difficulties lie in determining what is to be expected from states in relation to its population, and, moreover, what can be expected of other states and the international community in relation to developing countries'.[58]

In so far as a state's duty at the national level is concerned, one may disagree with the above argument for the reason that the Declaration clearly

53 Abi-Saab, op. cit., p 164.

54 Ibid.

55 Donnelly, op. cit., 499 (emphasis in original).

56 Yash Ghai, 'Human Rights and Governance: The Asia Debate', *Australian Year Book of International Law* 15, 1994, 1–34 at 9–10.

57 DRD, Arts 2(3), 3(1) and 8.

58 Lindroos, op. cit., p 34.

sets out what the state has to do for the realization of the RTD. Article 3(3) provides that 'states have the . . . duty to formulate national development policies'. Article 8 says:

> States should undertake, at the national level, all necessary measures for the realization of the [RTD] . . . shall ensure . . . equality of opportunity for all in their access to basic resources, education, health services, food, housing, employment and the fair distribution of wealth . . . ensure women have an active role in development.

The most important part of the state's duty, which the Declaration proclaims, is the principle of participation. What is, however, not clear is how the state can be compelled to fulfil this duty. This question relates to another jurisprudential issue called justiciability that is discussed later in this chapter.

Regarding the state's duty at the international level, there is no doubt that some confusion revolves around the jurisprudence of the RTD. The Declaration stresses the need for promoting the rapid development of the developing countries.[59] To this end, the Declaration uses the words 'duty to cooperate', 'the duty to take steps, individually and collectively' and 'effective international co-operation is essential'.[60] These words are patently devoid of a mandatory effect, creating a problem of justiciability. Moreover, it is not clear what exactly the states should collectively do to promote the rapid development of the developing countries.

Peoples as a subject

The next issue is whether peoples are a subject of the RTD. The word 'peoples' has been used in the Declaration in three different places. Firstly, in Article 1(1) the RTD is proclaimed as an inalienable human right of all peoples. Secondly, Article 1(2) provides that the RTD 'also implies the full realization of the right of peoples to self-determination'. Thirdly, in Article 5 the word appears in the context of the elimination of the flagrant violation of the human rights of peoples and the refusal to recognize their fundamental right to self-determination. The use of the word 'peoples' in the Declaration is vague and uncertain.

The Global Consultation on the RTD noted that difficult questions are raised by the word 'people'.[61] The Consultation also observed that the status of 'peoples' as the beneficiaries of the RTD is not necessarily the same as is understood in the context of the right to self-determination.[62] The

59 DRD, Art. 4(2).
60 Ibid. Arts 3(3), 4(1) and (2).
61 Report of the Global Consultation on the Right to Development, CHR Res. 1989/45, para. 80.
62 Ibid.

Consultation, however, 'generally felt that the term people should encompass groups within the State, such as indigenous peoples and minorities, as far as the [RTD] is concerned'.[63] Perusal of the report of the OEWG shows that the word 'peoples' is generally used to refer to the population of the state.[64] The various UN forums such as the Commission, the General Assembly and the Independent Expert on the RTD give no explanation of the word 'peoples'.[65] However, it is also used for making references to the RTD of different groups such as ethnic, linguistic, religious and indigenous and vulnerable groups such as migrants, persons with disabilities, children and persons affected with HIV/AIDS.[66] The African Charter on Human Rights mentions the RTD as a peoples' right.[67] While rights of 'peoples', 'nations' and 'groups' are widely referred to both in the official documents and in academic commentaries, these terms are still not clearly and unanimously defined.[68] Hence, the word 'peoples' remains an unsettled issue of the jurisprudence of the RTD.[69]

Individual as a subject

The Declaration pronounces that the RTD is the right of every human person.[70] It further proclaims that the human person is the central subject of development and should be the active participant and beneficiary of the RTD.[71] It further provides that the constant well-being of the entire population and of all individuals should be the aim of the national development policies.[72] The Vienna Declaration has also reiterated the central position of the human person in the process of development.[73] One commentator has rightly raised a preliminary question as to whether the subject of a right and the beneficiary of a right are not the same.[74] The former can claim a right in accordance with the domestic procedural laws; the latter cannot do so.[75] The

63 Ibid.

64 E/CN.4/2001/26, Report of the Open-Ended Working Group on the Right to Development.

65 See Philip Alston, 'Peoples' Rights: Their Rise and Fall' in Philip Alston (ed.), *The Rights of Peoples*, Oxford, Oxford University Press, 2001, pp 259–93 at pp 285–6.

66 E/CN.4/2001/26, p 41.

67 See the African Charter on Human and Peoples' Rights, Art. 22.

68 Lindroos, op. cit., p 34. See also Tatjana Asnbach, 'Peoples and Individuals as subject of the right to development' in Subrata Roy Chowdhury et al. (eds), *The Right to Development in International Law*, Dordrecht/London, Martinus Nijhoff Publishers, 1992, pp 155–65.

69 See Salomon, op. cit., pp 9–10.

70 DRD, Art. 1(1).

71 Ibid. Art. 2(1).

72 Ibid. Art. 2(3).

73 Ibid. Art. 10.

74 See Salomon, op. cit., p 30.

75 Ibid.

individual as a subject can claim a human right against the state under domestic human rights law. But the individual is a subject of a human right in international law in a very limited sense, i.e. under the optional protocol to the ICCPR.[76] Lindroos argues that treating individuals 'as mere beneficiaries seems misleading, since individuals can make claims at the national level' and they 'are not necessarily considered as subjects of international law'.[77] This issue will be further discussed in the next chapter as one of the weaknesses of the Declaration.

It is not a problem to identify the individual as a subject of the RTD.[78] As will be seen later in this chapter, the subject or right-holder is one of the essential characteristics of a right. The enforcement of the right would face a serious challenge if the right-holder is not specific. The critics of the RTD also admit that recognition of the individual as a subject of a human right to development is not a conceptual problem.[79] Academically, this issue appears to raise little conflict of opinion. It does not, however, resolve the jurisprudential controversy entirely. The contentious issue is that the RTD is to be recognized as a right of the state or of peoples. The RTD of the state will create an enabling environment for the realization of an individual RTD. In this context Bedjaoui views the RTD as 'much more a right of the state or of the people, than a right of the individual'.[80] The individual dimension of the RTD cannot be separated from its collective dimension. Recognition of the developing countries as a special category of states in international economic law is, in the ultimate analysis, aimed at improving the well-being of the peoples and all individuals in those countries. Where the state claims the RTD as a beneficiary at the international level, it holds a duty, at the national level, to fairly and equitably distribute those benefits among all individuals and the entire population on the strength of a rights-based approach to development.

CONTENT

In order to acquire a full juridical status, the content of the RTD needs to be specifically defined. A close analysis of the Declaration shows that the content of the RTD can be seen as comprising three categories: as an individual right, as a collective right and as both an individual and a collective right. Shown in Table 3.1, these categories are, however, not considered rigid.

76 Ibid. p 31; the European Convention on Human Rights also provides a procedure for individual human rights complaints.

77 Ibid.

78 Abi-Saab, op. cit., p 168.

79 Donnelly, op. cit., 500.

80 Bedjaoui, op. cit., p 1184.

Table 3.1

Individual right (RTD at the national level)	*Collective right (RTD at the international level)*	*Both Individual/Collective right*
Inalienable human right of every person (Art. 1(1))	And all peoples (Art. 1(1))	Development . . . a comprehensive economic, social, cultural and political process . . . aims at the constant improvement of the well-being of the *entire population and of all individuals* . . . their active, free and meaningful participation (Preamble, para. 2)
Human person the central subject, active participant and beneficiary of the RTD (Art. 2(1))	Self-determination of peoples . . . sovereignty over natural resources (Art. 1(2))	Well-being of *entire population and all individuals*, participation in development, fair distribution of economic benefits (Art. 2(3))
Equality of opportunity for all in their access to basic resources, education, health services, food, housing, employment and fair distribution of income; ensuring women's role in development; eradication of all social injustices (Art. 8(1))	Promotion of new international economic order (Art. 3(2)); rapid development of developing countries (Art. 4(2))	Elimination of massive and flagrant violations of human rights of *peoples and human beings* affected by conflict of one form or the other (Art. 5)
Creation of conditions favourable to the RTD at the national level (Art. 3(1))	Conditions favourable to the RTD at the international level (Art. 3(1))	
	Dividends of international peace/disarmament to be used for development, particularly of the developing countries (Art. 7)	
	Popular participation in all spheres as an important factor of development (Art. 8(2))	

Individual right

As an individual right, the content of the RTD may be seen in Article 1(1), which asserts it as an inalienable human right. This Article needs to be read jointly with Articles 2, 6 and 8. Articles 2 and 8 portray broadly the means and ends of the RTD. The former provides that 'the improvement of the well-being of the entire population and all individuals' shall be the aim of national development policies. The guiding principles of such a policy shall be participation,[81] equity and justice. The latter articulates that the steps to be taken shall guarantee 'equality of opportunity for all' in economic development (e.g. access to basic resources, employment and fair distribution of income) and social development (e.g. education, health, food and housing).[82] Coupled with Article 8, Article 6(3) requires the states to adopt 'all necessary measures' and remove 'obstacles to development'. Moreover, Article 3(1) provides that 'conditions favourable to the realization of the [RTD]' are to be created by the state at the national and international levels.

Collective right

The content of the RTD, according to Bedjaoui, comprises firstly, *erga omnes* claims (rights or obligations towards all), and secondly, a right, due from other states or the international community.[83] The first implies that the state must be 'master in his own house' by having meaningful exercise of permanent sovereignty over its natural resources, in the absence of which world peace is in danger. 'State sovereignty, permanent sovereignty over natural resources and the [RTD]', argues Bedjaoui, are inseparable from each other and the RTD thus deserves to be recognized as *jus cogens*.[84] The second includes the due rights of the state in the global distribution of wealth and the right 'to receive a fair share of what belongs to all'.[85]

Article 1(1) of the Declaration makes a reference not only to the individual human right but also to a collective RTD.[86] The promotion of a new international economic order constitutes the main content of the right in its collective form.[87] It has the following elements. Firstly, the rapid development of developing countries is the end of such an international order that is to be based on sovereign equality, interdependence, mutual interest and cooperation among all states.[88] Secondly, the means for achieving this end is the individual and collective responsibility of states to formulate international development policies for the realization of the RTD.[89] Thirdly,

81 Konrad Ginther, 'Participation and Accountability: Two Aspects of the Internal and International Dimension of the Right to Development', *Third World Legal Studies*, 1992, 55–77 at 57.

82 Lindroos, op. cit., p 44.

83 Bedjaoui, op. cit., pp 1188–91.

84 Ibid.

85 Ibid. p 1192.

86 See, generally, Arjun Sengupta, 'The Right to Development as a Human Right', Xaviour-Bagnoud Centre Harvard School of Public Health and Human Rights. Online. Available at: <www.hsph.harvard.edu/fxbcenter/FXBC_wp – Sengupta.pdf> 1–16 at 3 (accessed 7 May 2009).

87 DRD, Art. 3(3).

88 Ibid. Arts 4(2) and 3(3).

89 Ibid. Art. 4(1).

'[s]tates have the primary responsibility for the creation of national and international conditions, favourable to the realization of the [RTD]'.[90] Fourthly, the dividends of international peace and security are to be utilized for the RTD of the developing countries.[91] Fifthly, the RTD means the right to self-determination of peoples, particularly to exercise their full sovereignty over their natural wealth and resources.[92] In a nutshell, the collective dimension of the RTD implies that the international community has a duty to cooperate with the state in the realization of the RTD at the national level.

The right to a process of development

According to the Independent Expert,[93] the RTD comprises the following contents:

- an inalienable human right,
- a right to the process of development, and
- every human person's entitlement to the process of development.

The Independent Expert has explained in his various reports how the RTD is a right to a process of development. In this respect, he has carried out a textual analysis by referring to various articles of the Declaration.[94] Development must be a process that leads to the realization of human rights. The process of development must also aim at the principles of equity and social justice. The Independent Expert, however, differentiates the process of development from its outcome in the following words:

> The process must be distinguished from the outcomes of the process. The realization of different rights (i.e. civil and political rights, as well as economic, social and cultural rights) may be the specific outcomes of several policy programmes. But the right to those outcomes is quite different from the right to the process that produces those outcomes.[95]

Defending his view that the RTD is a right to a ('particular') process of development being necessary, the Independent Expert argues that without its being a right to a process, 'designing any mechanism or policies for realizing the [RTD] to development with any degree of precision would not be

90 Ibid. Art. 3(1).
91 Ibid. Art. 7.
92 Ibid. Art. 1(2).
93 Independent Expert, First Report, paras 36–46.
94 Ibid. See also DRD, e.g. Arts 1(1), 2(3), 6 and 8.
95 Ibid. para. 22.

possible'.[96] From a review of the first four reports of the Independent Expert, the following picture emerges:

1 The RTD is a right to a process of development in which 'all human rights and fundamental rights can be fully realized'.[97]
2 The process of development envisages an integrated approach of all the human rights as well as the enjoyment of all the fruits (outcomes) of development, and based on such principles of equity and justice as participation, accountability, transparency, non-discrimination and the rule of law.[98]
3 The integrated approach does not imply the RTD as a sum total of existing rights (value addition). The process of development aims at expansion of the opportunities and enhancement of the capabilities of the entire population, particularly the most disadvantaged sections.[99]
4 The [RTD] is described as a 'vector' of different elements. These elements include different rights – civil and political and economic, social and cultural – coupled with the rate of growth in economic resources.[100] These elements are interdependent (complementarities) on each other. 'An increase in the value of the [RTD] . . . will be defined as an improvement in the value of all the elements of the vector . . . or at least in one element of the vector while no other element deteriorates.'[101]

Osmani argues that the RTD should not be defined 'exclusively as a right to a process of development'. The reason he gives is that such a view makes the RTD only instrumentally valuable, ignoring the outcome (e.g. equity and sustainability) that has an intrinsic value in the concept of the RTD.[102] He further argues that viewing the process of development as instrumentally valuable is also harmful to the concept of the RTD itself because there could be no one process that could be agreed upon. Disagreement among people over a certain process of development can lead to 'a conflict of rights', which will be ultimately harmful to the whole tradition of human rights.[103]

While Osmani disagrees with the view of the Independent Expert that the RTD is a process of development because it does not allow trade-offs among

96 Ibid. para. 7.
97 See DRD, Art. 1(1).
98 Independent Expert, Second Report, paras 17 and 22.
99 Independent Expert First Report, para. 47.
100 Independent Expert Second Report, para. 23; Third Report, paras 8–10; Fourth Report, para. 4.
101 Ibid.
102 S.R. Osmani, 'Some Thoughts on the Right to Development', in *The Right to Development Book, Reflections on the First Four Reports of the Independent Expert on the Right to Development*, Geneva, Franciscans International, 2004, pp 34–45, at p 36.
103 Ibid. p 37.

different rights, he argues that the Independent Expert has included civil and political rights alongside economic, social and cultural rights in a vector representation[104] of the RTD. Hence, 'it is only logical to define the RTD in the space of outcome rather than as a right to a process of development'.[105] Osmani also views the participatory process of development as incomplete. He argues that the element of participation makes the process of development valuable in itself, 'not merely as an instrument for achieving socio-economic or civil-political rights'.[106] He maintains that the RTD is a combination of both substantive rights (civil-political and socio-economic rights) and certain process-related principles, such as participation, non-discrimination, transparency and accountability. Thus he proposes what he calls 'an alternative formulation' of the RTD (which he claims to be consistent with Article 1(1) of the Declaration) that includes both the right to a process and the right to outcomes:

> [1] The right to development is the right of everyone to enjoy the full array of socio-economic-cultural as well as civil-political rights equitably and sustainably and [2] through a process that satisfies the principles of participation, non-discrimination, transparency and accountability.[107] [added Numbers]

While one may not entirely disagree with Osmani's view, the third and fourth reports of the Independent Expert clearly include the outcomes perspective of the process of development. The third report argues that the vector approach of the process of development includes the principles of participation, non-discrimination, transparency and accountability 'and sharing of the fruits or outcomes of the process'.[108] The fourth report addresses this issue more precisely: 'the outcomes of the development, as well as the way the outcomes are realized, constitute the process of development which is regarded as a human right.'[109]

Moreover, if the RTD is the right to enjoy social, economic, cultural as well as civil and political rights, as the first part of Osmani's proposed formulation suggests, it makes the RTD a mere synthesis of these two categories of rights. Thus it weakens the foundational strength of the RTD articulated in the Declaration because it ignores the value added by the RTD, i.e. the indivisibility and interdependence of all human rights. The proposition cannot be said to have properly captured the essence of Article 1(1) of the Declaration.

104 See Independent Expert Second Report, para. 23. See also Independent Expert Third Report, paras 8–10; Fourth Report, para. 4.

105 Osmani, 'Some Thoughts on the Right to Development', op. cit., p 37.

106 Ibid. p 38.

107 Ibid.

108 Independent Expert Third Report, para.10.

109 Independent Expert Fourth Report, para. 2.

The Declaration does not express the content of the RTD in a concrete and solid form. At the national level, it is to be developed by the state by formulating national development policies favourable to the realization of the RTD. Such policies need to be crystallized into law by establishing a comprehensive legal and institutional framework in order to transform the objectives of development into claims or entitlements of the beneficiaries/right-holders, with corresponding obligations on the part of the duty-bearers.[110] This will lead to empowerment of the poor and the vulnerable sections of the society to enable them to participate in the process of decision-making for the formulation and implementation of sustainable development policies.[111]

The concreteness of the content of the RTD at the international level is more problematic and challenging. The reason is that the Declaration is not an international treaty of a binding nature. The content of a collective RTD, therefore, is an issue of customary international law. At present, the legal value of the principle of cooperation in international law is a highly contested topic. However, some rules and policies of international economic law show a strong tendency towards a hard law position. A typical example is the special and differential treatment of the developing countries in various international instruments, particularly in the WTO constitution, which recognizes these rules in some provisions.[112]

But the substantial issue is the enforceability or justiciability of the RTD, which is examined below.

JUSTICIABILITY

Whose duty is it to enforce the RTD? The question of enforceability or justiciability involves a discussion on the relationship of rights with duties and obligations. The main argument here is that perfect obligations, recognized as the technical tools for realizing human rights, are not sufficient. Imperfect obligations also require due consideration to address the issue

110 Arjun Sengupta, 'On the Theory and Practice of the Right to Development', *Human Rights Quarterly* 24, 2002, 837–89, at 846.

111 Independent Expert Second Report, para. 26.

112 Special and differential treatment aims to provide a variety of concessions to developing countries under the WTO/GATT law. These include access to the markets of the developed countries on preferential basis, longer periods for tariff phase-downs, flexibility of rules and capacity building in the implementation of multilateral trade agreements and technical assistance. See Part IV of GATT, 1994. See, generally, Faizel Ismail, 'Mainstreaming Development in the World Trade Organization', *Journal of World Trade* 39(1), 2005, 11–21. For a discussion on the link between special and differential treatment and the RTD, see Abdulqawi A. Yusuf, 'Differential Treatment as a Dimension of the Right to Development' in R.-J. Dupuy (ed.), op. cit., pp 233–45.

of justiciability. It is argued that to achieve justiciability, the focus of the discussion on rights, duties and obligations needs to be shifted from analytical to ethical jurisprudence. An examination of the Maastricht Guidelines for the implementation of economic, social and cultural rights, and the pluralistic foundations of human rights, would further help to clarify imperfect obligations. First, let us explain the distinction between perfect and imperfect obligations. A perfect obligation is that kind of obligation which identifies a specific duty-holder in case a right is violated. In this kind of obligation, the agent of the duty is specific and clearly defined. Another element of a perfect obligation is the involvement of a judicial process, such as a court of law. As regards an imperfect obligation, the duty-holder is not precisely defined and a judicial mechanism for the enforcement of a right is not necessarily involved. For example, to honour my right not to be subjected to torture or to cruel, inhuman or degrading treatment, the state has a perfect obligation not to violate my right (i.e. non-violation by the state's agents/officials), to prevent third persons from violation, and to punish them for such violation through a court of law. The state has an imperfect obligation to fulfil my right to an adequate standard of living by taking some policy measures such as creating job opportunities.

The Declaration uses different words with respect to the obligations of enforcing the RTD, such as 'responsibility', 'duty', 'the primary responsibility', 'shall take resolute steps', 'should cooperate', 'should take steps', 'should promote', 'should undertake' and 'should encourage'.[113] The Declaration specifies that the obligations for the enforcement of the RTD lie with three actors, viz. the individual, the state and the international community. These three actors, as shown in Diagram 3.1, being interdependent, can help each other in the enforcement of both the individual and the collective RTD.

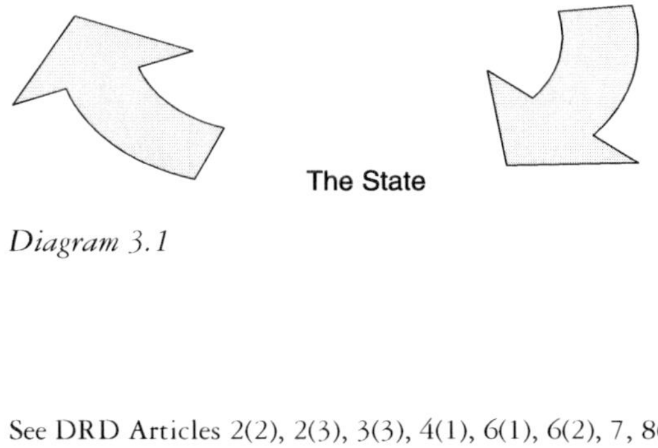

Diagram 3.1

113 See DRD Articles 2(2), 2(3), 3(3), 4(1), 6(1), 6(2), 7, 8(1) and 8(2).

Rights and duties in analytical jurisprudence

In a legal sense, the concept of right denotes 'an advantage or benefit conferred on a person by rules of a particular legal system'.[114] Salmond defines rights as 'interests protected by rules of right, that is, by moral or legal rules'.[115] Generally, a right is understood as a claim which has a corresponding duty or obligation to be respected and realized. The word obligation is generally used synonymously with the word duty. The two are, however, different in legal parlance. A duty 'is an act, which one ought to do, an act the opposite of which would be a wrong'.[116] A duty is also defined as 'a legal disadvantage, that which is owed or due to another and should be satisfied'.[117] An obligation signifies a legally essential bond between two or more legal persons, which creates mutually enforceable rights and duties.[118] A tie or a bond is a necessary element of obligation.[119] In a contract of sale, for example, a seller has a right to receive the price and a duty to deliver the property, and a buyer has a right to receive the property and a duty to pay the price. Thus obligation involves both right and duty. A duty may be moral or legal. The difference between the two is that only neglect of the latter involves a responsibility through a specific enforcement mechanism.

A right has three characteristics, viz. the subject or right-bearer – the person in whom the right is vested, the object or a duty-holder – the person who has a correlative duty with respect to the fulfilment of the right, and the content – which specifies the act or omission in favour of the right-bearer. In a wider sense, it is not always necessary for rights to have corresponding duties. Hohfeld, an American jurist, almost a century ago, challenged the express or implied assumption that all legal relations could be understood through the rights – duties correspondence alone.[120] A brief description of Hohfeld's views may help to explain the legal concept of rights. Hohfeld argued that it is only in the narrow sense that a right (or claim) has a correlative duty. In a broader sense, three other distinct concepts, viz. privilege, power and immunity, help in a proper understanding of rights. Hohfeld presented these basic concepts in the scheme shown in Table 3.2:[121]

114 David Walker, *Oxford Companion to Law*, Oxford, Clarendon Press, 1980, p 1070.

115 P.J. Fitzgerald, *Salmond on Jurisprudence*, London, Sweet & Maxwell, Twelfth Edition, 1966, p 217.

116 Ibid. p 216.

117 Walker, op. cit., p 385.

118 Fitzgerald, op. cit., p 446; Walker, op. cit., p 897.

119 T.E. Holland, *The Elements of Jurisprudence*, Oxford, Clarendon Press, 13th Edition, Impression of 1928, p 245. See also L.B. Curzon, *Dictionary of Law*, London, Pitman Publishing, 4th Edition, 1993, p 266.

120 Wesley Newcomb Hohfeld, *Fundamental Legal Conceptions, As Applied in Judicial Reasoning* (edited by Walter Wheeler Cook, with a new foreword by Arthur L. Corbin), New Haven, Yale University Press, 1919, p 35.

121 The Table reproduced from ibid. p 36.

Table 3.2

Jural Opposites	Right No-right	Privilege Duty	Power Disability	Immunity Liability
Jural Correlatives	Right Duty	Privilege No-right	Power Liability	Immunity Disability

Source: Wesley Newcomb Hohfeld, *Fundamental Legal Conceptions, As Applied in Judicial Reasoning* (edited by Walter Wheeler Cook, with a new foreword by Arthur L. Corbin), New Haven, Yale University Press, 1919, p 36.

Thus in the right–duty relationship (or claim rights), 'if X has a right [or claim] against Y that he shall stay off the former's land . . . Y is under a correlative duty towards X to stay off the place'. X has the privilege (or liberty) to enter upon his/her own land. In other words, X, having the privilege, is under no duty; Y has 'no-right'. Thus duty is the opposite and no-right is the correlative of privilege. Note the word 'no-right', invented by Hohfeld, indicates the absence of a right. X has also the right to alienate his land. This right of X has no corresponding duty. In Hohfeld's scheme, this kind of a right is called power (or ability). If X exercises his/her power (or ability), say, by selling the land to Y, X alters the rights and duties of Y. Thus Y is under a liability, i.e. his rights and duties, as regards X's land, are altered by X. Power (or ability) is the correlative of liability. The absence of power (or ability) is disability. The word right is also used in the sense of immunities, which means exemption from the power (or ability) of someone. In this situation, the rights and duties of one person are protected from the power (or ability) of another person. Most constitutionally guaranteed fundamental rights may be seen in this sense. Thus citizens enjoy immunity rights, such as rights to life, speech, religion, etc., while the legislature is under a disability to exercise the power of abridging such rights, which it would otherwise have (no doubt, in an emergency situation, such rights may be suspended or abridged). The opposite of immunity is liability, i.e. the absence of exemption.

How far does the Hohfeldian model inform the debate on the concept of rights, particularly in the context of the RTD? Hohfeld believed that none of the concepts, i.e., rights, privileges, powers and immunities, function alone, but all are related.[122] Thus a right (or claim) could be seen in juxtaposition to privilege, power and immunities. The right to life, for example, is a right (or claim) of one to live, having corresponding duties on the part of others (including government) not to hinder one's exercise of this right; liberties (or privileges) to preserve, protect and promote one's life in a manner one values; and immunities provide constitutional and statutory safeguards against abridging this right in any way.

122 Ibid. p 60.

In the Hohfeldian scheme, for the exercise of a right, the existence of a duty-holder is a must. However, critics argue that such a scheme does not clarify the concept of duty. Suppose A has a right (or claim) to X against B, who has a correlative duty to A in relation to X. Hohfeld leaves unspecified the concept of duty *owed to* A, that is, the concept of a claim right possessed by A. It is unclear whether, and in what ways, a duty *owed to* an entity A (e.g. the duty not to trespass on A's land) differs from a duty merely *concerning* an entity A (e.g., the duty not to destroy unowned works of art – a duty which, presumably, is not owed to anybody).[123]

The Hohfeldian scheme is confined to legal rights and duties or perfect obligations alone and, as such, it is merely professional and technical. It does not adequately inform a theory of rights in which the RTD could find expression. The concept of the RTD needs to be explained in the moral and political visions known as, to quote Dworkin, 'ethical jurisprudence', which means 'the study of what the law ought to be'.[124] In the current debate over the nature and justiciability of human rights, particularly of controversial rights like the RTD, attention needs to be diverted, from what rights and duties are, to what rights and duties should be.

Rights as goals: ethical jurisprudence

In ethical jurisprudence, the RTD, being a comprehensive process of economic, social and political development, may be defined as a goal-right – a right that can be understood as a political aim. How can it be realized? A challenge that the RTD faces is: what is the nature of the obligation for the implementation of this right? The controversy over the issue of justiciability is due to different approaches (i.e. positivist versus behavioural) to the concept of rights and obligations, particularly in the area of human rights. The legal positivists (e.g. Donnelly and Nozick), who take a strictly legal view of human rights, argue that human rights are specific and entail clear obligation on the part of the duty-holders, hence are justiciable. This school of thought sees only civil and political rights as human rights. The other group (e.g. Sen, Alston and Abi-Saab) believes that there are various levels of obligations such as respect, protection and fulfilment of human rights (also called perfect and imperfect obligations). In their view, *all* human rights may not be enforced through courts. This group favours a much wider scope of obligations, as their main concern is with the enforcement of economic, social and cultural rights and the RTD. The legal positivist group is mainly concerned with

123 Alon Harel, 'Theories of Rights' in Martin P. Golding and William A. Edmundson (eds), *Philosophy of Law and Legal Theory*, Oxford, Blackwell, 2005, pp 191–206, at p 193 (emphasis in original).

124 Ronald Dworkin, *Taking Rights Seriously*, London, Duckworth, First Edition, 1977, (2005 Impression, with reply to critics), p 2.

what are known as constraint-based rights, a view advanced by Nozick.[125] The behaviouralists take a goal-based view of rights, which is advocated by Dworkin and Sen and closely connected with his capability approach, discussed in the previous chapter.

According to the legal positivists, rights are constraints on social action. If a right has accrued to an individual in accordance with some morally just procedures of ownership, transfers and rectification, it shall not be violated in any way. The constraint thus operates as an obligation on others not to interfere with the right. This concept of obligation cannot move beyond the element of a constraint. It stresses the protection of a right simply because the right has been acquired through some morally just procedures. For example, A has a right to a piece of land because A has acquired its ownership through a procedure, say, purchase, which is morally just. It does not, however, take into consideration the fact that A's right to a piece of land has enabled him to feed his family (a necessary consequence of A's right).[126] In Hohfeld's sense, A can exercise a claim over the property as rights, privileges, powers and immunities, while others have duties, 'no-rights', liabilities and disabilities. In the light of this non-consequentialist view of rights, the nature of the obligation is negative only. Thus, while others are under a constraint not to interfere with A's right of ownership of a piece of land, they are under no obligation to help A make the piece of land cultivable.[127] If such an obligation to help A is recognized, it can help realize A's rights to a decent standard of living that may, in turn, lead to the fulfilment of his other rights such as the right to food. Why do others have no such obligation? Nozick answers:

> Rights do not determine social ordering but instead set the constraints within which a social choice is to be made . . . If entitlements to holdings are right to dispose of them, then social choice must take place *within* the constraints of how people choose to exercise these rights.[128]

Those who take such a view of rights do not believe in the indivisibility, interdependence and interrelatedness of human rights. For example, talking about the realization of social and economic rights, Maurice Cranston says that like civil and political rights, these 'rights can not be transformed into positive rights'.[129]

125 Robert Nozick, *Anarchy, State and Utopia*, Oxford, Basil Blackwell, 1974.

126 S.R. Osmani, 'Poverty and Human Rights: Building on Capability Approach', *Journal of Human Development* 6(2), 2005, 205–19, at 210. The example used by the writer is modified here.

127 Ibid.

128 Nozick, op. cit., pp 165–6 (emphasis in original).

129 Maurice Cranston, *What are Human Rights?* London, The Bodley Head, 1973, p 66.

On the other side, in Sen's goal-based view, rights are seen as goals,[130] which, as noted above, a political system pursues for social and economic development. Dworkin argues that goals (or political aims) and rights or duties can justify each other. In the context of goals, Dworkin classifies rights into background rights or institutional rights. The former 'provide justification for political decision by society in abstract'.[131] The latter 'provide a justification for a decision by some particular and specified political institution'. Dworkin also divided rights into those which are 'abstract' – general political aims; and those which are 'concrete' – 'precisely defined so as to express more definitely the weight they have against other political aims on particular occasions'.[132] Sen is of the view that rights are derived from goals. In other words, goal-based rights determine social ordering. If rights are goal-based, they create an obligation on the part 'of anyone who can help'[133] (also called an imperfect obligation). This approach extends the scope of the obligation to positive freedom (also positive rights),[134] but it does not reject negative freedom (negative rights advocated by the constraint-based theory of rights).[135]

It is thus established that a constraint-based view of rights significantly fails to address the implementation of *all* human rights, most particularly the economic, social and cultural rights, let alone the RTD. The obligations, which the current international human rights law imposes, on the state (the principal duty-bearer), is not confined to the constraint of non-violation alone.[136]

The Maastricht Guidelines

As part of the attempt to clarify the nature of obligations, reference may also be made to the Maastricht Guidelines on the violation of economic, social and cultural rights, which describe three categories of obligations: to respect, to

130 Sen, 'Rights as Goals' in S. Guest and A. Milne (eds), *Equality and Discrimination: Essays in Freedom and Justice*, Stuttgart, Franz Steiner, 1985, pp 11–25 (hereinafter Sen, 'Rights and Goals').

131 Dworkin, op. cit., pp 90–3.

132 Ibid.

133 Sen, 'Rights as Goals', op. cit., p 15. See also Sen, *Development as Freedom*, op. cit., p 227.

134 Civil and political rights are usually referred to as negative rights and economic, social and cultural rights are also usually referred to as positive freedoms. For a more detailed discussion on the distinction between the two freedoms, see Berlin, op. cit., pp 121–34.

135 Sen, 'Rights as Goals', op. cit., p 18. The linkage of the goal-rights system to capabilities is established thus: 'The capabilities are one way of characterising positive freedom, and they can be seen as right – positive right to do this or be that' at p 16. See also Sen, 'Rights and Agency', *Philosophy and Public Affairs* 11(1), 1982, 1–39, at 15 and 38–9. See also Sen, 'Consequential Evaluation and Practical Reason', *The Journal of Philosophy* 97(9), 2000, 477–502, at 495.

136 Osmani, 'Poverty and Human Rights', op. cit., 210.

protect and to fulfil.[137] The first category requires the state to refrain from any interference with the rights of the individual. The second category mentions the duty of states to prevent violation of rights by third parties. The last category obliges the states to formulate a broad-based policy that includes 'appropriate legislative, administrative, budgetary, judicial and other measures towards the full realization of such rights'.[138] Some commentators are of the view that the first two categories, i.e. the obligation to respect and the obligation to protect or ensure, can be grouped as perfect obligations and the last category, i.e. the obligation to fulfil or provide, can be one of imperfect obligations, to which can be added also the obligation to promote.[139] The imperfect obligations to fulfil or provide involve policy formulation, as the Maastricht Guidelines have noted. The obligation to promote is another kind of imperfect obligation, which enjoins the state to launch awareness campaigns to bring about changes in the 'attitudes and behaviour of the population in such areas as lifestyles, nutrition and harmful traditional practices'.[140]

Very recently one commentator has drawn some fine distinctions between enforceability and justiciability by arguing that the former requires means (or resources), but no specific duty-holder; while the latter needs legal procedures and a properly defined duty-holder.[141] 'Thus, while justiciability of a right implies its enforceability, it is not a necessary requirement for a right to be enforceable.'[142] It follows that justiciability is not essential because the human rights law is following the concept of 'implementation' and 'supervision'.[143]

If the RTD is pursued as a goal, it will be easier to realize this right. However, fundamental changes, obviously in the socio-economic conditions at the national as well as the international level, will be necessary.[144] At the national level, this will involve legislative, administrative, budgetary and judicial measures and at the international level, a duty of cooperation.

137 'The Maastricht Guidelines on Violation of Economic, Social and Cultural Rights', *Human Rights Quarterly* 20, 1998, 691–704 at 693–4.

138 Ibid.

139 Stephen Marks, 'The Human Rights Framework for Development: Seven Approaches' in Sengupta, et al. (eds), op. cit., pp 23–60 at pp 45–6. Noting that this categorization of obligations 'applies in general to the understanding' of rights and duties in international human rights. Stephen Marks, however, notes: 'In practice, it is somewhat artificial to call obligations to respect and protect "perfect" and those to promote and provide "imperfect" since examples may be given where the duty-holder and the specific behaviour are not easily identified with respect to the former and where this specificity may exist to the degree that a judicial remedy is appropriate for the latter.'

140 Ibid.

141 Manimary Sengupta, 'The Right to Development and Human Rights: A Social Choice Approach to Implementation and Measurement', in Sengupta, et al. (ed.) op. cit., pp 321–49 at p 323.

142 Ibid.

143 Alston, 'Making Space for New Human Rights', op. cit., 35.

144 Alston, Synder et al. (eds), op. cit., p 820.

The pluralistic foundations of human rights

The current debate over the issue of the justiciability of economic, social and cultural rights and the RTD has also led to a discussion regarding the nature of all human rights. Those (for example Donnelly) who deny the RTD as a human right argue that the notion of collective rights is a departure from the natural rights philosophy.[145] According to this view, human rights could not be social rights because they 'are clearly and unambiguously conceptualized as being inherent to humans and not as the product of social co-operation'. (Note the similarity between Donnelly and Nozick.) 'These rights', it maintains, 'are conceptualized as being universal and held equally by all; that is, as natural rights.'[146] The language of the UDHR, it is argued, is significantly similar to that of many eighteenth-century declarations of rights, e.g. the Virginia Declaration of 1776, the American Declaration of 1776 and the French Declaration of 1789, which proclaimed natural rights.[147]

The other view (espoused by, for example, Alston, referring to Van Dyke) argues that the natural rights theory, as the basis of human rights, has now been challenged by the supporters of the social rights.[148] Van Dyke's criticism of Hobbes and Locke shows that irrespective of the social contract, individuals from their birth have a group identity (even as a symbol of survival), which would have been more vivid during the times of Hobbes and Locke than today.[149] It is further argued that the concept of solidarity rights is indicative of the dynamism of human rights, and even said that the advocates of natural rights theory 'run the risk of being rebuffed on the ground of undue conservatism or short-sighted resistance to development which in the long term are assumed to be irresistible'.[150] Alston argues that the USA view of human rights and its consequential opposition to the RTD, is mainly derived from the American Declaration of Independence and not from the UDHR.[151] He is also of the view that there is a need to challenge the model of UN human rights as absolutely based on natural rights theory because the international human rights law is based on pluralistic foundations, being accommodative of diverse cultures and to elicit universal acceptability.[152] Note here the similarity of Alston's view with Rawls's overlapping consensus in which a

145 Donnelly, 'In Search, of a Unicorn', op. cit., 497.

146 Donnelly, 'Human Rights as Natural Rights', *Human Rights Quarterly* 4, 1982, 341–405 at 401 (hereinafter Donnelly, 'Natural Rights').

147 John Morsink, 'The Philosophy of the Universal Declaration', *Human Rights Quarterly* 6(3), 1984, 309–34 at 310, 311.

148 Alston, 'Making Space for New Human Rights', op. cit., 27.

149 Vernon Van Dyke, *Human Rights, Ethnicity and Discrimination*, 10 Contributions in Ethnic Studies, Westport, Connecticut, Greenwood Press, 1985, p 199.

150 Philip Alston, 'A Third Generation of Solidarity Rights', *Netherlands International Law Review* 29, 1982, 307–22 at 314.

151 Alston, 'Making Space for New Human Rights', op. cit., p 35.

152 Ibid. pp 28–30.

political conception of justice is 'affirmed by the opposing religious, philosophical and moral doctrines likely to thrive over generations'.[153] This view also comes very close to Sen's coherence critique of human rights ('culture and human rights'), which says, 'the value of freedom is not to be confined to culture only, and that the Western traditions are not the only ones that prepare us for a freedom-based approach to social understanding'.[154] In fact one scholar recognized, in 1969, after twenty years of the UDHR, that changes in different aspects of human life may necessitate either a conceptual change in human rights or the creation of new human rights.[155] The UDHR does not ignore the contributions of the community in shaping the personality of the individual; it goes beyond the natural rights theory.[156] Moreover, the association of civil and political rights with negative duty and social and economic rights with positive duty is superfluous because both sets of rights need positive ('prevention') as well as negative ('promotion or protective') measures.[157]

Keba M'baye suggests that the Aristotelian theory of natural law alludes to the group more than the human person.[158] He further argues that from the very beginning, the movement for individual rights in Europe, from the fifteenth century to the twentieth century, group feelings/the collective aspect, social equity and justice remained essential parts of the struggle as a revolution against class domination.[159] Marxist revolution, M'baye maintains, made it clear that an individual requires not only political protection but also fulfilment of his/her needs, which was further incorporated in the UN system as freedom from want; thus human rights and peoples' rights are based on economic equality and liberty.[160] Citing the example of Islam which has the concept of brotherhood, that is solidarity, as its main teaching, M'baye is of the view that religion also encourages peoples' rights.[161]

Justiciability at the national level

The duty for the implementation primarily lies on the state, whereas the individual is the beneficiary of the RTD.[162] The state should perform this

153 John Rawls, 'The Idea of an Overlapping Consensus', *Oxford Journal of Legal Studies* 7, 1987, 1.
154 Sen, *Development as Freedom*, op. cit., p 240.
155 Richard Bilder, 'Rethinking International Human Rights Law: Some Basic Questions', *Wisconsin Law Review*, 1969, 171–217 at p 173.
156 Sengupta, 'The Right to Development as a Human Right', op. cit., p 9.
157 Ibid.
158 M'baye, in Bedjaoui (ed.), op. cit., p 1043.
159 Ibid.
160 Ibid. pp 1044–5.
161 Ibid. p 1043.
162 DRD, Art. 3(1).

duty by devising a development programme.[163] The Declaration provides two main guiding principles for a development programme aimed at the realization of the RTD: (1) 'active, free and meaningful participation' and (2) 'the fair distribution of benefits' (justice and equity). The objectives of a development programme should be respect for and observance of all human rights and to eliminate obstacles to development. A state implementing the RTD will need to prioritize certain human rights. The question is, what is the nature of the obligations? The obligations necessary for the enforcement of the RTD are more in the nature of imperfect obligations.[164] 'That will not, however, make the RTD invalid or unrealizable' through perfect obligations.[165] There are a number of agents of duty, such as state institutions and non-state actors, such as Civil Society Organizations (CSOs). These agents have different kinds of obligations. Some institutions are well defined and have specific roles in the implementation process. The role and function of others may not be specifically and precisely defined. Thus the responsibilities in relation to the process of development and human rights vary from institution to institution. For instance, the role of the national courts in respecting and protecting human rights is an example of a perfect obligation, though the obligations for some human rights, such as economic and social rights, are not the same as those of civil and political rights. The state performs imperfect obligations through other institutions of its executive organ, which formulate development policies. An example of such institution is the Planning and Development Commission of Pakistan, the apex planning and coordination body of the country, which prepares the national development programme and reviews and evaluates its implementation. The work of this institution is to be guided by the Principles of Policy enunciated in the constitution of Pakistan. The implementation of these principles is subject to the availability of resources; and not enforceable through the judicial process (perfect obligations). Various non-state actors, such as CSOs, for example, the national human rights commissions, also play an important role in supporting both perfect and imperfect obligations through active and meaningful participation in the formulation, implementation and evaluation of development policies, helping courts in cases regarding the protection and promotion of human rights. The state is, however, responsible for coordinating the activities of all public-sector organizations and for involving non-state actors.[166] The RTD programme also requires that the state ensures 'the most efficient provision of goods and services and changes in the institutions and social arrangements to realize a set of targeted objectives as human rights, identified as expansion of capabilities and freedoms'.[167] The justiciability of the RTD at

163 Ibid. Art. 3(2).
164 Sengupta, 'On the Theory and Practice of the Right to Development', op. cit., 856.
165 Ibid. 857.
166 See Independent Expert Fourth Report, para. 18.

the national level, in Pakistan, will be discussed in greater detail in Chapters 6 and 8. National action for the implementation would not be possible independently of the international community.

Justiciability at the international level

The Declaration says that the states have the prime responsibility for creating favourable international conditions for the implementation of the RTD.[168] The main instrument of implementation of the RTD at the international level is cooperation among states. The Declaration provides that the states should cooperate with one another in accordance with the principles of international law concerning friendly relations, to eliminate obstacles to development, to focus on the rapid development of developing countries, and to promote respect for and observance of all human rights for all without any kind of distinction or discrimination.[169]

The nature of international obligations is more uncertain and vague than national-level obligations. No specific international organization/institution can be called a duty-holder of the RTD. The claim is thus generally addressed to everyone who can help. The obligations of the international community to help implement the RTD of developing countries include the transfer of technology, access to markets, adjusting the rules of operation of international trade and the IFIs, protection of intellectual property and foreign aid.[170] The resolution of these issues, through multilateral and bilateral dimensions of cooperation 'requires intensive review from the point of view of meeting the obligations of international co-operation with States trying to realize the [RTD]'.[171]

The growing concern for human rights in the development cooperation of bilateral and multilateral donors, as discussed in Chapter 2, is not specific to the RTD, but may prove helpful in promoting the RTD. The Independent Expert has proposed a Development Compact model (see Chapter 4) for the implementation of the RTD at the international level. The proposed Development Compact seeks to develop a strategy for international cooperation between the international community and a developing country wishing to implement the RTD.

167 Ibid. para. 20.

168 DRD, Art. 3 (1).

169 Ibid. Arts 3(2), (3), 4(2), 6(1).

170 Independent Expert Fourth Report, para. 43. See also Independent Expert Third Report, para. 34.

171 Ibid. para. 44. Third Report, para 35.

Rights and duties in Islamic jurisprudence

According to Islamic jurisprudence, rights are broadly divided into two, viz. public and private.[172] The former are known as the rights of God, not in the literal sense, but for the reason that they are concerned with society at large and not merely with the individual.[173] The latter are those rights which are of the individuals and have no direct bearing on the society at large, for example, enforcement of a contract and protection of property.[174] The main distinction between the two lies in the identification of the duty-holder, which is the state in case of the former, but not in case of the latter.[175] This distinction is, however, not rigid. Some rights may be both public and private at the same time; the one taking priority over the other.[176] A further classification of public rights would show that there are many rights, having both perfect and imperfect obligations, that have significant implications for the RTD. For example, the payment of *zakat* (an obligatory poor rate) and tithe are public rights enforceable (and, as such, justiciable) through perfect obligations. The performance of some religious duties is a public right, the non-performance of which involves atonement as an obligation. The act of atonement, as an imperfect obligation, includes fasting (i.e. a spiritual act) and feeding and clothing the poor. This concept of imperfect obligation appears to be similar to Sen's view that a claim can be generally addressed to anyone who can help. While Sen emphasizes the element of a right, the Islamic concept of imperfect obligation stresses the element of a duty. Thus a person liable for performance of atonement is bound to search out the deserving poor to provide them with food, clothing and other basic needs. Chapter 7 will reconceptualize the RTD in the context of Islamic law.

CONCLUSION

The chapter argued that there is lack of consensus of academic opinion regarding the claim that the right to self-determination and Article 28 of UDHR are the sources of the RTD. Given the fact that the RTD is a claim of developing countries on the international community as well as an individual human right, the right of people to self-determination to pursue their economic and social development requires an international order (Art. 28 UDHR) which may create favourable conditions for the realization of human rights. Regarding the subjects of the RTD, even the critics of the RTD admit that the individual as the subject of the RTD appears to be less problematic than

172 Rahim, op. cit., p 201.
173 Ibid.
174 Ibid. p 202.
175 Ibid.
176 Ibid.

the state and/or peoples as subjects. The reason is that human rights are basically the rights of the individual, while collective rights, by definition, could not be human rights. The content of an individual RTD is to be formulated in the form of a national development policy. There is, however, much difficulty in developing the content of a collective RTD.

The jurisprudential controversies can be narrowed down to two issues. Firstly: the justiciability of the RTD even as an individual right. Secondly: the collective dimension of the RTD as a human right and its justiciability as such. As seen above, the controversy is due to a difference of approach towards the current international human rights law from the perspective of philosophical foundations (natural rights theory or positivism) and the principle of cooperation as a source of obligation in international law. So far as the first issue is concerned, there is a growing tendency towards the clarification of the nature of obligations. It was argued above that all human rights need to be seen as goal-rights (a behavioural approach). The goal-rights system is an extension of the capability approach and widens the scope of the obligation and helps to overcome the issue of justiciability. At the national level, such goal-rights, including the RTD, could be enforced by means of both perfect and imperfect obligations. No doubt, the basic idea underlying human rights is the requirement to respect the dignity and worth of the human person. But, as the behavioural approach argues, accepting the importance of the individual as a member of society is a must if the notion of collective rights is to be acknowledged. This view sounds convincing as, in many societies, the individual is not separable from the society. In short, while the RTD has still to move forward, the thrust of the debate is in favour of the RTD as a human right.

The second challenge involves the principle of international cooperation and will be discussed in detail in Chapter 5. Suffice it to say here that the principle of cooperation is the main characteristic of post-war international law. The UN Charter itself can be understood as having brought two developments, viz. a shift of international law from coexistence to cooperation, and the rise of the individual as a subject of international law.[177] Given the inability of the developing countries, the principle of cooperation is indispensable for the realization of the RTD. Since the post-Cold War era, the RTD has gained an 'enduring relevance' in international development policy.[178] In this respect, the Commission (now the Council) on Human Rights has formed many working groups to clarify the content and scope of the RTD so as to pursue its realization at the international and national levels. The realization of the RTD through the policy proposals of these working groups is the main subject of the discussion in the next chapter.

177 Rich, op. cit., 290. See also H. Lauterpacht, *International Law and Human Rights*, New York, Frederick A. Praeger, Inc., 1950, pp 27–45.

178 Alston, 'Revitalising UN Work', op. cit., 249.

4 The declaration and the working groups

INTRODUCTION

While some theoretical issues still haunt the true legal concept of the RTD, the direction of the debate has significantly diverted towards the practical issue of its implementation. During the past two decades, remarkable work has been done in the UN to bring about a policy shift in development practice. In 1992, the General Assembly requested the Secretary-General to prepare an agenda for development.[1] The report submitted by the Secretary-General in 1995 records that the UN has started 'a process of re-examination and redefinition of development'.[2] In this context, the 1990s witnessed major changes in the linkage between human rights and development. This linkage has found expression in the rights-based approach to development, which is increasingly gaining currency as a major policy goal. The main source of this linkage lies in the concept of the RTD that recognizes development as a comprehensive economic, social, cultural and political process in which all human rights and fundamental freedoms can be fully realized. Between 1992 and 2001, a series of major international conferences and events have been held on: the environment, human rights, population, social development, women, the fiftieth anniversary of the UDHR and racism.[3] All these conferences have made explicit references to the RTD. As cmpared to the 1980s, during which decade the RTD was entangled in ideological rivalry, the changes in the 1990s opened up many possibilities for the promotion of the RTD.

1 UNGA Res. A/47/181, 22 Dec. 1992.

2 Boutros Boutros-Ghali, *An Agenda for Development*, New York, United Nations, 1995, p 1. The report of the Secretary-General underlines peace, economic growth, the environment, justice, democracy and good governance as dimensions of development.

3 World Conference on environment and development (Rio de Janeiro, Brazil, 1992), Human Rights (Vienna, Austria, 1993), population and development (Cairo, Egypt, 1994), social development (Copenhagen, Denmark, 1995), women (Beijing, China, 1995) and celebration of the fiftieth anniversary of UDHR (1998), World Conference against Racism, Racial Discrimination, Xenophobia and Related Intolerance (2001).

The Commission established as many as four working groups, the last one being an OEWG, to pave the way for the implementation of the RTD. These working groups have been engaged to clarify the scope and content of the RTD, and to identify obstacles to and suggest recommendations for the implementation of the RTD at the national and international levels. While there is a growing literature on the academic issues surrounding the RTD, the reports of the working groups on the RTD have received little attention in the research-based analysis. The contributions of the working groups could not be ignored in a discussion regarding the existence of the RTD in customary international law vis-à-vis state practice. The reason is that the Commission, as a permanent subsidiary body of the General Assembly in the field of human rights, provides a helping hand to the General Assembly in the progressive development of international law. The Commission's working groups formulate policy proposals for the implementation of the RTD, at the international level through international cooperation, and at the national level through the adoption of the proposal in national development policies. The issue of the implementation of the RTD pursued in the Commission is, therefore, the main theme of this chapter. The chapter argues that despite some efforts to depoliticize the debate over the implementation of the RTD, no consensus has, so far, been developed between the developing and developed countries in the working group. This lack of consensus is a challenge to the implementation of the Declaration through international cooperation.

The Commission has appointed various working groups on the RTD. The first working group, appointed in 1981, drafted the Declaration. In 1989, a Global Consultation was organized by the Secretary-General. Two more working groups were appointed in 1993 and 1996 respectively. In 1998, the OEWG, which is still working, was appointed. This working group was also assisted by an Independent Expert, appointed by the Commission. In 2004, a high-level Task Force was established by the Commission.

The chapter looks at the deliberations of the first working group and the drafting of the Declaration and this is followed by a textual analysis of the declaration. It then examines the suggestions of the Global Consultation and the two working groups. In order to look at the current status of the RTD, the last part focuses on the Development Compact model suggested by the Independent Expert and the reports of the Task Force submitted to the Commission.

THE FIRST WORKING GROUP AND THE DRAFTING OF THE DECLARATION

The working group report

In a 1981 resolution,[4] the Commission decided to establish a working group[5] on the RTD.[6] The mandate of the working group was:

> [T]o study the scope and content of the [RTD] and the most effective means to ensure the realization in all countries, of the economic, social and cultural rights enshrined in various international instruments, paying particular attention to the obstacles encountered by developing countries in their efforts to secure the enjoyment of human rights.[7]

The working group focused on: firstly, the scope and content of the RTD; secondly, the most effective means to ensure the realization of economic, social and cultural rights; thirdly, the obstacles faced by developing countries in the enjoyment of human rights; and fourthly, suggesting concrete proposals for implementation of the RTD and a draft international instrument on the subject.

First, regarding scope and content,[8] some experts from developing countries expressed the opinion that the RTD is both a collective and individual right, whereas other experts from Western countries held a contrary view. There was relatively more agreement over the individual RTD. The individual RTD was, however, seen as a combination of all the rights of the individual (synthesis right). Some experts traced the basis of the RTD in various international instruments, such as the UN Charter and the resolutions of the General Assembly.[9] This view was countered by some other experts, who argued that such instruments have no legal status. Regarding the legal nature of the RTD, one view was that it is a human right. The other view was that it is a moral imperative. Some experts viewed the collective dimension of the RTD as more important, while others laid greater emphasis on the individual aspect of the right.

4 CHR Res. 36/1981.

5 The working group held twelve sessions. At the eighth and ninth sessions, held in 1984, it adopted a report (E/CN.4/1985/11) which the Commission transmitted to the General Assembly, through the Economic and Social Council, enabling the Assembly to adopt the Declaration on the Right to Development.

6 E/CN.4/1489, Report of the working group. The working group comprised 15 governmental experts on the basis of geographical distribution. They were from Algeria, Cuba, Ethiopia, France, India, Iraq, the Netherlands, Panama, Peru, Poland, Senegal, Syria, the USSR, the USA and Yugoslavia.

7 CHR Res. 36, op. cit.

8 Ibid. paras 15, 20, 26, 28, 30, 32 and 33.

9 For example, the Declaration on friendly relations and the establishment of the NIEO discussed later in this chapter.

Secondly, with respect to the realization of economic, social and cultural rights,[10] the experts generally emphasized that national efforts for the realization of the RTD shall include the full realization of all human rights and fundamental freedoms, equality of opportunity to the basic sources and services for all, full participation of all people, particularly vulnerable sections of society, such as women, minorities and children, social-sector reforms, the encouragement of democracy and the preservation of cultural values. There were discussions about whether international action should include the establishment of an NIEO with the aim of achieving a just and equitable participation of all countries in the decision-making activities of the international economic institutions. Some experts were of the view that the granting of non-reciprocal preferential treatment, the implementation of the third development decade, cooperation in the areas of scientific and cultural development and foreign investment may lead to the active promotion of social and economic development in the developing countries.

Thirdly, deliberating upon the obstacles to the enjoyment of human rights,[11] many experts observed that the main obstacles faced by developing countries are colonialism, racism and the arms race. Other obstacles included unjust international trade and financial rules and the transfer of technology. At the national level, lack of social-sector development (i.e. education, health and absolute poverty) and a weak democratic system were seen as obstacles to the enjoyment of human rights. The principle of participation by all segments in the process of development received wide attention. The experts agreed that violation of human rights cannot be justified to achieve the end of development.

Fourthly, the experts agreed to prepare a draft declaration[12] on the RTD, with a possibility of preparing a more binding instrument in future.

An analysis of the working group report

The experts were sharply divided over the jurisprudential issues pertaining to the scope and content of the RTD. As discussed in the previous chapter, the division may be attributed to the approach towards the legal position of human rights, and the corresponding duties and obligations in the Western countries. But the fact cannot be ignored that the experts' negotiations followed the lines of their respective governments' political and ideological positions. During that time, in the USA, the then Reagan Administration was strongly opposed to the notion of the RTD. Thus the atmosphere, during which the negotiations were held, was politically antagonistic to the notion of the RTD. In such a situation, as Alston observed, the working group could

10 E/CN.4/1489, paras 34–39.
11 Ibid. paras 40–43.
12 Ibid. paras 44–48.

not be totally blamed for its failure.[13] It is also worth mentioning that most of the experts believed that the RTD is a synthesis of existing human rights. Thus, they were not clear about its real nature and scope.

The drafting of the Declaration

The Commission asked the working group to prepare a draft declaration on the RTD.[14] In 1982, the working group initiated the drafting process by considering the guidelines and provisions for the preamble and then considered the operative part in three parts, viz. principles and objectives, means, and general provisions.[15]

Moving forward, in 1983, the working group considered the drafts submitted by the non-aligned group, France and the Netherlands, and some other proposals.[16] Two experts were requested to prepare a 'Technical Consolidated Text' (TCT). The TCT was prepared[17] and, in 1984, the experts discussed it in detail, particularly 'articles 2 to 4 concerning the responsibility for development in its individual and collective dimensions, and the elements involved in the effective realization of the [RTD]'.[18] However, the experts could not arrive at a consensus.[19]

At the eighth and ninth sessions, the working group discussed the TCT and various other draft proposals submitted by the experts.[20] In the Commission, the debate was dominated by political differences between the developing and the developed countries. The differences had blocked progress over the preparation of the draft declaration. In the meanwhile, Yugoslavia submitted a compromise draft.[21] The Yugoslav draft, though it revealed sufficient improvements over the TCT, omitted some key elements of the collective dimension of the RTD. The omissions were related to the participation of the developing countries in global economic decision-making, the claim of development assistance by the developing countries against the developed countries, bridging the gap between the rich and the poor countries, and the well-being of all peoples, particularly in the developing countries.[22] The Yugoslav draft visualized the RTD as a synthesis right, not an independent

13 Alston, 'Revitalising UN Work', op. cit., 220.
14 CHR Res. 1984/16.
15 See *Year Book of the United Nations*, Leiden, Martinus Nijhoff Publishers, vol. 36, 1982, p 1091.
16 E/CN.4/1984/13, Report of the working group's Sixth and Seventh sessions. See also *UN Year Book* vol. 37, 1983, p 854.
17 E/CN.4/1984/Annex II, the text of the TCT.
18 *UN Year Book*, vol. 38, 1984, p 835.
19 Ibid.
20 E/CN.4/1983/13 and E/CN.4/1985/11, reports of the working group.
21 E/CN.4/1985/62 Annex, Yugoslav draft.
22 Ansah, 'The RTD in Malawi', op. cit., p 39.

right.[23] There was a mixed reaction to the draft, with the two groups of countries partly supporting and partly opposing it. However, despite the deadlock in the negotiation, the Commission decided to send the Yugoslav draft to the General Assembly.[24]

The Secretary-General forwarded the Yugoslav draft to the Council and the General Assembly. The Council approved the Commission's decision to send the Yugoslav draft to the General Assembly.[25] In the Council, almost all the developed countries strongly opposed the transmission of the Yugoslav draft to the General Assembly. Japan, Sweden, Finland and Iceland thought it premature to send the draft to the General Assembly.[26] The then Federal Republic of Germany (FRG) vocally raised the key issue of the legal status of the RTD and maintained that consensus was indispensable if the RTD was to become recognized as a universal right.[27] The FRG thought it illogical to discuss the implementation of the RTD before there was an accepted definition of the RTD.[28]

The Third Committee of the General Assembly discussed the draft declaration. France and the Netherlands proposed incorporation of Article 1, paragraph 2, of the ICCPR into the provisions pertaining to the right to self-determination.[29] Pakistan also proposed an amendment as a new Article 4.[30] Since no consensus was arrived at during its fortieth session, the General Assembly, therefore, on the recommendations of its Third Committee, decided to postpone the discussion to its forty-first session in 1986.[31]

The draft declaration was considered in the forty-first session (1986) and passed by a recorded vote of 146 in favour, 1 against (USA), with 8 abstentions (mostly developed countries). Among those who voted in favour were a number of developed countries, including Australia, Canada, France, the Netherlands and New Zealand. The draft proposed by Pakistan was adopted as a separate resolution.[32]

While explaining their votes, the developed countries launched a systematic attack on various aspects of the RTD.[33] The delegate from the USA

23 Ibid. p 40.
24 CHR Res. 1985/43; See also *UN Year Book*, vol. 39, 1985, p 879.
25 Economic and Social Council Decision 1985/149 adopted by a roll-call vote, 37 countries voted in favour, 9 against, with 6 abstentions. Most of those, which either voted against or abstained, were developed countries.
26 *UN Year Book*, vol. 39, 1985, p 880.
27 Ibid.
28 Ibid.
29 Ibid.
30 Ibid.
31 Ibid.
32 UNGA Res. A/41/133. Since the main thrust of this resolution was that national efforts to achieve the RTD were dependent on international action based on a comprehensive NIEO, therefore, most of the developed countries either voted against it or abstained from voting.
33 See *UN Year Book*, vol. 40, 1986, p 720.

maintained that conceptually the RTD of peoples is inconsistent with the human rights of the individual. The USA rejected the linkage between disarmament and development, as described in Article 7 of the Declaration. This latter view was also shared by the UK. Denmark, Iceland, Sweden and the UK did not agree with the connection between an NIEO and protection and promotion of human rights. The UK also opposed the RTD as a human right[34] as well as the indivisibility and interdependence of human rights.[35] The UK delegate agreed that promotion of development is an obligation of the state, but disagreed that such an obligation commands legal value in international law. The FRG shared the view with the USA by saying that the RTD would adversely affect the existing human rights agenda. Similarly, Finland, Denmark, Iceland, Sweden and Norway expressed the fear that the collective dimension of the RTD would endanger the protection of individual human rights by state authorities. Japan objected to the duty of cooperation spelt out in some articles of the Declaration and maintained that the duty of cooperation under Article 56 of the UN Charter is not legally binding. After the adoption of the Declaration, the Commission convened the working group to submit proposals regarding concrete measures to promote the RTD.[36] The expert from the USA actively objected to the mandate of the working group and decided to quit the deliberations.[37] The drafting history of the Declaration will be commented upon below when the weaknesses of the Declaration are discussed.

THE MAIN FEATURES OF THE DECLARATION

Before turning to a discussion of other working groups set up for the realization of the RTD, it is necessary to critically discuss some of the main features and weaknesses of the Declaration.

Unity of human rights

The most striking feature of the Declaration is that it proclaims the unity of all human rights. Article 6 of the Declaration says: 'all human rights and fundamental freedoms are indivisible and interdependent'. The article also emphasizes that first- and second-generation human rights should be treated equally, and that their implementation, promotion and protection should be considered urgently. The call for the unity and interdependence of human rights is not a new one. This issue had been pursued since 1957 in various General Assembly resolutions, particularly the 1969 Declaration on Social

34 DRD, Art. 1.
35 Ibid. Art. 6.
36 E/CN.4/1987/10, Report of the tenth session of the working group.
37 Statement by the representative of the USA, annexed in ibid.

Progress and Development.[38] It was three years after this declaration that Keba M'baye announced the concept of the RTD in 1972. It was pursued vigorously thereafter and, after five years, the Commission recognized the RTD as a human right. Thus the RTD concept not only provided an effective forum of discussion on this issue, but also paved the way for the integration of human rights with development at the policy level. The Declaration thus made a significant contribution to the RTD agenda through this change and the subsequent follow-up of the issue in the various working groups on the RTD and in the global conferences on human rights, most particularly the Vienna Conference, 1993.

It was noted above that developed countries opposed the notion of indivisibility and interdependence of human rights during the drafting of the Declaration. The fact remains that the RTD as a legal concept is still opposed by those countries. Yet the integration of human rights in their development assistance policies (and also those of some multilateral donor agencies) clearly explains that they see economic, social and cultural rights as no less important than civil and political rights. The indivisibility and interdependence of human rights, as set in by the Declaration, has created a wide scope for human rights lawyers at the domestic level and at the international level. A broad interpretation of human rights by lawyers in the context of social justice may help bridge the traditional gap between the negative and the positive rights. As will be seen in the context of Pakistan in Chapter 6, there is evidence that the scope of negative rights is extended to positive rights. For example, the right to life is interpreted as inclusive of a right to a decent standard of living. Such a judicial approach may facilitate the process of development by compelling the state to take positive action.

Participation

Another important feature of the Declaration is the principle of participation.[39] The Declaration builds up a comprehensive concept of participation:

38 UNGA Res. 2542 (XXIV); See also UNGA Res. 1161 (XII), 1957 in which the UNGA declared that balanced and integrated economic and social development would, *inter alia*, lead to the observance of, and respect for the human rights and fundamental freedoms of all. The indivisibility and interdependence of all human rights was proclaimed on the occasion of a world conference in Tehran in 1968: 'Since human rights and fundamental freedoms are indivisible, the full realization of civil and political rights without the enjoyment of economic, social and cultural rights is impossible. The achievement of lasting progress in the implementation of human rights is dependent upon sound and effective national and international policies of economic and social development.'

39 As a concept popular participation caught the attention of the Commission and ECOSOC in 1983/84, a time when the drafting of the DRD was under discussion by the working group. In 1984, the Secretary-General submitted a 'preliminary report on an analytical study he was undertaking on the right to popular participation in its various forms as an important factor in the full realization of all human rights'. See *UN Year Book*, vol. 38, op. cit., p 836.

1 Every human person and all peoples have a right of participation in the process of development.[40]
2 Participation must be active, free and meaningful not only in the process, but also in the outcome of development policies.[41]
3 The Declaration shows a special concern for the participatory role of women in the process of development.[42]
4 Finally, the Declaration requires states to encourage popular participation in development and in the full realization of all human rights.[43]

The Declaration requires the state to create an enabling environment for encouraging popular participation in development. At the national level, the state must discharge its duty of formulating appropriate national policies in such manner as ensures the genuine participation of the entire population and all individuals.[44] The importance of participation has emerged as a result of the failure of development policies in developing countries in the past. This failure is mainly attributed to the central role of the political, social, economic and legal institutions of the state in the implementation of development strategies. In other words, the fruits of development strategies could not effectively and meaningfully trickle down from top to the bottom, i.e. to the common people as they remain marginalized and excluded. An important reason for this failure is the absence of accountability of the state's institutions. The right of participation emphasizes the involvement of the beneficiaries at all stages, viz., the formulation, implementation, monitoring and evaluation of development policies. The principal methodology of this bottom-up approach is the reformation of the states' institutions with a view to making them more accountable and their performance more transparent in the process and the outcomes of development. Thus the right of participation breaks the traditional monopoly of the state institutions to ensure empowerment of the people at large. In other words, the traditional democratic institutions such as 'representative democracy and techno-bureaucratic administration' are no longer considered sufficient in the governance structure.[45] However, it is important to note that participation does not aim to make the state altogether irrelevant. Being a cardinal principle of good

40 DRD, Art. 1(1).
41 Ibid. Art. 2(3).
42 Ibid. Art. 8.
43 Ibid. Art. 8(2).
44 Ginther, 'Participation and Accountability', op. cit., 75; see also Konrad Ginther, 'The domestic policy function of a right of peoples to development: popular participation a new hope for development and a challenge for the discipline', in S.R. Chowdhury et al. (eds), *The Right to Development in International Law*, The Hague, Kluwer Law International, 1992, pp 35–41.
45 Archon Fung and Erik Olin Wright, 'Deepening Democracy: Innovations in Empowered Participatory Governance', *Politics and Society* 29(1), March 2001, 5–41.

governance, participation requires the state institutions to take on board the people and/or their CSOs in the decision-making process vis-à-vis development policies. The right of participation is increasingly receiving attention in national and international development policies aimed at a rights-based approach.[46] Participation is one of the core principles of a PRSP. The PRSP is a national policy document a country has to prepare as a precondition for claiming financial assistance from the IFIs. In the context of Pakistan's PRSP, participation will be discussed in detail in Chapter 8.

International cooperation

The basic tenet of the collective dimension of the RTD (i.e. as a right of the state) is solidarity, which means international cooperation among states. International cooperation can facilitate participation by developing countries in the international economic system. Article 3(2) connects the realization of a collective RTD with the duty of cooperation among states. In this respect, it makes a reference to the General Assembly Declaration on friendly relations. The Declaration lays down seven principles of friendly relations and cooperation, the most relevant one here being the duty of the states to cooperate with each other in accordance with the UN Charter. This area of cooperation includes the promotion of economic stability and progress, and the universal observance of, and respect for, the human rights and fundamental freedoms of all. Article 3(3) provides that such a duty of cooperation should aim at ensuring development and eliminating obstacles to development. The article explains that the cooperation shall promote an NIEO. Emphasizing continuous efforts for the promotion of development in developing countries, Article 4(2) says that 'effective international cooperation is essential' to allow and facilitate a participatory role for the developing countries in international economic policies.

Bedjaoui argues that since the international legal order is essentially of an inter-state character, therefore, the RTD would be meaningful in international law only when the RTD of the state is given predominance over the RTD of the individual.[47] Bedjaoui even believes that confining the RTD to its individual dimension, i.e. a claim of the individual against her state, would be dangerous.[48] He argues that even if the state wants to realize the RTD of the individual, favourable international conditions are essential.[49] Bedjaoui is

46 See, generally, S.R. Osmani, 'Participatory Governance and Poverty Reduction' in Alejandro Grinspun et al (eds), *Choices for the Poor: Lessons from national poverty strategies*, UNDP. Online. Available at: <http://www.undp.org/dpa/publications/choicesforpoor/ENGLISH/CHAP05.PDF> (accessed 24 June 2007), pp 121–43.

47 Bedjaoui, op. cit., p 1180.

48 Ibid.

49 Ibid.

right in stressing the international dimension of the RTD, but the Declaration makes the RTD the prime responsibility of the state. The importance of the international conditions cannot be overlooked, but the international community cannot be wholly responsible for the RTD.

The concept of development

Before looking at the meaning of the word 'development' in the context of the RTD, it is necessary to have a basic understanding of it. Thirwall argues that 'development' implies change.[50] In this sense, it describes the process of economic and social change.[51] According to Todaro and Smith:

> In strictly economic terms, *development* has traditionally meant the capacity of a national economy, whose initial economic condition has been more or less static for a long time, to generate and sustain an annual increase in its gross national income (GNI) at rates of 5% to 7% or more. A common alternative economic index of development has been the use of rates of growth of income per capita to take into account the ability of a nation to expand its output at a rate faster than the growth rate of its population.[52]

In this perspective, development is seen as simple economic growth.[53] Until the 1950s and 1960s, 'development' was seen in the sense of mere economic growth. However, while in these decades many countries were able to achieve their economic growth targets, such an increase in economic growth had little impact on the standard of living of the people.[54] In the 1970s, it was thought necessary to redefine the concept of 'development' so as to address wide social and economic issues such as the elimination of poverty, inequality and unemployment.[55] Since the 1980s, 'development' is understood as a change in

50 A.P. Thirwall, *Growth & Development*, New York, Palgrave Macmillan, seventh edition, 2003, p 19.

51 Ibid.

52 Michael P. Todaro and Stephan C. Smith, *Economic Development*, Harlow, Addison Wesley, ninth edition, 2006, p 15. The authors define GNI as 'the total domestic and foreign output claimed by residents of a country. It comprises *gross domestic product (GDP)* plus factor incomes accruing to residents from abroad, less the income earned in the domestic economy accruing to persons abroad.' The GDP is 'the total final output of *goods* and *services* produced by the country's economy, within the country's territory, by residents and non residents, regardless of its allocation between domestic and foreign claims.' See at p 815.

53 Jay Drydyk, 'When is Development More Democratic', *Journal of Human Development* 6(2), 2005, 247–67, at 249.

54 Todaro and Smith, op. cit., p 16.

55 Ibid.

the entire social system.[56] Thus development is 'a multidimensional process involving major changes in social structures, popular attitudes, and national institutions, as well as the acceleration of economic growth, the reduction of inequality and the eradication of poverty'.[57] M'baye, the founding father of the RTD, saw development in the following perspective:

> Economic growth must be accompanied by social and cultural progress; this means, to put it simply, that it must be accorded a human dimension. The increase in per capita [Gross National Product] GNP is of no avail if it does not at the same time take into account educational and cultural progress, and in a general manner, if it does not observe and develop the values of civilization of the group and their participation in universal civilization . . . to develop is to improve human life first in quantity, but ultimately in quality.[58]

Bedjaoui, another pioneer of the RTD, sees it as 'the development of all men and the whole man'.[59] In the context of the RTD, 'development' could be understood with reference to two aspects, viz. economic growth and human development. Economic growth means the expansion of national income and output in terms of GNP. By contrast, human development is not confined to the rise or fall of the GNP; it aims at 'expanding the choices people have to lead lives that they value . . . and it is thus about much more than economic growth, which is only a means – if a very important one – of enlarging people's choices'.[60] In other words, human development identifies the human person as the central subject of development. By linking it with human rights, the RTD adopts a more holistic approach to such a concept of human development. This is illustrated in the second preambular paragraph of the Declaration, which defines development as:

> Development is a comprehensive economic, social, cultural and political process, which aims at the constant improvement of the well-being of the entire population and of all individuals on the basis of their active, free and meaningful participation in development and in the fair distribution of benefits resulting therefrom.

56 Brian Chi-ang Lin, 'A New Vision of the Knowledge Economy', *Journal of Economic Survey* 21(3), 2007, 553–84, at 564.

57 Ibid. 17.

58 Quoted in H.G. Espiel, op. cit., 202.

59 See generally Bedjaoui, *Towards a New International Economic Order*, op. cit., p 73.

60 See definition of human development, online. Available at <http://hdr.undp.org/hd/> (accessed 26 Feb. 2009).

The Independent Expert on the RTD has endorsed Sen's view on development,[61] most notably the capability approach, discussed in Chapter 2. According to Sen, development is 'a process of expanding the *real freedom* that people enjoy'.[62] Social and political conditions of human life, e.g. education, health, liberty and participation, play important roles in the process of development that enhance freedom.[63] In Sen's opinion, freedom is necessary for development for two reasons: growth is basically evaluated to find out whether it has enhanced freedoms (an *evaluative reason*) and development can be achieved if people have meaningful freedom in the economic, social and political spheres of life (an *effective reason*).[64] Sen believes 'poverty as well as tyranny, poor economic opportunities as well as systemic social deprivation, neglect of public facilities as well as intolerance or overactivity of repressive States'[65] not only are obstacles to development, but also limit freedom (which Sen calls 'unfreedom'). Sen further argues that public policy based on an adequate development *process*, including economic, social and political institutions/organizations, enhances capabilities (or eliminates sources of 'unfreedom').[66] Public participation in this *process*, on the other hand, should also 'effectively influence the direction of such public policy'.[67] Almost in the same fashion, Eide argues that when development as a process of change creates worse conditions than before or significantly fails in getting what *could* have been achieved, it leads to mal-development.[68] Eide further argues that the international economic order, with both its elements of dominance and dependence, is a contributing factor to mal-development, causing 'unfreedoms' – inequality, poverty, malnutrition, bad health, low levels of education and cultural onslaught.[69]

The Declaration does not suggest a specific model of economic development. Any model of development that people may choose, however, should aim at the realization of the RTD for every individual and all people. To achieve this purpose, the Declaration lays down broad guidelines. Article 8 enunciates that the states are under the obligation to devise policies at the national level that lead to the provision of equality of opportunity for every one, including women, to basic resources, education, health services, food,

61 The Independent Expert First Report, para. 55.

62 Sen, *Development as Freedom*, op. cit., p 3 (emphasis added).

63 Ibid. p 5.

64 Ibid. pp 4 and 19 (emphasis in original).

65 Ibid. p 3.

66 Ibid. pp 8, 9 and 18.

67 Ibid.

68 Asbjorn Eide, 'Maldevelopment and the "Right to Development": A Critical Note with a Constructive Intent' in R.-J. Dupuy, op. cit., pp 397–416 at p 401 (emphasis in original). See, generally, Theo C. van Boven, 'The Right to Development and Human Rights', *The Review of the International Commission of Jurists* 28, 1982, 49–56.

69 Ibid. 405–11.

housing, employment and the fair distribution of income and popular participation in the activities of development and the realization of human rights.[70] In order to enable the state to create such conditions for the realization of the RTD for its people, the Declaration suggests that the members of the international community have a duty to cooperate among themselves.

The concept of development envisaged by the Declaration shows its ability to adapt to the different models of development which different states have adopted.[71] Alston notes that, being 'open ended and indeterminate', the Declaration shows dynamism to adjust to changing circumstances.[72] Some have argued that the Declaration provides an ethical foundation for human dignity-based development.[73] Does such development include sustainable development?

Sustainable development

According to the Brundtland Report, '[S]ustainable development is development that meets the needs of the present without compromising the ability of future generations to meet their own needs'.[74] Commentators argue that this is a generally accepted definition of sustainable development.[75] The Brundtland Report suggests that sustainable development has three components: first, environment, which should be protected 'by gradually changing the ways in which we develop and use technology'. Second is 'social equity', which means that the developing countries should be allowed to pursue their development to meet their basic needs such as employment, food, energy, water and sanitation. Third, while pursuing their economic growth, the developing countries should be allowed to achieve a growth of equal quality to the developed countries.[76]

The Declaration does not expressly recognize sustainable development. However, since the 1990s, it has been widely recognized in various international conferences that sustainable development and the RTD are mutually interdependent.[77] For example, principle 3 of the Rio Declaration provides that the RTD must be fulfilled so as to equitably meet the developmental and

70 DRD, Articles 2(3), 3 and 8.

71 Orford, op. cit., p 145.

72 Alston, 'Revitalising UN Work', op. cit., 221.

73 Yash Ghai, *Whose Right to Development?*, Human Rights Unit Occasional Paper, Human Rights in Development Series, Commonwealth Secretariat, London, 1989, p 3.

74 World Commission on Environment and Development, *Our Common Future*, Oxford, Oxford University Press, 1987, p 43. See also Amin U. Sarkar, 'Sustainable development and technology', *The Environmentalist* 17, 1997, 97–102.

75 Lindroos, op. cit., p 62.

76 Brundtland Report, p 43.

77 See Lindroos, op. cit., p 63.

environmental needs of present and future generations.[78] In 1993 and 1996, the working groups on the RTD also made specific references to sustainable development.[79] The current working group in its eighth session held in March 2007 also endorsed the relevance of sustainable development for the RTD.[80] Despite all this, one must appreciate that the possibility of a clash between environment and development cannot be ruled out.[81] Such a clash creates interesting but complex issues from the perspective of the RTD. The developing countries think that the developed world is responsible for environmental degradation. They are of the view that the developed world should help them in ensuring sustainable development. As one commentator has aptly put it:

> And the principle of 'common but differentiated responsibility' acknowledges that the North is, and historically has been, most responsible for the crisis – and has more resources, as well as a greater responsibility for resolving it. The South must also play its role – but must be helped with financial resources and technology transfer, and should not be made to bear an unfair share of the burden of global adjustment.[82]

Looking at this issue from the perspective of the RTD, it appears that the duty of international cooperation for the realization of the RTD should extend to the realization of sustainable development. Both sustainable development and the RTD require a duty of international cooperation, particularly on the part of the developed world to assist the developing countries in pursuing sustainable development. At the national level, developing countries face the challenge of accommodating economic growth with sustainable development.[83] The element of active, free and meaningful participation, a key feature of the RTD, is helpful in meeting the challenge of sustainable development. This will require the protection and promotion of many human rights such as the right to have access to information, the right to free speech and the right to education. Sustainable development shows signs of progress in those countries where participation, particularly in urban development

78 Rio Declaration on Environment and Development, 1992.

79 E/CN.4/1994/21, para. 7; E/CN.4/1996/24, para. 76.

80 A/HRC/4/47, paras 27 and 35; See also E/CN.4/2004/WG.18/2, para. 21.

81 Lindroos, op. cit., p 63. For example, The Rio Declaration on environment and development, 1992; Vienna conference on human rights, 1993; the world summit for social development, 1995; and, the Beijing Declaration, 1995.

82 Martin Khor, 'Paradigm Clash', *Our Planet*, Feb. 2007. Online. Available at: <http://www.unep.org/pdf/Ourplanet/2007/february/en/OP-2007-02-en-ARTICLE8.pdf> (accessed 19 June 2007).

83 See for example, *Case Concerning the Gabcikovo-Nagymaros Project*, op cit., 7. In this case, a judge of the ICJ discussed the RTD from the perspective of sustainable development. This case will be further discussed in the next chapter.

planning, is actively and meaningfully encouraged at the grass-roots level.[84] Pakistan's PRSP, the current development policy document, expressly links the poverty reduction programme to sustainable development (see Chapter 8). Chapter 6 will discuss the role of Pakistan's judiciary in the protection of the environment through a wider interpretation of human rights.

WEAKNESSES OF THE DECLARATION

Vague and imprecise

The language of the Declaration is vague, imprecise and unclear in some respects. Firstly, it is not clear whether the individual is the subject or the beneficiary of the RTD.[85] As discussed in the previous chapter, 'the individual as a subject' and as a 'beneficiary' create jurisprudential confusion and vagueness, which significantly reflect on the problems involved in the justiciability of the RTD. Moreover, the state is not specifically mentioned as a subject of the RTD.[86] The Declaration merely provides that the state has the right and duty to formulate development policies.[87]

Secondly, while the principle of cooperation is one of the main features of the RTD, the language of the Declaration does not couch it in precise terms. A close reading of the Declaration would show that the words used are neither mandatory nor consistent. For example, Article 3(2) says that 'the realization of the RTD *requires full respect* of the principles of international law concerning friendly relations and cooperation'. With respect to the formulation of international development policies for the realization of the RTD, Article 4(1) says, 'States have the *duty to take steps*, individually and collectively.' Article 4(2) is a very important provision because it deals with development cooperation and foreign development assistance to the developing countries. It provides:

> *Sustained action is required* to promote more rapid development of developing countries. As a complement to the efforts of developing countries, *effective international cooperation is essential* in providing these countries with *appropriate means* and facilities to foster their comprehensive development. [Emphasis added]

84 See, for example, Rualdo Menegat, 'Participatory democracy and sustainable development: integrated urban environment management in Porto Alegre, Brazil', *Environment and Urbanization* 14, 2002, 181–206.

85 Lindroos, op. cit., pp 30–1.

86 Maria Magdalena Kenig-Witkowska, 'The UN Declaration on the Right to Development in the light of its Travaux Preparatoires' in S.R. Chowdhury et al. (eds) *International Law and Development*, Dordrecht, London, Martinus Nijhoff Publishers, 1988, pp 381–7, at p 382.

87 DRD, Art. 2(3).

The language in the first sentence is problematic because it does not identify who is required to sustain action. In other words, who is the duty-holder, if there is a duty at all? Moreover, it does not speak explicitly about the mandatory nature of development aid provided by the developed countries to the developing countries. The second part is vague and ambiguous because 'appropriate means' is a very general phrase. Similarly, the words 'should cooperate' are used for the promotion of all human rights without any distinction.[88] The word 'duty' has been used in two provisions: Articles 3(3) and 4(1). The former says that the states have *the duty to cooperate* with each other in ensuring development and eliminating obstacles to development. The latter pronounces that '[t]he states have *the duty to take steps*, individually and collectively, to formulate international development policies with a view to facilitating the full realization of the [RTD]'.

The advocates of the RTD usually refer to Articles 55 and 56 of the UN Charter as having a general recognition in international law, but some commentators are of the view that 'the formulation of this principle remains rather abstract and permits a relatively wide margin of discretion regarding its practical interpretation and application'.[89]

Thirdly, Article 6 requires states to cooperate for the observance of all universal human rights, to eliminate obstacles to development resulting from failure to observe civil, political and economic, and social and cultural rights, and to ensure that human rights are indivisible and interdependent. This, arguably, makes the RTD a mere synthesis of the existing human rights. Such a synthesis does not make it a separate right in itself. As one critic puts it, 'affirming that all people have the RTD, and that . . . development consists of and is realized through the realization of every existing right category of human rights, adds nothing to our knowledge. It adds only verbiage.'[90]

A compromise document

As discussed above in the drafting history, the Declaration was adopted as a compromise document. Developed countries strongly opposed the collective dimension of the RTD. There was no consensus in the working group in the Commission or the General Assembly.[91] As noted above, there was even strong opposition to the transmission of the draft declaration to the General Assembly. The negotiations over this issue had reached a stalemate, and in order to break the stalemate, a compromise draft was submitted. The

88 Ibid. Art. 6(1).

89 Danilo Turk, 'Participation of Developing Countries in Decision-Making Process', in Chowdhury, et al (eds), op. cit., pp 341–57, at p 342. See also, generally, Lindroos, op. cit., p 38.

90 Uvin, op. cit., p 43.

91 Milan Bulajic, 'Principles of International Development Law' in Chowdhury, et al. (eds), op. cit., pp 359–69, at p 360.

developing countries wanted to move quickly towards a declaration the whereas developed countries wanted to continue with the discussion. Kiwanuka argues that 'if more time had been given to the working group, the distance between the main opposing groups would have been narrowed'.[92] Kiwanuka maintains that the USA, for example, changed its position of overall opposition and submitted its own draft proposal to the working group. The proposed draft recognized the RTD as 'the human right of every person, individually or entities established pursuant to the right of association'.[93] In the wake of some discussion, the proposal was also amended to include 'people', which was omitted in the first draft.[94] The draft further narrowed the controversy when it recognized that 'equality of opportunity is a prerogative of both nations and individuals who make up the nations'.[95] Although six developed countries abstained from voting and only the USA voted against the Declaration, this position emerged as a consequence of extensive negotiations and compromise.[96] While abstention can be legally termed as acquiescence, the view that it does not amount to a genuine consensus cannot be simply dismissed.

Reference to the NIEO

It was explained in Chapter 2 that the NIEO was a movement launched by the developing countries in the 1960s, for structural reforms in the then international economic order. The developing countries thought their struggle for a new global economic order was an item of unfinished business left over from the course of their political emancipation. The developed countries, on the other hand, strongly opposed this demand. The RTD debate was initiated in the early 1970s, a time when the NIEO movement was at its peak.[97]

The Declaration does not make a clear and explicit reference to the specific NIEO declaration of the General Assembly. However, in its preambular paragraph 15 and Article 3(3), the Declaration makes a vague reference to the promotion of an NIEO. This vague reference is due to a compromise between the developed and developing countries because the former were opposed to a direct and explicit reference to the NIEO resolutions of the General

92 R.N. Kiwanuka, 'Developing Rights: The UN Declaration on the Right to Development', *Netherlands International Law Review* 35, 1988, 257–72, at 267.

93 Ibid.

94 Ibid.

95 Ibid.

96 Ibid. 261.

97 See generally, *North-South: A Programme for Survival*, Report of the Independent Commission on International Development Issues, The MIT Press, Cambridge, Massachusetts, 1980, Eighth Printing, 1986. The Commission, also known as the Brandt Commission, carried out an in-depth study of the international development issues vis-à-vis the NIEO. The Brandt Commission also put forward recommendations for resolving such issues.

Assembly. Despite this vague reference, the Declaration reflects the rivalry of the two groups over the NIEO. As discussed above, a Pakistan-sponsored amendment to the draft declaration was rejected because it reflected the main principles of the NIEO movement. One obvious reason for the rejection was that such an amendment was likely to jeopardize the compromise by which the parties had arrived at the draft declaration. The proposed amendment was adopted as a separate resolution on the RTD.[98] It follows that this connection has posed challenges of both legal recognition and implementation of the Declaration at the international level.

Women's rights

In Article 8, the Declaration spells out women's RTD: 'effective measures should be undertaken to ensure that women have an active role in the development process.' Another provision emphasizes that states should cooperate to promote all human rights without any distinction as to race, sex, language or religion.[99] Other articles make more implicit references to women's role by using words such as 'every human person', 'all people' and 'entire population'. Some critics have raised objections to the feminist perspective of the RTD. The weaknesses of the Declaration may be analysed from two perspectives, viz. the feminist and cultural.

The feminist critique is carried out by Charlesworth. Her first argument is that Article 5 of the Declaration does not include discrimination against women as one of the examples of massive and flagrant violation of human rights.[100] Her second argument, relating to women's role in a model of development, appears to be more general. Charlesworth is of the view that any model of development that is based on the RTD must address women's role effectively and meaningfully because economic inequality constitutes the crux of the RTD. Her argument is directed to developing countries only (using the term 'Third World'). It seems difficult to carve out a universally accepted role for women in a human rights-based development programme where human rights face a cultural critique.

Regarding the cultural critique, it can be argued that the Declaration, by

98 UNGA Res. A/41/133. Those who voted against were Belgium, Canada, France, FRG, Italy, Japan, Luxembourg, the Netherlands, Portugal, the UK and the USA. Belgium, Canada, France and the Netherlands had favoured the DRD. Countries who abstained were Australia, Austria, Denmark, Finland, Ireland, Norway and Sweden. Among these countries, Australia favoured the DRD. The remainder had abstained from voting on the DRD.

99 DRD, Art. 6(1).

100 Hilary Charlesworth, 'The Public/Private Distinction and the Right to Development in International Law', *Australian Year Book of International Law*, 1999, 190–204 at 196. For further discussion on human rights and cultural relativism, see also Hilary Charlesworth, *The Boundaries of International Law: The Feminist Analysis*, Manchester, Manchester University Press, 2000, pp 201, 222–44.

referring to human rights, presupposes the universality of the current international human rights regimes. However, it is not so. In fact, there is a complex debate over the cultural origin and evolution of contemporary human rights. In the human rights literature, this issue is known as cultural relativism.[101] In many non-Western societies, the current human rights standards are not seen as universal.[102] Particular reference may be made to Muslim societies, where the current human rights are seen by some as the tool of Western ideological imperialism and as the cultural invasion of many non-Western ideologies, cultures and religions.[103] The problem of cultural relativism can pose potential problems for the implementation of the Declaration through international cooperation at the international level. This subject will be discussed in detail in Chapter 7 in the context of Pakistan. The current working group has recognized that women play a key role in development.[104]

REALIZATION OF THE RTD

After the adoption of the Declaration by the General Assembly, the first working group, while continuing its work, considered the realization of the RTD. The USA strongly objected to the issue of the realization on the ground that since the RTD has not been defined and lacks consensus, no question of its realization arises.[105] Despite opposition to the realization of the RTD, the Commission continues to make efforts for its recognition.

The global consultation

In 1989, the Commission invited the Secretary-General to organize a global consultation on the realization of the RTD.[106] The consultation was to involve

101 Michael Freeman, 'Human Rights and Real Cultures: Towards a Dialogue on "Asian Values" ', *Netherlands Quarterly of Human Rights* 16(1), 1998, 25–39. For a discussion on cultural relativism and the UDHR, see Philip Alston, 'The Universal Declaration at 35: Western and Passé or Alive and Universal', *The Review of the International Commission of Jurists* 31, 1983, 60–70.

102 See, e.g., J. Donnelly, 'Human Rights and Human Dignity: An Analytic Critique of Non-Western Conceptions of Human Rights', *The American Political Science Review* 76, 1985, 303–16; Nie Jing-Bao, 'Cultural Values Embodying Universal Norms: A Critique of a Popular Assumption about Cultures and Human Rights', *Developing World Bioethics* 5(3), 2005, 251–7; Bony Ibhawoh, 'Between Culture and Constitution: Evaluating the Cultural Legitimacy of Human Rights in the African States', *Human Rights Quarterly* 22, 2000, 838–60.

103 Baderin, op. cit., p 13; Martin, op. cit., 827–45.

104 See E/CN.4/2001/26, paras 59–61.

105 Ansah, 'The RTD in Malawi', op. cit., p 47.

106 CHR Res. 1989/45.

experts from a wide spectrum, having relevant experience in human rights and development issues at the national level. The experts were also to include, at the international level, representatives of the UN specialized agencies, regional inter-governmental organizations and interested non-governmental organizations (NGOs), active in human rights and development work. The aim of the consultation was to:

> Focus on the fundamental problems posed by the implementation of the [Declaration], the criteria which might be used to identify progress, and mechanisms for evaluating and stimulating such progress.

Although participation in the consultation was more representative of the developing countries, the views expressed in the discussion on key jurisprudential issues, such as the content and scope, subjects and justiciability of the RTD, remained highly divided as between the developed and the developing countries. There was, however, a detailed discussion on the national dimension of the RTD. The participants observed that development strategies should be determined by the peoples concerned about them and should be adapted to their particular conditions and needs.[107] The consultation concentrated on how to integrate human rights in UN operational activities.[108]

The consultation outlined basic elements of national development policies for the realization of the RTD. The crucial role of participation was accentuated.[109] The participants noted that a weak constitution and excessive bureaucratization lead to the social exclusion of the poor. It was also pointed out that local cultural and historical values and institutions can play the role of 'mediating structures' or 'intermediary groups' in creating an enabling environment for effective participation.[110] Changes in the concept of the welfare state and legal assistance to the extremely poor and vulnerable were viewed as more important factors in effective and meaningful participation. Specific perspectives of the RTD, such as women, indigenous peoples and the extremely poor,

107 Global Consultation on the RTD, paras 154–155.

108 R.L. Barsh, 'The Right to Development as a Human Right: Results of the Global Consultation', *Human Rights Quarterly* 13, 1991, 322–38.

109 Global Consultation on the RTD, paras 114–126.

110 The Consultation made a reference to the African Charter on Human and Peoples' Rights, 1981 and the Lomé III Convention, 1985. For example, Article 121 of the Lomé III Convention provided that the participation and continuous involvement of grass-roots communities in developmental operations should be ensured. The Lomé Convention was an aid and trade agreement between the European Communities (EC) and African Caribbean and the Pacific Countries (ACP). First signed in 1975 at Lomé, Togo, for a period of five years, it was renegotiated twice, each for the same period, Lomé II (1980) and III (1985). Lomé IV was signed in 1990 for ten years and ended in 1999. In the year 2000, Lomé IV was replaced by the Cotonou Agreement. Lomé I was signed by 46 countries, the Cotonou Agreement by 77 countries.

were also discussed.[111] At the international level, the consultation, inter alia, suggested that both the UN bodies and specialized agencies should incorporate the RTD in their mandates. Further, it was recommended that a high-level committee of independent experts be appointed with a mandate to make recommendations for the realization of the RTD.

The consultation scored some successes. The link between human rights and development was 'considerably strengthened': firstly, the UNDP's first human development report stressed the link between human freedom and human development.[112] Secondly, the fourth UN Decade of Development also emphasized that 'development should enhance the participation of all men and women in economic and political life, protect cultural identities'.[113] Thirdly, a visible change was also witnessed in the position of the USA and the EU during the General Assembly's sixty-eighth session (1990), which considered the report of the consultation.[114] The RTD resolution was adopted without vote[115] as the USA finally decided not to participate in the vote and explained that the report had some 'positive elements'. Germany observed that the consultation was 'a step in the right direction'.[116] The Commission did not consider the proposal for a committee of independent experts.[117]

The second and third working groups

The Commission established one working group in 1993 for a period of three years[118] and another working group (called the Inter-governmental group of experts) in 1996 for a period of two years.[119] Like the Global Consultation, the purpose of both groups was the implementation of the RTD. No substantial difference could be found in the work of the two groups. The 1993 working group observed that the main obstacles at the international level were: the negative effects of globalization, the heavy debt-burden, financial conditionalities and decreasing aid flows.[120] The 1996 working group recommended a dialogue of all parties, preferably in the Council and continued coordination between the High Commissioner for Human Rights and the IFIs so that the latter could mainstream the RTD in their policies. Further suggestions included an equitable distribution of global economic gains,

111 Global Consultation on the RTD, para. 1.
112 UNDP, *Human Development Report*, 1990, p 16.
113 UNGA Res. A/45/199, para. 13.
114 Barsh, op. cit., 336.
115 UNGA Res. A/45/97.
116 Barsh, op. cit., 336–7.
117 See Ansah, 'The RTD in Malawi', op. cit., p 100.
118 CHR, Res. 1993/22.
119 CHR, Res. 1996/15.
120 See the working group's reports such as E/CN.4/1994/21; E/CN.4/1995/11; E/CN.4/1996/10.

with increased participation from the developing countries and an increase in the foreign aid of developed countries (i.e. 0.7 per cent GDP).[121] The views of the two groups regarding the implementation of the RTD at the national level were also more or less the same. Both urged the states to respect and protect human rights and fundamental freedoms and introduce legal and constitutional changes for this purpose. They also stressed the promotion of good governance, accountability, participatory democracy, sustainable development and the rule of law.

The representatives of various UN agencies, treaty-monitoring bodies and international organizations appeared before the 1993 working group and submitted their statements regarding the mainstreaming of the RTD in development policies. Among them, of significant importance is the statement of the representative from the Economic Commission for Europe, according to which 'international cooperation for the implementation of the RTD could have three objectives: specify the content of the right; evaluate progress realized and define the conditions for its joint implementation by the actors of development'.[122] This indicates a willingness on the part of the European countries to support the implementation of the RTD. The first session of the 1996 working group was attended by the ILO and the IMF; observers from the member states of the Commission were some of the key opponents of the RTD, such as Germany, Japan, the UK and the USA. The working group was informed that a consultation between the High Commissioner for Human Rights and the World Bank had taken place and many aspects of cooperation had been discussed.

The two working groups made no significant contribution towards the implementation of the RTD. The political rivalry between the developing and the developed countries continued. The dialogue in these forums, particularly in the Global Consultation, was, however, not altogether fruitless. The issue of the link between human rights and development received more serious consideration. Some Western countries also softened their tone on the RTD. Even in the two working groups, representatives of the international development community, e.g. the observer of the IMF, participated in the deliberations. Thus these forums did provide an opportunity to both the supporters and the opponents of the RTD to express their respective contentions and understand each other's views. It was this continuity of the dialogue that paved the way for further efforts towards the implementation of the RTD. If the proposals made by the working groups for the realization of the RTD at the international level are implemented, this can strengthen international cooperation. Moreover, the implementation of the proposals may create an enabling environment for the RTD at the national level. The working groups' proposals for the realization of the RTD at the national level, such

121 E/CN.4/1997/22.

122 E/CN.4/1996/10, para. 13.

as the protection of human rights and fundamental freedoms, good governance and the rule of law, are helpful for the promotion of the RTD. As this book argues, such proposals require strong judicial institutions, which have the prime responsibility of protecting human rights and fundamental freedoms.[123] The next section analyses those efforts and focuses on the reports of the Independent Expert and the Task Force.

THE CURRENT STATUS OF THE REALIZATION

The independent expert and the task force

Taking note of the above suggestion, the Commission established an OEWG, with the following mandate:[124]

> (i) To monitor and review progress made in the promotion and implementation of the [RTD] . . . at the national and international levels, providing recommendations thereon and further analysing obstacles to its full enjoyment, focusing each year on specific commitments in the Declaration;
>
> (ii) To review reports and any other information submitted by States, United Nations agencies, other relevant international organizations and non-governmental organizations on the relationship between their activities and the [RTD].

The mandate also included advice to the Office of the High Commissioner for Human Rights (OHCHR) with regard to the implementation of the RTD and suggestions for possible programmes of technical assistance to those countries which were interested in the promotion of implementation of the RTD. The Commission also appointed an Independent Expert with high competence in the area of the RTD with a mandate:

> [T]o present to the working group at each of its sessions a study on the current state of progress in the implementation of the [RTD] as a basis for a focused discussion, taking into account, *inter alia*, the deliberations and suggestions of the working group.

Up until June 2007, the OEWG had held eight sessions. The Independent Expert had submitted six reports, which were discussed in the sessions of the OEWG. Since the main focus, as stated above, is on the work of the

123 The role of the judicial institutions of Pakistan in the area of human rights, governance and social justice will be focused upon in the next part of this book.

124 CHR, Res. 1998/72.

Independent Expert, therefore, the reports of the Independent Expert are discussed and critically evaluated below.

The Development Compact (DC)

The Independent Expert on the RTD has carried out in-depth studies on the current progress in the implementation of the RTD. In his first report, he suggested the implementation of the RTD principally by collective action.[125] He proposed a Development Compact, which can be implemented through a step-by-step approach, 'in tandem with the growth of both the international and the national economies, and also the strength of the human rights movements'.[126]

The proposed Development Compact model is based on an arrangement between the developing countries and the international community, including the UN system, bilateral donors and IFIs, to the effect that the latter will provide required assistance to the former for implementation of their programmes of adjustment and reform.[127] A step-by-step mechanism is suggested whereby agreement for such a Development Compact can be reached.[128] Those steps are, firstly, cooperation to achieve, as a high-priority objective, a few rights (e.g. the rights to food, education and health), but without ignoring or violating other rights. Secondly, an organization (e.g. the Development Assistance Committee (DAC) of the Organization of Economic Cooperation and Development (OECD)) could be requested to coordinate the negotiations for a development programme. Thirdly, developing countries that wish to implement the RTD should ask the DAC for a Development Compact. The development programme proposed by such countries shall cover all aspects of the RTD, i.e. integration of human rights with development. Fourthly, a support group of the DAC comprising the IFIs, the UN specialized bodies and major donor countries 'will scrutinize, review and approve the targets and policies of the programme, examine the obligation specified and identify the respective responsibilities of its members in fulfilling those obligations'. Fifthly, the developing countries should bring their national laws in line with international human rights instruments. The proposed development programme shall be designed in consultation with civil society. The national human rights commissions and authorities can monitor the implementation of the programme and can adjudicate complaints concerning violation of human rights. Sixthly, the programme should clearly set out different steps, which shall clearly specify the reciprocal duties and

125 Independent Expert First Report, para. 58.

126 Ibid. para. 67.

127 Ibid. para. 65.

128 Independent Expert Fourth Report, paras 54–63; see also Second Report, paras 67–71; Third Report, para. 43; Fifth Report, para. 14(C).

obligations of the developed and developing countries involved in the exercise. Seventhly, a burden-sharing approach should be taken regarding debt, financial restructuring, investment and international trade and financial rules. Finally, the Development Compact would also require the setting-up of a financial facility called the Fund for Financing Development Compacts, to which the members of the DAC of the OECD shall contribute in the form of 'callable commitments', for which a mechanism may be established with the help of the support group. The Independent Expert has also proposed that the rights to food, primary health care and primary education may be considered by a Development Compact as the minimum indicators of the RTD.[129]

At the national level, it is suggested that the above rights should be justiciable and the individual should be able to claim them from the state in the same manner as other civil and political rights.[130] Moreover, a state's poverty eradication policies shall be guided by a rights-based approach to development, having elements of participation, transparency, accountability and non-discrimination with a view to enhancing capabilities.[131] The Independent Expert has stressed that the development programme shall not ignore the importance of economic growth in terms of GDP; moreover, the realization of some rights shall not violate other rights.[132]

As duty-holders of the RTD, human persons, states and the international community should have an agreement on the realization of the RTD and they should 'work together according to a programme and some binding procedures' to respect the agreement; one procedure suggested is the promulgation of the laws (at the national level) that would make the RTD a legal right.[133] The study also observes that at the international level, a different procedure or programme can be agreed upon by the duty-holders.[134]

The Independent Expert has also carried out country-specific studies, which were of significance to the Development Compact.[135] In this respect, he has analysed the New Partnership for Africa's Development (NEPAD), comparing it with the Development Compact (DC).[136] The Independent Expert argues that the NEPAD 'policy framework is very similar to the approach spelt out in the development compact'.[137] He further observes that the African Peer Review Mechanism (APRM) is an operational institution of

129 Independent Expert First Report, para. 69.

130 Ibid. para. 70.

131 Independent Expert Third Report, para. 38.

132 Ibid. para.14; Fourth Report, paras 10, 11 and 12.

133 Independent Expert Second Report, para. 9.

134 Ibid.

135 Independent Expert Fifth Report.

136 The NEPAD, launched in 2001, by the Organization of African Unity, now the African Union (AU), is an initiative that brings together economic growth and social and political development, e.g. the promotion of democracy, human rights, poverty eradication and good governance. The initiative works with the World Bank, the IMF and the African Development Bank.

137 Independent Expert Fifth Report, para.18.

the NEPAD that has a close similarity with the 'mechanism for ensuring the assessment of the "mutuality of the obligations" between the developing countries and the international community'.[138] However, a major difference is that the NEPAD does not specifically declare a linkage with human rights.[139] Moreover, the Independent Expert has also compared other international development frameworks sponsored by the UN and IFIs (CDF, PRSP, and CCA-UNDAF) to the Development Compact. The Independent Expert has found these development initiatives to be consistent with the Development Compact. However, these initiatives do not specifically recognize the link between human rights and development.[140] The Independent Expert has also carried out a preliminary study of the impacts of globalization on the RTD.[141] According to this study globalization can help promote the RTD. Firstly, developing countries must link their development policies with equity and social justice. Secondly, developing countries need to be integrated into the world economy.

Debate in the working group

The idea of the proposed Development Compact was presented by the Independent Expert to the various sessions of the OEWG. The Independent Expert, while defending his proposal, stated that though the idea of a Development Compact is not new, the previous proposals lacked a human rights approach to development.[142] It was also stressed that instead of creating a new Development Compact, existing development partnerships should be strengthened.[143] The Independent Expert also clarified that the monitoring mechanism in the proposed Development Compact would not lead to conditionality for development assistance.[144] The Independent Expert further suggested that the monitoring mechanism could be made possible through the existing national human rights commissions.[145] The delegates also debated certain other issues such as the mandate, the resources and the necessary expertise, and the role of the donor agencies in the monitoring

138 Ibid. para. 20. 'The African Peer Review Mechanism (APRM) is an instrument voluntarily acceded to by the member states of the African Union as an African self-monitoring mechanism.' Online. Available at: <http://www.nepad.org/2005/files/documents/49.pdf> (accessed 21 June 2007).

139 Ibid. para. 24.

140 Ibid. paras. 33–49.

141 E/CN.4/2003/WG.18/2, Independent Expert's Sixth Report (Preliminary study of the independent expert on the right to development, on the impact of international economic and financial issues on the enjoyment of human rights, submitted in accordance with Commission resolutions 2001/9 and 2002/69).

142 E/CN.4/2001/26, First session of the OEWG, para. 69. The study was discussed by the OEWG in Feb. 2004, E/CN.4/2004/WG.18/2.

143 Ibid. See also E/CN.4/2003/26, Fourth session, para. 19.

144 Ibid. para.70.

145 Ibid. Second session, para. 90.

bodies to deal with violations of the RTD.[146] While collaborating with the Independent Expert over the international dimension of the RTD, the OEWG observed: 'There was no State [RTD]. However, there was an obligation to take multilateral actions to ensure the formulation of development policies that were conducive to the enjoyment of the [RTD].'[147] Delegates commented on the concept of 'mutuality of obligations' and sought clarification that it would not affect the country ownership of development policies.[148] Some delegates also observed that the 'mutuality of obligation' should ensure a redress mechanism in the case of non-fulfilment of international obligations.[149]

A critical appraisal of the Development Compact

As noted above, the Independent Expert is of the view that existing development initiatives share some norms with his proposed Development Compact, but they do not recognize the centrality of human rights and the principles of a rights-based approach. These missing links could be added to the existing development frameworks. A question arises why the Independent Expert proposes a Development Compact as a new development framework. According to Laure-Helene Piron, the existing approaches have resulted from 'national and international negotiations, and have taken time to become established and effective'.[150] Thus, the case for adding an RTD dimension to the existing development framework appears to be stronger than the case for the proposed Development Compact. However, international consensus, particularly the willingness of the developed countries, would be extremely important for making the existing development approaches consistent with the RTD-Development Compact. Piron also argues that developed countries do not make human rights an objective; rather the eradication of poverty is the main target of their development policies.[151] The role of the support group in the proposed Development Compact may adversely affect the country ownership[152] of an RTD-based development programme, which a developing country may wish to implement. The country ownership is one of the key principles of the existing development initiatives such as the CDF, PRSP and

146 Ibid. paras 94–95.

147 E/CN.4/2002/28/Rev.1, Third session, para. 44.

148 E/CN.4/2003/26, Fourth session, para. 19.

149 Ibid.

150 Laure-Helene Piron, 'Are "Development Compacts" Required to Realise the Right to Development?' in *The Right to Development Book, Reflections on the First Four Reports of the Independent Expert on the Right to Development*, Geneva, Franciscans International, 2004, pp 46–61 at p 56. See also Rajeev Malhotra, 'Right to Development: Where Are We Today?' in Sengupta et al. (eds), op. cit., pp 127–52. Sengupta, 'Realizing the Right to Development', *Development and Change* 31, 2000, 553–78.

151 Piron, op. cit., p. 56.

152 Ibid. p 57.

others. A further critical examination would show that the proposed Development Compact stresses international cooperation as the main tool in the realization of the RTD. Most of the developing countries claim that they are not satisfied with the global financial and trade institutions. The aid policies of developed countries are still guided by their political interests and historical relations.[153] The Development Compact model does not envisage how the individual, not a party to an agreement for a Development Compact, can make a claim at the international level.[154] It is unlikely that the DAC members would be willing to participate in an RTD-Development Compact with those developing countries (if they wish to pursue it) that are seen as posing challenges to the political hegemony of the developed countries. This approach appears to be too simple because it does not propose how such cooperation can in practice be achieved in a world where political and economic interests are sharply divided.

The proposal of the Independent Expert could also be seen as problematic at the national level. The reason is that most developing countries, except a few African countries, have not incorporated the RTD, either in their constitutions or in their development policies. Secondly, it is true that a country has to design an RTD-based development policy of its own, keeping in view its social and economic needs. But the approach of the Independent Expert does not recognize the importance of the specific values and belief system[155] of the people of a country wishing to adopt a Development Compact model. As noted above, it is far from clear that international cooperation, especially from the developed countries, for such a development plan, would really be possible. Indeed this area is one of considerable tension in the contemporary global environment where development is seen by some as modernization and Westernization. The proposed RTD-Development Compact model, therefore, seems to give priority to economic development over the social and cultural values of a country.

The high-level task force

The high-level task force was established by the Commission resolution 2004/49 on the recommendation of the OEWG at its fifth session.[156] For its

153 Ibid.

154 Ibid. pp 57–8.

155 Alfredo Sfeir-Younis, 'The Right to Development: The Political Economy of Implementation' in *The Right to Development Book*, op. cit., pp 46–61 at p 56.

156 E/CN.4/2004/23. Prior to the Fifth session, the Office of the High Commissioner for Human Rights (OHCHR) convened a two-day high-level seminar, 'Global Partnership for Development', which was attended by experts from human rights, development, trade and financial institutions. The objective of the seminar was 'to review and identify effective strategies for mainstreaming the [RTD] in the policies and operational activities of the major international organisations/institutions'. For a separate note of the OEWG session, see E/CN.4/2004/23/Add.1.

first report, the task force was to consider three issues for analysis and recommendation by the OEWG: firstly, obstacles and challenges to the implementation of the MDGs in relation to the [RTD]; secondly, social impact assessments in the areas of trade and development at the national and international levels; thirdly, best practices in the implementation of the [RTD]. The task force held its first meeting in December 2004.[157] Among the state members of the Commission, who participated in the meetings as observers, were some key opponents.[158] Experts from international organizations also participated in both meetings.[159]

The task force held its second meeting in November 2005. It concentrated on devising criteria for assessing MDG 8, developing global partnerships for development, from the perspective of the RTD.[160] Among the criteria suggested, were the need to find out to what extent the partnership reflects 'human rights standards and a rights-based approach', the right of each state to determine its own development policies, and promote good governance and the rule of law.[161] The task force emphasized that the states should not put aside their human rights obligations under international instruments when negotiating in other forums, such as those relating to international finance and trade.[162] The value added of the RTD with the global partnership for development was seen in three ways: human rights and the RTD should be explicitly incorporated in the existing partnership for development and its corresponding accountability mechanism; monitoring the implementation of the MDGs through the existing human rights instruments; 'the need to translate abstract human rights principles into practical policy recommendations that could be used by practitioners on the ground'.[163] The task force concluded that global partnerships are parts of the implementation of the RTD. It also concluded that human rights experts and representatives of the multilateral trade and development bodies and IFIs can continue to collaborate with each other in order to make practical suggestions for the implementation of the RTD.[164]

In its third meeting held in January 2007, the task force focused on applying the criteria to particular partnerships for development.[165] The task force

157 E/CN.4/2005/WG.18/2.

158 They were Germany, Japan, the UK and the USA. In the second meeting, the UK did not participate as an observer.

159 Such as the UNDP, UNICEF, UNCTAD, the IMF, the World Bank and the WTO.

160 E/CN.4/2005/WG.18/TF/3.

161 Ibid. para. 82.

162 E/CN.4/2005/WG.18/TF/3, para. 21.

163 Ibid. para. 44.

164 Ibid. paras 48–49.

165 A/HRC/4/WG.2/TF/2. The focus was on three partnerships for development: The APRM, the Economic Commission for Africa (ECA) and the Paris Declaration for Aid Effectiveness.

found no evidence of mainstreaming human rights, including the RTD, into those partnerships for development. However, it concluded that the criteria were important because they facilitate current and future partnerships to explicitly factor in more essential elements of the RTD.[166]

Evaluation of the task force reports

The task force constituted a platform for discussion between experts from the human rights and development areas in order to 'strengthen the global partnership for development by bridging diverse perspectives'.[167] The conclusion and recommendations of the task force are worth assessing, since they clearly link the MDGs to human rights, including the RTD.[168] The task force recommended that the MDGs should be clearly and rigorously mapped, for the policy makers and development practitioners, against the provisions of the relevant international human rights instruments, which can facilitate implementation of the MDGs. The first meeting of the task force was significant for two reasons. Firstly, the World Bank and the IMF remained consistently engaged with the task force. Such engagement was significant because of the enormous influence of the rules and policies these organizations have on the implementation of the RTD at the national and international levels. Secondly, the task force agreed that various principles of the Declaration provided guidelines to international development and financial institutions. Those principles are: the unity of all human rights; a holistic view of human rights and development; development as a comprehensive process, which includes poverty reduction; empowerment of people; the human person as the central subject of development; and the role and responsibilities of the state and the international community in the implementation of the RTD.

However, the first meeting of the task force failed to agree on the rights-based approach as a sufficient mechanism for the implementation of the RTD. Some experts thought this approach to be sufficient, but others believed that the RTD 'embraced and exceeded a rights-based approach'. The rights-based approach to development recognizes the obligation of the state and grants legitimacy to peoples' claims/rights; equality and non-discrimination; participation; and accountability. However, the working group recognized the multifaceted nature of the RTD and agreed that a rights-based approach contributes to the realization of the RTD.[169] On the negative side is the lack of clear support from three developed countries in the working group, which

166 Ibid. para. 54.

167 Margot E. Salomon, 'Towards a Just International Order: A Commentary on the First Session of the UN Task Force on the Right to Development', *Netherlands Quarterly of Human Rights* 23(3), 2005, 409–38, at 410.

168 The first report of the Task Force was debated in the Sixth session of the working group. See report of the Sixth session, E/CN.4/2005/25.

169 Ibid. para. 46.

adopted the conclusions and recommendations of the task force. Australia, Canada and the USA dissociated themselves from the consensus, while Japan joined the consensus, but expressed reservations over the issues of trade and debt relief.[170]

During the seventh session of the working group, the report of the second meeting of the task force was severely criticized by developing countries for its emphasis on the national dimension of the RTD. Delegates, presumably from the developing countries, observed that the report of the task force placed emphasis 'excessively on national rather than international responsibilities of States'.[171] Malaysia, in a general statement made on behalf of the NAM and China, 'noted with concern the absence of tangible progress in the Operationalisation of the [RTD] . . . since the adoption of the Declaration . . . in 1986'.[172] The Group of African States also joined with NAM and China to express concern over the focus on the national dimension of the RTD in the report of the task force.[173] Developed countries, on the other hand, reiterated that the states have the primary responsibility for the respect of all human rights, including the RTD.[174] In the eighth session of the working group, Australia, Canada and the EU did not join the consensus over paragraph 52 in which the working group agreed that the ongoing work of the task force may evolve into an international instrument of a binding nature.[175]

CONCLUSION

The debate on the implementation of the Declaration is still ongoing. The reports of the Independent Expert, particularly his idea of a Development Compact, and of the task force have been debated in the OEWG at length. In the light of the debates, some positive elements may be noted here. The active participation of the IMF, the World Bank, the WTO and other international agencies may be seen as beneficial in terms of their willingness to mainstream the RTD in their policies. The statement of the Economic Commission for Europe before one of the working groups shows that the European nations seem willing to work for the implementation of the RTD. The proposed model of a Development Compact is open-ended and the reports of the Independent Expert show that other models may be adopted or the existing development frameworks could be attuned to the principles of an RTD-based approach. In this respect, the statement of the representative of the IMF that a PRSP could be linked to human rights, if a country so wishes, is very

170 Ibid. para. 32.
171 E/CN.4/2006/26, para. 22.
172 Ibid. para. 17.
173 Ibid. para. 19.
174 Ibid. para. 18.
175 A/HRC/4/47, para. 52 and Annex III.

significant. The appointment of the Independent Expert and the task force itself indicates the depoliticization of the debate. However, the debate over their reports still remains entrenched in political rivalries between developing and developed countries. This means that a consensus is still lacking.[176] The proposal for a Development Compact is not recognized, nor are the recommendations of the task force agreed upon by all members of the OEWG. Nevertheless, the idea of integrating human rights into the existing development initiatives, such as the PRSPs, seems viable for the following reasons. Firstly, such initiatives have already become effective after negotiations between countries and the IFIs. Secondly, it will put the responsibility squarely on the shoulders of developing countries, in line with the Declaration, which provides that the primary responsibility for the RTD lies with the state. Consequently, developing countries will be obliged to make and fulfil their political commitment, which is otherwise missing. Thirdly, in addition to states' responsibility, the international community still cannot be absolved of its obligation of cooperation. But international cooperation, the main bone of contention in the entire RTD debate, also requires a political commitment on the part of the international community, particularly the developed countries, and this too is missing. The main reason that these political altercations will continue is that the international community, particularly its developed nations, still does not appear to accept the notion of international cooperation as a legal obligation. As a resolution of the General Assembly, the Declaration is merely a recommendation. This basic flaw prompts a question: do the underlying principles of the RTD command recognition in customary international law? The answer to this question will be considered in the next chapter.

176 In its comments on the conclusions adopted by the OEWG at its third session, the USA appreciated the efforts of the working group, but observed: 'The US has fundamental differences with the text's conclusions and recommendations and therefore must dissociate itself with the same. We note that there is still no consensus on the precise meaning of the [RTD]' (Annex III, report of the Third Session).

Part II

The RTD in international law

5 The legal status of the RTD in public international law

INTRODUCTION

Part I mainly analysed the conceptual basis of the RTD and the political and jurisprudential controversies surrounding it. The results of the analysis are: firstly, conceptually underpinned by the capability approach, the RTD is a holistic concept of development and human rights. Secondly, the collective dimension of the RTD as well as the justiciability of both collective and individual RTD remain as unresolved issues. Thirdly, as an individual right, the RTD is less problematic. While the goal-rights system may resolve the issue of justiciability, particularly at the national level, the promotion of the RTD at the international level largely hinges on the principle of cooperation. It was seen in the previous chapter that international cooperation is one of the key features of the Declaration. This chapter looks at the legal value of international cooperation in international law and argues that if international cooperation for development and human rights is recognized as a source of obligation, the RTD may become an established right in international law. 'Established' here means recognition by the international community.

The Declaration provides that states have the duty to cooperate with each other for the realization of the RTD. There are several methods of international cooperation, including foreign aid or Official Development Assistance (ODA), capital flows, transfer of technology, access to markets through trade liberalization, debt forgiveness and bilateral and multilateral assistance to developing countries to implement economic reforms. Each of these areas of international cooperation has implications for the RTD. However, in order to provide a focused discussion on international cooperation, the chapter examines the customary status of the practice of the developed countries in foreign aid only.

The chapter evaluates the legal status of the Declaration in light of formal sources of international law, particularly custom. The focus is on the legal status of foreign aid as a tool of international cooperation. The chapter also examines the Declaration with reference to general principles of law, soft law and 'new sources' such as consensus, cooperation and interdependence.

Finally, various factors responsible for determining the legal effect of a General Assembly resolution are applied to the Declaration.

SOURCES OF INTERNATIONAL LAW

Article 38(1) of the Statute of the ICJ describes the following sources of international law:

- a international conventions, whether general or particular, establishing rules expressly recognized by the contesting states;
- b international custom, as evidence of general principle accepted as law;
- c the general principles of law recognized by civilized nations;
- d subject to the provisions of Article 59, judicial decisions and the teachings of the most highly qualified publicists of the various nations, as subsidiary means for determination of rules of law.

These are called the formal (also traditional) sources of international law. International law, traditionally, needs the consent of states in order to be binding on states. Given the fact that international law is still law in the making, in a dispute between two states, the principal question of law that usually arises pertains not only to the existence of the legal rule relied on by one state, but also to the binding value of that legal rule on the other party (state).[1] As Thirlway has put it, 'a rule may exist conceptually, as a proposal or a draft, and later come to be accepted as binding. The problem may then be to determine at what moment the rule acquired the status of a rule of existing, binding, law.'[2] For the existence of a rule of law, reference is normally made to the formal sources of international law, as listed above. As international law governs relations between states, therefore, rules may derive their existence from other sources such as treaties between the states, the jurisprudence of international tribunals, a resolution of the General Assembly, a proposal of the International Law Commission, or even a textbook.[3] These sources are called material sources of international law. If two states have agreed in a treaty between them as to the application of a certain rule, that rule shall apply between them, the treaty being the material source of that rule. For other states that rule becomes customary rule. In practice, however, treaties and custom are commonly used as sources of international law. As compared to custom, a treaty clearly lays down the rights, duties and obligations of the states parties to it. The states can enter into law-making treaties (such treaties

1 Hugh Thirlway, 'The Sources of International Law' in Malcolm D. Evans (ed.) *International Law*, Oxford, Oxford University Press, 2003, pp 117–44 at p 118.

2 Ibid.

3 Ibid.

create the same obligation on all parties and regulate their conduct over a long period of time[4]). Multilateral treaties, for example the WTO, constitute the source of obligation for the member states. Article 3(2) of the WTO's Dispute Settlement Understanding (DSU)[5] features the rule enunciated in Article 31(3)(c) of the Vienna Convention on the Law of Treaties,[6] and as such reconciles public international law with the WTO law. 'Some authorities have viewed certain [General Assembly] declarations as augmenting the modern body of treaty law.'[7] As the Declaration on the RTD is not a treaty, therefore, its legal status may be investigated in custom as a source of international law.

CUSTOM

Although a resolution in itself is not binding, yet it may lay down principles of international law and be, or purport to be, declaratory.[8] A declaratory resolution becomes binding on the basis of customary law.[9] According to Article 38(1)(b) of the Statute of the ICJ, international custom is applicable as evidence of a general practice accepted as law. The law relating to custom is highly contentious in theory and much more complex in practice.[10] In the present-day world of a communication revolution and globalization, fresh state practices are emerging in new areas, for example, cyber law and Information Technology (IT) law. The situation is becoming more complex, because of conflict not only among individual states, but also between groups of states, owing to a remarkable growth in regionalism. Some international lawyers attribute the importance of custom in contemporary international law to economic relationships among states, conflict between groups of states,

4 Peter Malanczuk, *Akehurt's Modern Introduction to International Law*, London/New York, Routledge, 7th Edition, 1997, p 37.

5 It reads: 'The Members recognize that [the dispute settlement system of the WTO] serves to preserve the rights and obligations of Members under the covered agreements, and to clarify the existing provisions of those agreements in accordance with customary rules of interpretation of public international law. Recommendations and rulings of the [Dispute Settlement Body] DSB, cannot add to or diminish the rights and obligations provided in the covered agreements.'

6 Article 31(3)(c) says: 'There shall be taken into account, together with the context: any relevant rules of international law applicable in the relations between the parties.'

7 Christopher C. Joyner, 'U.N. General Assembly Resolutions and International Law: Rethinking the Contemporary Dynamics of Norm-Creation', *California Western International Law Journal* 11, 1981, 445–78, at 456.

8 Ian Brownlie, *Principles of Public International Law*, Oxford, Clarendon Press, 6th Edition, 2003, p 633.

9 Blaine Sloan, 'General Assembly Resolutions Revisited (Forty Years Later)', *British Year Book of International Law* LVIII, 1987, 39–150 at 68 (hereinafter Sloan, *BYIL* 1987).

10 Michael Akehurst, 'Custom as a Source of International Law', *The British Year Book of International Law* XLVII, 1974–75, 1–53 (hereinafter Akehurst, *BYIL* 1974–75).

and growth of those parts of customary international law which have been considered more or less accepted by the newly independent states.[11]

It is generally accepted that custom has two elements: *opinio juris* and state practice.[12] However, the position of *opinio juris*, as a necessary element, is disputed by few scholars. With respect to their binding effect, the General Assembly resolutions can be divided into two categories. Firstly: those resolutions, which have a binding effect. They include, among others, the approval of budgets, the adoption of rules of procedure and the establishment of subsidiary organs.[13] Secondly: those resolutions which are recommendations. The General Assembly may make recommendations on a variety of matters, among others, any matter or any question within the scope of the Charter, the encouragement of progressive development of international law and the promotion of international cooperation in the economic, social, cultural, educational, and health fields, and assisting in the realization of human rights and fundamental freedoms for all without distinction as to race, sex, language, or religion.[14] The recommendations (also called 'declarations'[15]) are not legally binding. The Declaration, as a General Assembly resolution, falls into the second category, i.e. recommendation. The legal value of such recommendations is a controversial issue in international legal scholarship. A brief look at the word 'recommendation' is, therefore, necessary.

What is meant by 'recommendation'?

One view is that a 'recommendation' is simply a recommendation and as such has no legal value. This view is shared by Brierly,[16] Kelsen,[17] Higgins[18] and Judge Lauterpacht,[19] to name a few. Another view is that a 'recommendation' has no legal value, yet it has a moral force. This view, expressed by Judge

11 Cassese, *International Law in a Divided World*, para.100.

12 Sloan, *BYIL* 1987, op. cit., 72.

13 See UN Charter, Arts 17, 21 and 22.

14 Ibid. Arts 10–14.

15 'In the United Nations practice, a "declaration" is a formal and solemn instrument, suitable for rare occasions when principles of great and lasting importance are being enunciated, such as a Declaration on Human Rights. A recommendation is less formal. There is probably no difference between a "recommendation" and a "declaration" . . . as far strict legal principle is concerned.' See E/CN.4/L.610, cited in Joyner, op. cit., 456.

16 Brierly, *The Law of Nations*, Oxford, Clarendon Press, 1963, p 107.

17 Hans Kelsen, *The Law of the United Nations*, London, Steven & Sons Limited, 1950, pp 195–6, 198–216.

18 Roslyn Higgins, *The Development of International Law through the Political Organs of the United Nations*, Oxford, Oxford University Press, 1963, p 5.

19 1955 WL 2 (I.C.J.), 1955 I.C.J. 67, *Voting Procedure on Questions Relating to Reports and Petitions Concerning the Territory of South-West Africa*, p 67 at p 120.

Klaestad,[20] is widely supported by scholars.[21] A third view is that a 'recommendation' has a legal value for a number of reasons, most notably, its role in customary international law. Those who support this view include Judge Alvarez[22] and Blaine Sloan.[23] The present study also supports this view because it offers a constructive basis for assessment of whether the Declaration is part of customary international law. As will be seen below in examining Sloan's approach, the last view demonstrates a shift from the complex debate surrounding the binding value of the resolutions towards an effort to consider their role in the creation of customary international law. The ICJ has given considerable judicial weight to the General Assembly resolutions in *Nicaragua v The United States* (merits). The Court observed:

> The parties . . . accept a treaty-law obligation to refrain in their international relations from the threat or use of force against the territorial integrity or political independence of any State, or in any other manner inconsistent with the purposes of the United Nations. The Court has however to be satisfied that there exists in customary international law an opinio juris as to the binding character of such abstention. This opinio juris may, though with all due caution, be deduced from, inter alia, the attitude of the Parties and the attitude of States towards certain General Assembly resolutions, and particularly resolution 2625(XXV) entitled 'Declaration on Principles of International Law concerning Friendly Relations and Co-operation among States in accordance with the Charter of the United Nations' . . . the Declaration approved by resolution 2625(XXV), which set out principles which the General Assembly declared to be 'basic principles' of international law.[24]

The ICJ has referred to the RTD in the *Case Concerning the Gabcikovo-Nagymaros Project*, a dispute between Slovakia and Hungary over the construction of a dam.[25] Judge Weeramantry in his separate opinion made reference to

20 Ibid. p 88.

21 Blaine Sloan, 'The Binding Force of a "Recommendation" of the General Assembly', *The British Year Book of International Law* XXV, 1948, 1–33 (hereinafter Sloan, *BYIL* 1948). See also D.H.N. Johnson, 'The Effect of Resolutions of the General Assembly of the United Nations', *British Year Book of International Law* XXXII, 1955–56, 97–122 at 106.

22 See individual/dissenting opinion of Judge Alvarez in the following cases: 1951 WL 12 (I.C.J.), 1951 I.C.J. 116, *Fisheries Case, United Kingdom v Norway* (contentious), Individual Opinion of Judge Alvarez [Translation], p 145 and 1951 WL 3 (I.C.J.), 1951 I.C.J. 15, *Reservation to the Convention on the Prevention and Punishment of the Crime of Genocide, Dissenting Opinion*, p 49 at p 52 (Advisory Opinion of the Court).

23 Sloan, *BYIL* 1948, op. cit.; See also Sloan, *BYIL* 1987, op. cit., 68.

24 1986 WL 522 (I.C.J.), 1986 I.C.J. 14, *Case Concerning Military and Paramilitary Activities in and against Nicaragua (Nicaragua v United States of America)*, at pp 99–100, 107.

25 *Case Concerning the Gabcikovo-Nagymaros Project*, op. cit., 7. In 1977, Hungary and Czechoslovakia entered into a treaty to construct dams and barrages along the Danube river in the

the RTD in the context of sustainable development. Judge Weeramantry is of the opinion that the consideration of development needs to be weighed against the consideration of environment because, he maintains, the RTD and the right to environmental protection are important principles of the current international law.[26] Citing the Declaration, Weeramantry observed:

> It is thus the correct formulation of the [RTD] that that right does not exist in the absolute sense, but is relative always to its tolerance by the environment. The [RTD] as thus refined is clearly part of modern international law. It is compendiously referred to as sustainable development.[27]

While the Declaration as a recommendation of the General Assembly was not the core issue in this case, the judicial notice taken by the court has positive implications for the legal status of the RTD. Judge Weeramantry's opinion has a good persuasive value and seems to be a strong move towards a judicial recognition of the RTD. However, two points appear to be worth noting. Firstly, the Declaration was examined exclusively from the perspective of sustainable development. It is for this reason that one commentator has aptly termed it 'a reductionist view of the [RTD]'.[28] Secondly, the Declaration was not examined by a majority of the members of the court. Thus the opinion lacks a judicial unanimity of the court.

Sloan argues there are three situations in which the recommendations of the General Assembly may be legally binding, viz., (1) special agreement or consent of states, (2) custom and (3) the authority inherent in the General Assembly.[29] The first situation, which relates to treaty obligations, is not relevant to the present discussion because the Declaration is not a treaty, whereas custom – *opinio juris* and state practice – will be discussed below.

Regarding the third situation, i.e. authority inherent in the General Assembly, two aspects deserve to be mentioned here, viz. the General Assembly 'is an organ of an entity having separate legal personality' and it is a

two countries. In 1989, Hungary abandoned the project because of perceived environmental risks. Czechoslovakia unilaterally proceeded and constructed another dam. As a result the waters of the Danube river were diverted without the consent of Hungary. Hungary terminated the treaty in 1992. As the negotiations between Hungary and the new Slovak republic failed, both countries submitted their dispute to the ICJ.

26 Ibid. Separate opinion of Judge Weeramantry, p 89.

27 Ibid. p 92. See, generally, Afshin A-Khavari and Donald R. Rothwell, 'The ICJ and the Danube Case: A Missed Opportunity for Environmental Law', *Melbourne University Law Review* 22(3), 1998, 507–36.

28 Bunn, op. cit., p 132.

29 Sloan, *BYIL* 1948, op. cit., 16.

congress of the whole world.[30] It has become an inherent power of the General Assembly to adopt resolutions, so a state is legally bound by a resolution if it has voted in favour of it with an intention to be bound by it. In other words, a resolution has a binding effect on that state. In the case of a state that has voted against a resolution, its position can be seen within the meaning of *lex ferenda*[31] (what the law ought to be). However, a dissenting state has obligations of good faith and the duty of cooperation under the Charter and cannot simply ignore a resolution.[32] An interesting point, which Sloan makes, is that the limitation of the General Assembly is not due to the recommendatory value of its resolutions, but because of the principle of sovereign equality of states and their domestic jurisdiction. Changes in international society affect these principles of sovereign equality and domestic jurisdiction. The General Assembly, as an agent of the international community, fills the vacuum.[33] Sloan further argues that the resolutions of the General Assembly should exert greater influence because they represent the will of the majority and are expressions of world public opinion.[34] There is also a growing body of literature on the view that the resolutions of the General Assembly have the effect of 'soft law', a phrase used for non-binding resolutions of international organizations, including the UN General Assembly.[35]

Opinio juris

Mendelsen defines *opinio juris* as a 'belief in (or claim as to) the legally permissible or obligatory nature of the conduct in question, or of its necessity'.[36] *Opinio juris* is a belief of a state (a psychological factor; also called a subjective element) as to the obligatory nature of a custom in international law.[37] A state's practice may be prompted by economic, political or military necessity (*opinio necessitates*). For example, exploitation of natural resources in the seabed is a state practice based on economic needs. Such practice may become *opinio juris* if a state starts believing that it is conforming to an international rule.[38]

It is widely held that state practice, unaccompanied by *opinio juris*, does not

30 Ibid. 22.

31 Ibid. 23.

32 Sloan, *BYIL* 1987, 43.

33 Sloan, *BYIL* 1948, 24. See also D.H.N. Johnson, op. cit., 97–122.

34 Ibid. 31.

35 See Alan Boyle, 'Soft Law in International Law-making' in Malcolm D. Evans (ed.) *International Law*, Oxford, Oxford University Press, 2nd Edition, 2006, pp 141–58.

36 Maurice Mendelson, 'The Subjective Element in Customary International Law', *British Year Book of International Law* LXVI, 1995, 177–208 at 195 (hereinafter Mendelson *BYIL* 1995).

37 See generally *North Sea Continental Shelf Case* [ICJ Reports, 1969], pp 3, 44. Available online at: <http://www.icj-cij.org/docket/files/51/5535.pdf> (accessed 14 March 2009).

38 Antonio Cassese, *International Law*, Oxford University Press, 2001, p 120.

amount to practice.[39] The General Assembly provides an effective forum for states to express their opinions regarding resolutions involving general norms of international law. Such resolutions, if adopted with a majority vote, establish the evidence of *opinio juris*. Some resolutions are 'convenient material sources of law, inasmuch as they state, with apparent authority, propositions of general law, and are often assented to by a very large majority of the members, and thus of the states of the world.[40] Some examples in point are the declarations on friendly relations, the NIEO, permanent sovereignty over natural resources, decolonization and outer space. The resolution on outer space is said to have constituted state practice and *opinio juris* instantly. This resolution, known as 'instant custom',[41] signifies that firstly, a long state practice is not necessary. Secondly, *opinio juris* alone is sufficient for the creation of customary rule. Thirdly, substantial consensus or a majority vote can help facilitate the creation of customary rule.

Scholastic opinion about *opinio juris* is divided. Keeping in view the difficulty involved in determining the existence of *opinio juris*, some writers argue that other elements of custom, such as duration ('long practice is not necessary'), uniformity and consistency of practice,[42] need to be resorted to. Akehurst notes that Kelsen and Guggenheim argued that *opinio juris* may be done away with by giving more weight to consistency of practice.[43] Recently, another writer, Mendelson, has strongly attacked *opinio juris* as a necessary element of custom, arguing that state practice is the only information regarding the external conduct of a state's behaviour.[44] Having challenged the very view that custom is based on consent of the states, he argues that 'general customary rule binds States who have given no intimation of such consent'.[45] Mendelson maintains that *opinio juris* may be *sufficient* but not *necessary* for the basis of obligation. The view that *opinio juris* is not necessary is not widely supported. The two-element theory of custom is an established doctrine of international law.[46] In a number of cases, the ICJ has ruled that

39 Akehurst, *BYIL* 1974–75 op. cit., 31.

40 Thirlway, op. cit., p 139.

41 Ben Cheng, 'United Nations Resolution on Outer Space: "Instant" International Customary Law?' *Indian Journal of International Law* 5, 1965, 23–48. Under this resolution, the USA and the former USSR, the only two big powers having the technological resources to exploit outer space, agreed with each other over the use of outer space. The concept of 'instant custom', however, is a disputed issue of international law. See Oscar Schachter, *International Law in Theory and Practice*, Martinus Nijhoff, 1991, p 88. See also Sloan, *BYIL* 1987, 89.

42 See Brownlie, op. cit., pp 7–8.

43 Akehurst, op. cit., 34. Both of them are, however, said to have changed their views later on.

44 Mendelson, *BYIL* 1995, op. cit., 178. Mendelson has traced back his theory to Lazare Kopelmenas. See also Lazare Kopelmanas, 'Custom as a Means of the Creation of International Law', *British Year Book of International Law* XVIII, 1937, 127–51.

45 Mendelson, op. cit., 178.

46 M. Dixon, *Text Book on International Law*, Oxford, Oxford University Press, 5th Edition, 2005, p 32. See also Thirlway, op. cit., p 122.

opinio juris is a necessary element of customary law. The *Nicaragua* case is a good precedent on this point. Hence, *opinio juris* is extremely important for ascertaining whether practice amounts to a customary rule or not.

Looking at the Declaration in light of the above discussion, it is clear that it was not a consensus document. It was adopted by a majority vote. It was favoured by 146 countries, opposed by 1 (USA), whereas 8 abstained. Those who abstained included key Western donor countries. This situation can be analysed with reference to three questions. First, did the supporting votes of those who favoured the Declaration, amount to *opinio juris*? It is generally held that a General Assembly resolution has a binding effect on those states who cast positive votes in favour of that resolution. When the drafting process of the Declaration was set in motion, members of the first working group expressed the intention that in future a binding instrument would be adopted (Chapter 4). That opinion indicated that the delegates did not intend to propose a legally binding instrument at the very outset. The fact that the Declaration was adopted as a compromise instrument further indicates that the intention of the General Assembly was neither to declare an existing law nor to crystallize an emerging law. But the intention was to chart a course for future development of a customary rule (*lex ferenda*). With the exception of a few African states, most of those states who have favoured the Declaration, have not incorporated the RTD as a right in their constitutions. Thus the mere fact that the Declaration was adopted by a majority of votes does not appear to be sufficient for *opinio juris*. However, the linkage of human rights with development policies in these countries could be seen as an indication of a change in their attitude. A further change could be seen by reading a 1999 General Assembly resolution on the RTD, which proposed to the OEWG that it should consider a convention on the RTD.[47] Those who favoured that resolution intended to have a binding instrument on the RTD. Those who opposed the proposal, clearly did not want to have a binding and legally enforceable instrument. The consensus over the RTD on the occasion of the Vienna Conference, 1993, could be further evidence of a change in the belief as to the binding authority of the Declaration.

Secondly, what is the legal value of abstention? Abstention could be considered as both tacit approval and rejection of a resolution.[48] The role of six Western countries, which abstained from the voting, was crucial for the implementation of the Declaration. It may be argued that their abstention from voting had a negative effect. However, recent trends in the voting

47 UNGA Res. A/54/175. Some paragraphs of this resolution, including para. 21, which proposed a convention, were subjected to separate voting. The paragraph was adopted by 112 votes to 43, with 2 abstentions. Those who voted against were Western countries, including the USA.

48 I.C. MacGibbon, 'Customary International Law and Acquiescence', *British Year Book of International Law* XXXIII, 1957, 114–45, at p 132. Sloan, *BYIL* 1987, op. cit., 131.

pattern in the General Assembly appear to be encouraging signs for recognition of a customary status for the Declaration (see Chapter 2).[49]

Thirdly, what is the impact of the one negative vote by the USA? A short answer to this question is that as a dissenting state, the USA is not bound by the Declaration. The USA has been opposing the Declaration since its inception. Therefore, its position is that of a 'persistent objector' (a state which 'opposes the [customary] rule in the early days of the rule's existence (or formation) and maintains its opposition consistently thereafter'[50]). However, the USA joined the consensus over the RTD at the Vienna Conference, 1993. This raises the question of whether the USA can still be called a 'persistent objector'.[51] If a certain resolution enjoys the persuasive force of an existing obligation, a persistent objector may be said to be bound by that obligation.[52] Schachter argues that the negative vote of South Africa to the resolution declaring apartheid illegal, did not mean that the resolution was deprived of its evidentiary force as an interpretation of the Charter obligations under Articles 55 and 56.[53] The apartheid resolution cannot be treated on a par with the Declaration for the reason that the former had a persuasive power because of the support of nearly all states.[54] Moreover, the apartheid resolution laid down precise obligations on South Africa to put an end to its apartheid policies. The Declaration neither got that level of support nor asserted specific and precise obligations on any state. However, like the apartheid resolution, the Declaration also interprets Articles 55 and 56 of the Charter by referring to the duty of international cooperation (solidarity) for the realization of the RTD. The implications of the duty of cooperation may be analysed in regard to the practice of the developed countries in the area of foreign aid.

State practice

The main question is whether the practice of the developed countries in foreign aid, the main tool of international cooperation, is accompanied by *opinio juris*. In answering this question, a brief look at the practice of foreign aid is necessary. The focus is on the practice of the members of the DAC of the OECD in foreign aid.[55] Some member states of the DAC, for example, the USA, Australia, Canada and Western European

49 The effect of abstention from the voting process is discussed further below.

50 Akehurst, *BYIL* 1974–75 op. cit., p 24.

51 The legal value of the concept of a 'persistent objector' will be discussed later in this chapter. .

52 Schachter, 1991, op. cit., p 91.

53 Ibid.

54 Ibid.

55 The DAC comprises 22 members. They are: Australia, Austria, Belgium, Canada, Denmark, Finland, France, Germany, Greece, Ireland, Italy, Japan, Luxembourg, the Netherlands, New Zealand, Norway, Portugal, Spain, Sweden, Switzerland, the UK and the USA.

countries, generally share a common position on the RTD. According to Akehurst:

> State practice means any acts or statement by a State from which views about customary law can be inferred; it includes physical acts, claims, declarations *in abstracto* (such as General Assembly resolutions), national laws, national judgements and omissions.[56]

This means that a resolution itself, being one of the 'collective pronouncements of States must be considered as a part of State practice'.[57]

The developed countries have a long practice of providing development assistance or foreign aid to the developing countries. The Declaration does not specifically recognize foreign aid as a right of the developing countries. However, it asserts in general terms that 'effective international cooperation is essential in providing these countries with appropriate means and facilities to foster their comprehensive development'.[58]

A foreign aid programme was started unilaterally by the USA in 1949, and this was followed by Western countries in 1951.[59] Since the 1960s, the General Assembly has passed many resolutions which set specific targets for foreign aid by the developed countries. Thus, in the light of the General Assembly resolutions adopted in 1960[60] and 1970[61], respectively, an annual target for ODA of 0.7 per cent of GNP has been set for all DAC members. These resolutions of the General Assembly are of no binding value. The ODA has hardly achieved the target set by the General Assembly resolutions.[62] It was planned to achieve the target by 1985.[63] Through a 1980 General Assembly resolution, a new target of 1 per cent was fixed.[64]

The OECD countries 'have adopted the promotion of Third World development as one of their serious and most demonstrated national objectives'.[65] The DAC members exchange views with each other about their

56 Akehurst, *BYIL* 1974–75 op. cit., 53.

57 Ibid.

58 DRD, Art. 2(4).

59 Rich, op. cit., 304.

60 UNGA Res. 1522 (XV) 15 Dec. 1960.

61 UNGA Res. 2626 (XXV) 24 Oct. 1970. See also World Bank, 'Pages from World Bank History: the Pearson Commission'. Online. Available at: <www.worldbank.org> (accessed 28 Feb. 2009). The Pearson Commission was formed in 1968 by the World Bank, comprising Lester B. Pearson and seven other members, who presented the report on 15 Sept. 1969, with the mandate to map out an aid strategy.

62 Independent Expert Fourth Report, para. 71.

63 Development Co-operation Review, p 81, 1981, quoted in Rich, op. cit., 304.

64 UNGA Res. A/35/56, para. 24.

65 *Development Co-operation Review*, p 27, 1981, quoted in Rich, op. cit., 304.

performance.[66] This practice of development aid has gained widespread currency as developed countries' practice at the international level. The intention of the aid-supplying countries may be judged from the fact that from the very inception, targets for the aid money were being fixed[67] and objectives announced.[68] In 2006, the total ODA of DAC members was 0.30 per cent of members' combined GNI.[69]

The UN Independent Expert on the RTD has observed that since the second half of the 1990s, the development cooperation policies of the DAC of OECD and the bilateral donor agencies 'have started integrating a human rights approach into a country's development programme'.[70] The Independent Expert has further observed that a development compact model, proposed by him, may be created in light of the programmes proposed in some of the policy studies of the DAC and the bilateral donor agencies.[71] The OECD is also committed to helping the developing countries achieve the MDGs,[72] recognizing the vital role of human security, democracy, good governance, human rights and the rule of law in the process of development. In 2005, the OECD designated poverty as 'the issue of the year', stressing that progress:

> [W]on't happen unless rich countries deliver the trade and other reforms that will give poor countries a chance to earn their own keep. But aid does matter and we have to get the best possible bang for our aid buck in terms of real improvements in poor people's lives.[73]

66 Roland Rich, 'The Right to Development: A Right of Peoples?' in James Crawford (ed.) *The Rights of Peoples*, Oxford, Clarendon Press, 1988, pp 39–54 at p 47.

67 Ibid. The writer says that the UN first set quantitative targets in the 1960s; for the 1970s the ODA target was 0.7% of GNP for DAC members (Rich, op. cit., p. 304) For the year 2000, it was USD53.7 billion.

68 See for example, J.P. Pronk, 'Human Rights and Development Aid', *International Commission of Jurist Review* 18, 1977, 33–9. At that time, Pronk, who was the Netherlands Minister for Development Aid, argued, 'Dutch development policy, impliedly, if not explicitly, aims at human rights promotion', at 37.

69 See OECD report dated 3 April 2007. Online. Available at: <http://www.oecd.org/document/17/0,3343,en_2649_201185_38341265_1_1_1_1,00.html> (accessed 27 June 2007).

70 Independent Expert Fourth report, para. 49; First report, para. 84.

71 Ibid. First report, para. 84. Those studies include: DAC, *Shaping the 21st Century: The Contribution of Development Cooperation*, OECD, 1996; White Paper by the UK Secretary of State for International Development, *Eliminating World Poverty: A Challenge for the 21st Century*, 1997.

72 See OECD DAC, *Development Co-operation Report, 2006*, p 29. Online. Available at: <http://caliban.sourceoecd.org/pdf/dac06/01.pdf> (accessed 27 June 2007).

73 OECD Development Directorate, *Doing Aid Better*, A comment piece by Donald J. Johnson, Secretary-General of the OECD, and Richard Manning, Chair of the OECD Development Committee. Online. Available at: <www.oecd.org> (accessed 28 June 2007).

It is thus clear that the practice of foreign aid has been followed by developed countries for more than fifty years generally and consistently. As stated above, a long practice is not necessary; rather uniformity and consistency matter much in customary law. Thus the customary value of this practice cannot be plainly dismissed.

The question is whether the practice of most of the donor countries, except the USA (a 'persistent objector'), amounts to acceptance of an obligation, particularly under the General Assembly resolutions. In other words, is the practice accompanied by *opinio juris*? In answering these questions, the following observations of Akehurst provide a good starting point:

> Most if not all, developed countries give aid to poorer countries and would probably admit that they have a moral obligation to do so, but how many of them recognize a legal obligation to give aid? Conversely, there are many illogical distinctions and exceptions in customary law which have grown up for *historical reasons*, but which cannot be regarded a response to moral or social needs.[74]

Schachter underscores the legal importance of development aid practice in the following words:

> What is striking about [aid] is not so much of its espousal by the large majority of poor and handicapped countries but the fact that it has been accepted – by and large – by the more affluent countries to whom the demand is addressed. The evidence for this can be found not only in international resolutions with which the rich countries have concurred but also, and more convincingly, in the series of actions by them to grant assistance and preferences to those in less developed countries . . . the scale and duration . . . demonstrate the practical acceptance of a responsibility based on the entitlement of those in need.[75]

From these statements, it appears that the developed countries may, at best, consider development aid as their moral obligation. Some countries such as Austria and Switzerland have made foreign aid a part of their municipal laws.[76] Denmark and Norway have imposed a tax regarding

74 Akehurst, *BYIL* 1974–75 op. cit., p 35; Emphasis added. Historical reasons seem to refer to the colonial past.

75 Oscar Schachter, 'The Evolving International Law of Development', *Columbia Journal of Transnational Law* 15, 1976, 1–16, at 9–10.

76 Rich, Crawford (ed.), op. cit., p 47, mentions Austrian Federal Law of 10 July 1974; Swiss Federal Law of 19 March 1976. The mandate of the Swiss Agency for Development and Co-operation is based on the Federal Law on International Development Cooperation and Humanitarian Aid enacted on 19 March 1976. Available at: <http://web.mit.edu/urbanupgrading/upgrading/resources/organizations/sdc.html> (accessed 28 June 2007).

aid.[77] It seems that these countries regard development aid as a legal obligation. However, a number of developed countries appear to regard development aid only as a moral obligation.[78] For example, in a 1997 White Paper on international development cooperation, the UK government noted: 'We all have a moral duty to reach out to the poor and the needy.'[79] Some countries, for example, the USA, is pursuing aid as a foreign policy goal. Since the USA regularly opposes the RTD, therefore, its practice is examined separately.

Is the USA a 'persistent objector'?

The USA has spelt out its position on the question of 'persistent objector' as follows:

> *Dissenting views and new State* . . . [I]n principle a dissenting State which indicates its dissent from a practice while the law is still in the process of development is not bound by that rule of law even if after it matures . . . A State that enters the international system after a practice has ripened into a rule of international law is bound by it.[80]

The USA position, described in Chapter 2, is briefly revisited here. Firstly, development comes about not as a matter of legal claim or right but because of economic liberties. Secondly, economic, social and cultural rights can be realized progressively. Thirdly, the language of the RTD is not clear. Fourthly, the Commission on Human Rights has no jurisdiction over trade and financial matters. Fifthly, 'the [USA] is firmly opposed to the idea of regulating State behaviour to conform to the RTD or any elements thereof'.[81]

77 Rich, Crawford (ed.), op. cit., p. 47. 'Norway has had such a tax since 1963; Denmark's excise tax on coffee serves the same purpose.'

78 According to an Australian government statement, 'Australia gives aid because we want to help those less fortunate than ourselves.' Online. Available at: <http://www.ausaid.gov.au/makediff/whatis.cfm> (accessed 6 July 2007).

79 The UK's 1997 White Paper op. cit., see also White Paper by the UK Secretary of State for International Development, 'Eliminating World Poverty: Making Globalisation Work for the Poor', 2000, para. 348, which says, 'The UK government has worked within the G8 to put development issues higher on the agenda, ranging from debt relief, aid untying . . . We believe that the G8 has a duty to take forward action on [the] issues.' Online. Available at: <http://www.dfid.gov.uk/Pubs/files/whitepaper2000.pdf> (both accessed 6 July 2007).

80 Restatement of the Foreign Relations Law of the United States (Revised), Tentative Draft No. 6, 12 April 1985, (Comment (d) to s. 102), quoted in Jonathan I. Charney, 'The Persistent Objector Rule and the Development of Customary International Law', *The British Year Book of International Law* LVI, 1985, 1–24 at 2–3.

81 For a detailed discussion on these points, see Stephen Marks, 'The Human Right to Development: Between Rhetoric and Reality', *Harvard Human Rights Journal* 17, 2004, 137–68, 143–51. Arguments regarding the Millennium Challenge Account are mainly based on Stephen Marks.

It is clear that the USA has regularly opposed the RTD and its position appears therefore to be that of a 'persistent objector'. There are, however, two exceptions to this opposition. First, it supported the Vienna Declaration and Programme of Action, which reaffirmed the RTD as enunciated in the Declaration 'as a universal and inalienable right and integral part of fundamental human rights'.[82] The USA delegate, Nancy Rubin, stated before the Commission on Human Rights: 'in Vienna, we affirmed the RTD as a universal and inalienable right with the human person as the central subject of development.'[83] On a recent occasion, the USA reiterated: 'there was broad consensus on certain basic truths such as the affirmation in the Vienna Declaration that the human person was the central subject of development.'[84] This statement appears to support Article 2(1) of the Declaration, which also says that 'the human person is the central subject of development'. Secondly, the USA has also supported the establishment of the OEWG and the appointment of the Independent Expert on the RTD in 1998.[85]

Thus it may be argued that the USA is no longer a 'persistent objector'. A question arises: can the strong opposition of a big power like the USA prevent or delay the creation of a customary rule? Commentators argue that the concept of 'persistent objector' has lost its legal importance because of the 'community oriented configuration of international relations' and lack of 'firm support in State practice and international case law for a rule' regarding it.[86] One commentator observes that it 'has no legitimate basis in the international legal system'.[87] Regarding a big power's opposition to a customary rule, one may argue that the growing interdependence (or community-oriented international relations) of states, particularly in this era of globalization, coupled with the assertive role of developing countries in international law, has a strong negative influence on the notion of a big power's role in customary international law. In the contemporary world, 'it is extremely difficult for an individual State to eschew the strong pressure of the vast majority of members of the community.'[88] Since 2002, the USA has been pursuing a development cooperation programme called the Millennium Challenge Account (MCA). The developing countries asking for funds under the MCA have to show their commitment to these goals: (1) good governance or ruling justly, comprising control of corruption, respect for human rights and the rule of law; (2) investing in people, such as in education and health;

82 Vienna Declaration, Article 10.
83 Quoted in Marks, 'Rhetoric and Reality', op. cit., 151.
84 Ibid.
85 Ibid.
86 Cassese, *International Law*, op. cit., p 124.
87 Charney, op. cit., 21.
88 Cassese, *International Law*, op. cit., p 124.

and (3) sound policies for a free market economy.[89] One commentator argues that the MCA has clear similarities with the RTD Development Compact.[90] However, President George W. Bush categorically stated: 'States . . . have no obligation to provide guarantees for implementation of any [RTD].'[91]

It may be concluded that developed countries consider foreign aid as a moral obligation rather than a legal obligation. While aid is a 'standard practice for richer states', most of these countries seem reluctant to recognize it as a legal obligation.[92] In the 1980s, the aid policy of the OECD was based on three principles, viz. 'national self interest, unabashed humanitarianism and global system maintenance'.[93] Until the 1980s, most of the leaders[94] of the developing countries viewed the aid of the Western powers to the developing countries (most of which were their former colonies) as reparation for the colonial past. The 1990s witnessed a growing call for development aid as a rights-based approach to development, which thus created hopes for promotion of the RTD. In 2000, the MDGs were set as a pathway towards global justice. Critics argue that the recent diversion of aid flows to the 'war on terrorism' is seen as a shift from the objective of helping the poor to pursuance of foreign policy goals.[95] Given this position of the developed countries, which involves a conflict between their (state) practice and *opinio juris*, it is necessary to examine the legal status of the Declaration in relation to the general principles of law.

GENERAL PRINCIPLES OF LAW

According to Article 38(1)(c) of the Statute of the ICJ, 'the general principles of law recognised by civilised nations' are ranked as the third source in the hierarchy of the sources of international law. However, the status of the 'general principles', as sources of international law, is a disputed issue among

89 Details of the Millennium Challenge Account (MCA). Online. Available at <http://www.whitehouse.gov/infocus/developingnations/millennium.html> (accessed 6 July 2007).

90 Marks, 'Rhetoric and Reality', 157.

91 Ibid. 135.

92 See Michael Akehurst, *A Modern Introduction to International Law*, London/New York, Routledge, 6th Edition, 1987 (reprinted 1993), p 236. See also Isabella D. Bunn, 'The Right to Development: Implications for International Economic Law', *American University Journal of International Law Review* 15, 1999–2000, 1425–68, at 1454.

93 Development Co-operation Review, p 81, 1981, quoted in Rich, 'The Right to Development on Emerging Human Right' 305.

94 See generally, Zulfikar Ali Bhutto, 'Is Aid Charity?' in Hamid Jalal and Khalid Hasan, (eds) *Reshaping Foreign Policy: A collection of articles, statements and speeches by Zulfikar Ali Bhutto*, Politics of the People, Lahore, Classic, Politics of the People Volume One, 1948–1966, p 151.

95 Christian Aid, *The Politics of Poverty: Aid in the New Cold War*. Available at: <http://www.un-ngls.org/orf/politics%20of%20poverty.pdf> (accessed 15 March 2009). See also Canadian Council for International Co-operation, *Reality of Aid 2004*. Online. Available <http://www.ccic.ca/e/docs/002_aid_roa_2004.pdf> (accessed 29 July 2007).

international lawyers. Some argue that general principles of law constitute the affirmation of natural law principles. Others are of the view that the general principles do not constitute a separate source, but are parts of treaty and custom.[96] It is also argued that 'these principles constitute merely a function of the court permitting it to reach a judgment when no treaty or custom is available'.[97] These controversies are not resolved. As one writer observes: 'There is no unanimity among scholars as to the nature of the principles, which may be invoked under this head.' There are broadly two possible interpretations.'[98] Firstly, the general principles are those principles which are common to all or the majority of the national legal systems.[99] Some of those principles are *res judicata*, estoppel and good faith. Secondly, general principles include those principles which are 'applicable directly to international legal relations, and general principle applicable to legal relations generally'.[100] These include the principles of consent, reciprocity, good faith, the freedom of the seas and the legal validity of agreements.[101] Being directly related to state practice, these principles have close similarities with international customary law.[102] But they are different from customary law because 'they have been so long and so generally accepted as to be no longer *directly* connected with state practice'.[103]

Many General Assembly resolutions are cited as examples of the general principles of international law. The UDHR, as a General Assembly resolution, is an example of the general principles derived from a national legal system.[104] Other General Assembly resolutions such as those on genocide, racial discrimination, outer space, friendly relations, and the seabed illustrate general principles which have emerged directly from international consensus.[105]

Is the Declaration a part of the general principles of international law? In answering this question, international cooperation, a key feature of the Declaration, may be examined. The principle of international cooperation is one of the purposes of the UN. In addition to Articles 55 and 56 of the Charter, international cooperation is reiterated in a long series of General

96 Malcolm N. Shaw, *International Law*, Cambridge University Press, 5th Edition, 2003.

97 Sloan, *BYIL* 1987, op. cit., 78. See also Wolfgang Friedmann, 'The Uses of "General Principles" in the Development of International Law', *American Journal of International Law* 57, 1963, 279–99. See further Lord McNair QC, 'The General Principles of Law Recognized by Civilized Nations', *British Year Book of International Law* XXXIII, 1957, 1–19.

98 Thirlway, op. cit., p 131.

99 Ibid.

100 Ibid.

101 Brownlie, op. cit., p 18.

102 Mestdagh, 30–53 at 39.

103 Brownlie, op. cit., pp 8–19.

104 Philip Alston, 'Conjuring Up New Human Rights: A Proposal for Quality Control', *American Journal of International Law* 78, 1984, 607–21, 614.

105 Sloan, *BYIL* 1987, op. cit., p 80.

Assembly resolutions, conventions, recommendations and international conferences.[106]

The duty of cooperation envisaged by the Declaration may be seen in relation to good faith as a general principle of international law. But for practical purposes, the principle of cooperation mentioned in Article 56 of the UN Charter is abstract and the states have a wide margin of discretion to disregard it (Chapter 4). This is also true about Article 2(2) of the Charter which says that all member states should fulfil their obligations in good faith. Commentators, however, argue that good faith applies in the case of existing rules of international law, as it is not 'in itself a source of obligation'.[107] There is no acceptance of cooperation in good faith with particular reference to the RTD. It was concluded in Chapter 4 that a consensus between the developing and the developed countries over the implementation of the RTD is still lacking. Thus the Declaration is not established as a general principle of international law. It is important to note that the role of the General Assembly resolutions is also seen as what is known as soft law.

IS THE DECLARATION A SOFT LAW?

The term soft law refers to those international instruments which are of a non-binding nature. Soft law evokes a 'transitional stage in the development of norms where their content is vague and their scope imprecise'.[108] The resolutions of international organizations, particularly those of the General Assembly, are considered to be soft law instruments.[109] However, 'soft law' is a contentious issue in contemporary international law.[110] It is generally held that soft law creates a fertile ground for the development of hard law rules.[111] Current human rights law – grown from the UDHR, a resolution of the General Assembly – is a typical example of a soft law,[112] crystallized into a hard law. The RTD is also seen as a part of human rights discourse. The

106 See UDHR Arts 22 and 28; ICESCR, Arts 2(1), 11(2); CRC, Arts 4 and 24(4), The Vienna Declaration and Programme of Action, 1993; Millennium Declaration, 2000, MDG 8. See also Committee on Economic, Social and Cultural Rights, General Comment No. 2.

107 Shaw, op. cit., p 98.

108 Rene Jean Dupuy, 'Declaratory Law and Programmatory Law: From Revolutionary Custom to "Soft Law" ', in R.K. Akkerman et al. (eds) *Declarations on Principles, A Quest for Universal Peace*, Leyden, A.W. Sijthoff, pp 247–57, at p 252.

109 Sloan, *BYIL* 1987, op. cit., 106–107. The non-binding agreements and voluntary codes of conduct for transnational corporations are also categorized as soft law instruments.

110 Ibid.

111 C.M. Chinkin, 'The Challenge of Soft Law: Development and Change in International Law', *International and Comparative Law Quarterly* 38, 1989, 850–66.

112 See Ignaz Seil-Hohenveldern, 'International Economic "Soft Law" ', *Recuiel des Cours 163*, 1979–II, 165–246, at 195.

legal status of the Declaration, therefore, may be seen more conveniently as soft law.

Commentators see the RTD as an economic expression of the right of self-determination. For example, Chinkin argues: 'The concepts inherent in the use of soft law forms in international economic relations are the forces for development and change. They both cause change and are consequential upon it.'[113] Chinkin further argues, '[e]conomic development necessitates the resolution of international claims for the allocation of resources according to principles of distributive justice, in conjunction with notions of affirmative action and entitlement so as to achieve substantive equality of States.'[114] This statement pertinently argues that the RTD is raised as a claim by the developing countries against the developed countries for an equitable distribution of global economic resources. Such claims were initially spelt out in the NIEO declarations, which were in the nature of soft law.[115]

The RTD appears to fit well with the notion of what Dupuy calls programmatory law.[116] Dupuy elaborates the notion of the programmatory nature of resolutions as follows:

> Certain resolutions are prospective in nature. They proclaim principles which are not yet respected in practice. As regards the resolutions, they are found at an intermediate level between the declaratory instrument and the recommendation pure and simple. Their provisions often contain purposes and principles which themselves are rather fluid in their formulation and their substance.[117]

The prospective nature of the Declaration is demonstrated in its language. The Declaration provides that the states have a duty to cooperate to ensure development and eliminate obstacles to development,[118] to take steps individually and collectively to formulate international development policies for the realization of the RTD[119] and to cooperate with a view to promoting, encouraging and strengthening respect for the human rights and fundamental rights of all without any discrimination or distinction.[120] The Declaration's purposes of 'global equity' and 'justice' and its principle of 'cooperation'

113 Chinkin, op. cit., p 853.

114 Ibid.

115 For the legal value of the NIEO resolutions, see, generally, Thomas M. Franck and Mark M. Munansangu, *The New International Economic Order: International Law in the Making?*, Geneva, United Nations Institute for Training and Research (UNITAR), 1982.

116 See Bunn, op. cit., p 125.

117 Dupuy, op. cit., p 254.

118 DRD, Art. 3(3).

119 Ibid. Art. 4(1).

120 Ibid. Art. 6(1).

are, with reference to Dupuy, 'rather fluid in their formulation and their substance'.

Soft law has the potential to influence national legal systems and policies.[121] International human rights law has been adopted by almost all countries in their respective domestic legal systems and their domestic courts are applying it. The Declaration, too, can influence state laws and policies because it enjoins the states to undertake, at the national level, all necessary measures for the realization of the RTD[122] and to take steps 'to ensure the full exercise and progressive enhancement of the [RTD], including the formulation, adoption and implementation of policy, legislative and other measures at the national and international levels'.[123]

THE RTD AND 'NEW SOURCES'

There is a view that the formal or traditional sources are not sufficient to keep international law abreast with the changing needs of the time. Sir Robert Jennings observed in 1964 that '[a] fresh approach to [the] whole question of sources is much needed'.[124] In the early 1980s, Jennings reiterated that Article 38 of the Statute of the ICJ:

> [I]s a 1920 draft and not always well-suited to international law in the 1980s. So we must use it, by interpreting where need be . . . whether it is now of itself a sufficient guide to the content of modern international law.[125]

Among the new sources of international law are the interrelated principles of consensus, cooperation and interdependence, which are also of significant relevance to the Declaration.[126] The debate about these new sources began in the late 1950s. Prominent international lawyers, such as Falk, Friedmann, Fenwick, Jenks and Weeramantry, have written in favour of these new sources.

Richard Falk argues that 'there is discernable a trend from consent to

121 Chinkin, op. cit., p 863.

122 Ibid. Art. 8(1).

123 Ibid. Art. 10.

124 See also Sir Robert Jennings, 'Recent Developments in the International Law Commission: Its Relation to the Sources of International Law', *International and Comparative Law Quarterly* 13, 1964, 385–97, at 387.

125 Sir Robert Jennings, 'What is International Law and how do we tell it when we see it?' *The Cambridge-Tilburg Law Lectures*, 3rd series, 1980, London/Deventer, Kluwer, 1983, p 5.

126 Other principles include 'recognition and acceptance, community expectations, vacuum filling and such concepts as a general will, judicial conscience or manifest community intent.' See Sloan, *BYIL* 1987, op. cit., 90–95.

consensus as the basis of international obligations'.[127] He attributes this change, among others, to a growing interdependence in economic and social activities. Falk emphasizes the need for reinterpretation of the basis of obligation in international law on sociological grounds due to the emergence of newly independent states in Africa and Asia and their active participation in international law.[128] Falk grounds his theory on: (a) a jurisprudential basis for attributing a limited legislative status to those resolutions of the General Assembly that are supported by consensus of the members, and (b) the 'legislative competence [which] has made or might continue to make a contribution to world legal order'.[129]

With reference to the General Assembly resolutions, consensus is understood in two senses, viz., procedure and substance. Sloan argues:

> As a procedure, consensus is a method for reaching a decision without voting in the absence of formal objection. From the point of view of substance, a consensus is normally a compromise in which opposing views are reconciled . . . In the consensus process, the majority forgets its right to impose a text on the minority, but in turn expects good faith acceptance of the consensus text.[130]

It is clear from this statement that consensus is a tool of cooperation among the states. Since the Declaration (1986), the General Assembly has adopted a number of resolutions on the RTD without a vote: they were for the years 1987, 1989–1996 and 2000, respectively.[131] The rest, for the years up to 2006, were subjected to a vote; the USA opposed almost all of them. Commentators argue that the voting process alone is not an effective process of law-making through consensus.[132] It is 'the actual generality of acceptance including all of the states with substantial interest in the subject' that is necessary for consensus.[133] Given the persistent opposition of the USA and the absence of clear and consistent support from the major Western donor

127 Richard A. Falk, 'On Quasi-Legislative Competence of the General Assembly', *American Journal of International Law* 60, 1966, 782–91 at 785. For criticism of Falk, see N.G. Onuf, 'Professor Falk on Quasi-legislative Competence of the General Assembly', *American Journal of International Law* 64, 1970, 349–55, at 352.

128 Falk, op. cit., 782.

129 Ibid. 783.

130 Sloan, *BYIL* 1987, op. cit., 91–2.

131 See Record of the UNGA resolutions. Online. Available at: <http://www.un.org/documents/resga.htm> (accessed 28 Oct. 2006).

132 Stephen M. Schwebel, 'The Effect of Resolutions of the U.N. General Assembly on Customary International Law', *Proceedings of the American Society of International Law*, 1979, 301–9, at 302.

133 Quincy Wright, 'Custom as a Basis for International Law in the Post-War World', *Texas International Law Forum* 2, 1966, 147, 158, quoted in Anthony D'Amato, 'On Consensus', *Canadian Year Book of International Law* 8, 1970, 104–22, at 108.

countries,[134] the consensus arrived at the Vienna Conference, 1993, could be merely hortatory and a good faith consideration.

The importance of cooperation is emphasized by Friedmann in these words: 'a developing cooperative international law represents community aspects, rather than society aspects, in the relations between States and nations.'[135] He advocated an inclusive role for the developing countries, the individual and other non-state actors in social and economic development through a universal and dynamic public international law.[136] Fenwick stated that the story of the 'new' international law (a reference to the post-Second World War period) is incomplete without 'the new areas of economic and social co-operation'.[137] Fenwick argued that 'the declarations and the resolutions of the General Assembly are slowly acquiring an authority beyond the legal obligation of the document [the Charter]'.[138] The views of Friedmann and Fenwick reinforce the duty of cooperation as it is visualized in the Charter of the UN and elaborated in the Declaration. Cooperation is also considered a tool of interdependence. Brierly argued that fundamental rights ('self-preservation, independence, equality, respect and intercourse') and consent of the states, as the sources of obligation, have negative consequences, and therefore 'it is certainly desirable to move towards interdependence'.[139] Jenks comprehensively developed the notion of interdependence. He argued that 'the only principle adequate for the purpose under modern conditions can be expressed in one word: interdependence'.[140] His view could be seen to be very close to the normative force of the Declaration when he links interdependence with equality of opportunity and economic security.[141] A later authority on these 'new sources' of international law is Judge Weeramantry, who observed:

> International law has moved progressively from the notion of mere tolerance of other states and co-existence with them to the notion of co-operation. The movement from co-existence to active co-operation necessitates a more collective approach to the problems facing us. We are witnessing an exceptional growth of collectivist ideas in displacement of some of the strong individualism of the past.[142]

134 They are referred to as Key Donor Countries (KDC) and listed as such in Chapter 2, above.

135 Wolfgang Friedmann, 'The Changing Dimensions of International Law', *Columbia Law Review* 62, 1962, 1147–65, at 1162.

136 Ibid. 1150.

137 Charles G. Fenwick, 'International Law: Old and New', *American Journal of International Law* 60, 1966, 475–83, at 481.

138 Ibid. 480.

139 Brierly, *The Law of Nations*, op. cit., p 49; See also Brierly, *The Basis of Obligation in International Law*, Oxford Clarendon, 1958, pp 51–65.

140 C. Wilfred Jenks, *Law, Freedom and Welfare*, London, Stevens & Sons, 1968, p 71.

141 Ibid. p 78.

142 C.G. Weeramantry, *Universalising International Law*, Leiden, Martinus Nijhoff Publishers, 2004, p 222.

However, international cooperation for the promotion of the RTD is facing a challenge in the UN because firstly, there is no consensus over the mechanism for the implementation of the RTD. This view was discussed in Chapter 4 above. Secondly, international development cooperation, as discussed above in this chapter, is not considered a legal obligation in international law. On balance, however, the growing change in the attitude of European countries indicates progress, albeit slow, in the implementation of the RTD.

THE VALUE OF THE DECLARATION: DETERMINING FACTORS

Finally, it may be seen how the non-binding resolutions of the General Assembly contribute to the customary rule of international law. It is generally agreed that each and every resolution needs to be seen in the light of a number of factors.[143] These factors include: the language of the resolution, the voting strength, implementation and follow-up and state practice.[144] Sloan has examined in detail as many seventeen factors. It seems pertinent to examine the Declaration in the light of some of those factors.[145]

Competency of General Assembly

There is no need to emphasize that the General Assembly is the main organ of the UN and a highly representative body of the international community. It has been regularly adopting declaratory resolutions for the last six decades. Sloan stated in 1987: 'it is much too late in the history of the UN to raise the issue with respect to [the] competence of the General Assembly.'[146] Thus the competency of the General Assembly is not in question. Sloan has argued that this power of the General Assembly, irrespective of its being inherent or acquired, having never been objected to by any state, 'is now firmly established . . . beyond any rational challenge or dispute'.[147]

143 Sloan, *BYIL* 1987, op. cit., 125.

144 Ibid. 127–38. See also Wil D. Verwey, 'The New International Economic Order and the Realisation of the Right to Development and Welfare – A Legal Survey' in Frederick E. Synder (eds), et al. pp 825–49 at p 833; Obed Asamoah, 'The Legal Effect of Resolutions of the General Assembly', *The Columbia Journal of Transnational Law* 3(2), 1965, 210–30, at 228.

145 Sloan, *BYIL* 1987, op.cit., 125. Other factors are: Method of preparation, Effective power, Cumulative factor – repetition and recitation, Opinion of jurists, Judicial decisions, Public opinion, Morality and Credibility.

146 Ibid.

147 Ibid. 45.

'The nature and content'

The nature of the Declaration is that of a General Assembly resolution. The Declaration provides that the states have the right and duty to cooperate with each other for the realization of the RTD.[148] It also underlines the importance of effective international cooperation to help the developing countries in promoting their comprehensive development.[149] The assertion of developing countries that they have a collective RTD is a highly political issue in the North–South relations.

'Time and circumstances'

The NIEO movement lost much of its heat during the drafting period of the Declaration, yet its influence was strongly felt in international relations. The linking of the RTD to the NIEO by the developing countries was one of the crucial elements in the controversies during the drafting of the Declaration. The then USA government was highly sceptical of the Declaration at that time. The effect of these circumstances was that the Declaration could not command a consensus of the developed countries at the time of its adoption by the General Assembly.

'Terms and intent' or language

The language of the declaration must be precise and mandatory. Resolutions embody general principles or specific rules.[150] Commentators say that certain methods, such as assessment of the language of the resolution and of the rights and duties of the states that it delineates, coupled with the support of other countries that it receives (voting, discussed below), may be applied to transform the resolution into international law.[151] As Abi-Saab argues, the degree of concreteness of the content is one of the three factors determining the legal weight of General Assembly resolutions.[152]

Chapter 4 argued that the language of the Declaration is vague and imprecise. However, some degree of concreteness in the language of a few articles may be found. For example, Article 2(1) says that 'the human person is the central subject of development'. Article 6(2) clearly asserts that 'all human rights and fundamental rights are indivisible and interdependent'. Similarly Article 8 guides the state to devise a comprehensive national development policy and to encourage the participation of all, including women. The cumulative effect of the above provisions is that the Declaration guides a

148 DRD, Art. 2(3).

149 Ibid. Art. 4(2).

150 Asamoah, op. cit. 228.

151 Falk, op. cit., 786.

152 Quoted in Cassese, *International Law in a Divided World*, Oxford Clarendon Press, 1986, para. 107.

state's development programme towards ensuring the well-being of all people, avoiding trade-offs among human rights, and encouraging participation of all people, including women.

'Voting pattern'

The degree of support for a resolution reflects the will of the states.[153] However, the Declaration was overwhelmingly supported by the developing countries only. Eight countries, including six major Western countries, abstained from voting and the USA cast a negative vote.

In the context of a conflict in the voting trend, it is difficult to derive a solid result. As discussed in Chapter 2, some RTD resolutions were adopted without a vote. This fact points to growing support for the Declaration. The positive votes of some major Western donor countries in the 2003–2005 resolutions further indicate a strong move towards increasing acceptability of the RTD. Many commentators admit that the vote on the Declaration shows popular support among states.[154] However, a genuine consensus has yet to develop. It is important to note that most of the developing countries have been consistently casting votes in favour of the RTD resolutions. This means that those states 'will act according to' the terms of those resolutions, 'even if [they are] not legally bound to do so'.[155]

'International organization practice'

The RTD has not been specifically mainstreamed by any international organization in its law and policies. However, the African [Banjul] Charter on Human and Peoples' Rights, a regional treaty, has incorporated the RTD as a human right in its Article 22. But 'the Charter has not effected radical changes'.[156] However, recently an African Court on Human and Peoples' Rights has been established. The judicial practice of this regional court will be significant for the RTD in future.[157] The SAARC Social Charter, adopted

153 Asamoah, op. cit. 228.

154 Brownlie, *The Human Right to Development*, op. cit., para. 59; see also generally Wade Mansell and Joanne Scott, 'Why Bother About the Right to Development?', *Journal of Law and Society* 21(4), 1994, 171–92 at 175.

155 Dixon, op. cit., p 46.

156 L. Amede Obiora, 'Beyond the Rhetoric of a Right to Development', *Law & Policy* 18, 1996, 355–418, at 380. See Andre Mbata B. Mangu, 'The Changing Human Rights Landscape in Africa: Organisation of African Unity, African Union, New Partnership for Africa's Development and the African Court', *Netherlands Quarterly of Human Rights* 23(3), 2005, 379–408.

157 Article 24 of the Protocol established the court. It read: 'The Protocol shall come into force thirty days after fifteen instruments of ratification or accession have been deposited.' The International Federation for Human Rights (FIDH) has issued a report, which says that the Union of Comoros deposited the fifteen instruments of ratification on 26 Dec. 2003 and the Protocol came into force on 25 Jan. 2004.

in 2004, specifically refers to the RTD as one of the principles, goals and objectives. It is yet to be seen what practical steps the SAARC countries will take to mainstream the RTD in their development policies.

Human rights are increasingly being incorporated by international organizations in their development activities. There is growing evidence of this practice in the UN bodies, particularly the UNDP, which explicitly recognizes the potential of the RTD for sustainable development.[158] In 2003, the OHCHR published guidelines on a human rights approach to poverty-reduction strategies.[159] The law and practice of the WTO regarding the special category status of the developing countries may be considered a dimension of the RTD:

> The WTO Agreements contain special provisions which give [the] developing countries special rights and which give [the] developed countries the possibility to treat developing countries more favourably than other WTO Members. These special provisions include, for example, longer time periods for implementing agreements and commitments or measures to increase trading opportunities for developing countries. These are referred to as the 'special and differential treatment' [S & D] provisions.[160]

Implementation or follow-up mechanism

Implementation includes observation, control and follow-up measures.[161] The annual General Assembly and the Commission's resolutions reinforce the normative force of the RTD.[162] The deliberations of the Global Consultation, the OEWG and the reports of the Independent Expert provide ample evidence of implementation and follow-up studies.

'Community values, needs and expectations'

The emphasis on the duty of cooperation, self-determination, sovereignty over natural resources, international peace and security, principles concerning

158 UNDP, 'Integrating human rights with sustainable development', a UNDP Policy Document, January 1998. Online. Available at: <www.undp.org> (accessed 9 July 2007).

159 Paul Hunt, Manfred Nowak and S.R. Osmani, *Guidelines: A Human Rights Approach to Poverty Reduction Strategies*. Online. Available at: <http://www.unhchr.ch/development/povertyfinal.html> (accessed 9 July 2007).

160 Available at: <www.wto.org> (accessed 9 July 2007).

161 Sloan, *BYIL* 1987, op. cit., 134.

162 Salomon, Arjun Sengupta, op. cit., p 27.

friendly relations, the need for an NIEO and respect for human rights underlined by the Declaration may be seen as the values, needs and expectations of the international community. Firstly, international cooperation, as the Declaration asserts, is one the purposes of the UN. Under Article 56 of the Charter, all the members have promised to 'take *joint and several actions in co-operation* with the Organization' to realize the ideals of 'higher standards of living, full employment, and conditions of economic and social progress and development' laid down in Article 55. These articles of the Charter are, as Higgins comments:

> [P]recise legal obligations binding on all States . . . the Charter being an international treaty, members are bound by each and every clause in it, none of which may be deemed 'more binding' than others.[163]

Secondly, the General Assembly resolutions regarding the other community values, needs and obligations, mentioned above, provide enough 'legislative energy' to the duty of cooperating to work for the economic and social progress in the less developed countries.[164] This duty of cooperation, according to Verwey, exists in international law because 'a *basic* commitment has thus been established in the form of a binding treaty obligation'.[165] Thirdly, the UDHR has attained the status of a primary duty of the states because of the states' practice to consider it as an obligation.[166] The protection of and respect for human rights has attained the status of *jus cogens* (the peremptory norm of international law) which enjoys hierarchical superiority over all the other rules of international law.[167] Moreover, this obligation has been recognized by the international community on many occasions.[168] Recent examples are the Rio Declaration, 1992, the Vienna Declaration, 1993, the Beijing Conference, 1995, etc. Fourthly, it may be argued that the provisions of the ICESCR[169] have created a legally binding obligation for non-state parties (and a binding obligation for those states which are party to the Covenant)

163 Higgins, op. cit., p 129.

164 Asamoah, op. cit., 223

165 Verwey, op. cit., p 828 (emphasis in original). See also Maria Magdalena Kenig-Witkowska, 'Development ideology in international law' in S.R. Chowdhury et al (ed.), op. cit., pp 35–41.

166 Ibid. p 829. See also generally, J. Shand Watson, *Theory & Reality in the International Protection of Human Rights*, New York, Transnational Publishers, Inc., 1999, chapter V: General Assembly Resolutions as a Source of Human Rights, pp 107–38.

167 See, generally, Cassese, *International Law*, op. cit., p 118.

168 Such as in GA resolution 1514(XV), the Proclamation of Tehran, 1968 and the Convention to Prevent and Punish the Acts of Terrorism Taking the Form of Crimes against Persons and Related Extortion that are of International Significance, 1971.

169 For example, Article 11, paras 1 and 2.

nationally as well as internationally in general customary international law.[170] This view may be extended to the RTD for the reason that human rights are 'indivisible, interdependent and interrelated'. Fifthly, the General Assembly and the Commission[171] have, in many resolutions, articulated the opinion that the international economic order is unjust. Thus the establishment of the NIEO is essential for the realization of the human rights laid down in the UDHR, particularly the economic, social and cultural rights.[172]

CONCLUSION

This chapter has analysed the Declaration in light of both traditional sources and 'new sources' of international law. The Declaration is not a treaty. The analysis, therefore, focused on custom. Given the complexity involved in the process of creating customary rules, the controversy over the legal effects of General Assembly resolutions is still unresolved. For the existence of a customary rule:

> [W]hat is sought for is a general recognition among states of a certain practice as obligatory . . . this test of general recognition is necessarily a vague one; but it is the nature of customary international law . . . not susceptible of exact or final formulations.[173]

The consistency with which development aid, a tool of international cooperation, is pursued by developed countries through their practices amounts to a general recognition. But most developed countries consider aid as a moral obligation. It is clear that while a general and consistent (state) practice is there, *opinio juris* is missing. Thus cooperation in the form of development aid is not recognized as a source of legal obligation in international law. Regarding the general principles of law, the chapter has argued that there is no acceptance of cooperation in good faith, particularly in relation to the RTD. However, the states have a general duty (even the USA, which opposed the Declaration) to consider the Declaration in good faith. If indeed viewed in good faith, the Declaration may provide strong holistic support to a growing consensus on human rights and development and may strengthen international development cooperation with equity and justice.

170 Verwey, op. cit., p 830. See Magdalena Sepulveda, 'Obligations of "International Assistance and Co-operation" in an optional protocol to the International Covenant on Economic, Social and Cultural Rights', *Netherlands Quarterly of Human Rights* 24(2), 2006, 271–303.

171 UNGA Res. A//32/130 and Res. A/34/46; CHR Res. 4 (XXXV) and 6 (XXXVI) referred to above in Chapter 2.

172 Verwey, op. cit., p 831.

173 Brierly, op. cit., p 61.

'New sources' such as consensus, cooperation and interdependence have great significance for the Declaration, for the reason that cooperation is one of the main features of the Declaration and is related to consensus and interdependence. No clear picture emerges from the analysis of the Declaration vis-à-vis various factors responsible for determining the legal value of the Declaration. For example, the language of the Declaration is imprecise and vague and the voting pattern on the RTD resolutions in the General Assembly is diverse. The chapter has established that being programmatory in nature, the Declaration, at best, appears to be a soft law. Like many other General Assembly resolutions, for example the UDHR, the Declaration has a strong moral force. However, it must be appreciated that the recognition of the Declaration is not entirely dependent on its international dimension. In fact, the Declaration asserts that the primary responsibility for the realization of the RTD lies with the state. The next part of the book examines the judicial practice of Pakistan vis-à-vis the RTD.

Part III

The RTD at the national level

Pakistan as a case study

6 The nature and extent of the realization of the RTD in Pakistan

INTRODUCTION

The analysis in Parts I and II has demonstrated that firstly, jurisprudentially, the RTD at the national level is less problematic and, secondly, the Declaration as a soft law influences domestic laws. The Declaration emphasizes that the state has the prime responsibility to create conditions both at the national and international levels that are favourable to the realization of the RTD.[1] The Declaration further proclaims that 'States should undertake, at the national level, all necessary measures for the realisation of the RTD'.[2] Moreover, it also enjoins the 'State to take steps to eliminate obstacles to development resulting from failure to observe civil and political rights, as well as economic, social and cultural rights'.[3]

This part of the book now moves to examine the national dimension of the RTD from the standpoint of state practice. Using Pakistan as a case study, it analyzes the experience of the judiciary in the protection and promotion of the fundamental rights. Chapters 6 and 7 focus on the role of the superior judiciary in the areas of PIL and interpretation of the *Shari'ah*, respectively. Chapter 8 focuses on the reform in the lower courts through the current PRSP.

The detailed reasons using for Pakistan as a case study have already been mentioned in Chapter 1. This chapter looks at the nature and extent of the realization of the RTD in the 1973 constitution of Pakistan. The main argument is that a wider interpretation of fundamental rights by the superior courts through PIL may promote the RTD in Pakistan.

The chapter takes a brief look at the current economic conditions and constitutional dilemmas of Pakistan and their impact on the promotion of the RTD. It also compares the features of the Declaration and Pakistan's constitution and examines the nature of constitutional obligations necessary for the

1 DRD, Art. 3(1).
2 Ibid. Art. 8(1).
3 Ibid. Art. 6(3).

realization of the RTD at the national level. The constitutional obligations are then examined from the perspective of fundamental rights jurisprudence developed by Pakistan's superior courts to address wider issues of social justice, having significance for the RTD.

THE POLITICAL ECONOMY OF PAKISTAN

Economy: far from distributive justice

Pakistan's economic growth was better in earlier decades. The average GDP growth of 6.0 per cent in the 1980s declined to 4.0 per cent in the 1990s.[4] According to the Human Development Report (HDR), 2007–08, 17 per cent of Pakistan's population lives on less than US$1 per day.[5] Pakistan ranks at number 77 on the Human Poverty Index (HPI-1).[6] Life expectancy at birth in 2005 was 64.6.[7] The adult literacy rate for children aged 15 years and above, in 2005, was 49.9 per cent.[8] The number of physicians available per 1,000,000 persons was only 74.[9] Public expenditure on health and education in 2004 and 2005 was 0.4 and 2.3 per cent of GDP, respectively.[10] As against this, Pakistan's military expenditures are 3.5 per cent of its GDP; whereas debt servicing gnaws away 2.2 per cent.[11] According to official reports, economic growth rose by an average of 7.5 per cent during 2005–2007.[12] However, Pakistan's performance on the MDGs is very poor. Almost half of the country's children of primary-school age are without education and there is a wide gender disparity in enrolment in the rural areas. The MDG of universal primary education (MDG 2) cannot be achieved with a meagre budget of just 2.3 per cent of GDP. According to a recent UNESCO report, Pakistan is one of the countries which are at risk of not achieving the literacy goal by 2015.[13] The performance on maternal health and child mortality goals is depressing.

While the economy shows overall good performance, the fruits of economic growth have been far from equitably distributed.[14] Such a situation is a challenge for the RTD at the national level because the Declaration provides

4 *Economic Survey of Pakistan*, 1999–2000, p 1. Online. Available at: <http://www.paksearch.com/Government/STATISTICS/Survey00/OVERVIEW.html> (accessed 23 July 2007).

5 UN, *Human Development Report*, 2007–08, Table 3, p 239.

6 Ibid.

7 Ibid. Table 1, p 245.

8 Ibid. Table 1, p 231.

9 Ibid. Table 6, p 249.

10 Ibid. and Table 11, p 267.

11 Ibid. Table 19, p 296.

12 *Economic Survey of Pakistan*, 2006–07, Finance Department, p 1.

13 UNESCO, *Education for All, Global Monitoring Report*, 2006, p 70.

14 *The News International*, Islamabad, 12 Sept. 2006.

that the state has a duty to ensure a fair distribution of the benefits arising out of a development policy.[15]

Constitution-making: still a dilemma

Constitution-making has proved to be an arduous task in Pakistan. Since independence, Pakistan has produced three constitutions; in 1956, 1962 and 1973, respectively. As many as seven provisional and interim constitutions, including four produced by the military regimes, were adopted.[16] During the last sixty years, the military have ruled the country for about thirty years. The preparation of the first constitution took eight years. The first Constituent Assembly was created under the Indian Independence Act, 1947. It was a sovereign law-making body, having the power to frame a constitution for the country. Until the framing of the new constitution, the country was to be governed under the Government of India Act, 1935. On 12 March 1949, the Constituent Assembly passed the Objectives Resolution, which was made the preamble to all three constitutions. With the passage of time, the Objectives Resolution has assumed greater importance. In 1985, the military regime of General Zia declared it a substantive part of the 1973 constitution under a new Article 2-A.

The constitution-making process had many problems. In 1953, the Governor-General dismissed the elected Prime Minister and his government. When the constitution was prepared in 1954, the Governor-General dismissed the Constituent Assembly. On a writ petition, the Sind High Court (then the Chief Court) ruled that the act of the Governor-General was illegal and without authority. That ruling was challenged in the Supreme Court (then the Federal Court), which validated the dismissal of the Constituent Assembly.[17] The draft constitution prepared by the new Constituent Assembly came into force on 23 March 1956. The constitution of 1956 provided a political system based on a federal structure, with an Islamic ideology.[18] It included a list of fundamental rights, Directive Principles of Policy and an

15 DRD, Art. 2(3).

16 The provisional and interim constitutions were: The Government of India Act, 1935, adopted through the Pakistan (Provisional Constitution) Order, 1947; The Law (Continuous in Force) Order, 1958; The Provisional Constitutional Order, 1969; The Interim Constitution of 1972; The Laws (Continuous in Force) Order, 1977; the Provisional Constitutional Order of 1981 and the Provisional Constitutional Order 1, of 1999.

17 *Maulvi Tamiz-ud-Din Khan v Governor-General of Pakistan*, PLD 1955 F.C. 240. A new Constituent Assembly was elected by the members of the provincial Assemblies.

18 It may be pointed out that few changes were made to the Objectives Resolution as the preamble of the Constitution of 1956. After the clause regarding the sovereignty of Allah, a new clause was added: 'Whereas the founder of Pakistan, Quaid-e-Azam Mohammad Ali Jinnah, declared that Pakistan would be a democratic state based on Islamic principles of justice.' From the opening clause of the preamble dealing with the sovereignty of God, the reference to the delegation was dropped. The new clause reads: 'Whereas sovereignty over

independent judiciary. The Islamic provisions were separately listed. However, the first constitution proved to be short-lived. In 1958, the President of Pakistan abrogated it, dissolved the national and provincial assemblies and imposed martial law. The fundamental rights were taken away and the courts were divested of the powers to take cognizance of the violation of the fundamental rights. The action of the President was legitimized by the Supreme Court in a constitutional case.[19] However, the President himself was deposed the same year by Ayub Khan, the then Commander-in-Chief of the Army, who imposed martial law.

The second constitution was adopted by the military regime of Ayub Khan in 1962.[20] The 1962 constitution was based on a presidential form of government. It recognized the fundamental rights of the citizen. For the Islamization of laws, two institutions, viz., an advisory Council of Islamic Ideology and an Islamic Research Institute, were established. The Principles of Policy included, among others, the fair treatment of minorities, promotion of the interests of backward peoples, education, raising the standard of living through distributive justice and the provision of basic necessities.[21] The 1962 constitution remained in force till 1969, when Ayub Khan handed over the power to another military regime, which again imposed martial law. The legality of the new military regime was queried in a constitutional petition, which was accepted and the regime was declared illegal.[22] General elections were held in 1970 and for the first time, the National Assembly was elected on the basis of adult franchise. In 1971, soon after the elections, due to serious political differences, East Pakistan seceded from West Pakistan and emerged as the independent state of Bangladesh. In 1972, an interim constitution was adopted. By 1973, a new constitution (the third) was passed by the National Assembly. The 1973 constitution retained almost the entire Objectives Resolution as the preamble and included a long list of fundamental rights and the Principles of Policy. It provided a parliamentary form of government and an independent judiciary. It also included the Islamic provisions and an Islamic Ideology Council, which was to play an advisory role in the Islamization of laws. The issue of provincial autonomy was also given due attention.

The general elections in 1977 created political differences among the political parties, which resulted in a military *coup d'état* by the Army Chief,

the entire Universe belongs to Almighty Allah alone, and the authority to be exercised by the people of Pakistan within the limits prescribed by Him is a sacred trust.' See Rubya Mehdi, *The Islamization of the Law in Pakistan*, Nordic Institute of Asian Studies, Surrey, Curzon Press, 1994, p 80.

19 *The State v Dosso and others*, PLD 1958 SC 533.

20 In February 1960, Ayub Khan appointed a Constitutional Commission, which submitted its report in April 1961. The Report of the Commission was published in 1962.

21 The Constitution of 1962, Articles 7–8.

22 *Miss Asma Jilani v Government of Pakistan*, PLD 1972 S.C. 139. See also *The State v Zia-ur-Rehman*, PLD 1973 SC 49.

Zia, and the removal of the government of Prime Minister Zulfikar Ali Bhutto. The action of Zia was upheld by the Supreme Court in 1977.[23] The 1973 constitution was amended many times; to date seventeen amendments have been adopted. The most important was the eighth amendment, by which the military regime in 1985 validated all the laws and regulations passed by the martial law regime. It also made the Objectives Resolution, as stated above, a substantive part of the constitution, conferred upon the President a discretionary power to dissolve the National Assembly, and established a Federal Shariat Court (FSC). Zia launched a massive Islamization of laws programme, which will be discussed in the next chapter. Zia invoked his discretionary power in 1987 by dismissing the government which had been elected in 1985.[24] Civilian rule returned to Pakistan in 1988 after the death of Zia. However, between then and 1993, two elected governments were dismissed by the President,[25] one of which was restored by the Supreme Court.[26] General elections were held in 1997, as a result of which an elected government took office. The President's discretionary power to dissolve the National Assembly was taken away by the 1997 thirteenth Constitutional Amendment.

In October 1999, General Musharraf dismissed the elected government in a successful coup, an action that was upheld by the Supreme Court.[27] In a 2001 controversial referendum, General Musharraf became the President. General elections were held in 2002 in which the pro-Musharraf party came to power. Through the Legal Framework Order, 2002, the power of the President to dissolve the National Assembly, was revived.

Pakistan's role in the USA-led war against terror created external as well as internal pressure on the Musharraf government. The USA and the West continually demanded that Pakistan should fight the growing militancy inside the country, particularly in the tribal areas adjoining Afghanistan. The frequent bombardment by American forces on Pakistan's tribal areas in search of the Taliban militants also exerted tremendous internal pressure on the government. The growing judicial activism of the Supreme Court, too, notably the cases of missing persons allegedly picked up by intelligence agencies on suspicion of their involvement in terrorist activities, proved a challenge for the government. The suspension of the former Chief Justice Iftikhar Choudhry, on 9 March 2007 unleashed an unprecedented judicial crisis. Chief Justice Choudhry was restored by the Supreme Court, but the issue of

23 *Begum Nusrat Bhutto v Chief of Army Staff*, PLD 1977 SC 657.

24 The elected government of Muhammad Khan Junejo was dismissed by Zia. Political parties were not allowed to participate in the 1985 elections.

25 The elected governments of Benazir Bhutto and Nawaz Sharif were dismissed by President Ghulam Ishaq Khan in 1990 and 1993, respectively.

26 *Muhammad Nawaz Sharif v President of Pakistan*, PLD 1993 SC 473.

27 *Wasim Sajjad and others v Federation of Pakistan*, PLD 2001 SC 233. See also *Zafar Ali Shah and others v General Pervez Musharraf, Chief Executive of Pakistan*, PLD 2000 SC 869.

Musharraf's eligibility for the office of President for a second term again brought his government to a head-on collision with the superior judiciary. To avoid an apparent rejection of his candidature, Musharraf imposed emergency rule on 3 November 2007, dismissing Chief Justice Choudhry and about sixty other superior court judges. While Musharraf was successfully elected as President for a second term, his party suffered a stunning defeat in the general elections on 18 March 2008. Having remained under constant pressure since March 2007, Musharraf finally resigned in July 2008. Most of the military interventions were legitimized by the judiciary. Musharraf's emergency rule, too, was validated by the post-Chief Justice Choudhry Supreme Court.[28] This raised questions about the judiciary's independence and impartiality at key moments of constitutional crisis. One critic sarcastically observed, '[T]he Supreme Court had always upheld rule of law . . . even *Martial Law.*'[29] The present democratically elected government is facing almost the same challenges to achieve the goal of a true constitutional democracy.

It seems pertinent to describe two constitutional dilemmas. First: the Islamic concept of the state. Politicians and intellectuals are still sharply divided over the Islamic concept of the state. One group, which may be called the modernists, argues that Pakistan should be a modern secular state. The other group – Islamic activists – is of the view that Pakistan should be an Islamic state.[30] Pakistan's role in the Afghan *Jihad* against the former Soviet Union in the 1980s as well as the current 'war on terrorism' has further increased the tension between the Islamic activists and the modernists. The public at large see the role of the USA in Afghanistan and the hot pursuit of the Taliban in the tribal areas of Pakistan as an invasion and a grave threat to Islamic values.[31] This public reaction has led to a growing call for the promotion of Islamic values as a constitutional obligation of the state.[32]

28 *Tika Iqbal Muhammad v General Pervez Musharraf*, PLD 2008SC178.

29 Khalid Akhter, 'Judicial Glasnost', *The Muslim*, 3 Dec. 1989 (emphasis added), quoted in Mansoor Hassan Khan, 'The Concept of Public Interest Litigation and its Meaning in Pakistan', *PLD Journal*, 1992, 84.

30 The words: 'modernist' and 'Islamic activist' are borrowed from Charles H. Kennedy, 'Repugnancy to Islam – Who Decides? Islam and Legal Reform in Pakistan', *International and Comparative Law Quarterly* 41, 1992, 769–87. Some other words are also used, such as 'secularist' for the first group and 'traditionalist' and 'conservative' for the second group.

31 A survey conducted by a US-based independent poll organization – Terror Free Tomorrow – in August 2007 showed that 66 per cent of Pakistanis think the 'war against terror' is against Islam and Muslims. Online. Available at: <http://www.terrorfreetomorrow.org/upimagestft/Pakistan%20Poll%20Report.pdf> (accessed 14 Sept. 2007).

32 In recent years, a controversy has ensued between the Islamic activists and the modernists over women's rights and the *Hisba* bill. The Protection of Women (Criminal Laws Amendment) Act 2006 was passed by the parliament in 2006. The *Hisba* bill was passed by the *Muttahid Majlis-e-Amal* (MMA – a coalition of religious parties that ruled the NWFP from 2002 to 2007) in the provincial assembly on 13 Nov. 2006. The *Hisba* bill was initially passed by the NWFP Assembly in 2005. The President sought the opinion of

The second dilemma is federalism, involving the relationship between the centre and the provinces. It has been a complex and sensitive issue since independence. The equitable distribution of the natural resources of the provinces has been a source of dispute among the provinces, on the one side, and between the provinces and the centre, on the other. The constitution provides an institutional mechanism in the form of the Council of Common Interests and the National Economic Council. But these two institutions have yet to play an effective role in the promotion of federalism. The most pressing issues of federalism in Pakistan today are the royalties to the North West Frontier Province (NWFP) for its hydro-electric power resources, to Baluchistan for its natural gas wealth, and the dispute over the construction of a proposed Kalabagh dam. Other issues of federalism include the share of the provinces in the employment quota in the centre-controlled civil and military services, language and ethnicity. The Musharraf government proposed a law on provincial autonomy, which never saw the light of day. The present government has proposed a constitutional package, which is yet to be submitted to the parliament. The suspension of the Chief Justice – Iftikhar Choudhry – on 9 March 2007 and the imposition of a state of emergency on 3 November and the sacking of about sixty superior court judges, including the Chief Justice, created a constitutional crisis involving the executive–judiciary relationship.[33]

The above-noted challenges as well as constitutional dilemmas have deep repercussions for the RTD at the national level. Frequent political instability has obfuscated the chances of developing a genuine and healthy democratic culture in Pakistan. While an elected government was formed after the 2002 elections, real power remained vested in the office occupied by Musharraf. Genuine political participation was, therefore, not seen in the country. The policies on the war against terror were not taken through a process of democratic deliberations. Neither the parliament nor civil society was consulted in the formulation and implementation of these policies. The element of participation, a necessary ingredient of the RTD, was thus ignored. No doubt, economic growth is showing a relatively upward trend, but this is not accompanied by equity and justice, which are the linchpins of the RTD approach. Moreover, the current economic growth is unable to promote and realize all human rights and fundamental freedoms, particularly the rights to health and education. The lack of a true and meaningful federalism, too, has

the Supreme Court (Advisory Jurisdiction) on the bill. By its August 2005 decision, the Court declared that the bill violated fundamental rights such as the freedom of assembly and equality of citizens. The judgment is available at <www.supremecourt.gov.pk//judgment.htm> (accessed 29 Aug. 2007). The bill was amended to meet the deficiencies pointed out by the Court and again passed by the Assembly in 2006. The President also sought the opinion of the Court on the second bill. The Supreme Court found some parts of the bill to be in conflict with the Constitution.

33 The Chief Justice challenged the validity of the proceedings against him. A larger bench of the Court accepted his plea and on 20 July 2007 directed that he be reinstated.

negative consequences for the national dimension of the RTD. The royalties issue, referred to above, demonstrates that the state is unable to discharge its duty of ensuring the fair distribution of the benefits of its development policies.[34] The highly centralized legislative and executive authority of the central government denies the provinces the power of decision-making in the formulation, implementation and monitoring of development policies. Such a situation cannot encourage public participation as an essential element of the process of development, as envisaged by the Declaration. The control of the main core of the bureaucracy by the central government also badly affects public participation. Here a reference may be made to the Global Consultation on the RTD, which emphasized that 'excessive bureaucratization' is a hurdle to public participation in development.[35] This has created the need for urgent civil service reform. Despite an increase in the number of women's seats in the parliament and local government, the plight of women continues unabated. A recent incident of burying some young women alive in Baluchistan is a flagrant human rights violation and a denial of women's role in national life, in violation of Article 8(1) of the Declaration. In short, lack of democracy, misallocation and/or unfair distribution of resources, centralization and abuse of power and violation of women's rights are the main obstacles to the RTD in Pakistan.[36] Can the national dimension of the RTD address these obstacles?

THE NATIONAL DIMENSION OF THE RTD

The Declaration

According to the Declaration, the principal features of a national development policy are:[37]

- Effective and meaningful participation of the individual in the development process, including decision-making;[38]
- That the individual would have equal opportunity of access to resources;[39]
- Fair distribution of benefits that accrue from such a process of development;[40]

34 See the DRD, Art. 2(3).

35 The Global Consultation on the RTD, op. cit., para. 14.

36 See generally, Yash Ghai, 'Redesigning the State for "Right Development"' in B.A. Andreassen and Stephen Marks (eds), *Development as a Human Right, Legal, Political and Economic Dimensions*, Harvard School of Public Health, Cambridge, Massachusetts, Harvard University Press, 2006, pp 141–66.

37 See, generally, The Independent Expert, First Report, op. cit., para. 45.

38 DRD, Arts 1, 2(3) and 8.

39 Ibid. Art. 8.

40 Ibid. Arts 2 and 8.

- Respect for civil and political, as well as economic, social and cultural, rights;[41]
- Effective measures to ensure for women an active role in the development process.[42]

A national development policy should aim at realizing human rights in their totality. Owing to resource constraints, the implementation of rights may be prioritized. However, such prioritization should not be done in a manner that may lead to the improvement of one right and the violation or retrogression of another right.[43] It is necessary that a state accepts international human rights standards. In this respect, legislative and constitutional changes are necessary so that the state should guarantee the precedence of treaty law over internal law. Such changes should reflect the state's treaty obligation directly in the national legal order.[44] The states' policies should guarantee the availability of and access to goods and services for all, particularly the poor and vulnerable groups, who should have access to the productive assets. Availability depends on economic growth, whereas access means the distribution of resources and their benefits to all without any discrimination.[45] As an inalienable human right, the RTD is a right to a process of development, to which everyone is entitled. Such a process means a national programme or strategy for development.[46]

Pakistan's role in the mainstream RTD debate

Pakistan has been participating in the RTD discussions in the UN and other international forums. It was a member of the second working group and an observer in the first and third working groups. During the drafting of the Declaration, Pakistan proposed a new Article 4, as an amendment in the draft. The proposed amendment, which was aimed at the international dimension of the RTD, was rejected, but was adopted as a separate resolution of the General Assembly.[47] Pakistan has favoured all the General Assembly resolutions on the RTD and participated in several international conferences which have reiterated the RTD as a human right.[48] During a 1996 session

41 Ibid. Preamble and Arts 6 and 9.

42 Ibid. Art. 8.

43 Independent Expert, Second Report, para. 25; Third Report, para. 24.

44 See Report of the Inter-governmental Group of Experts on the Right to Development, E/CN.4/1998/29, para. 65.

45 Independent Expert, Fourth Report, para. 20. The property rights and legally acquired rights of people in conflict-ridden areas should be ensured.

46 Ibid.

47 UNGA Res. A/41/133.

48 These include, for example, the 1993 Vienna conference on human rights and the 1994 Cairo conference on population and development.

of the Commission, the Pakistani delegate suggested the appointment of a special rapporteur on the RTD 'with a mandate to review current economic and social policies of States and propose ways in which the [RTD] could be promoted universally'.[49] In a year 2000 address to the General Assembly, a Pakistani delegate said that the Millennium Declaration committed the world leaders to make the [RTD] a reality for everyone.[50] The eleventh workshop on regional cooperation for the promotion of human rights in the Asia–Pacific region, which was hosted by Pakistan in 2003, affirmed that all human rights, including the RTD, are indivisible, interdependent and interrelated.[51] In 2005, a Pakistani delegate stressed before the working group the importance of the international dimension of the RTD.[52] Pakistan has attended all except the 2006 session of the current RTD working group. It appears that Pakistan is playing a more active role in promoting the international dimension rather than the national dimension of the RTD.

The SAARC Social Charter makes the RTD one of its objectives. Pakistan's action plan under this charter does not explicitly refer to the RTD, but refers to a rights-based approach in governance reforms.[53] It is necessary to examine the main features of the RTD in the practice of Pakistan.

Constitutional mechanisms versus the features of the RTD

The constitution provides that subject to available resources, the state shall secure the well-being of all people by raising their standard of living and provide basic necessities of life, such as food, clothing, housing, education and medical relief, for all such citizens.[54] The Declaration proclaims that states have the duty to formulate appropriate national development policies that aim at the constant improvement and well-being of the entire population and of all individuals. Moreover, the state shall undertake all necessary measures for the realization of the [RTD] and shall ensure, *inter alia*, equality

49 See statement of the then Foreign Minister of Pakistan. Online. Available at: <http://www.scienceblog.com/community/older/archives/L/1996/A/un960574.html> (accessed 29 Nov. 2006).

50 See statement of the then Foreign Minister of Pakistan, in the UNGA on 18 Sept. 2000. Online. Available at: <http://www.un.org/ga/webcast/statements/pakistanE.htm> (accessed 29 Nov. 2006).

51 Available at: <http://www.unhchr.ch/html/menu6/islamabad.htm> (accessed 29 Nov. 2006).

52 See statement of the Deputy Permanent Representative of Pakistan. Online. Available at: <http://missions.itu.int/~pakistan/2005_Statements/CHR/CHR_Item_7_Statement_22_March_2005.htm> (accessed 29 Nov. 2006).

53 Pakistan Plan of Action to Implement SAARC Social Charter. Available at: <http://www.mopd.gov.pk/usefull%20links/Economics/SAARC%20SOCIAL%20CHARTER.pdf> (accessed 27 Feb. 2009).

54 The Constitution of Pakistan, Art. 38.

of opportunity for all in their access to basic resources, education, health services, food, housing, employment and fair distribution of income.[55]

The constitution guarantees fundamental rights, including equality before the law, freedom of thought, expression, belief, faith, worship and association, subject to law and public morality.[56] The Declaration, on the other hand, states that development is a comprehensive economic, social, cultural and political process. It further proclaims that human rights and fundamental freedoms are indivisible and interdependent.[57]

The constitution provides that steps shall be taken to ensure the full participation of women in all spheres of national life.[58] The Declaration also provides that the state should take effective measures to ensure that women have an active role in the process of development.[59]

The constitution obliges the state to enable the people of different areas to participate in all forms of national activities.[60] The Declaration, on the other hand, requires the state to encourage popular participation in all spheres as an important factor in development and in the full realization of all human rights.[61]

However, not all the features of the Declaration are reflected in the constitution. For example, the indivisibility and interdependence of human rights, as an important feature of the Declaration, is missing from the constitution.[62] The fundamental rights guaranteed in the constitution are mostly civil and political rights. Economic, social and cultural rights reflected in the Principles of Policy are subject to the availability of resources and are not justiciable.[63] The Declaration makes it a duty of the state to take steps to eliminate obstacles to development resulting from the failure to observe civil and political rights, as well as economic, social and cultural rights.[64] The constitution, on the other hand, provides no such mechanism for the elimination of obstacles that may arise from failure of respect for and observance of all human rights. Promotion and protection of human rights through a process of development is another feature of the Declaration that is absent in the constitution.

The nature of the constitutional obligations

The RTD may involve both perfect and imperfect obligations, but it is not necessary that both must be involved. The former are also understood as

55 DRD, Arts 2(3) and 8(1).
56 Ibid. The Objectives Resolution, paras 8 and 9.
57 DRD, Preamble para. 2 and Art. 6.2.
58 The Constitution, Art. 34.
59 Ibid. Art. 8(1).
60 The Constitution, Art. 37(f).
61 DRD, Art. 8(2). See also Arts 1(1), 2(1) and 2(3).
62 Ibid. Art. 6(2).
63 The Constitution, Arts 29 and 30.
64 DRD, Art. 6(3).

specific and justiciable, while the latter are understood as unspecific and non-justiciable. The enforcement of the fundamental rights and the Objectives Resolution (Art. 2-A) clearly requires perfect obligations. The superior courts have powers under the constitution and the local subordinate courts under the statutory laws, to protect fundamental rights. The responsibility for the implementation of the Principles of Policy lies on 'each organ and authority of the State, and [on] each person performing on behalf of an organ or authority of the State',[65] but it is not enforceable through a court of law.[66] Thus two of the three constitutional mechanisms, viz., the Objectives Resolution and the fundamental rights, create perfect obligations, while the third mechanism, i.e., the Principles of Policy, create imperfect obligations. Pakistan's current Poverty Reduction Strategy Paper (PRSP) is a development programme, which fits with the Principles of Policy, and therefore creates imperfect obligations. The strategy of the courts is two-pronged: firstly, to ensure that the state discharges its perfect obligations of protecting fundamental rights. Secondly, the courts interpret fundamental rights broadly enough so as to make them supplementary to the Principles of Policy. This strategy, adopted in the PIL, creates better prospects for the promotion of the RTD.

PUBLIC INTEREST LITIGATION: PROSPECTS FOR THE RTD

The concept of PIL is a new phenomenon of modern judicial systems that bridges the gap between law and socio-economic development. It emerged in the USA in the 1960s as a public interest law movement for securing welfare rights, such as the rights of the poor and unrepresented class, the protection of the environment, and the security of the interests of consumers, racial and ethnic minorities and others.[67] In South Asia, PIL emerged in India in the early 1980s and in Pakistan in the late 1980s.

Conceptual basis

Pakistan's true constitutional rule was marred by prolonged political instability. Fundamental rights were suspended during these constitutional crises and the superior courts had no authority to issue any writs to enforce them.[68]

65 Ibid. Art. 29(1).

66 Ibid. Art. 30(2).

67 Arun Ray, *Public Interest Litigation and Human Rights in India*, New Delhi, Radha Publications, 2003, p 70. See also Faqir Hussain, 'Public Interest Litigation in Pakistan', *PLD Journal 1993*, 72–83; Nasim Hassan Shah, 'Public Interest Litigation as a means of social justice', *PLD Journal 1993*, 31–4 at 34.

68 The last occasion on which fundamental rights were suspended was on 3 Nov. 2007 when the former president, General Musharraf, imposed a state of emergency.

After the revival of the constitution in 1985, the judiciary had an opportunity to respond to the challenge of protecting fundamental rights. The judges used PIL as a viable option 'to provide citizens with the opportunity to voice their opinions and redress their grievances – a responsibility in the first instance to the polity'.[69] The judicial approach of the mid-1980s revealed an appreciation of the need for a change in approach to protect the basic rights of the people. The speeches of the then Chief Justice show that the judiciary realized that social justice was the principal issue which the courts should uphold. From the perspective of sociological jurisprudence, the Chief Justice envisaged judicial activism through PIL as a means of social justice:

> [T]he function of adjudication is not only to solve disputes, but also to give meaning to public views . . . [T]his approach . . . indicates the importance of considering the dispute settlement process as a method of resolving social conflicts through the application of a system of flexible rules of law that should be meant to promote human welfare.[70]

The PIL movement continued in the 1990s, and in recent years it gained new vigour, particularly during the time of the Chief Justice Choudhry. In August 2006, the Supreme Court declared that its '*suo motu* jurisdiction . . . is a source of strength for the rule of law, good governance and awareness of legal rights'.[71] Thus the judiciary recognized their vital role in the contemporary scheme of governance.[72] How the judiciary in Pakistan exercised their legal authority to serve the cause of social justice can be judged by analysing selected case law.

An analysis of case law

Under the constitution, the traditional requirement of *locus standi* is not an impediment in the way of the Supreme Court if a matter is of public importance and involves the enforcement of a fundamental right.[73] Barring a few exceptions,[74] in the past, the courts refrained from taking *suo motu* action.[75] However, the trend was significantly changed in the well-known PIL case of

69 Paula R. Newberg, *Judging the State: Courts and Constitutional Politics in Pakistan*, Cambridge University Press, 1995, p 235.

70 Muhammad Haleem, 'Law, Justice and Society', *PLD Journal 1986*, 205–12.

71 *The News International*, Islamabad, 16 Aug. 2006.

72 Ray, op. cit., p 64.

73 Constitution of Pakistan, 1973, Art. 184(3). Under Art. 199(1)(a)(i), (ii) and (c)), *locus standi* is necessary for the exercise of power by the High Court except in cases of *habeas corpus* and *Quo warranto*.

74 *Mian Fazal Jan v Lahore Development Truts*, PLD 1969 SC 223 at p 231.

75 See, for example, *Tariq Transport Company, Lahore v Sargodha-Bhera Bus Service*, PLD 1958 SC 437; *Muhammad Botta v Commissioner Sargodha*, PLD 1973 Lah. 580; *Province of East Pakistan v M.D. Mehdi Ali Khan*, PLD 1959 SC 387; the court categorically ruled that

Benazir Bhutto in 1988. Ms Bhutto, the chairperson of Pakistan's People's Party, challenged certain amendments introduced in the Political Parties Act 1962, contending violation of fundamental rights: freedom of association[76] and equality of citizens.[77] *Locus standi* was set up as a preliminary objection. The court ruled that *locus standi* may be dispensed with in case of violation of fundamental rights of a class or a group of persons who are unable to seek redress from the court.[78]

The courts also relaxed the method of drafting a petition, the manner of its submission and the filing of the affidavit,[79] and the rules as to proof of claim. Thus actions were taken on a letter from residents of a certain area,[80] a telegram[81] and newspaper reports.[82] The court observed that its approach should be dynamic, progressive and liberal in the PIL cases. The latest case law demonstrates that any member of the public can maintain an action for judicial redress of a public injury arising from the violation of a constitutional provision, or a law or a public duty.[83]

Right to life (Article 9)

The interpretation of this right by the courts is wide enough to serve the purpose of the RTD. In *Shehla Zia*, the Supreme Court held:

> The word 'life' in the Constitution has not been used in a limited manner. A wide meaning should be given to *enable a man not only to sustain life but to enjoy it* . . . the Constitution guarantees dignity of man [Article 14] and also right to 'life' under Article 9 and if both are read together, [the question] will arise whether a person can be said to have [the] dignity of man if his right to *life is below bare necessity* [*i.e. without*] *proper food, clothing, shelter, education, health care, clean atmosphere and unpolluted environment*.[84]

In *Pakistan Chest Foundation*, the court banned cigarette commercials on electronic media as part of the right to life.[85] These decisions are unique for

the petitioner cannot move the court *pro bono publico*, p 408; *Akhtar Abbas v Nayyar Hussain*, 1982 SCMR 549. See also *Tariq Transport Company, Lahore v Sargodha-Bhera Bus Service*, PLD 1958 SC 437.

76 The 1973 Constitution, Art. 17.

77 Ibid. Art. 25.

78 *Benazir Bhutto v Federation of Pakistan*, PLD 1988 SC 416 at p491. See also *Ardeshir Cowasjee v Multiline Associates, Karachi*, PLD 1993 Kar. 237, p 253.

79 Human Rights Cases Nos 9 and 20 of 1992 in Hussain, op. cit., 80.

80 *Shehla Zia v WAPDA*, PLD 1994 SC 693.

81 *Darshan Masih v The State*, PLD 1990 SC 513.

82 *The State v Senior Superintendent of Police*, PLD 1991 Lah. 224.

83 *Wattan Party v Federation of Pakistan*, PLD 2006 SC 697.

84 PLD 1994 SC 693 at p 714 (emphasis added).

85 1997 CLC 1379.

the RTD in many respects. Firstly, they give a liberal interpretation to the term 'life', and recognize the right to a clean environment, which is not specifically guaranteed in the constitution. Secondly, as is clear from the italicized parts in the above quoted passage, they complement many rights including the rights to food, education and health, nominated by the Independent Expert on the RTD for immediate action. Thirdly, the scope of the right to life as one of the civil and political rights is extended to both second- and third-generation rights, e.g., the rights to education, health and a decent standard of living (economic and social rights) and the right to a clean environment (third generation). In this way, the court's rulings may be seen as having endorsed the indivisibility and interdependence of human rights. The obligation of the state for the promotion of these rights falls within the ambit of the Principles of Policy. Here a perfect obligation to ensure the right to life is extended from mere personal security to a dignified life that requires a range of policy measures on the part of the state. Fourthly, arguably, these decisions may be interpreted as being consistent with the capabilities approach. As Sen would argue, the prime concern is the capability not only to live but to live long and to have a good life.[86]

Prohibition of forced labour (Article 11)

Pakistan, as a signatory to many international instruments regarding forced labour, also has international obligations regarding the abolition of bonded labour.[87] The Supreme Court examined this issue closely in *Darshan Masih*. Action was taken on a telegram sent by bonded labourers working in brick-kilns. The labourers contended that they had been illegally detained by their employers. The Court advised the government to pass the necessary legislation to abolish bonded labour in the country. As a result, the government enacted the Bonded Labour System (Abolition) Act, 1992.[88] The Act prohibits any custom, tradition, agreement or contract that allows bonded labour.[89]

86 Sen, *Development as Freedom*, op. cit., p 14.

87 The UN Supplementary Convention on the Abolition of Slavery, the Slave Trade, and Institutions and Practices similar to Slavery, 1956. The Convention was ratified by Pakistan in 1958; ILO Convention No. 29 concerning Forced Labour, 1930, ratified by Pakistan in 1957; ILO Convention No.105 concerning the Abolition of Forced Labour, 1957 ratified by Pakistan in 1960; the 1989 UN Convention on the Rights of the Child, Article 32 of which guarantees children's protection from economic exploitation and from performing any work that is likely to be hazardous or to interfere with the child's education. The Convention was ratified by Pakistan in 1990.

88 The Bonded Labour System (Abolition) Rules 1995 were also framed.

89 Section 5 of the Act reads: 'Any custom or tradition or practice or any contract, agreement or other instrument, whether entered into or executed before or after the commencement of this Act, by virtue of which any person, or any member of his family, is required to do any work or render any service as a bonded labourer, shall be void and inoperative.'

In this case, the Court interpreted the right to life as including freedom of movement, freedom of trade, business or profession and equality of citizens. This case has had a positive impact on the promotion of the RTD in Pakistan. Firstly, the intervention of the Court in the matter indicates that the government failed to protect the fundamental rights of its citizens. Respect for human rights and fundamental freedom is a key feature of the Declaration. Secondly, the Court's direction to the government to pass the necessary legislation indicates the failure of the government to discharge its constitutional (imperfect) obligations under Article 37 of the Principles of Policy, which provides that the state shall promote social justice and eradicate social evils, including ensuring just and humane conditions of work. Thus the Court's decision transformed an imperfect obligation into a perfect obligation. Thirdly, the Court's ruling, that the recovery of the *peshgi* amount through a normal civil suit will create problems (such as engaging a lawyer) for the bonded labourers, reflects how the present adversarial system of litigation in Pakistan affects the right of the extremely poor to access justice. Although there is no reference to the Declaration or any other international instruments, the ruling of the Court clearly resonates with the report of the Global Consultation, which says that legal assistance to the extremely poor, the bonded labourers in the present context, is one of the elements of the RTD as a human right at the national level.[90]

In the 2006 *Human Rights Case No. 5091*, the Court took action on the complaint of a detained labourer, sent by post, and ordered 18 bonded labourers to be set free. The Court recommended: firstly, that section 5 of the Act should be reviewed by the legislature. The Court made this recommendation while taking notice of the fact that the culprits had attempted to avoid criminal liability on different pretexts, including that the labourers were working voluntarily at the brick-kiln. The Court directed that provincial governments shall adhere strictly to section 5 of the Act. Secondly, the provincial governments were directed to adopt a system for the registration of brick-kilns and to adopt a regular record of their workforce. Thirdly, the police and local government institutions were directed to ensure the implementation of the Act if any violation were reported to them. The Court further advised that provincial governments could seek assistance from the Free Legal Aid Committees working in all provinces under the control of Provincial Bar Councils.

Pakistan's current PRSP has proposed a number of policy interventions to eliminate bonded labour, notably to make the laws on bonded labour consistent with international human rights standards.[91] It appears that despite these

90 See the Global Consultation, para.120.

91 Others are: to undertake a series of purposive studies; to provide training to District *Nazims* (head of a district government) and members of the Vigilance Committees on human rights and bonded labour concerns; and to develop a partnership with the stakeholders, employers, and workers to secure a more harmonious relationship. See Pakistan's Poverty Reduction Strategy Paper, para. 6.25.

policy measures, things have not changed. There are 1.7 million bonded labourers in the country.[92] The Act is 'extremely poorly enforced'.[93] The Court made no reference to the Principles of Policy. However, the impact of the above-mentioned recommendations for the Principles of Policy is that they may help secure just and humane working conditions and ensure equitable adjustment between employers and employees.[94] Moreover, the recommendations will further augment the policy measures proposed in the PRSP.

Freedom of association (Article 17): political participation

In 1989 Ms Bhutto challenged[95] certain legal requirements regarding election symbols.[96] The Court ruled that the issue of election symbols was a part of the right to form a political party under Article 17(2) of the constitution. In *Nawaz Sharif*, the Court held that freedom of association not only includes the right:

> [T]o form a political party, contest elections under its banner but also, after successfully contesting the elections, the right to form Government if . . . in possession of the requisite majority . . . the dismissal of the Prime Minister [and] the National Assembly [are] violative of Fundamental Right 17.[97]

In 1993, the government of the Prime Minister, Nawaz Sharif and the National Assembly were dismissed by the President of Pakistan. Nawaz Sharif challenged the dismissal. The Court held the dismissal action to be illegal and restored the government led by Nawaz Sharif. In this case, political participation was recognized as a right.

From the perspective of the RTD, it may be argued that the Court recognized the role of participation. Although the Court did not mention the RTD, recognition of participation has positive implications for the RTD. The following observations of the Court are worth noting here: 'No section of the citizenry no matter how small it might be, should be deprived of equal participation in the national life.'[98] In the context of the RTD, participation in politics is not strictly different from participation in development.

92 Human Rights Commission of Pakistan (HRCP), *The State of Human Rights, 2006*, p 251. Online. Available at: <http://www.hrcp-web.org/ar_home_05.cfm> (accessed 27 June 2007).

93 Ibid.

94 The 1973 constitution, Arts 37 and 38.

95 *Benazir Bhutto and another v Federation of Pakistan and another*, PLD 1989 SC 66.

96 The Representation of People Act 1962 was challenged.

97 *Muhammad Nawaz Sharif v President of Pakistan*, PLD 1993 SC 443.

98 Ibid.

Equality of citizens (Article 25)

Regarding equality rights, two cases may be mentioned here. In *Azizullah Memon*, the Court found that a tribal law of Baluchistan Province contravened, among others, Article 25.[99] In *Al-Jehad Trust*, it was held that fundamental rights must be extended to Northern Areas of Pakistan.[100] Both cases made references to international human rights law. In the former case, the Court took a broader view of equality before the law and access to justice and referred to Article 10 of the UDHR and Article 14 of the ICCPR – the right to a fair trial by an independent and impartial tribunal established by law. In this case, too, the Court emphasized the need for progressive and dynamic interpretation of the Constitution.

In the latter case, the Court observed: 'even under the [UDHR], to which Pakistan is a signatory, human beings have some basic fundamental rights irrespective of their origin or status'.[101] The Court also made reference to Articles 1–13, 15 and 21 of the UDHR and reproduced them in its judgment. The Court extended human rights to a group of people of a particular area. For the people of tribal areas, these decisions opened up new vistas of social justice based on the equality of all citizens.[102] The extension of fundamental rights to the people of the underdeveloped areas is helpful in facilitating people's participation in development.[103] Moreover, the reference to the UDHR indicates that the Court wants the state to respect its obligation under international human rights instruments.

Women's rights

Article 25 also prohibits discrimination on the basis of sex. However, the moves towards Islamization of the law and society have important implications for women's rights, particularly in family and criminal laws. As argued above, the role of Islam in the constitutional framework of Pakistan is a constitutional dilemma. The issue of women's rights in Islam is a serious and contentious issue between the modernists and the Islamic activists. Pakistan has also acceded to the Women's Convention, with the reservation that the Convention is subject to Pakistan's constitution. Women's rights activists are pursuing various strategies for reforms at the legislative and policy levels.[104] The Women's Protection Act 2006, which replaced the controversial *Hudood* law, is an example in point.

99 PLD 1993 SC 341. Baluchistan (Criminal Law (Special Provisions) Ordinance (II of 1968)).

100 1999 SCMR 1379.

101 Ibid. p 1393.

102 Asif Saeed Khan Khosa, 'Judiciary's Role towards Promotion of Social Justice: The Pakistan Experience', PLD 1995 SC Journal Section, 79–102 at 85.

103 Siobhan Mullally, ' "As Nearly as May Be": Debating Women's Human Rights in Pakistan', *Social & Legal Studies* 14(3), 2005, 341–58, at 342.

104 Ibid.

The superior courts have also interpreted various fundamental rights, particularly Article 25, to protect women's rights, such as the rights to free legal aid and access to justice,[105] property, particularly in inheritance,[106] and education.[107] The courts have also intervened in criminal matters involving women's status. A noteworthy example is a *suo motu* notice of an increase in the number of women being killed apparently because of the bursting of oil stoves used for cooking purposes.[108] The Court conducted an investigation itself and summoned the family of a deceased female, the police department, stove manufacturers, and other concerned governmental and non-governmental agencies, to ensure that such incidents should not occur in future. The Court also held that the right to life includes a happy and joyful married life, criticizing police highhandedness in treating a married woman.[109] There are a large number of unreported cases regarding women's status in which *suo motu* actions were taken by courts, particularly in relation to police excesses against women.[110] These cases, which involved various human rights such as the rights to property, education and life, ensured inexpensive and expeditious justice, which is an obligation of the state under the Principles of Policy. The political participation of women has increased as 43,000 women were elected as councillors in local government elections in 2005.[111] However, the protection of women's rights (the fundamental rights provisions) and ensuring their full participation in all spheres of national life (the Principles of Policy and Art. 8 of the Declaration) still remain challenging tasks for Pakistan.

Protection of the environment

Pakistan is committed to sustainable development. This is clear from its PRSP.[112] PIL has also been effectively and meaningfully extended to the right to a clean environment despite the fact that the constitution does not recognize such a right. The leading cases are *Shehla Zia*, discussed above, and the *Human Rights Case (Environmental Pollution in Baluchistan)*.[113] In the latter case, the Court took action on its own regarding the dumping of nuclear waste in Baluchistan. In both cases, the Court interpreted the right to life

105 *Fazal Jan v Roshan Din*, PLD 1992 SC 811.
106 *Ghulam Ali v Mst. Ghulam Sarwar Naqvi*, PLD 1990 SC 1.
107 *Shirin Munir v Government of Punjab*, PLD 1990 SC 295.
108 *State v Senior Superintendent of Police*, Lahore, PLD 1991 Lah. 224.
109 *Sajida Bibi v Incharge, Chouki No. 2 Police Station Saddar, Sahiwal*, PLD 1997 Lah. 666, p 670.
110 Khan, op. cit., pp 89–90.
111 HRCP, op. cit., p 200.
112 See Pakistan's Poverty Reduction Strategy Paper, paras 6.27–6.32. See also Government of Pakistan's National Environmental Policy, 2005.
113 PLD 1994 SC 102. Pakistan introduced the Environmental Protection Act in 1997, which replaced the Environmental Protection Ordinance of 1983.

broadly enough so as to include the right to a clean environment. In the former case, the Court also directed the Water and Power Development Authority (WAPDA) to initiate public consultation procedures along the lines of the USA Public Service Commission, to hear complaints before commencing its work on the projects. In *Shehla Zia*, due to the absence of clear scientific proof, the Court followed the precautionary principle of environmental law and relied on Principle 15 of the Rio Declaration.[114] The following remarks of the Court regarding the binding force of the Rio Declaration are relevant here:

> Pakistan is a signatory to this Declaration . . . although it has not been ratified or enacted, the principle so adopted has its own sanctity and should be implemented, if not in letter, at least in spirit. An international agreement between the nations if signed by any country is always subject to ratification, but it can be enforced as a law only when legislation is made by the country through its legislature. Without framing a law in terms of the international agreement the covenants of such agreement cannot be implemented as a law nor do they bind down any party. This is the legal position of such documents, but the fact remains that they have a persuasive value and command respect . . . environment is an international problem and every nation has to cooperate and contribute and for this reason the Rio Declaration would serve as a great binding force.

This case is closely related to the RTD. Firstly, the recognition of the right to a clean environment provides a good precedent for the RTD. Both are third-generation human rights, not recognized in the constitution. Secondly, the Court's reliance on the Rio Declaration creates a possibility for reliance on the RTD Declaration in similar cases in future. Moreover, the Court's view that the Rio Declaration has a persuasive value suggests that it is not willing to regard similar Declarations, including the RTD Declaration, as legally binding instruments. Thirdly, it gives jural authority to the right of participation in the decision-making process of development projects. Hence, it has a direct nexus with a rights-based approach to development.

Moulvi Iqbal Haider is a recent example of recognition of public participation in development projects.[115] In this PIL case, the Capital Development Authority (CDA) leased a public park to a private business enterprise for conversion into a commercial park. The Court held that the CDA denied the general public and other stakeholders the opportunity of consultation in the process of decision-making. Environmental protection was not a direct issue

114 Principle 15 of the Rio Declaration reads: 'Where there are threats of serious or irreversible damage, lack of full scientific certainty shall not be used as a reason for postponing cost-effective measures to prevent environmental degradation.' The Rio Declaration was endorsed by the General Assembly, see UNGA Res. A/47/190.

115 *Moulvi Iqbal Haider v Capital Development Authority*, PLD 2006 SC 394.

in this case. However, the emphasis laid down on participation has implications for environmental protection. The Environmental Protection Act 1997 provides that every review of an environmental impact assessment shall be carried out with public participation.

The Principles of Policy

The Principles of Policy, which reveal a charter of social and economic justice, are not justiciable. However, case law suggests that PIL jurisprudence has been extended into this domain as well. In a number of cases, the courts expressly referred to the Principles of Policy while dealing with fundamental rights issues. While interpreting the constitution, the approach of the Court, notably in the *Benazir Bhutto* and *Nawaz Sharif* cases, was based on the following principles. Firstly, the court followed the rule of dynamism, i.e. the constitution should be interpreted keeping in view the demands of a progressive society. Thus in *Benazir Bhutto*, the Court remarked that its approach of progressive interpretation of the constitution 'is in tune with the era of progress and is meant to establish that the Constitution is not merely an imprisonment of the past, but is also alive to the unfolding of the future'.[116] Secondly, different parts of the constitution have to be read in harmony with one another. Following this rule of harmony in *Benazir Bhutto*, the Court held that the fundamental rights and the Principles of Policy 'are the conscience of the Constitution, as they constitute the main thrust of the commitment to socio-economic justice'.[117] The rule of harmony was also followed in other cases.[118] Thirdly, the Court adopted the rule of consistency. Thus it was held that while implementing the directive Principles of Policy, the state is under an obligation to make no law that removes or abridges fundamental rights.[119] The Court also held that the Principles of Policy are, in an indirect sense, justiciable.

In a *suo motu* action regarding a rape case, reference was made to Articles 31, 34, 37 and 38 of the Principles of Policy.[120] The Court stressed the importance of launching social uplift programmes in rural areas to improve the conditions of the poor and illiterate people especially womenfolk, in accordance with Islamic principles.

The Principles of Policy were also expressly relied upon in *Mst. Zaib-un-Nisa*[121] and *Mst. Saima v The State*.[122] In the former case, the petitioner was

116 PLD 1988 SC 416, at 490.

117 PLD 1988 SC 416, at p 489.

118 *Aziz Sheikh v The Commissioner of Income-Tax Investigation, Lahore*, PLD 1989 SC 613, at p 625; *Shirin Munir v Government of Punjab*, PLD 1990 SC 295.

119 PLD 1988 SC 416.

120 *Mst. Nasreen v Fayyaz Khan*, PLD 1991 SC 412.

121 *Mst. Zaib-un-Nisa v Government of the Punjab, Education Department*, 1995 CLC 1281, p 1284.

122 PLD 2003 Lah. 747.

appointed by the Metropolitan Corporation, Lahore, as a teacher, but she was not paid a salary for more than two years. The Court ruled that by not paying a salary to the petitioner, the Education Department of the Punjab acted contrary to Article 38 of the Principles of Policy. In the latter case, the Court relied on Article 35 of the Principles of Policy along with Article 16 of the Women's Convention.

It is clear from the foregoing analysis that the superior courts consider the Principles of Policy as supplementary to the fundamental rights. In none of the cases above did the courts make reference to the availability of resources for realization of the Principles of Policy. This shows that the courts believe that even with resource constraints, the executive could meet the specified obligation either by reallocating the resources or by improving the efficiency of the resources. Though the Principles of Policy are not expressly referred to in each and every PIL case, yet a wider interpretation of fundamental rights does have implications for such principles. Moreover, the rules of interpretation of the constitution, viz., dynamism, harmony and consistency, allow room for the Principles of Policy.

Problems and prospects of PIL

While PIL is a helpful tool of social justice, it has problems. Firstly, there is a danger of abuse by private interests. Alive to this danger, courts have always taken into account the bona fides of the petitioner and cautioned that vexatious and frivolous petitions may lead to an abuse of the process of the court.[123] Secondly, the implementation of decisions is another problem of PIL. Notwithstanding the judgments of the courts, the situation has not changed; blatant violations of human rights still continue.[124] For instance, the bonded labourers' conditions remain extremely poor. Thirdly, the courts' views in similar cases are inconsistent. For example, in 2002, the Sindh High Court dismissed as many as 94 cases of bonded labourers. Blatant violations of women's rights, particularly honour killings, continue. Fourthly, a lack of resources is another impediment to the process of implementation. The constitution provides that the Principles of Policy are dependent on the availability of resources.[125] Pakistan has no case law regarding such a plea.[126] However, in some cases, Indian courts have rejected the plea of lack of funds.[127]

123 *Tariq Saeed v Director, Anti-Corruption Establishment*, 1996 MLD 1864.

124 Centre for Development and Human Rights, *The Right to Development: A Primer*, New Delhi/London, Sage, 2005, p 247.

125 The 1973 constitution, Art. 29(2).

126 Werner Menski et al, *Public Interest Litigation in Pakistan*, Karachi, Pakistan Law House/Platinum Publishing, 2000, p 86.

127 *Municipal Council, Ratlam v Shri Vardichand and Others*, 1980, quoted in Centre for Development and Human Rights, op. cit., p 242; *Kishen Pattanayak v State of Orissa*, AIR 1989 SC 677, quoted in Menski, et al, op. cit., p 85.

Fifthly, the courts' jurisdiction in PIL cases is limited to fundamental rights. Thus PIL provides a 'piecemeal approach to justice [that] does not allow for implementation of comprehensive and systematic human rights agenda'.[128] Sixthly, commentators argue that protection of one human right by way of PIL may sometimes lead to violation of other human rights.[129] For example, the closure of a pollution-creating industry protects the right to a clean environment, but violates the right to livelihood of its workers.[130] Such a situation contradicts the RTD approach, which requires that protection of one right shall not violate any other.[131]

There is also a lack of awareness about PIL in the legal community. International human rights instruments are rarely referred to by courts. The Declaration has never been cited in any case. In neighbouring India, the highest court specifically referred to the Declaration in one case only.[132]

Finally, it is also argued that PIL may lead to judiciary–executive confrontation.[133] In light of the current judicial crisis in Pakistan, this issue needs to be separately examined vis-à-vis the RTD.

Impact of the current judicial crisis

Judges have clarified that while dealing with PIL cases, 'they are not acting as [a] parallel government'.[134] Despite this, it appears that PIL led to the creation of confrontation between the executive and judiciary. The Judicial Conference, held in August 2006, reiterated the importance of PIL. However, as noted above, Chief Justice Choudhry was suspended on 9 March 2007 and then dismissed along with sixty other judges on 3 November 2007, when emergency rule was imposed. Judicial activism led by Justice Choudhry was used as one of the justifications for the imposition of emergency rule in two respects: firstly, the judiciary's role with respect to the government's fight against terrorism; and secondly, judicial interference in government policy and bureaucracy.[135] Regarding the first, the Proclamation of Emergency reads:

> Some members of the judiciary are working at cross purposes with the executive and legislature in the fight against terrorism and extremism

128 Centre for Development and Human Rights, op. cit., p 249.

129 Ibid. p 248.

130 *M.C. Mehta v Union of India and Others*, AIR 1996 SC 2231; *Almitra H. Patel v Union of India*, 2000, 3 SCC 166, quoted in Centre for Development and Human Rights, op. cit.

131 Ibid. p 248.

132 Ibid. p 243.

133 Ray, op. cit., p 75.

134 P.N. Bhagwati, 'Judicial Activism and Public Interest Litigation', *Columbia Journal of Transnational Law* 23(3), 1985, 561–75 at 576; Haleem, op. cit., 211.

135 *Tika Iqbal Muhammad Khan v General Pervez Musharraf*, PLD 2008 SC 615, at 619–20.

> thereby weakening the Government and the nation's resolve and diluting the efficacy of its actions to control this menace.

With respect to the second, the relevant paragraph is as follows:

> The humiliating treatment meted out to government officials by some members of the judiciary on a routine basis during court proceedings has demoralized the civil bureaucracy and senior government functionaries, to avoid being harassed, prefer inaction.

Upholding these and many other justifications, the Supreme Court ruled that judicial activism pursued by Chief Justice Choudhry eroded the trichotomy, i.e. the separation of the powers under the Constitution. The Court held:

> Unfortunately, some members of the superior judiciary by way of judicial activism transgressed the constitutional limits and ignored the well-entrenched principle of judicial restraint. Thousands of applications involving individual grievances were being processed as suo motu cases ostensibly in the exercise of power under Article 184(3) of the Constitution, which provision is resorted to [for] the enforcement of fundamental rights involving questions of law of general public importance.[136]

The Court also observed that 'the former Chief Justice [Iftikhar Choudhry] interfered [with] and interrupted the working of each and every department/office of the government'.[137] Since 3 November 2007, the number of *suo motu* notices has been significantly reduced. In recent months, the PIL movement has lost the vigour that was seen before that date. It was argued above that the PIL movement has positive prospects for RTD-friendly human rights jurisprudence. It appears that a decline in the PIL movement will have a negative impact on a rights-based jurisprudence, particularly the RTD. Arguably, however, the decline may not last long. Firstly, in recent years, PIL has gained a high degree of populism, notably due to increasing awareness about the rule of law and good governance in civil society as well as the role of an increasingly free electronic media in Pakistan. With the lawyers' movement for the restoration of Chief Justice Choudhry and other deposed judges continuing unabated, this populism appears likely to grow more in future. Secondly, economic underdevelopment and political instability coupled with dysfunctional public institutions will create justifications for intervention by the Court. Indeed, as argued above, in numerous cases the Court has expanded the fundamental rights to the Principles of Policy in matters of public

136 *Tika Iqbal Muhammad Khan v General Pervez Musharraf*, PLD 2008 SC 615, at 625; also see PLD 2008 SC 178.

137 Ibid. p 633.

importance. Thirdly, some of the deposed judges have now been restored. The possibility of their resorting to PIL in future cannot be absolutely ruled out.

CONCLUSION

This chapter has argued that while the RTD is not explicitly recognized in the constitution of Pakistan, most of its key features are compatible with the Objectives Resolution, the fundamental rights and the Principles of Policy. Pakistan supports the RTD in the UN, but only its international dimension. This reflects a lack of commitment to recognizing and implementing the RTD at the national level. However, the three constitutional mechanisms mentioned above create both perfect and imperfect obligations for the state institutions to pursue an RTD-based programme of development. Frequent political instability and constitutional dilemmas have had negative effects on the development of the RTD in Pakistan. The chapter has established that superior courts can play a vital role in the promotion of the RTD at the national level by broadly interpreting the fundamental rights, particularly through PIL. In other words, PIL jurisprudence creates scope for the promotion of the RTD. The reiteration of PIL in the 2006 International Judicial Conference widened this scope. PIL has the potential to influence legislative measures and policy options to promote the RTD within the framework of the constitution. This movement may, therefore, help Pakistan to go along with the suggestions of the Independent Expert on the RTD regarding legislative and constitutional changes for implementing the RTD at the national level. There is little or no reference to international human rights instruments in the case law (and no reference to the Declaration at all). This reflects partly a lack of awareness on the part of legal and judicial professionals and partly the recognition of the fact that the international instruments, in the form of declarations, are not regarded by courts as legally binding. Awareness of international human rights instruments, including the Declaration, may enable the petitioner(s) or other PIL activists to press into service, or even for the courts to take into consideration, Pakistan's obligation under international human rights instruments, including the Declaration. The post-emergency situation appears to make the future of PIL uncertain. However, there are some positive factors, which may limit the negative influence of the current judicial crisis on PIL and thereby the RTD. The next chapter examines the RTD in Pakistan from the perspective of the Islamic concept of social justice.

7 Reconceptualizing the RTD in Islamic law

INTRODUCTION

The purpose of this chapter is to examine the concept of the RTD in Pakistan from the perspective of Islamic law (the *Shari'ah*). The chapter mainly examines the role of the *Shari'ah* in the promotion of the RTD and the implications of the struggles for Islamization on the promotion of the RTD in Pakistan. Islam is the state religion of Pakistan. The 1973 constitution of Pakistan has many clear provisions, which provide for the establishment of an Islamic society. The Objectives Resolution proclaims: 'the principles of democracy, freedom, equality, tolerance and social justice, as enunciated by Islam, shall be fully observed in Pakistan.' This clause indicates that Islam shall be the guiding principle for the whole political system of Pakistan. The role of Islam in the political system, however, remains the most challenging task. The military regime of General Zia-ul-Haq (1977–1988) launched a widespread Islamization movement, which led to concerns being raised at home and abroad, particularly by human rights activists.

This chapter looks at the meaning, sources and purpose of the *Shari'ah*. It then examines the Islamization movement of the Zia regime, its implications for the RTD and the role of the judiciary in the interpretation of the Islamic laws introduced as part of Islamization. It is argued that the purpose of the *Shari'ah* is *maslahah* (promotion of public interest and welfare and the prevention of harm). It then looks at whether the principles and institutions of the *Shari'ah* may promote the RTD even if there remain some differences between the two. Finally, the chapter examines the implications of the doctrine of *maslahah* for other Muslim countries.

SHARI'AH: MEANING, SOURCES AND PURPOSE

Meaning of the *Shari'ah*

According to Ahmad Zaki Yamani, '[t]he word [*Shari'ah*] literally means "the path to follow", and it is the name given to the all-embracing legal system that regulates the lives of Muslim everywhere.'[1] Esposito defines *Shariʿah* as:

> [A] comprehensive law or way of life governing all of man's activities, both his duties to God (*ibadat*) such as worship and fasting, and his duties to his fellow man (*muʾamalat*) which encompass both public and private law . . . [it is a] divine guidance for the individual and the national community.[2]

In a socio-political context, the *Shariʿah* 'is an essential expression of Islam that supplies the vital link between its faith and the socio-political order'.[3] It is clear from the above views that the *Shariʿah* is a body of Islamic law, which covers both the spiritual and temporal aspects of the lives of Muslims. In other words, for a Muslim, nothing lies outside *Shariʿah*. It is a complete code of life. Sometimes, the nature of the *Shariʿah* is confused with its sources and methods.[4] The *Shariʿah* refers to the principal sources of the revealed text of the law – the Qurʾan and the Sunnah.[5] The word *fiqh* (literally: understanding) is used for the methods of the *Shariʿah*. *Fiqh* is the work of jurists (*fuqaha*) aimed at the elaboration, interpretation and application of the revealed text of the law.[6] The *Shariʿah* is divine and immutable, while *fiqh* may change as time and circumstances demand.[7] Islamic law is the sum total of the *Shariʿah* and *fiqh*.[8] The difference between the *Shariʿah* and *fiqh* is of relatively recent origin in the history of Islamic jurisprudence. In the classical literature of Islamic law, the word '*Shariʿah*' was used for all Islamic legislation.[9]

As the *Shariʿah* developed with the passage of time, four major schools (*madhabs*) of Islamic jurisprudence in the majority Sunni sect emerged. They were: Hanafi, Shafi, Maliki and Hanbali.[10] In the Shia sect, *Ithna Ashari*

1 Ahmad Zaki Yamani, 'The Eternal Sharia', *New York University Journal of International Law and Politics* 12, 1979, 205–12, at 205.

2 John L. Esposito, 'Perspectives on Islamic Law Reform: The Case of Pakistan', *New York University Journal of International Law and Politics*, 13(1), 1980, 217–45 at 218–19.

3 Quoted in Deina Abdelkader, *Social Justice in Islam*, Herndon, Virginia, USA, International Institute of Islamic Thought, 2000, p 44.

4 Baderin, op. cit., 2003, p 33.

5 The terms Qurʾan and Sunnah are explained in Chapter 1 and will be further explained below.

6 Baderin, op. cit., p 34. See also 'Islamic Law' in John L. Esposito (ed.), *Oxford Dictionary of Islam*, Oxford, Oxford University Press, 2003 (hereinafter *Oxford Dictionary of Islam*). Online. Available at: <http://www.oxfordreference.com/views/ENTRY.html?subview=Main&entry=t125.e1107> (accessed 11 Jan. 2007).

7 Ibid.

8 Ibid.

9 See 'Shariah', *Oxford Dictionary of Islam*, op. cit.

10 Abu Hanifah (699–767 C.E./80–148 A.H.), Al-Shafi (767–820 C.E./150–204 A.H.), Malik Ibn Anas (715–795 C.E./93–179 A.H.) and Ahmad Ibn Hanbal (780–855 C.E./164–241 A.H.) were the leading jurists after whom the four Sunni schools were named.

(Twelvers; twelve *imams*), the *Zaydi* and the *Ismaili* appeared as the major schools.[11] Sunnis and Shias differ on who has the power to interpret the *Shari'ah*. Sunnis hold the view that the scholars had this right.[12] Shias initially gave this right only to an *imam* (the ruler), who should be a descendant of the Prophet.[13] 'When the line of the appropriate descendants ended, this tradition was reinterpreted to grant judicial authority to the *fuqaha* [jurists] as the imam's representatives.'[14]

The four Sunni schools have differences of opinion on legal matters, but their principles of law are substantially the same. Similarly, the Shia schools differ from each other in some details, but generally have a common vision of the law. Sunnis and Shias have a consensus on some aspects of the *Shari'ah*. All the schools of jurisprudence agree that the Qur'an and the Sunnah are the primary sources of the *Shari'ah*. The arguments of this chapter are based on the Sunni jurisprudence of the Hanafi School, which is the predominant School in Pakistan.

Primary sources: the Qur'an and the Sunnah

The formal or primary sources of the *Shari'ah* are the Qur'an and the Sunnah. The Qur'an is believed to be the exact word of God, revealed to Prophet Muhammad (may God's blessings be upon him). It is not strictly a legal code, but contains some legal rules in some parts. Scholars are not unanimous about the exact number of legal texts in the Qur'an.[15] The words of the Qur'an are immutable for Muslims, who are bound to obey and follow them in letter and spirit. The Qur'an says: 'Verily this is a Revelation from the Lord of the Worlds.'[16] 'This Qur'an is not such as can be produced by other than Allah.'[17]

A.H. stands for After Hijra (migration); C.E. means Christian Era. The Islamic calendar started from the time of the migration of the Prophet Muhammad (may God's blessings be upon him) from Makkah to Madina, which took place in 622 C.E.

11 Baderin, op. cit. p 38.

12 See 'Islamic Law', *Oxford Dictionary of Islam*, op. cit.

13 Ibid.

14 Ibid.

15 Kamali argues that 350 to 500 verses describe the legal texts, see M. Hashim Kamali, *Principles of Islamic Jurisprudence*, Cambridge, Islamic Text Society, 2000, pp 19–20. See also Kamali, 'Sources, Nature and Objective of Shari'ah', *Islamic Quarterly* 33, 1989, 215–35, at 219. Coulson holds the view that nearly 80 verses deal with legal matters, see N.J. Couslon, *A History of Islamic Law*, Edinburgh, Edinburgh University Press, 1964, p 12. Professor Munir says that about 600 verses indicate legal rulings; 400 pertain to *ibadat*, the remainder to *mu'amalat*. About 70 verses relate to trade and finance; 13 to oaths; 30 to crime and sentencing; 10 to constitutional and administrative laws; and 25 to international law and Prisoners of War (POW) (personal communication, Muhammad Munir, Professor of Islamic Law, International Islamic University, Islamabad, March 2008).

16 The Holy Qur'an, 26:192.

17 Ibid. 10:37.

The major areas covered by the legal texts are marriage, divorce, polygamy, the status of women, inheritance, property, the payment of *zakat*, the rights of orphans, adultery, homicide, usury, prohibition of the use of alcohol, and so on. The Qur'anic texts (both legal and non-legal) were elucidated and applied by the Prophet Muhammad as a prophet and judge.[18] Generally, the Qur'an expresses basic values rather than specific rules.[19] Sometimes, the procedure is also laid down. This necessitates interpretation and creates scope for *ijtihad* (literally: striving, meaning independent human reasoning).[20]

The Sunnah is the second formal source of Islamic law. It constitutes the practices of the Prophet Muhammad, which include his sayings, deeds and tacit approvals. The status of the Sunnah as a formal source of the *Shari'ah* is proved from the Qur'an: 'Nor does he [the Prophet] say (aught) of (his own) Desire'[21]; 'He who obeys the Messenger, obeys Allah.'[22] Muslims generally believe that the Sunnah is divinely inspired. During the Prophet's lifetime, the words and the practices of the Prophet were proofs for all Muslims. Since the Sunnah was collected and recorded after the death of the Prophet, therefore, the scholars of later generations have developed certain rules for ascertaining their authenticity.[23] Like the Qur'an, the Sunnah is of binding nature. The Sunnah expounds law in three ways, viz. firstly, it may simply reiterate or corroborate a ruling laid down in the Qur'an; secondly, it may explain, clarify and interpret the Qur'anic text; and, thirdly, it may provide instructions on matters not expressly covered by the texts.[24] The last-mentioned category shows that the Sunnah is also an independent source of the *Shari'ah*.

Besides the Qur'an and the Sunnah, another source of Islamic law is *ijma* (consensus of opinion). '*Ijma* . . . is agreement of the jurists . . . in a particular age on a question of law.'[25] As a valid technique, *ijma* is supported by certain texts of the Qur'an and the Sunnah. The Qur'an says, 'Obey Allah and obey the Messenger, and those charged with authority among you.'[26] The Prophet said, '[M]y followers will never agree upon what is wrong.'[27] *Ijma* is resorted to in a situation which is not covered by the Qur'an and the Sunnah. Shias think the

18 Baderin, op. cit., p 35.

19 M. Hashim Kamali, 'Law and Society, the Interplay of Revelation and Reason in the Shariah' in John L. Esposito (ed.), *The Oxford History of Islam*, Oxford, Oxford University Press, 1999, pp 107–53, at p 138.

20 M. Hashim Kamali, 'Fundamental Rights of the Individual: An Analysis of Haqq (Rights) in Islamic Law', *American Journal of Islamic Social Sciences* 10(3), 1993, 340–66, at 354.

21 The Holy Qur'an, 53:3.

22 Ibid. 4:80.

23 Kamali, 'Sources, Nature and Objective of Shari'ah', op. cit., at 222.

24 Ibid. 222–3.

25 Rahim, op. cit., p 115.

26 The Holy Qur'an, 4:59.

27 Ibid.

approval of the *imam* is necessary for *ijma*.[28] In solving a particular problem, these sources of law are hierarchically applied. However, if these sources are silent, a judge/jurist has to exercise *ijtihad* by a number of juristic techniques.

Juristic techniques

In order to keep the *Shari'ah* abreast with the challenges posed by changing conditions, the rules laid down in these primary sources are modified through various techniques of juristic deduction. These techniques are mostly the product of *fiqh*. The principal technique of juristic deduction is *ijtihad*, which is based on human reasoning. *Ijtihad* deals with new circumstances, which are either not explicitly covered by the primary sources or require changes and modifications in the text of the law. *Ijtihad* takes various forms such as *Qiyas* (analogical deduction), *istihsan* (juristic preference), *maslahah* (public interest) and *urf* (custom).

Qiyas (analogy), which means 'measuring', 'accord', 'equality', is resorted to when a particular matter is not covered by the Qur'an, Sunnah and *ijma*. It is an extension of the text of the law to a matter which is governed not by the language of the text, but by the reason of the text.[29] The reason of the text means the *illah* (effective cause). *Illah* is 'the fact, circumstance, or consideration which the Lawgiver has had in regard in laying down the law embodied in a text'.[30] If a rule of law based on analogy is opposed to equity or fairness, a jurist may depart from it and prefer a solution that serves justice, equity and public interest. This method of deduction is called *istihsan* (juristic preference or equity), which literally means considering something good and preferable.[31] The doctrine of *istihsan* was developed by Hanafi jurists. Muslim scholars argue that *istihsan* is equivalent to the English legal concept of equity because both seek equity and fairness and allow a departure from a rule of law the enforcement of which may cause inconvenience and hardship. However, the difference between the two is that the former is based on the values of the *Shari'ah* and the latter on natural law.[32]

Similar to *istihsan* is *maslahah* (literally: public interest or welfare), which is based on the consideration of securing public interest or welfare and preventing harm. Both *istihsan* and *maslahah* are based on the concepts of public good and welfare. The two, however, differ from each other. The former seeks

28 Kamali, 'Law and Society, the Interplay of Revelation and Reason in the Shariah', op. cit., p 121.

29 Rahim, op. cit., p 138.

30 Ibid. p 162.

31 *Istihsan* 'involves setting aside an established analogy in favour of an alternative ruling that serves the ideals of justice and public interest in a better way'. See M. Hashim Kamali, *Principles of Islamic Jurisprudence*, op. cit., p 324. See also M. Hashim Kamali, *Equity and Fairness in Islam*, Cambridge, Islamic Text Society, 2005, p 11.

32 Kamali, *Principles of Islamic Jurisprudence*, op. cit., p 323.

to expound the law from the existing sources, whereas the latter is not necessarily tied to existing sources; it 'can often consist of an original formula . . . and can bring independent legislation'.[33] However, it is necessary for *maslahah* to be based on the recognized proofs of the *Shari'ah*.[34]

Urf (custom) may also be used as a technique in the growth of the *Shari'ah*. The reforms introduced by the Qur'an and the Sunnah did not abolish all the pre-Islamic customs of Arabia. Some were endorsed by the Qur'an; others were followed by the Prophetic Sunnah. The companions and successors of the Prophet also gave due weight to customs in the development of the *Shari'ah*. Custom is a source of law provided it is not against the *Shari'ah*.

The views of different schools of jurisprudence differ regarding the juristic techniques. Some schools of Shias do not recognize *ijma* as a source.[35] Similarly, differences of opinion exist among the jurists of the four Sunni schools over the concept of *maslahah*. However, despite their differences, all the schools are regarded as valid and Muslims are free to follow any school of thought of their choice.

The purpose of the *Shari'ah*: the doctrine of *maslahah*

The principal objective of Islamic law is the achievement of *maslahah*, which literally means 'benefit' or 'welfare'.[36] A number of Qur'anic injunctions justify *maslahah*.[37] Expressing the purpose of the prophet-hood of Muhammad, the Qur'an says, '[W]e have not sent you but as a mercy for all creatures.'[38] The Qur'an proclaims itself to be 'a healing to the (spiritual) ailments of the hearts' and a 'Guidance and Mercy' for the believers and mankind.[39] Both the institution of prophet-hood and the Qur'an, being sources of mercy, aim to ensure the welfare and interests of the public at large. Thus the laws of the Qur'an are aimed at securing benefit and preventing harm to the people, as another verse reads: 'God never intends to impose hardship upon people.'[40]

During the early period of the development of Islamic jurisprudence, *maslahah* was given importance. After the Prophet's death, *maslahah* was the key objective of his successors and companions in applying and interpreting the revealed texts as well as in developing new rules. Some evidence from the practice of the companions and the successors of the Prophet, is available in its

33 Kamali, *Equity and Fairness in Islam*, op. cit., p 27.
34 Ibid.
35 Rahim, op. cit., p 117.
36 Kamali, *Principles of Islamic Jurisprudence*, op. cit., p 351.
37 See M. Hashim Kamali, 'Have we Neglected the Shari'ah–Law Doctrine of Maslahah?' *Islamic Studies* 27(4), 1988, 287–303, at 291.
38 The Holy Qur'an, 21:107; See also M. Hashim Kamali, 'Maqasid al-Shariah: The Objectives of Islamic Law', *Association of Muslim Lawyers Newsletter* 3, 1998, 1–7, at 1.
39 The Holy Qur'an, 10:57.
40 Ibid. 5:6.

support. 'Umar ibn al-Khattab, a close companion of the Prophet and the second caliph, suspended the enforcement of amputation of [the] hand, a kind of punishment called *hadd* (prescribed in the Qur'an) for the offence of theft during a period of widespread famine.'[41] In this particular situation, the caliph departed from a ruling of the Qur'an to meet the exigency of a new situation, viz. the famine.

All the schools of Sunni jurisprudence agree that if *maslahah* is consistent with Islamic law, it must be supported.[42] However, the chief proponents of *maslahah* were Maliki jurists, who considered it independent of the primary sources. Shatibi (died 790 A.H./1388 C.E.), a Maliki jurist, defines *maslahah* as follows:

> That which concerns the subsistence of human life, the completion of man's livelihood, and the acquisition of what his emotional and intellectual qualities require of him, in an absolute sense.[43]

Shatibi maintains, '[t]he primary objective of the Lawgiver is the *maslahah* of the people'.[44] Thus scholars of Islamic law use the words *maslahah* and *maqasid* (objectives) synonymously. Shatibi has divided *maslahah* (the plural of *masalih*) into three categories. They are essentials (*daruriyyah*), exigencies (*hajiyyah*) and embellishments (*tahsinyyah*).[45] Essentials are the spiritual and material things, which are five: religion, human life, progeny, material wealth and human reason. These five essentials – i.e. the first category of *maslahah* – are generally seen as the objectives of the law (*maqasid al-Shari'ah*). Exigencies are those the absence of which will cause distress and hardship; they include enjoyment of the lawful and good things in life. These objectives take into consideration the mitigating circumstances to

41 Kamali, *Principles of Islamic Jurisprudence*, op. cit., p 325. 'Umar did *ijtihad* on many occasions to secure *maslahah*.' With the consideration of achieving *maslahah*, the first Caliph Abu Bakr 'collected and compiled the scattered records of the Qur'an'; the third Caliph Uthman 'validated the right to inheritance of a woman whose husband had divorced her in order to be disinherited', the fourth Caliph, Ali, 'held craftsmen and traders responsible for the loss of goods that were placed in their custody', see p 355.

42 Hanbali jurists support *maslahah* for the same reasons as Malikis do. Shafi jurists validate it only when it is supported by the Qur'an and the Sunnah. Hanafi jurists treat it as part of *istihsan* (juristic preference/equity). See Deina Abdelkader, op. cit., p 51.

43 M. Khalid Masud, *Shatibi Philosophy of Islamic Law*, Islamabad, Islamic Research Institute, International Islamic University, 1995, p 151. Shatibi mainly built his views on al-Ghazzali (d.505/1111), a Shafi jurist, who saw *maslahah* as 'the preservation of the *maqasid* (objectives) of the law, which are the preservation of religion, life, reason, descendants and property'. See p 139.

44 Ibid.

45 Ibid. p 152. See also Al-Raysuni, op. cit., p 108. See also Wael B. Hallaq, *A History of Islamic Legal Theories, An Introduction to Sunni Usul al-Fiqh*, Cambridge, Cambridge University Press, 1997, p 168.

alleviate hardships.[46] Embellishments are those things which are not as important as the others, but which enhance the function of the other two.[47] These ameliorative requirements promote quality of life; they include 'commendable habits and customs, the observance of rules of etiquette and a high moral standard'.[48] All three categories of *maslahah* are linked to each other. Each category needs to be promoted separately as well as in relation to the others.

It is clear from the foregoing account that the primary sources provide the basic norms. The principle of *ijtihad* provides wide scope for independent human reasoning to transform the basic norms into the existing conditions of human life. The relevance of *maslahah* to the RTD is examined below.

MASLAHAH AND THE RTD

General relevance of *maslahah* to the RTD

The RTD is a right of the individual and all peoples.[49] The national development policies of the state should 'aim at the constant improvement and the well being of the entire population and of all the individuals'.[50] Thus both the individual and the people are the focus of the Declaration. However, at the national level, the starting point of the RTD is the promotion and protection of individual rights. *Maslahah*, on the other hand, secures public interest and welfare. In other words, the starting point of *maslahah* is the interest and welfare of the people. How then is *maslahah* relevant to the RTD?

The relevance of the two concepts may be seen in the following ways. First, generally, *maslahah* does not 'preclude individual benefit or welfare to ensure protection of human rights'.[51] The welfare of the individual promotes the welfare of the community and vice versa.[52] It may be appreciated that the notions of interest and welfare, public as well as individual, are different from human rights in the sense that the latter are specific in content, aim at the protection of the rights of the individual and entail obligations. Moreover, promoting the former does not necessarily constitute a rights-based approach to development. For instance, the accountability of the duty-bearer is an essential part of the rights-based approach. Accountability may be desirable

46 Al-Raysuni, op. cit., p 109. See also Masud, op. cit., p 152.

47 Ibid.

48 Ibid.

49 DRD, Art. 1(1).

50 DRD, Art. 2(3).

51 Baderin, op. cit., p 43. See also M. Hashim Kamali, *The Dignity of Man: An Islamic Perspective*, Cambridge, Islamic Text Society, 2002, first published by Ilmiah Publishers, Kuala Lumpur, Malaysia, 1999, p 91. See also Kamali, 'Fundamental Rights of the Individual', op. cit., at 362.

52 Ibid.

in promoting the notions of public and individual interest and welfare, but not intrinsic to them. However, both are closely linked to each other because human beings are the ultimate beneficiaries of public interest and welfare. Despite the above-noted differences, *maslahah* provides strong holistic support to a rights-based approach because, in addition to its being an objective of juristic deduction, it is also the main guideline for socio-economic policy and legislation. Scholars have extended the scope of *maslahah* to include some contemporary issues, which may include the realization of the RTD. Among contemporary scholars, Yusuf al-Qaradawi has included human dignity, freedom, social welfare and human fraternity.[53] Kamali has added economic development, protection of the environment and the development of science and technology as crucially important themes of *maslahah* for the whole Muslim world.[54] The vibrant nature of *maslahah* is well articulated by Kamali:

> The doctrine of *maslahah* is broad enough to encompass within its fold a variety of objectives, both idealist and pragmatic, to nurture the standards of good government, and to help develop the much needed public confidence in the authority of statutory legislation in Muslim societies. The doctrine of *maslahah* can strike a balance between the highly idealistic levels of expectation from the government on the part of the public and the efforts of the latter to identify more meaningfully with Islam.[55]

Secondly, *maslahah* is in harmony with the objectives of Islamic law, which, as noted above, are the protection of life, religion, family, property and reason. At the national level, a Muslim country may integrate *maslahah* with the RTD because the Declaration does not suggest any specific model of development policies for the realization of the RTD. Thus the five essentials of the first category of *maslahah* (given above), may form the content of an RTD-based development policy in a Muslim state like Pakistan. Indeed, the five essentials overlap with some of the basic human rights,[56] listed in the UDHR such as the rights to life, family, property and religion.[57] However, the use of the words 'rights' or 'human rights' for these objectives of Islamic law is of fairly recent origin.[58] Efforts were made to codify these essentials in

53 Yusuf al-Qardawi, *Madkhal li Dirasah al-Shari'ah*, p 75, cited in Kamali, 'Maqasid al-Shariah: The Objectives of Islamic Law', op. cit., at 4.

54 Ibid.

55 Kamali, 'Have we Neglected the Shari'ah–Law Doctrine of Maslahah?' op. cit., 287–8.

56 Kamali, 'Fundamental Rights of the Individual: An Analysis of Haqq', op. cit., 355.

57 See the UDHR, Arts 3, 16–18.

58 See Ridwan Al-Sayyid, 'Contemporary Muslim Thought and Human Rights', *Islamochristiana* 21, 1995, 27–41, at 35.

the Universal Islamic Declaration of Human Rights (UIDHR).[59] Thus *maslahah* may promote human rights and welfare.[60]

Thirdly, the implementation of the *Shari'ah* requires the establishment of various public institutions, such as legal, social and economic, for the protection and promotion of the five basic objectives. The judicial process for imposing retribution (*Qisas*) for murder is aimed at the protection of life. Similarly, the *Shari'ah* protects property, the family and personal honour of the individual through legal punishments for theft, adultery and slanderous accusation.[61] The protection and promotion of the five objectives as well as other categories also requires an affirmative action policy through economic and social institutions to create opportunities for people. An affirmative action policy may be a poverty-reduction strategy and may also include an Islamization process. Once such a policy is linked to the RTD, it should be guided by two principles of the Declaration, viz. ensuring participation of people and the fair and equitable distribution of benefits among all peoples;[62] it should also reflect the key features of the Declaration (see Chapter 4). The policy would further demand that the promotion of a particular goal of Islamic law is related to human rights because the RTD aims to promote and protect human rights. In this way, the Declaration may help realize the goals of Islamic law. For example, the provision of all possible means of livelihood, by means of an RTD-based policy, will help protect life and promote a decent standard of living. This will also include the protection and promotion of the rights to work, food and health. The right to education will help facilitate the protection of human reason and intellectual well-being to promote arts, culture, sciences and civilization.[63] The protection of family or progeny will require, firstly, improving the status of women, for example by the provision of education, health care and fair employment opportunities; and the protection of their legal and social rights, for example equality before law, inheritance and access to justice. Secondly, the protection of family or progeny requires positive state obligations to improve child welfare and ensure protection of their rights. However, in the context of the RTD in a Muslim country like Pakistan, tension may arise between the protection and promotion of the objectives of Islamic law, on the one hand, and international human rights standards, on the other. There is a growing debate on the issue of conflict between human rights and Islamic law. It is necessary to discuss this issue.

59 Ibid. at 36. The UIDHR was adopted on 19 Sept. 1981 in Paris, France. It contains a list of 23 human rights. Another Declaration was adopted by the Organization of Islamic Conferences (OIC) at its nineteenth Conference in Cairo in 1990. It lists 25 rights.

60 Kamali, *The Dignity of Man*, op. cit., p 94.

61 Ibid. p 91.

62 DRD, Art. 3(2).

63 See Kamali, 'Maqasid al-Shariah: The Objectives of Islamic Law', op. cit., at 2.

Human rights and Islamic law

The Declaration makes a reference to the UDHR and the two human rights covenants and urges the protection and promotion of all human rights, civil and political as well as economic, social and cultural. The Declaration may be said to presuppose the universality of human rights. A country wishing to implement the Declaration would need to make legislative and constitutional changes to allow the precedence of international human rights law over its national laws,[64] and to ensure respect for all human rights and the active role of women in the process of development. Pakistan is a signatory to the ICESCR, Conventions on the Rights of the Child (CRC), and the Convention on the Elimination of All Forms of Discrimination against Women (the Women's Convention) (with some reservations), but not a signatory to the ICCPR. The constitution provides fundamental rights, which are mostly the same as those listed in the UDHR. However, the Islamization movement in Pakistan, coupled with a general view that Islamic law are in conflict with the international human rights standards, is linked with the question of incompatibility between the two. This issue requires a brief analysis of the debate on the universality of human rights and the challenge of cultural relativism.

The challenge of cultural relativism

The advocates of universality argue that 'if human rights are, literally, the rights (every) one has simply because one is a human being, they would seem to be universal by definition'.[65] The universality of human rights is mainly supported by Western states and Western legal scholarship; they subject human rights 'to complete West-oriented interpretations'.[66] Donnelly, for instance, argues that 'the idea of human rights was first articulated in the West . . . it is particularly suited . . . and thus of widespread contemporary relevance *both in the West and the Third World*'.[67] Charlesworth argues that 'modern human rights law derives primarily from Western philosophical thought'.[68] Regarding the role of other cultures in the ideology of human rights, Charlesworth says, '[human rights law] has *some resonance* in other cultural traditions'.[69] After this passing reference to the role of non-Western cultures, she further traces the roots of human rights in Judaeo-Christian

64 See Report of the Inter-governmental Group of Experts on the Right to Development, E/CN.4/1998/29, para. 65.

65 Jack Donnelly, 'Cultural Relativism and Universal Human Rights', *Human Rights Quarterly* 6(4), 1984, 400–20, at 400.

66 Baderin, op. cit., p 26.

67 Donnelly, op. cit., 303 (emphasis added).

68 Charlesworth, op. cit., p 201.

69 Ibid. (emphasis added).

morality, natural law and the French and American revolutions.[70] This claim has its critics. For example, Sen argues that the Western concept of freedom is not the only basis of human rights.[71]

Cultural relativism is 'the position according to which local cultural traditions (including religious, political and legal practices) properly determine the existence and scope of civil and political rights enjoyed by individuals in a given society'.[72] The advocates of cultural relativism argue that there exists no universal moral or legal rule for judging human rights.[73] They contend that the idea of the present human rights law is based on the Western philosophy of secularism and is exploited by the West to maintain its dominance. They argue that in case of conflict between international human rights and their own cultural standards, the latter shall prevail.[74]

It is generally held, particularly in the West, that Islamic law is incompatible with human rights law.[75] Some Western scholars hold that what Muslim scholars allege as human rights in Islam are 'only duties of rulers and individuals'.[76] The reason behind this thinking is the avowed assumption that the current human rights are secular in nature. Some advocates of universal human rights argue that human rights are not granted by God or Nature, but arise from human action.[77] This state of affairs has pushed those who look at the human rights discourse from a religious perspective, into a defensive position.[78]

The Qur'an makes no formal distinction between human rights and ordinary rights.[79] Normally, the Qur'an expresses legal rulings in the form of commands and prohibitions.[80] Out of such rulings, rights and obligations arise either expressly or implicitly in the light of textual interpretation and the goals of the *Shari'ah*.[81] For example the right to life is derived from the Qur'anic commandment: 'kill not a soul which God has made sacrosanct save in the cause of justice.'[82] The right to privacy is embodied in a legal

70 Ibid. p 202.

71 Amartya Sen, *Development as Freedom*, op cit., p 240. See also Jerome J. Shestack, 'Philosophic Foundations of Human Right', *Human Rights Quarterly* 20, 1998, 201–34, at 206.

72 Fernando R. Teson, 'International Human Rights and Cultural Relativism', *Virginia Journal of International Law* 25(4), 1985, 869–98, at 870.

73 Ibid.

74 See Charlesworth, op. cit., p 202.

75 Baderin, op. cit., p 3.

76 Donnelly, 'Human Rights and Human Dignity', op. cit. p 306.

77 Jack Donnelly, *Universal Human Rights in Theory and Practice*, Ithaca, New York/London, Cornell University Press, 2003, p 17.

78 See Michael Freeman, 'The Problem of Secularism in Human Rights Theory', *Human Rights Quarterly* 26, 2004, 375–400.

79 Kamali, 'Fundamental Rights of the Individual', op. cit., 354.

80 Ibid. 352.

81 Ibid. 354.

82 The Holy Qur'an, 17:33.

injunction in the form of a prohibition: 'O believers! Enter not houses other than your own until you have asked leave.'[83] A number of other human rights such as the right to life,[84] equality before the law,[85] freedom of expression[86] and freedom of conscience and religion,[87] to name just a few, may be derived from the verses of the Qur'an.[88]

In his 'Farewell Sermon' on Mount Arafat, Saudi Arabia, on the occasion of his last pilgrimage, the Prophet declared the equality of all people, the sanctity of their lives, the freedom of their religion and speech and a number of other basic rights. He proclaimed:

> O mankind! The Arab is not superior to a non-Arab, nor vice versa; the white has no superiority over the black, nor vice versa; and the rich has no superiority over the poor. All of you are Adam's descendants and Adam was made of earth.[89]

After the death of the Prophet, the rightly guided caliphs of Islam established numerous precedents of human rights. For example, 'Umar had a Christian house-boy; he never compelled the Christian to embrace Islam.'[90]

However, despite apparent similarities, there are conceptual differences between the two traditions. Firstly, modern human rights are secular and derived from natural law. The Islamic concept of human rights, on the other hand, is based on divine scripture, i.e. the Qur'an and the Sunnah.[91] Secondly, the former is based on the state–individual relationship and has nothing to do

83 Ibid. 24:27.

84 'If any one slew a person – unless it be for murder or for spreading mischief in the land – it would be as if he slew the whole people: and if any one saved a life, it would be as if he saved the life of the whole people. Then although there came to them Our apostles with clear signs, yet, even after that, many of them continued to commit excesses in the land' (5:32).

85 'O mankind! We created you from a single (pair) of a male and a female, and made you into nations and tribes, that ye may know each other (not that ye may despise (each other). Verily the most honoured of you in the sight of Allah is (he who is) the most righteous of you. And Allah has full knowledge and is well acquainted (with all things)' (49:13).

86 'Allah The most Gracious! It is He Who taught the Qur'an; [He] Created Man [and] Taught him eloquent speech' (55:1–4).

87 'Let there be no compulsion in religion: Truth stands out clear from Error: whoever rejects evil and believes in Allah hath grasped the most trustworthy hand-hold that never breaks. And Allah heareth and knoweth all things' (2:256).

88 A number of other rights recognized by the Qur'an are the right to work (4:32 and 62:10), the right to privacy (24:27), freedom of association (3:110), the right to basic necessities (51:19), and the right to justice (5:3, 5:8 and 4:135).

89 Tahir Mehmood, 'The Islamic Law of Human Rights', *Islamic and Comparative Law Quarterly* IV(1&2), 1984, 32–44, at 32.

90 Ibid. 35. For many other precedents, see Sheikh Showkat Hussain, 'Human Right in Islam: Principles and Precedents', *Islamic and Comparative Law Quarterly*, III(2) 1983, 103–28.

91 See Ebrahim Moosa, 'The Dilemma of Islamic Rights Scheme', *Journal of Law and Religion* 15(1/2), 2000–2001, 185–215.

with race, religion, colour and sex.[92] The individual has the right to be protected from abuses of state authority. The latter is primarily based on the God–human being relationship in which both the ruler and the ruled are subject to the laws of God.[93] These differences, however, do not mean that these systems are the antithesis of one another.[94] Nor does it mean that Islamic rights should be denied a role in the promotion and protection of human rights.[95]

A growing body of literature on human rights in Islam shows that Islam fully recognizes the concept of human rights.[96] After carrying out an article-by-article comparison of the ICCPR and ICESCR with Islamic law, Baderin concludes that 'there is certainly a human rights discourse in Islamic law . . . [and] there is a wide positive common ground between international human rights law and Islamic law'.[97] A more recent study is the work of Shah, which has shown that 'the rule and spirit of the [Qur'an] are compatible with the [Women's] Convention except in the areas of sexual relations outside marriage'.[98]

The differences between international human rights law and Islamic law can pose challenges to the implementation of the Declaration in Pakistan and other Muslim countries. The areas of tension generally relate to the equality rights of women and minorities and the criminal law. Take, for instance, women's rights. Article 11 of the Women's Convention (also Art. 6 of ICESCR) provides equality of men and women in employment opportunities. Article 25 of the constitution also safeguards this right of women. However, there is a difference of opinion among different schools of jurisprudence regarding the employment rights of women in certain areas, such as in the appointment of a woman as a judge. There is also a dispute over women's political rights such as in the appointment of a woman as a head of state. Resolution of these issues requires methodologies to achieve compatibility.

How to achieve compatibility

Various approaches are put forward regarding Islam and international human rights in the growing body of literature on the subject. Notable among them

92 Ibid. 202.

93 Kamali, 'Fundamental Rights of the Individual', op. cit., 342.

94 Baderin, op. cit., p 6.

95 Moosa, op. cit., 204.

96 See, for example, Mohamed Berween, 'Fundamental Human Rights: An Islamic Perspective', *International Journal of Human Rights* 6(1), Spring 2002, 61–78; Al-Sayyid, op. cit.; David L. Johnston, 'The Human Khilafa: A Growing Overlap of Reformism and Islamism on Human Rights Discourse', *Islamochristiana* 28, 2002, 35–53.

97 Baderin, op. cit., p 219.

98 Shah, *Women, the Koran and International Human Rights Law*, op. cit., p 231.

is a reconciliatory approach, which provides that the areas of conflict between the two may be reconciled and reformulated with international human rights standards.[99] The studies by Baderin and Shah, which are representative of the reconciliatory approach, and the interpretive approach, respectively, are analysed here. Baderin, who conducted his study in 2003, proposed the doctrines of *maslahah* and the 'the margin of appreciation' (a mechanism developed in the European human rights law, it is 'the line at which international supervision should give way to a State party's discretion in enacting or enforcing its laws').[100] Baderin argues that 'the margin of appreciation' is effectively applied by the European Court of Human Rights in several cases, while the Human Rights Committee has not formally adopted it, but has made an indirect reference to it in *Hertzberg v Finland*.[101] Baderin further argues that the doctrine will be useful in addressing issues such as the definition of family, homosexuality, blasphemy, abortion, and other moral questions in relation to Muslim state parties that apply Islamic law.[102]

Shah's study, which focuses on women's rights, appeared in 2006. Shah advocates an interpretive approach. This approach calls for the interpretation of the Qur'an in its proper context in three ways: (1) the historical context (i.e. the seventh century) in which the Qur'an was revealed, (2) the social context, i.e. taking consideration of the social conditions of Arab society, which was the main target audience of the Qur'an in the seventh century, and (3) the Qur'anic context, firstly: when and why was a verse revealed and secondly, what is the overall approach (intention) of the Qur'an?[103]

The interpretive approach is very similar to what is known as *maslahah mu'tabarah*, i.e. validated by primary sources. It calls for a proper contextual interpretation of the relevant Qur'anic verses, but does not preclude legislation in case the primary sources are silent on an issue. *Maslahah mursala* seeks new legislation on a subject which is neither supported nor opposed by a text. In case of a conflict between a revealed text of the *Shari'ah* and a human rights norm, greater compatibility may be achieved through the interpretive approach. In other cases, greater compatibility may be achieved through the doctrine of *maslahah*.

99 Ibid. p 8. Other approaches, mentioned by Shah, are the secular, the non-compatible and the interpretive. According to the secular approach, human rights are compatible with Islamic law without reference to religion. The non-compatible approach argues that they are distinct. The interpretive approach stresses the reinterpretation of Islamic law through *ijtihad* to meet the conditions of the day.

100 Baderin, op. cit., pp 42, 231.

101 Ibid. pp 231–2. *Hertzberg v Finland*, Communication No. R.14/61 (7 Aug. 1979), U.N. Doc. Supp. No. 40 (A/37/40) at 161 (1982). The complainants had prepared a TV programme regarding homosexuality, which was censured by the State Party. They alleged violation of Art. 19 of the ICCPR.

102 Baderin, op. cit., p 234.

103 Shah, op. cit., p 14.

A possible objection to the interpretive approach is that a revealed text can be interpreted in different ways, raising a question as to which interpretation should be followed. Different interpretations enable 'people in different regions and times in history to interpret scriptures in ways suitable to their needs'.[104] As regards *maslahah*, a likely objection is that it may be abused. The chances of abuse of *maslahah* may be checked by three conditions of *maslahah*: it must be genuine, general and in consonance with the primary sources of the law.

While tensions exist between Islam and human rights, they may generally promote each other. The tensions may be addressed through an interpretive approach and *maslahah* to pursue a rights-based approach to development. The question is whether Pakistan's policies for the implementation of Islamic law promote human rights. What are their implications for the RTD? The next section examines these issues.

ISLAMIZATION AND THE RTD IN PAKISTAN

Jinnah's vision of Pakistan

In Pakistan, political opinion on the Islamic concept of the state is sharply divided between two groups, viz., the modernists and the Islamic activists. The former believe that the founding father of the nation visualized Pakistan as a democratic state based on secularism, where religion would be a private affair of the individual. The modernists also argue that Islamic political parties in India, particularly Jamaat-e-Islami of Maududi, opposed the creation of Pakistan.[105] The activists are of the view that the country was established in the name of Islam; hence, Islamic law will reign supreme. In his famous speech delivered to the Constituent Assembly in 1947, Jinnah (1876–1948) said:

> You may belong to any religion or cast or creed – that has nothing to do with the business of the state . . . We are starting with this fundamental principle that we are all citizens of one state . . . in the course of time Hindus would cease to be Hindus and Muslims would cease to be Muslims, not in the religious sense, because that is the personal faith of each individual, but in the political sense as citizens of the state.[106]

104 Ibid. p 17.

105 Hamza Alvi, 'Ethnicity, Muslim Society, and the Pakistan Ideology' in Anita M. Weiss (ed.), *Islamic Reassertion in Pakistan: An Application of Islamic Laws in a Modern State*, New York, Syracuse University Press, 1986, pp 21–47, at p 35.

106 Quoted in Abdus Sattar Ghazzali, *Islamic Pakistan: Illusion or Reality*, Islamabad, National Book Club, 1997, p 6.

Jinnah also made specific references to Islam:

> The Muslims demand Pakistan, where they could rule according to their own code of life and according to their own cultural growth, traditions and Islamic law.[107]

Jinnah's views were significantly influenced by the ideas of Muhammad Iqbal (1877–1938), the poet philosopher.[108] The idea of a separate homeland with an Islamic identity, for the Muslims of India, was first presented by Iqbal.[109] In his works, both poems and prose, Iqbal advocated an Islamic renaissance through *ijtihad*.[110] Both Iqbal and Jinnah also saw the creation of a separate state as a means of improving not only the social but also the economic development of the Muslims. Thus in a 1937 letter to Jinnah, Iqbal wrote:

> The problem of bread is becoming more and more acute. The Muslim has begun to feel that he has been going down and down during the last 200 years . . . The question therefore is: how is it possible to solve the problem of Muslim poverty?[111]

In 1943, Jinnah condemned the exploitation of the poor at the hands of the rich and reminded them of the teachings of Islam.[112] In 1946, Jinnah reiterated: 'In Pakistan, we will do all in our power to see that everybody can get a decent living.'[113]

Though Jinnah made references to Islamic principle of social justice, he categorically opposed the rule of theocracy in Pakistan.[114] Jinnah was reported to have combined Islam with democracy: 'Islam and its ideals have taught us democracy. It has taught us equality of man, justice and fair play to everybody.'[115] Perhaps Anderson has made a more eloquent comment on the ideology of Pakistan:

107 Quoted in J.N.D. Anderson, 'Pakistan: An Islamic State?' in R.H. Holland and G. Schwarzenberger (eds), *Law, Justice and Equity*, London, Sir Issac Pitman and Sons Ltd., 1967, pp 127–36, at p 127.

108 Jinnah used Islam simply as 'the common cultural heritage and identity of [Indian] Muslims'. Iqbal saw Islam as a 'religio-social order . . . and Pakistan . . . an Islamic state, one whose institutions and law should be based upon Islam'. See John L. Esposito and John O. Voll, *Islam and Democracy*, Oxford, Oxford University Press, 1996, pp 102–23.

109 Akbar S. Ahmed, *Jinnah, Pakistan and Islamic Identity: The Search for Saladin*, London/New York, Routledge, 1997, p 74.

110 See Muhammad Iqbal, *The Reconstruction of Religious Thought in Islam*, London, Oxford University Press, 1934.

111 Ahmed, op. cit., p 76.

112 Ibid.

113 Ibid.

114 Ghazzali, op. cit., p 12; Ahmed, op. cit., p 177.

115 Ibid. p 13.

> [T]here could be no room for doubt . . . that two ambitions – the one to be an Islamic [state], and the other to be a modern, democratic State – are knit together in *the aspirations of the people* of Pakistan.[116]

All the constitutions attempted to create constitutional mechanisms for the establishment of an Islamic, but modern democratic state of Pakistan.

The Objectives Resolution

The Objectives Resolution spelt out the principles of an Islamic ideology. Firstly, sovereignty over the entire universe belongs to Allah Almighty. The people of Pakistan shall exercise sovereignty as a sacred trust from Allah Almighty and within the limits prescribed by Him. Secondly, the Islamic principles of democracy, freedom, equality, tolerance and social justice as enunciated by Islam shall be fully observed. Thirdly, the Muslims shall be enabled to order their lives in the individual and collective spheres in accordance with the teachings and requirements of the Qur'an and the Sunnah. Fourthly, adequate provision shall be made for the protection of the religious and cultural freedom of minorities.

Some non-Muslim members of the Constituent Assembly objected to the clause that proclaims the sovereignty of Allah, arguing that it would endanger the democratic character of the state.[117] Answering this objection, some Muslim members argued that this clause did not mean that Pakistan would be a theocratic state. It was argued that the constitutions of many modern states, for example, the Republic of Ireland, used similar words about God.[118] Moreover, by proclaiming the supremacy of God, the Objectives Resolution does not rule out a representative democracy.

The Objectives Resolution, with slight modifications, had the role of a preamble to the constitution and was the central ingredient of the ideology of Pakistan. In the case of *Zia-ur-Rehman*, the Supreme Court held that the Objectives Resolution is only a preamble; nevertheless, it was admitted as the *grundnorm* of the state.[119] In 1985, the Objectives Resolution was made a substantive part of the constitution by virtue of a new article 2-A.[120] Thus it became an enforceable provision of the constitution. All the constitutions adopted Islamic provisions, mostly similar in nature. The Islamic provisions of the 1973 constitution are briefly described below.

116 Anderson, op. cit., p 127 (emphasis added).

117 Mehdi, op. cit., p 74.

118 Ibid.

119 See *State v Zia-ur-Rehman*, PLD 1973 SC 49.

120 See generally, Charles H. Kennedy, 'Repugnancy to Islam – Who decides? Islam and Legal Reform in Pakistan', *International and Comparative Law Quarterly* 41, Oct. 1992, 769–87.

The Islamic provisions of the 1973 constitution

The constitution proclaims Pakistan as an Islamic Republic and Islam as the state religion of Pakistan.[121] It says that all existing laws shall be brought in accordance with the Injunctions of Islam as laid down in the Qur'an and the Sunnah, and no law shall be enacted which is repugnant to such injunctions.[122] In this respect, an Islamic Ideology Council has to make recommendations to the national and provincial legislatures.[123] The Council shall also make recommendations to these law-making bodies as to the ways and means of enabling and encouraging the Muslims of Pakistan to order their lives in accordance with the principles and concepts of Islam as enunciated in the Qur'an and the Sunnah.[124]

It is generally held that the Objectives Resolution and the Islamic provisions were adopted in all three constitutions as a compromise between the modernists and the Islamic activists.[125] Most of the Islamic provisions faced the problem of practical implementation. No constitution provided a precise definition of the Islamic concept of the state. The opinion of the constitutional institutions, notably the Council, concerning Islamization of the law has no binding effect on the government. All the constitutions attempted to create a balance between the modern concept of a nation-state and Islam. The military regime of Ayub did try to give a more secular shape to the 1962 constitution, but soon almost all the Islamic elements were restored as a result of opposition by the Islamic activists. The 1973 constitution was more Islamic than the two previous ones. The military regime of Zia (1977–1988) introduced an extensive programme to implement the Islamic provisions of the 1973 constitution and also introduced some constitutional reforms for this purpose. Despite all this, however, the central debate about the establishment of Islamic social justice, between the modernists and the Islamic activists, still remains unanswered. Rather, the conflict between the two groups has escalated further. One major reason for this is the support of the present Pakistani government for the US-led war against terrorism. The general suspicion among the masses is that the war against terrorism is a proxy war against Islam and the promotion of Islamic values in Pakistan. Pakistan is thus facing challenges in meeting its obligations under the international instruments. In such a scenario, the implementation of an international instrument, like the Declaration, in Pakistan requires a proper theoretical understanding of the Islamic principles of social justice.

121 Arts 1 and 2. Art. 41 of the constitution provides that both the President and the Prime Minister shall be Muslims.

122 The 1973 constitution, Art. 227.

123 Art. 228.

124 Under Art. 228, the national and/or a provincial legislature can also seek the opinion of the Council as to whether a proposed law is or is not against the Injunctions of Islam.

125 Mehdi, op. cit., pp 84–102.

The Islamic concept of social justice

As stated above, all the constitutions of Pakistan referred to the Islamic principles of social justice. What is meant by the Islamic concept of social justice? Neither the present nor the previous constitutions define this concept. A reference may, therefore, be made to the relevant Qur'anic injunctions and their commentaries. According to the Qur'an, justice is a divine Command: 'Allah commands justice, doing of good.'[126] The Qur'an says that justice is the purpose of the institution of prophet-hood: 'We sent aforetime Our messengers with clear Signs and sent down with them the Book and the Balance (of Right and Wrong) that men may stand forth in justice.'[127] The Qur'an also refers to justice as trust (*amanah*): 'Allah does command you to render back your trusts to those to whom they are due; and when you judge between man and man, that you judge with justice.'[128] This verse 'was an address primarily to those in charge of the community affairs [the rulers] who are the main audience of the Qur'anic verses enjoining the [trust] of establishing a just government'.[129] Within this broad concept, justice is the overriding objective of the Lawgiver. Justice as the basis of government appears to be a broad term, which may include social justice. Kamali argues that social justice 'refers to the structure and policies of a society, and to its political, legal, economic and social institutions'.[130] Choudhury and Malik have explained social justice as an objective of Islamic law that can be established 'through the process of managing and allocating physical and human resources in a way that harmonises the objective goals of distributive equity and economic efficiency'.[131] The practical realization of social justice, however, requires an institutional framework, which is to be devised by the Muslim community itself through *ijtihad* by interpreting the relevant rules of Islamic law.[132]

Moreover, the government of a Muslim state may formulate and enact, at its discretion, any suitable policies for the sake of good government in different areas ranging from domestic and foreign relations to constitutional, fiscal, administrative or judicial affairs, provided such policies do not conflict with the *Shari'ah*.[133] This doctrine of Islamic public law is known as *Siyasah Shar'iyah* (*Shari'ah*-oriented Policy).[134] A widely known concept of Islamic law, *Siyasah*

126 The Holy Qur'an, 16:90.

127 Ibid. 57:25.

128 Ibid. 4:58

129 M. Hashim Kamali, *Freedom, Equality and Justice in Islam*, Cambridge, Islamic Text Society, 2002, p 113.

130 Ibid. p 109.

131 See Masudul Alam Choudhury and 'Uzir Abdul Malik, *The Foundations of Islamic Political Economy*, London, Macmillan, 1992, p 1.

132 Kamali, *Freedom, Equality and Justice in Islam*, op. cit., p 109.

133 Ibid., pp 142–3.

134 See M. Hashim Kamali, 'Siyasah Shar'iyah or the Policies of Islamic Government', *American Journal of Islamic Social Sciences* 6(1), 1989, 59–80.

Shari'ah, extends to all kinds of government policies that are in the public interest and intended to prevent harm. In this way, it helps achieve the goal of *maslahah*. In other words, it is in harmony with the objectives of Islamic law.[135]

The Islamic concept of social justice as referred to in the constitution of Pakistan is understood in the above perspective. Despite a conflict of opinion between the modernists and the Islamic activists on the Islamic concept of the state, all the constitutions have reiterated the realization of the ideals of social justice as a goal of Islamic law. The implementation of Islamic law, however, has been a key challenge to successive governments in Pakistan. Widespread Islamization was carried out by the military dictator Zia. However, post-Zia governments have also taken some legislative measures to implement Islamization.

Zia's Islamization movement and the RTD

While Islamization has been pursued as a national goal since independence, it was General Zia who launched a comprehensive programme to achieve this goal.[136] Zia introduced changes mainly in three areas: the judicial system, the economy and education. The reform in the first two areas are relevant to the present discussion, and are briefly examined.

The judicial system

The Islamization of the judicial system started with a 1979 Presidential Order that established Shariat Benches in the High Court of each of the four provinces, with the power to strike down any law that is found repugnant to the injunctions of Islam. In 1980, the Federal Shariat Court (FSC) was established through a constitutional amendment.[137] The original jurisdiction of the FSC is to declare null and void a law or any provision of a law that is repugnant to the injunctions of Islam.[138] The constitution, the Muslim Personal Law and some financial/commercial laws were excluded from the court's powers.[139] However, in a year 2000 decision, the FSC ruled that it has jurisdiction to examine the provisions of the statutory Muslim Family Law.[140]

135 Ibid. 61.

136 General Zia seized power on 5 July 1977 in the wake of a coup.

137 According to Art. 203(C) of the constitution, the Federal Shariat Court comprises eight Muslim judges, including three judges from among *ulama* (Islamic law scholars), who are, or have been, qualified to be judges of the High Court.

138 Under Art. 203D, such law shall cease to have effect on the day the decision of the Court becomes effective.

139 The 1973 Constitution, Art. 203B(c).

140 See *Allah Rakha and others v Federation of Pakistan*, PLD 2000 FSC 1. The Court ruled that 'ouster of jurisdiction of Federal Shariat Court and for that matter of the Shariat Appellate Bench of the Supreme Court of Pakistan in the case of the Muslim Family Ordinance but was referrable to Muslim Personal Law of particular sects', p 28.

The decisions of subordinate courts passed under the *Hudood* laws are subject to appeal and revision by the FSC.[141]

In 1979, Zia introduced the *Hudood* laws dealing with adultery, fornication and rape; *Qazf* (false imputation of adultery); theft, armed robbery (*haraba*); the prohibition of alcohol (for Muslims only); and whipping. The last-mentioned law was abolished in 1996 except in *hadd* cases. These laws provide severe punishments subject to strict standards of evidence under law. For example, the offence of adultery carries the punishment of stoning to death if the accused makes a voluntary confession or four adult male eye witnesses testify to the charge. Theft and armed robbery are punishable with amputation of a hand. In 1984, the Evidence Act 1872 was amended and was given an Islamic title.[142] This law provided that a document executed in respect of financial or future obligations 'shall be attested by two men or one man and two women, so that the one may remind the other'.[143] In 1985, the words 'Majlis-e-Shoora' (Council of Consultation) were substituted for the word 'parliament' and the Objectives Resolution was made a substantive part of the constitution through a new Article 2A. In 1988, Zia promulgated a Shariat Ordinance.

After Zia's death in 1988, the Islamization movement continued. In 1988, President Ghulam Ishaq Khan promulgated a revised Shariat Ordinance. The Senate proposed a Shariat bill in 1990, which proved unsuccessful. In 1991, the Parliament passed the Enforcement of Sharīah Act. All this *Sharīah* legislation did not bring any substantive change. The jurisdiction of the FSC remained limited. In 1990, a new criminal law, the *Qisas* (retribution) and *Diyat* (blood money; monetary compensation) was introduced. This law deals with the offences of murder and different kinds of injury. According to this law most offences, including murder, are compoundable. However, it has outlawed an old custom of giving a woman in marriage to the complainant party in murder cases. The law also provides that a woman, as one of the legal heirs of the deceased, has to receive half-share in the amount of *diyat*, per her share in inheritance. General Musharraf (1999–2008) not only discontinued Islamization, but also made successful attempts to do away with the reforms introduced by Zia. Rather, he brought radical changes in the *Hudood* laws by introducing a Women Protection Act in 2006, amid protests from religious scholars.[144] The MMA-led government of the NWFP (2002–2007) introduced a *Hisba* bill in the provincial

141 The 1973 constitution, Art. 203DD.

142 *The Qanun-e-Shahadat Order* [the law of evidence] 1984.

143 Ibid. Art. 17(2).

144 According to this law, rape is now a *tazir* offence punishable with death or life imprisonment, fornication (*zina*) is punishable with five years' imprisonment and a fine of up to ten thousand rupees. A complaint of these offences can now be made to the court (instead of to the police) which is competent to try such offence.

legislature.[145] Musharraf twice challenged the constitutionality of the *Hisba* bill in the Supreme Court.

Economic reform

Among the economic reforms, the *Zakat* and *Ushr* Ordinance 1980 deserves to be mentioned here.[146] *Zakat* is one of the five pillars of Islamic faith. It is a charitable obligation on all financially sound Muslims, who must give away a proportion of their wealth (2.5 per cent of their savings and valuables kept for one lunar year, the total value of which is more than a basic minimum called *nisab*).[147] *Zakat* is distributed among eight categories of people: the poor, the destitute, those who collect *zakat*, those new Muslims whose hearts are to be reconciled with Islam, slaves, debtors, those who are doing *jihad* for the sake of Allah and wayfarers. *Zakat* has a key role in establishing economic and social justice;[148] hence it may be helpful for the promotion of the RTD in Pakistan.

The Ordinance recognizes that 'the prime objective of Zakat and Ushr, and disbursements therefrom, is to assist the needy, the indigent and the poor'. The law provides a compulsory deduction of *zakat* at the rate of 2.5 per cent on different kinds of assets, which include bank deposits such as savings, fixed deposit/saving certificates, annuities, life insurance policies, provident funds, and so on.[149] The law is applicable to Muslim citizens only. However, Shias

145 The Muttahid Majlis-e-Amal (MMA) was a coalition of religious parties that ruled the North West Frontier Province (NWFP) from 2002 to 2007. The bill was passed by the NWFP Assembly as part of their Islamization movement.

146 Other reforms include the Islamization of the banking and financial system, with the aim of eliminating interest (*riba*). In this respect, the *Mudaraba* Ordinance was introduced in 1981. *Mudaraba* is '[a] form of partnership where one party provides the funds while the other provides expertise and management. The latter is referred to as the *Mudarib*. Any profits accrued are shared between the two parties on a pre-agreed basis, while loss is borne by the provider of the capital.' See State Bank of Pakistan, *Annual Report, FY02*, pp 189–98. In 1991, the Federal Shariat Court declared interest to be un-Islamic. The decision was upheld by the Shariat Appellate Bench of the Supreme Court in a decision in 1999. Through its decision of 24 June 2002, the Shariat Appellate Bench of the Supreme Court reviewed its earlier decision and remitted the matter to the Federal Shariat Court for a fresh decision: *United Bank v M/s Farooq Brothers etc*. Online. Available at: <http://www.supremecourt.gov.pk//judgment.htm> (accessed 28 Aug. 2007).

147 The amount of *nisab* is 3 ounces or 87.48g of gold.

148 Grace Clark, 'Pakistan's Zakat and Ushr as a Welfare System' in Anita M. Weiss (ed.), *Islamic Reassertion in Pakistan: The Application of Islamic Laws in a Modern State*, New York, Syracuse University Press, 1986, pp 79–95, at p 82.

149 The Zakat and Ushr Ordinance, s. 3. The ordinance also provides payment of *zakat* on those assets which are not subject to compulsory *zakat*. They include gold, silver and other precious metals; cash money, prize bonds, agricultural produce and different kinds of animals, such as goats and camels. It also creates a comprehensive machinery of *zakat* administration, which includes *zakat* funds and *zakat* committees at the central, provincial and local levels (s. 7).

were exempted from the law because they opposed it on jurisprudential grounds.[150] Pakistan's current PRSP has proposed a *zakat* fund as a key social safety net for a diverse section of people and even institutions, such as hospitals and educational institutions.

Implications for the RTD

The Islamization of the legal and judicial system attracted widespread opposition from modernists and human rights activists, at home and abroad. They argued that the movement badly affected the rights of women and minorities and that Zia used it to gain legitimacy for his illegal regime.[151] Some argued that the Islamization movement appeared 'to be concerned with the husk and not the core of Islam'.[152] The *Hudood* law regarding sexual offences struck at the status of women because it required four adult male eye witnesses, as the standard of proof in rape cases. In the absence of such proof, the victim's allegation and/or pregnancy were considered sufficient to prove her guilt. Thus the law affected women's rights to equality, to a fair trial, to access to justice and to protection against cruel and inhuman treatment. One view is that the problem was due not to gender bias, but to the improper implementation of the laws.[153]

As an essential part of the Islamization movement, the *zakat* law combined 'elements of Islam's traditional religious welfare institution with those of a modern public welfare system'.[154] Initially, the *zakat* law led to a sectarian clash between Sunnis and Shias. The Shias objected to compulsory *zakat* for the reason that a government, which is not a legitimate successor of the Prophet, has no authority to collect *zakat*.[155] However, the law allowed them to claim exemption from compulsory payment of *zakat*. Other problems of the *zakat* system include lack of funds and male domination of the local *zakat* committees. Generally, the *zakat* system has been modestly successful in the rehabilitation of disabled people. Recent years have witnessed an increase in the number of *zakat* beneficiaries and the initiation of rehabilitation schemes for the beneficiaries, with a view to contributing to poverty

150 Ann Elizabeth Mayer, 'Islamization and Taxation in Pakistan' in Anita M. Weiss (ed.), *Islamic Reassertion in Pakistan: The Application of Islamic Laws in a Modern State*, New York, Syracuse University Press, 1986, pp 59–77, at p 72.

151 Mehdi, op. cit., p 32.

152 D. Taylor, 'The Politics of Islam and Islamization in Pakistan' in J. Piscatori (ed.), *Islam in the Political Process*, Cambridge, Cambridge University Press, 1983, p 181 cited in Niaz A. Shah, op. cit., p 106.

153 See C. Kennedy, 'Islamization in Pakistan: Implementation of the Hudood Ordinance', *Asian Survey* 28(3), March 1988, 313, cited in Ian Talbot, *Pakistan: A Modern History*, London, C. Hurst, 1998, p 276.

154 Clark, op. cit., p 79.

155 Ibid. p 81.

reduction.[156] But it still has a long way to go to achieve the goals of poverty reduction and redistribution of wealth. Moreover, it will remain too marginal to the national economy unless coupled with the elimination of *riba* (interest: usury) and redistribution of lands.[157]

The Islamization movement carried out both by Zia and by the post-Zia governments did not address wider issues of socio-legal importance. Like other developing countries, Pakistan's social, political, economic and legal institutions have a colonial legacy, where the relations between the state and the individual are generally problematic. Political domination by large landowners and ethnic division lead to poor public service delivery and growing inequality.[158] Equally problematic are the regional and global dynamics characterized by political interests such as security issues like terrorism and economic interest such as trade liberalization. The Islamization movement needs to address the growing problems between the state and the individual, on the one side and the impact of the problems of social and economic globalization, on the other. Unless the modernists and Islamic activists agree on common grounds to address these internal and external challenges, the Islamization movement will remain a tool of political expediency. This requires an RTD agenda – genuine participation, respect for and observance of human rights, particularly women's rights, and a comprehensive development policy.

Obviously, the impact of the Islamization on the RTD is negative. Firstly, the Islamization movement was the agenda of a military regime. It seriously lacked the element of participation – political participation – a key feature of the Declaration.[159] It was not initiated, debated and implemented through a process of democratic deliberation (*Shura*), nor were CSOs consulted. Moreover, the process of Islamization was also against the spirit of the Qur'an which emphasizes the role of consultation in all matters of public policy, saying: 'and consult them in the affairs (of moment)'.[160] Elections were held in 1985, but the political parties were not allowed to participate in the elections. The parliament formed as a result of those elections passed a con-

156 See Ishrat Hussain, 'Economic Reforms and Macroeconomic Management in Pakistan, 1999–2001'. Online. Available at: <www.sbp.org.pk>.

157 Grace Clark, 'Pakistan's Zakat and Ushr as a Welfare System', op. cit., p 92.

158 See William Easterly, 'The Political Economy of Growth Without Development: A Case Study of Pakistan', Paper for the Analytical Narratives of Growth Project, Kennedy School of Government, Harvard University, Development Research Group, World Bank, June 2001. Online. Available at <http://ksghome.harvard.edu/~drodrik/Growth%20volume/Easterly-Pakistan.pdf> (Accessed 29 Aug. 2007). See also Tariq Amin Khan, 'Economy, Society and the State in Pakistan', *Contemporary South Asia* 9(2), 2000, 181–95.

159 See DRD, Art. 2(3).

160 The Holy Qur'an, 3:15.

troversial eighth constitutional amendment bill that endorsed all the laws and regulations introduced by Zia.

Secondly, as noted above, the Islamization movement was not formulated as part of a broad-based national development policy that, as the Declaration provides, aims to provide for the constant well-being of the individual and the entire population. Thirdly, international human rights law was totally ignored. For example, no efforts were made to ratify the ICCPR and ICESCR, despite the fact that Pakistan fully supported the Declaration in the UN forums. As argued above, the objectives of Islamic law generally overlap with international human rights. Fourthly, the negative impact of the criminal laws reforms – the *Hudood* laws – on women's human rights directly violated Article 8 of the Declaration, which requires effective measures that are to ensure an active role for women in the process of development. Women's rights activists strongly opposed the reforms. Justice and equality are the objectives of the *Shari'ah* as well as of the Declaration. But the *Hudood* laws failed to realize these objectives since hundreds of women have suffered because of the erroneous application and interpretation of these laws.[161] Fifthly, the financial impact of the *zakat* law on fair and equitable distribution of wealth has been minimal.[162] The administration of *zakat* was dominated by males. Thus, in violation of Article 8 of the Declaration, the role of women in the formulation and implementation of *zakat* policy was ignored. In short, the Islamization movement did not focus on social and economic egalitarianism.[163] Finally, the independence of the judiciary was undermined by the introduction of a requirement compelling judges of the superior courts to take a fresh oath of office. This move had serious implications for the rule of law, which is a cornerstone of the rights-based approach to development. Stressing the role of the judiciary, the current working group has noted that a development programme should promote an independent legal system and encourage participatory, transparent and accountable government and management.[164] The Islamization movement was launched at a time when the RTD debate in the UN was at its peak. Pakistan actively supported the RTD at the international level, but totally ignored its importance at the domestic level.

Soon after the end of the Zia regime, the superior judiciary introduced an era of judicial activism in the form of a move to protect human rights through PIL. The intervention of the judiciary in the Islamization process is analysed in the next section.

161 Shah, op. cit., p 139.
162 DRD, Art. 2(3).
163 Talbot, op. cit., p 272.
164 E/CN.4/2001/26, First session, para. 136.

THE ROLE OF THE JUDICIARY

The courts are specifically empowered by the Enforcement of *Shari'ah* Act 1991 to carry out *ijtihad*.[165] Such *ijtihad* may be called judicial *ijtihad*.[166] The influence of the *Shari'ah* on judicial interpretation of human rights is briefly analysed here with reference to the case law.

Commentators argue that 'since the late 1960s, Pakistani courts have increasingly recognized and relied on principles of Islamic law'.[167] From the very beginning, the courts in Pakistan followed a progressive interpretation of the *Shari'ah*,[168] by applying *istihsan* (juristic preference/equity) to serve *maslahah*. An early example is the well-known case of *Khurshid Bibi v Muhammad Amin* in which the Supreme Court validated *khul*, a kind of separation that a wife can ask for without the consent of her husband.[169] The ruling was a clear departure from a rigid rule of the traditional law that *khul* was conditional on a husband's consent and the return of dowry by a wife. Justice Cornelius, a former Chief Justice of Pakistan, emphatically said in 1970, 'in Pakistan, the concept of the rule of law should indicate nothing else than [*Shari'ah*]'.[170]

The courts applied and elaborated Islamic social justice in a justiciable way. The courts held that a Muslim in a financially sound position is under a duty to support his poor and destitute relatives within the prohibited degrees (blood relations, to whom marriage is not permitted under Islamic law).[171] The Supreme Court also declared un-Islamic a customary practice of

165 However, the courts themselves recognized much earlier that they may do *ijtihad*. On this, see *Mst. Zohra Begum v Sh. Latif Ahmad Munawwar*, PLD 1965 (West Pakistan) Lahore 695. 'Where there is no Quranic or Traditional Text or an *Ijma* on a point of law, and if there is a difference of views between [scholars and jurists], a Court may form its own opinion on a point of law.'

166 See s. 4: '(a) while interpreting the statute-law, if more than one interpretation is possible, the one consistent with the Islamic principles and jurisprudence shall be adopted by the Court; and (b) where two or more interpretations are equally possible the interpretation which advances the Principles of Policy and Islamic provisions in the Constitution shall be adopted by the Court.'

167 Martin Lau, *The Role of Islam in the Legal System of Pakistan*, Leiden/Boston, Martinus Nijhoff Publishers, 2006, p 9.

168 See generally, Kamal F. Farouki, 'Pakistan Islamic Government and Society' in John L. Esposito (ed.), *Islam in Asia: Religion, Politics and Society*, Oxford, Oxford University Press, 1987, pp 53–78.

169 PLD 1967 SC 97.

170 A.R. Cornelius, 'Fundamental Rights under Shari'at', *PLD Journal*, 1970, 144–5 at 145.

171 *Haji Nizam Khan v Additional District Judge, Lyallpur*, PLD 1976 Lahore 930 and 950. This case was approved by the Supreme Court in PLD 1982 SC 139; for a similar precedent see also *Fazlul Quader Chowdhry v Muhammad Abdul Haq*, PLD 1963 SC 486; it was held that the courts can scrutinize the acts of other branches like the executive and legislature, though 'this power does not give to the Court any practical or real omnipotence' (at 521).

relinquishment by a woman, in favour of her male relatives, of shares in inherited property.[172] This case can be read as reflecting a clash between the customs of a patriarchal society and the dictates of religious laws.

The insertion of Article 2-A in the constitution further widened the scope for invoking the principles of Islamic justice, particularly in the cases pertaining to fundamental rights. Thus Article 2-A, which was a symbol of the Zia era, was effectively utilized by the courts in protecting fundamental rights. At a 1991 conference, the judiciary reiterated their commitment to protecting the fundamental rights of citizens in accordance with the tenets of Islam.[173] The Islamic facet in the constitutional and judicial system is the main distinguishing features of Pakistan in the area of PIL.[174] However, the court also ruled: 'even the fundamental rights as given in the Constitution must not violate the norms of Islam.'[175]

The courts have extended the scope of human rights by treating many of the social and economic entitlements of citizens as rights recognized by Islam. For example, the right to have the choice of a decent profession[176] and the right to a good reputation or a fair name are equal to the rights to life and property.[177] The scope of the right to justice is also extended to the right to hearing[178] and the right of appeal against conviction.[179] The right of a woman to have freedom to choose her spouse has recently been a subject of litigation in Pakistan. The cases of *Saima Wahid*[180] and *Humaira Mehmood*[181] reflect the judiciary's attempt to interpret Islamic law broadly. In both the cases, it was held that a woman can freely choose her spouse for marriage without the consent of her parents/guardian (*wali*). In the latter case, the court also cited Article 16 of the Women's Convention and the Cairo Declaration on Human Rights. Within the purview of Islamic law, these rights are among the objectives of the *Shari'ah*, i.e. the five essentials – life, property, reason, religion and family.

The role of the FSC in promoting *maslahah* through *ijtihad* deserves to be particularly examined here. The FSC may be said to be doing judicial *ijtihad*. In *Ansar Burney*, the court interpreted two Qur'anic verses regarding the status of women.[182] The first verse reads: 'And women shall have rights

172 *Pakistan, Federation of v Muhammad Ishaque*, PLD 1983 SC 273.

173 Judicial Conference, Quetta, 1991, details of proceedings in *PLD Journal* 1991, 126–39.

174 Mansoor Hassan Khan, *The Concept of Public Interest Litigation and its Meaning in Pakistan*, Karachi, Pakistan Law House, 1993, p 48.

175 *Zaheerudin v The State*, 1993 SCMR 1718.

176 *Federation of Pakistan and others v Public-at-Large and others*, PLD 1988 SC 202.

177 *Muhammad Akram v Mst. Farman Bi*, PLD 1990 SC 28; *Syed Ghayyur Hussain Shah and another v Gharib Alam*, PLD 1990 Lah. 432.

178 *Pakistan and others v Public-at-Large and others*, PLD 1987 SC 304.

179 *Pakistan through Secretary, Ministry of Defence v The General Public*, PLD 1989 SC 6.

180 *Abdul Wahid v Asma Jehangir*, PLD 1997 Lahore 301. See also PLD 2004 SC 210.

181 *Humaira Mehmood v State*, PLD 1999 Lahore 494.

182 PLD 1983 FSC 73.

similar to the rights against them, according to what is equitable; but men have a degree (of advantage) over them.'[183] The second verse is: 'Men are the protectors and maintainers of women, because Allah has given the one more (strength) than the other, and because they support them from their means.'[184] Ansar Burney challenged the appointment of women judges as being contrary to the above injunctions of the Qur'an. The court ruled that 'there is no express or even implied restriction on the appointment of a female [judge] in the Qur'an and Sunnah'. The court applied the doctrine of *ibahah* (permissibility) and observed that 'what is not prohibited by the Holy Qur'an and Sunnah is permitted, and the burden of proof that anything is prohibited is on the person who claims it be so'. The court held that the Arabic word *qawwam* (maintainers, protectors) used in verse 4:34 means the one who protects and maintains his wife. The court rejected the view that the word means that the man is sovereign: 'To call a man a sovereign or one who exercises full domination over the life and property of a woman . . . cannot be in accordance with the Qur'an and Sunnah.'

In another case, the court rejected the plea of a member of parliament for exemption from appearing in a court of law.[185] The petitioner claimed this privilege under a provincial law.[186] The court ruled that the granting of such privileges is contrary to the Qur'an and the Sunnah. The court applied and interpreted the Qur'an: 'O ye who believe! stand out firmly for justice . . . even as against yourselves, or your parents, or your kin, and whether it be (against) rich or poor.'[187]

The jurisprudence of the court in the *Hudood* laws introduced by General Zia is inconsistent. In several cases, the FSC corrected the decisions of the lower courts on a number of issues, for example, that a case of rape cannot be converted to that of *zina*[188] and the absence of marks of violence on the body of the victim is not a proof of crime.[189] The court's approach to the presence of pregnancy as a proof of guilt is inconsistent.[190] The requirement of four male eye witnesses for the proof of rape was held to be contrary to the Qur'an and Sunnah.[191]

Two recent constitutional cases regarding Islamization may be mentioned here. The first concerns the *Hisba* bill, introduced by the MMA government

183 The Holy Qur'an, 2:228.

184 Ibid. 4:34.

185 *Pakistan, Federation of v Hazoor Bakhsh* PLD 1988 FSC 283.

186 The NWFP Provincial Assembly (Powers, Immunities and Privileges) Act 1988.

187 The Holy Qur'an, 4:135.

188 *Mst. Taslem v The State*, PLJ 1996, FSC 138.

189 *Muhammad Nawaz v The State*, 1990 SCMR 886; *Muhammad Sadiq v The State*, 1997 PCr. LJ 546 (FSC); *Muhammad Qasim v The State*, 1997 PCr. LJ 10965 FSC.

190 See *Mst. Jehan Mina v The State*, PLJ 1983 FSC 134 (pregnancy was considered sufficient proof); *Mst Siani v The State*, PLD 1984 FSC 121 (pregnancy was not considered sufficient proof).

191 *Begum Rashida Patel v Federation of Pakistan*, PLD 1989 FSC 95.

of the NWFP in 2006, regarding which the President sought the opinion of the Supreme Court (advisory jurisdiction). The Court held that certain parts of the bill violated some fundamental rights, such as the freedom of assembly, association, trade, business or profession, speech, freedom to profess religion and to manage religious institutions and the equality of citizens.[192] It follows that the court considers it necessary that any piece of legislation that is in pursuance of Islamization should conform to the constitutionally guaranteed fundamental rights. The second case relates to the prohibition of interest (*riba*) in the banking system. Through its decision of 24 June 2002, the Shariat Appellate Bench of the Supreme Court reviewed its 1999 decision on the elimination of interest and remitted the matter to the FSC for a fresh decision.[193] This judgment indicates that a number of jurisprudential issues relating to *riba* are still unresolved despite the government's efforts to implement the earlier judgments of the court.

IMPLICATIONS FOR OTHER MUSLIM COUNTRIES

Almost all Muslim countries support the RTD in the UN. But, like Pakistan, most have not expressly recognized the RTD in their constitutions.[194] Nineteen Muslim countries recognize Islam as their state religion.[195] They have constitutional obligations to apply Islamic law at the domestic level. As discussed above, the constitutional role of Islam comes into conflict with international human rights. Moreover, there are also growing calls from the Muslim population of these countries for the imposition of Islamic law. These calls are related to wider issues of political, economic, social and cultural conditions of life, with Islamic law proposed as the main tool of change. Several reasons, which are relevant to the RTD, explain the Muslim peoples' desire for such a change, such as lack of genuine political participation and democracy,[196] poor institutions and a fair and equitable distribution of the gains of development. While these issues are common to all developing countries, their peculiarity in the Muslim countries lies in the fact that the Islamic activists seek their resolution through Islamic law. It was argued above that

192 *Reference by the President of Pakistan under Article 186 of the Constitution of the Islamic Republic of Pakistan*, 1973. The judgment is available at: <www.supremecourt.gov.pk//judgment.htm> (Accessed 29 Aug. 2007). See also I.A. Rehman, *A Tale of Two Bills*, *The Dawn*, 30 Nov. 2006.

193 The judgment is referred to above in the section on economic reform.

194 Benin, Cameroon and Uganda have recognized the RTD in their constitutions.

195 Afghanistan, Algeria, Bangladesh, Bahrain, Egypt, Iraq, Jordan, Kuwait, Libya, Malaysia, Mauritania, Morocco, Oman, Pakistan, Qatar, Saudi Arabia, Syria, Tunisia, Yemen.

196 See James P. Piscatori, *Islam in a World of Nation-States*, Cambridge, Cambridge University Press, 1986, p 32. For various approaches explaining Islamic activism, see Abdelkader, op. cit., pp 1–26.

notwithstanding some differences, *maslahah* may promote the RTD. All the Sunni schools of jurisprudence support *maslahah*. Every school can take *maslahah* into consideration to interpret the existing law or make new legislation in the absence of textual rule(s). Generally, *maslahah* appears to have positive implications for the promotion of the RTD in Muslim countries that follow Sunni jurisprudence. However, as discussed above, the promotion of the RTD through *maslahah* requires a movement well beyond mere jurisprudential interpretations. The process of Islamization, as discussed above, should address external challenges such as global security issues, notably the menace of terrorism and economic globalization, for example trade liberalization and internal challenges such as good governance, democracy, respect for human rights and a just and fair distribution of economic development.[197]

CONCLUSION

One must appreciate that the Islamization movement is a living reality in the social and political life of Pakistan. Even a secular government cannot totally ignore it. The promotion of the RTD in Pakistan, therefore, will depend on the specific policy of a particular government to achieve the goal of Islamic social justice. This chapter, however, has argued that theoretically the doctrine of *maslahah* can promote the RTD in Pakistan and other Muslim countries that follow Sunni law. Wider interpretation of Islamic law may address the problem of cultural relativism to promote and protect human rights, including the RTD, and may achieve *maslahah*. But it is necessary that Islamization should be pursued in the context of diverse internal and external challenges. The real hurdle in the promotion of the RTD in Pakistan is, however, created by first, the undue politicization of Islamic law and secondly, serious neglect of active, free and meaningful participation in the process of Islamization. Since independence, Islam has been much more in the politics than in the policy framework of the government. Zia's Islamization movement was a tool of political legitimacy; it did not focus on the core issue of social and economic development through Islamization. In the post-Zia era, efforts towards complete Islamization have continued. However, the question of the appropriate role of Islam in the political process remains an unresolved issue between the modernists and the Islamic activists.[198] Thus the executive and legislative authorities of the state are unable to establish good government (*Siyasah Shari'ah*) and thereby secure *maslahah*. However, on the

197 See generally, Radha D'Souza, 'The "Third World" and Socio-Legal Studies: Neo-Liberalism and Lessons from India's Legal Innovations', *Social & Legal Studies* 14(4), 2005, 487–513. Analysing India's judicial experience, the author argues that the readaptation of the sociological state (a colonial construction) in the Third World to the post-Cold War order must entail an immanent discourse of law.

198 Kennedy, op. cit., 769.

credit side a system of *zakat* has been established, and this has so far enjoyed a limited success. If the *zakat* system is improved, it may prove very helpful for the promotion of the RTD. The superior courts have interpreted Islamic law by taking due cognizance of social conditions. Thus it is the judiciary which has been relatively more successful in using *maslahah*, and which may play a more positive role in the promotion of the RTD. The role of the superior courts, however, is not sufficient. As this book argues, an effective and efficient judicial service at the grass-roots level is also necessary for the promotion of the RTD. The role of the judiciary in good governance is incomplete if its lower tier is not involved in broad-based governance reforms as part of a national poverty-reduction strategy. The next chapter looks at the implementation of the RTD in Pakistan through the current poverty-reduction programme, focusing on current judicial reforms.

8 Pakistan's poverty-reduction strategy and the RTD

INTRODUCTION

It was argued in Chapter 4 that if human rights are incorporated in the PRSP framework, it may provide a feasible way to realize the RTD because firstly, such a framework has become effective in the backdrop of negotiations between states and the IFIs. Secondly, it will place responsibility on the state, which has the primary duty, under the Declaration, to realize the RTD. This chapter mainly builds on the arguments made in Chapter 4 and looks at Pakistan's present PRSP vis-à-vis the RTD. It focuses on judicial reforms currently being pursued under the PRSP to see whether an effective and efficient judicial service at the grass-roots level can ensure the protection of fundamental rights.

From a constitutional perspective, Pakistan's development policy, notably the PRSP, must be guided by the Principles of Policy set out in the constitution. The principles require the state to secure, subject to available resources, an adequate standard of living for all without any discrimination by ensuring a fair distribution of wealth and means of production, providing basic necessities such as food, clothing, housing, health and by reducing income disparity.[1] In order to meet constitutional obligations, a national development policy must aim to realize these principles.

There is a growing debate about linking human rights to the PRSP. The significance of this linkage for the RTD has been recognized by the current working group during its debates on a Development Compact model, proposed by the Independent Expert for the realization of the RTD. The representatives of the IFIs have also expressed the view that instead of a Development Compact model, existing development frameworks, such as the PRSP, may be strengthened for the realization of the RTD. The UN's OHCHR has published 'Principles and Guidelines for a Human Rights Approach to Poverty Reduction

1 DRD, Art. 3(8).

Strategies'.[2] These guidelines can prove helpful in the promotion of the RTD.

The chapter gives a brief introduction to the PRSP framework and its relevance to the RTD and the OHCHR guidelines. It then examines the principles of the PRSP framework vis-à-vis the features of the Declaration and attempts to see its practical implications. Pakistan's PRSP and its implications for the RTD are separately discussed, with particular reference to the AJP, a current programme of reform for the lower judiciary, pursued under the PRSP. Finally, the judicial reform programme is examined through the lens of the OHCHR's guidelines about the right of access to justice.

THE PRSP FRAMEWORK

Introduction and background

The PRSP is a policy document of a country, which embodies a comprehensive programme of poverty reduction and the promotion of economic growth.[3] It outlines macroeconomic and social policies and structural changes to reduce poverty. Such policies include reforms in the financial sector, the devolution of power, improving good governance, investing in human capital, to name just a few. The preparation of a PRSP by a recipient country is a condition for debt relief and other financial assistance from the IFIs.[4] An essential feature of the PRSP is that it is to be prepared through a process of participation, involving various stakeholders at home, such as local CSOs and organizations abroad, such as the World Bank and the IMF.

The growing consensus over a broad definition of poverty as a failure of capability provides a theoretical underpinning to the PRSP. According to the capability approach (Chapter 2), poverty is defined as a failure to achieve basic capabilities, for example, freedom from hunger or to be able to take part in the life of the community. Since the 1990s, development practitioners have adopted this approach as an indication of human development. The

2 UNHCHR, 'Principles and Guidelines for a Human Rights Approach to Poverty Reduction Strategies'. Online. Available at: <www.ohchr.org/Documents/publications/poverty Strategiesen.pdf.> (Accessed 11 Nov. 2008) (hereinafter the guidelines).

3 See 'Poverty Reduction Strategies'. Online. Available at <www.worldbank.org> (accessed 9 March 2007).

4 The implementation of a PRSP was a requirement of the IFIs under the Heavily Indebted Poor Countries (HIPC) initiative, introduced by the World Bank and IMF in 1996, in order to help poor countries that were unable to manage their heavy burdens of debt. In 1999, this initiative was linked with poverty reduction. The IFIs now also require non-HIPC countries to have a PRSP as a pre-condition for giving concessional aid. Details online. Available at: <http://www.imf.org/external/np/exr/facts/hipc.htm> (accessed 9 March 2007).

UNDP Human Development Reports (HDRs) of 1993 and 1996 are examples in point.[5] The 1993 HDR says that human development means investing in human capabilities such as health, education and skills. The report maintains that the outcomes of development should be fairly and equitably distributed.[6] The 1996 HDR argues that economic growth should be linked to human development, poverty reduction and environmental protection.[7] The World Bank, in its 2000/2001 World Development Report, recognizes that a poverty reduction strategy should aim at the expansion of poor peoples' capabilities.[8]

Another reason for encouraging countries to draw up a PRSP was the desire to improve the effectiveness of foreign aid.[9] Commentators argue that aid effectiveness depends on democracy and good institutions.[10] In this respect, one commentator observes that development aid has shown good results in countries where institutions are strong enough to check the arbitrary use of power by government.[11] Thus political and civil liberties, such as freedom of speech and rights to association and assembly, create an enabling environment for accountability and participation. It was also recognized that the failure of development policies in many countries was due to lack of ownership of such policies by those countries.[12]

The guidelines

The guidelines were initially developed by the OHCHR in 2001 in response to a request made by the Committee on Economic, Social and Cultural Rights. The drafters observe, '[t]he value added by the human rights approach to poverty reduction consists both in the manner in which it departs from existing strategies and in the manner in which it reinforces them.'[13] The drafters argue that the guidelines 'elaborate and clarify certain principles that should guide the process of formulating, implementing and monitoring a poverty reduction strategy if it is to be consistent with a human rights approach'.[14]

5 UNDP, *Human Development Report*, New York/Oxford, Oxford University Press, 1993, p 3.
6 Ibid.
7 UNDP, *Human Development Report*, New York/Oxford, Oxford University Press, 1996, p 1.
8 World Bank, *Attacking Poverty, World Development Report, 2000/2001*, Oxford, Oxford University Press, 2000, p 32.
9 Gobind Nankani, et al., 'Human Rights and Poverty Reduction Strategies: Moving Towards Convergence?' in Alston and Robinson (eds), op. cit., 2005, pp 475–97, at p 476.
10 Ibid.
11 See Jakob Svensson, 'Aid, Growth and Democracy', *Economics and Politics* 11(3), Nov. 1999, 275–97, at 275.
12 Francis Stewart and Michael Wang, 'Poverty Reduction Strategy Papers within the Human Rights Perspective' in Alston and Robinson (eds), op. cit., pp 447–74, at p 447.
13 Guidelines, para. 17.
14 Ibid. para. 4.

The guidelines underscore the principles of a human rights-based approach to development and the value of such an approach to poverty reduction. In this respect, the guidelines observe that a human rights-based approach provides guiding norms and values to the institutions and policies of poverty reduction.[15] The guidelines also underline that '[an] international human rights framework provide[s] a compelling normative framework' to a poverty-reduction strategy because poverty is seen as a denial of human rights and human rights have the potential to empower the poor.[16] Moreover, the human rights-based approach has the potential to extend the scope of a poverty-reduction strategy from a needs-based to a rights-based approach. The latter approach creates a legal entitlement of the poor and a legal obligation on the duty-holder as the first step towards empowerment.[17]

The guidelines cover both the process and the content of the poverty-reduction strategy. Regarding the process, the guidelines provide advice to policy-makers to identify the poor from the perspectives of human rights and basic capabilities; to expressly identify the national and international human rights frameworks; to address inequality and discrimination as the causes of poverty; to develop indicators and benchmarks for progressive realization of human rights and to ensure participation and empowerment.[18] In this book, poverty is understood in this multidimensional perspective (Chapter 1).

For the content of a poverty-reduction strategy, the guidelines prescribe guidance regarding certain human rights at the national and international level, which are seen as relevant to a poverty-reduction strategy. At the national level, the guidelines include the rights to adequate food, education, decent work, adequate housing, personal security, access to justice and political rights and freedoms. At the international level, the right to international assistance and cooperation is included in the guidelines. Guideline 8, which pertains to the right of equal access to justice, will be analysed in detail in the context of Pakistan's current judicial reform, later in this chapter.

For each of these rights, the guidelines are developed methodically. Firstly, the importance of a human right is explored. Secondly, the scope and content of the right as set out in international human rights instruments is outlined.

15 Ibid. para. 16.

16 Ibid.

17 Ibid.

18 Ibid. Chapter II deals with the process of formulating, implementing and monitoring a human rights-based poverty-reduction strategy and sets out seven guidelines. Chapter III deals with the content of a human rights-based poverty reduction strategy and sets out one guideline each in respect of specific human rights standards such as the rights to work, adequate food, housing, health, education, personal security and privacy, equal access to justice and political rights and freedoms.

Thirdly, the guidelines identify 'key targets in relation to each right and lists, for each target, some indicators that will help assess the extent to which these targets are being achieved over time'.[19] Fourthly, the guidelines set out key features of a strategy for achieving the specified targets.[20]

The drafters of the guidelines have, however, indicated that the proposed indicators reflect the conditions of the poor and vulnerable sections of society and hence are not exhaustive.[21] Moreover, the drafters have also made it clear that the proposed strategies are limited to poverty reduction only.

PRINCIPLES OF THE PRSP AND THE RTD

The PRSP scheme is based on the following five core principles:[22]

- country-driven, promoting national ownership of development policy through broad-based participation of civil society;
- result-oriented and focused on outcomes that will benefit the poor;
- comprehensive in recognizing the multidimensional nature of poverty;
- partnership-oriented, involving coordinated participation of development partners (government, domestic stakeholders, and external donors); and
- based on a long-term perspective for poverty reduction.

The relevance of these principles to the RTD is discussed below.

Country ownership

The country ownership, a key characteristic of the PRSP framework, is intended to empower the state to initiate, outline and implement a poverty-reduction strategy itself. This feature of the PRSP is compatible with the Declaration, which emphasizes the responsibility of the state for designing a development policy.[23] It is also similar to the right of peoples to self-determination,[24] one of the sources of the RTD. The ownership of a policy

19 Ibid. para. 9.
20 Ibid.
21 Ibid. para 106.
22 See IMF, Poverty Reduction Strategy Papers (PRSPs). Online. Available at <http://www.imf.org/external/np/exr/facts/prsp.htm> (accessed 27 Apr. 2007).
23 See DRD, Arts 2(3), 3(1) and 8(1). See E/CN.4/2004/15, ODI, 'The right to development: study on existing bilateral and multilateral programmes and policies for development partnership', Independent Study by ODI, p 12 (hereinafter ODI Study).
24 See OHCHR, 'Human Rights and Poverty Reduction: A Conceptual Framework', New York/Geneva, United Nations, 2004, p 2. See also Nankani et al., op. cit., 484.

requires a perception of possession, which is a psychological factor.[25] A real change in perception is not possible without a change in the underlying realities.[26] However, mere ownership by the national government is not sufficient because governments 'are influenced by special (including their own private) interest rather than the people they supposedly represent'.[27] This is, however, not to say that governments are not legitimate representatives of the people. Genuine ownership means effective participation of all stakeholders.[28] It seems necessary that different national actors, beyond the state elites, arrive at a consensus over the proposed policies.[29]

How far, in practice, is a PRSP effectively owned by a state? In this respect, reference needs to be made to the practice of preparing the PRSPs in different countries. In the first instance, an inherent conflict may be seen in the PRSP scheme because, on the one side, it is a requirement for debt relief as well as other financial assistance, while on the other side, it is supposed to be nationally owned.[30] These two aspects of the PRSP are mutually contradictory because, if the submission of a PRSP is a condition for debt relief, how could it be based on national ownership? Moreover, the most important aspect of country ownership is the expectation of a change in donors' behaviour towards respecting the national priorities of a country and enhancing its capacity to realize such priorities.[31] Such an expectation seems unlikely to be fulfilled because the boards of the World Bank and the IMF play a dominant role in approving a PRSP. The World Bank and the IMF also play dominant roles in influencing macroeconomic policies, as part of the PRSPs.[32] This fact is gleaned from the reviews of the PRSPs of many countries in Africa,[33] Latin America and the Caribbean.[34] In some countries even government officials

25 Francis Stewart and Michael Wang, 'Do PRSPs Empower Poor Countries and Disempower the World Bank or is it the Other Way Round?', *Queen Elizabeth House Working Paper* No. 108, p 2. Online. Available at: <http://www3.qeh.ox.ac.uk/RePEc/qeh/qehwps/qehwps108.pdf> (accessed 24 March 2007) (hereinafter *Queen Elizabeth House Working Paper* No. 108).

26 Ibid.

27 Stewart and Wang, op. cit., p 452.

28 The guidelines No. 5, para. 76.

29 Laure-Helene Piron (ODI) with Alison Evans, 'Politics and the PRSP Approach: A Synthesis Paper', *Working Paper* 237, London, ODI, March 2004, 5.

30 ODI Study, op. cit., p 14.

31 Nankani et al., op. cit., p 484.

32 Stewart and Wang, op. cit., p 464.

33 Rosemary McGee with Josh Levene and Alexandra Hughes, 'Assessing Participation in Poverty Reduction Strategy Papers: A Desk-based Synthesis of Experience in sub-Saharan Africa', Brighton, Institute of Development Studies, Research Report 52, Feb. 2002, p 17. Online. Available at: <http://www.ids.ac.uk/ids/bookshop/rr/rr52.pdf>. The writers review the PRSPs of Ghana, Malawi, Mozambique, Tanzania and Zambia (accessed 12 March 2007).

34 ODI, 'Experience with Poverty Reduction Strategy Papers in Latin America and the Caribbean', PRSP Synthesis Note No. 5, February 2003. Online. Available at: <www.prspsythensis.org> (accessed 12 March 2007).

stated that the World Bank and the IMF compelled governments not to change the macroeconomic framework.[35] Hence, it is evident that the national ownership principle of the PRSP framework is not effectively enabling the state to fulfil its primary responsibility under the Declaration. It is further evident that the PRSP framework is not effectively promoting the right to self-determination.

Participation

Participation is a common principle both of the PRSPs and the RTD. A process of participation should involve the relevant stakeholders, particularly the poor sections of the society, to 'influence and share control over priority setting, policymaking, resource allocations, and/or programme implementation'.[36] Free, active and meaningful participation has the potential to promote and protect many human rights, such as the freedom of expression, assembly and association. Participation is an instrument of empowerment. Empowerment 'means enhancing the capacity of poor people to influence the state institutions that affect their lives, by strengthening their participation in political processes and local decision-making'.[37] The human rights approach to poverty reduction 'empower[s] individuals and communities by granting them entitlements that give rise to legal obligations on others'.[38] National empowerment may be achieved by giving an opportunity to all national actors, including government and the civil society, to participate in the formulation of policy.[39]

The World Bank has indicated five categories of participants. They are the general public; government institutions such as parliament, and local government bodies; CSOs such as women's rights activists, peasant associations, etc.; the private sector; and donors, bilateral as well as multilateral.[40] The participation of the general public and the government is directly relevant to the RTD because the RTD is a right of both the individual and people.[41] The CSOs, for example women's organizations, can prove helpful in ensuring that

35 Ibid. pp 464–5. See Irene Knoke and Pedro Morazan, 'PRSP: Beyond the Theory, Practical Experiences and Positions of Involved Civil Society Organisations', 2002. Online. Available at: <http://www.eurodad.org/uploadstore/cms/docs/suedwind_prsp_review.pdf> (accessed 12 March 2007). The writers review the PRSPs of Honduras and Kenya. See also Mishka Zaman, 'Are We Getting Lost in Exclusive Anti-poor, Adjustment Lending Policy Cycles?', *Action Aid Policy Briefs on PRSPs*, January 2002. Online. Available at: <http://www.esrftz.org/ppa/documents/aa_1.pdf> (accessed 12 March 2007).

36 Cited in Stewart and Wang, op. cit., p 453.

37 World Bank, *Attacking Poverty*, op. cit., p 39.

38 OHCHR, 'Human Rights and Poverty Reduction: A Conceptual Framework', op. cit., p 14.

39 *Queen Elizabeth House Working Paper* No. 108, op. cit., p 3.

40 Stewart and Wang, op. cit., p 453.

41 Ibid.

women have a role in the process of development.[42] Commentators argue that participation of the private sector in the PRSP scheme can play only an instrumental role in the promotion of human rights.[43] The participation of donors, particularly bilateral donors, is significant for the RTD because international cooperation is a key feature of the Declaration. However, it may be reiterated that control by the donor communities, particularly the IFIs, over decision-making, is creating a challenge for international cooperation.

The practical assessment of participation in different countries is the subject of academic studies. It is argued that in many countries the process of participation was guided and managed by government. Important national actors such as parliamentarians, trade unions, women's groups and marginalized sections of society were either missing or involved only marginally.[44] It is also said that the groups which did participate were carefully selected by the governments.[45] There are also examples which show that donors influenced the process of participation.[46] With the exception of a few countries, religious organizations were not involved in the process.[47] Moreover, participation took place over a very short period because donors expected the countries to submit their PRSPs very quickly.[48] Furthermore, the information available to participants was not only insufficient but also in foreign languages, mostly in English, which effectively hampered the process.[49] The process was not fully extended to the rural areas, where most of the poor population live.[50] The CSOs suggested recommendations on a variety of issues such as tax and civil services reforms, but those were not incorporated in the final version of the PRSPs.[51]

42 DRD, Art. 8(1).

43 Stewart and Wang, op. cit., p 453.

44 *Queen Elizabeth House Working Paper* No. 108, op. cit., p 11.

45 Catholic Relief Services, *Review of the Poverty Reduction Strategy Paper Initiative*, 2001, p 10. Online. Available at: <http://www.imf.org/external/np/prspgen/review/2002/comm/v2.pdf>. (Accessed 27 April 2007.) See also Stewart and Wang, op. cit., p 458.

46 For example, in Tanzania's Interim-PRSP, see Stewart and Wang, op. cit., p 456.

47 Ibid. p 458. For example, in Cameroon's PRSP, see Catholic Relief Services, op. cit., p 10.

48 Ibid. p 459. See also Action Aid, *Inclusive Circles Lost in Exclusive Cycles*, 2002, p 7. Online. Available at: <www.imf.org/external/np/prspgn/review/2002/comm/v2.pdf> (accessed 27 April 2007). Reviews Nepal's PRSP.

49 See Christian Aid, *Ignoring the Experts: Poor Peoples' Exclusion from Poverty Reduction Strategies*, p 14. Online. Available at: <http://www.imf.org/external/np/prspgen/review/2002/comm.pdf> (accessed 27 April 2007). Reviews Bolivia's PRSP.

50 Ibid. p 13.

51 Ibid. pp 464–5. For example in Bolivia, Honduras, Nicaragua, and Ghana. See Zaman, op. cit., p 8.

Other principles

Other principles of the PRSP framework may also be seen in relation to the RTD. The focus of the PRSP on result orientation and on the outcomes that will benefit the poor, is similar to the wording of Article 2(1) of the Declaration: 'the human person is the central subject of development.' The outcomes of a PRSP, in order to benefit the poor, may require, as the Declaration stresses, participation and the 'the fair distribution of the benefits' accruing therefrom. The principle of participation was discussed in detail above. Some features of a rights-based approach, such as transparency and accountability, may help achieve the outcomes that will benefit the poor.

The principle of comprehensiveness, which recognizes the multidimensional nature of poverty, also has some similarities with the RTD. As argued above, the recognition of a broad definition of poverty is of fundamental importance for the PRSP framework. In other words, the PRSP is supposed to build up a comprehensive diagnostic of poverty, which covers a wide spectrum, ranging from corruption to lack of access to justice, gender discrimination and regional disparities.[52] It recognizes the complementarity of different factors that cause poverty. It is argued that the indivisibility of human rights, a key feature of the RTD (Chapter 4), is consistent with the PRSP framework. A comprehensive concept of poverty endorsed in the PRSP framework helps in disaggregating the poverty data to identify different factors which cause poverty and affect the vulnerable poor sections of society.[53] A human rights-based approach can inform and support an integrated attack, through a PRSP, on these diverse causes of poverty.[54] However, it must be pointed out that a specific linkage of the PRSP to a human rights-based approach is essential, for the reason that in the present form the PRSP framework does not use the language of human rights.

The principle of partnership resonates with the principle of international cooperation. In other words, partnership indicates a compact between the states and the international community. Various international conferences on development in the 1990s as well as international efforts in the current decade are seen as representing a 'global compact' on poverty reduction.[55] However, as stated above, the interventionist role of donors in the preparation process of the PRSP is a challenge to international cooperation and thereby to the RTD.

The last principle, i.e. a long-term perspective for poverty reduction, generally appears to be consistent with the Declaration, which emphasizes the duty of the state to formulate appropriate development policies, aimed at the realization of the RTD. The bundle of measures laid down in Article 8(1)

52 Nankani et al., op. cit., pp 492–3.
53 Ibid.
54 Ibid.
55 See ODI Study, p 8.

requires long-term policies to support a poverty-reduction strategy based on a rights-based approach. The principle of accountability, for example, requires a broad system comprising different institutions: '[J]udicial (e.g. judicial review of executive acts and omissions), quasi judicial (e.g. ombudsman, international human rights treaty bodies), administrative (e.g. the preparation, publication and scrutiny of human rights impact assessments) and political (e.g. through parliamentary processes).'[56]

Similarly, the principle of participation requires the protection and promotion of civil and political rights, such as the freedom of expression, assembly and association. A full-fledged realization of these and other principles of a human rights-based approach to a poverty-reduction strategy will take time.[57]

PAKISTAN'S PRSP AND THE RTD

It may be observed that Pakistan's PRSP, like those of many other countries referred to above, is not specifically linked to human rights. The current literature on Pakistan's experience shows no evidence that Pakistan has used the guidelines proposed by the OHCHR. While the PRSP framework already has some similarities with human rights, it is clear from the above discussion that in practice many PRSPs fail to act as an instrument for promoting human rights. It seems necessary to examine the experience of Pakistan in the process and content of the PRSP and its relevance for the RTD from the perspective of national ownership and participation.

National ownership and participation

In November 2001, Pakistan prepared its Interim PRSP, and, in September 2004, its full PRSP, entitled: 'Accelerating Economic Growth and Reducing Poverty: The Road Ahead'.[58] For the full PRSP, the World Bank approved a Poverty Reduction Strategy Credit (PRSC) of US$300 million in September 2004 for a period of three years. A PRSP Secretariat has been established in the Ministry of Finance that coordinates, monitors and evaluates the progress of the PRSP. The process for preparing a revised PRSP for another three-year period has also been started by the PRSP Secretariat. The PRSP has four core elements:

56 OHCHR, op. cit., p 16.

57 Ibid.

58 Government of Pakistan, 'Accelerating Economic Growth and Reducing Poverty: The Road Ahead', Poverty Reduction Strategy Paper, Ministry of Finance, December 2003, para. 1.1. Online. Available at: <www.moe.gov.pk/prsps_03.pdf> (accessed 24 March 2007) (hereinafter Pakistan PRSP).

1 Accelerating economic growth, while maintaining macroeconomic stability;
2 Improving good governance;
3 Investing in human capital; and
4 Targeting the poor and vulnerable.

Looking at the trends of poverty, the PRSP acknowledges that during the 1990s, poverty increased by 6 percentage points from 26.1 per cent in 1990–91 to 32.1 per cent in 2000–01.[59] The PRSP recognizes that poverty is multidimensional and stresses the need to improve basic capabilities such as access to primary education, primary health care, drinking water, and access to justice.[60] It also recognizes the involvement of the poor as well as a broad-based alliance between civil society and the private sector in the formulation of policies and management of their affairs to achieve the objectives of the strategy.[61] The PRSP also aligns poverty reduction to the MDGs for sustainable development according to the targets proposed by national environmental plans and international summits.[62] The PRSP also proposes to give special attention to policy reforms, the promulgation and enforcement of environmental legislation and collaboration and coordination among stakeholders.[63] Two programmes, the utilization of the Zakat Fund as one of the key social safety nets[64] and the Islamization of the financial sector, indicate the continuation of efforts to incorporate the Islamic concept of social justice.[65] It is proposed that the Zakat Fund will be used as a major instrument of rehabilitation in the fields of education, health care and social welfare.

The government asserts that participation includes a comprehensive process of consultation on a range of issues, such as poverty measurement, education, health and gender mainstreaming.[66] The government also claims that

59 Ibid. para. 1.1.
60 Ibid. paras 1.6 and 3.1.
61 Ibid.
62 Ibid. paras 1.9, 6.32. The Pakistan Environmental Protection Council approved the National Environmental Action Plan (NEAP) in Feb. 2001. The PRSP also proposes to achieve the targets set out in the World Summit on Sustainable Development (WSSD) held in South Africa in 2004. The Plan of Implementation adopted at the WSSD sets out various targets for sustainable development. The targets include poverty, water, agriculture, health, biodiversity and natural resources. Online. Available at <www.worldsummit2002.org/> (accessed 16 July 2007).
63 Ibid.
64 Ibid. paras. 5.136, 5.146, 5.185 and 5.186.
65 Ibid. para. 5.25. The financial system reforms are pursued by the State Bank of Pakistan and the Ministry of Finance in compliance with the decision of the Supreme Court. For details of those measures, see *The State Bank of Pakistan Annual Report, FY02*, pp 189–98. Online. Available at: <http://www.sbp.org.pk/reports/annual/arFY02/chap10.pdf> (accessed 16 July 2007).
66 Ibid. para. 2.2.

the consultations included parliamentarians, civil society, NGOs and donors in various workshops and seminars on the subject of the PRSP.[67] The PRSP also shows that, at the grass-roots level, consultations were held through the Rural Support Programs Network in 49 districts[68] including Northern Areas and Azad Jammu and Kashmir (AJK).

As in other countries, the national ownership of and the participation in Pakistan's PRSP have also attracted criticism from commentators and the CSOs. One commentator argued that there is a 'lacklustre ownership of the PRSP in Pakistan [which can] severely curtail the potential for poverty reduction'.[69] Despite claims about participation, the government did not ensure active, free and meaningful participation. This fact is clearly demonstrated in the following statement by an anonymous government official, noted by a commentator:

> Consultation with civil society would take too long and NGOs would stall reforms because of politics. We need the participation of officials and agencies affected by reforms, not just civil society. Consultation cannot just be with NGOs . . . Consultative processes should be left to government as they should know and be able to decide what segments of society they need to deal with.[70]

A coalition of the CSOs led by an Islamabad-based think tank, the Sustainable Development Policy Institute, wrote to the Ministry of Finance raising serious concerns regarding both the national ownership of and the participation in the preparation of the PRSP.[71] Regarding the national ownership, the letter says, 'We are also deeply concerned about the . . . clear influence the IFIs are exerting on the Pakistani state.'[72] The letter rejects both the content and the process of the PRSP in Pakistan. It refers to a report of the IMF's

67 Ibid. paras 2.2–2.9.

68 In Pakistan, a province is divided into districts, and each district is a geographically defined administrative unit. In 2000, a devolution plan was introduced by the Military Government and in 2001 Local Government Ordinances were introduced in each province, under which the concept of district government was introduced. Elections to the district governments were held in 2001 and 2005. The total number of districts, including the capital city Islamabad, Northern Areas and the AJK, is 121.

69 Syed Mohammad Ali, 'Infusing Participation into Development Planning: A CSO Review of the PRSP'. Online. Available at: <http://www.policy.hu/ali/SAP%20review%20of%20PRSP.pdf> (accessed 24 March 2007).

70 Syed Mohammad Ali, 'Participation as the means to assess effectiveness of the Poverty Reduction Strategy Paper for Pakistan', IPF Research Paper, 2005–2006. Online. Available at: <http://www.policy.hu/ali/IPF%20research%20paper.pdf> (accessed 24 April 2007).

71 Notable CSOs are ActionAid Pakistan, South Asian Partnership Pakistan, the Human Rights Commission of Pakistan, the Pakistan Institute of Labour Education and Research (PILER) and the Pakistan Federal Union of Journalists.

72 Letter dated 20 Dec. 2002. Online. Available at: <http://www.eurodad.org/uploadstore/cms/docs/LetterCSOsPakistan.doc> (accessed 24 March 2007).

Independent Evaluation Office, which concludes that there is no genuine national ownership of the IFIs' policy prescriptions in Pakistan.[73] In an annex, the letter highlights the shortcomings in the process of participation. It disputes the government's claim of a comprehensive process of consultation and says that 'in reality the only "participatory" meetings that have taken place are those that have involved government functionaries with a scattering of individuals who have no formal affiliation with the government'.[74] The letter further adds that potential stakeholders such as political parties, trade unions, academics, peoples' movements, civic and professional bodies were not consulted.

Generally, Pakistan's PRSP appears to have some relevance to the RTD. The acknowledgement of a broad-based concept of poverty may reflect a comprehensive concept of development, as envisaged by the Declaration. The government's assertion regarding the participation of stakeholders may indicate its willingness to endorse participation as a necessary element in the process of development. In the introductory part of the PRSP, the government admits that it has the prime responsibility to improve the standard of living of its people. This acknowledgement may be seen as an acceptance of the moral obligation under the Declaration, which makes the realization of the RTD a primary duty of the state. The PRSP, however, does not use the language of human rights. This means that it does not seem to endorse a key feature of the Declaration. The non-existence of this linkage has deep and lasting repercussions on the RTD because the Declaration requires the state to promote and protect human rights through a development programme. A human rights-based approach demands equitable distribution of the benefits arising out of the development process. But the PRSP does not propose any meaningful strategy for equitable distribution, for example, land reforms.[75] As was seen above, despite some similarities, the PRSP framework of most countries does not meaningfully promote the RTD in practice. The PRSP of Pakistan is no exception. The reason for this, as stated above, is the absence of a specific link between human rights and the PRSP. On the other hand, some PRSP-related development programmes are funded by multilateral and bilateral donors who support a rights-based approach to development in Pakistan. Two such programmes may be mentioned here. Firstly, EIROP relates to improving the governance sector in the NWFP, in order to

73 See IMF's report, Part II, chapter IX, Pakistan, p 201. Online. Available at: <http://www.imf.org/external/np/ieo/2002/pu/file12.pdf> (accessed 24 March 2007).

74 Letter dated 20 Dec. 2002, op. cit.

75 See Ahmad Nawaz Hakro and Mustafa Talpur, 'A Civil Society Perspective on the Millennium Development Goals and the Poverty Reduction Strategy Paper: The Case of Pakistan', Commonwealth Foundation, 2005, p 11. Online. Available at: <http://www.commonwealthfoundation.com/uploads/documents/mdg_pakistan.pdf> (accessed 24 March 2007).

implement a successful devolution plan. In this respect, it seeks to enhance the capacity building, transparency and accountability of local governance institutions and access to public services, particularly justice for all and disadvantaged groups such as women and the poor.[76] EIROP claims to enable the NWFP to realize its obligations under international human rights instruments.[77] This programme is jointly funded by the UNDP and the SDC. Both of these donor agencies are committed to rights-based development in Pakistan.

Secondly, the UNDP is funding a project for legal aid services for the most disadvantaged, such as women and the poor.[78] This project is supplementary to the AJP, a judicial reform project which is analysed later in this chapter.

Regarding the first-mentioned programme, i.e. EIROP, the commitment of the donor agencies to a rights-based approach is clear. But Pakistan's commitment to a rights-based approach to development is not clear because there is no reference to any such approach in the national PRSP. EIROP is a programme of the NWFP. The PRSP of the NWFP mentions this programme,[79] but does not specifically mention a rights-based approach. Nor does it refer to human rights. However, in the area of women's role in development, the provincial PRSP makes a reference to Pakistan's obligations under the Women's Convention.[80] It is clear that no human rights were taken into consideration at the time of the formulation of the national or the provincial PRSPs. The guidelines proposed by the OHCHR may help integrate human rights into the PRSP framework provided a country has a commitment to realize the RTD. The significance of these guidelines for one PRSP project, viz. AJP, is analysed below.

AJP in the PRSP

Judicial reforms are part of the governance reforms entitled: 'Pillar Two: Improving Governance and Devolution'. The PRSP links judicial reforms to the governance issues. The government acknowledges the governance crisis and proposes to address this issue in different ways, such as devolution of power to the grass-roots level, improved access to justice, participation in the decision-making process, transparency and accountability.[81] While most of

76 See NWFP EIROP. Online. Available at: <http://www.eirop.org/> (accessed 24 March 2007).

77 Ibid.

78 See UNDP, 'Access to Justice Through Integrated Legal Aid Services', Project Document. Online. Available at: <http://www.un.org.pk/undp/governance/prodoc-a2j.doc> (accessed 14 Sept. 2007).

79 'Poverty Reduction Strategy Paper of the NWFP', p 19. Online. Available at: <http://nwfp.gov.pk/AISdownload_file.php?Distld=22&Langld=filed=305> (accessed 8 May 2007).

80 Ibid. p 26.

81 Pakistan PRSP, para. 5.80.

these components are also features of a rights-based approach to development, the PRSP does not specifically recognize the link between judicial reforms and human rights. This is clear from the following statement of the PRSP: 'The Government recognises that judicial, legal and police reforms are essential to establish the rule of law and enforcement of contracts that will *stimulate economic growth and encourage private investment – both local and foreign*.'[82] It is evident that the approach of the PRSP is focused on economic growth, not human rights. The PRSP does not realize that judicial reforms are equally necessary for the promotion and protection of human rights. However, it needs no emphasis that the judiciary plays a key role in the promotion and protection of human rights. Access to justice is a recognized human right, which not only is a right in itself, having an intrinsic value, but also has an instrumental importance in promoting and protecting other human rights, such as the right to a fair trial.[83] The AJP is funded by the Asian Development Bank (ADB) with a loan facility of US $350 million. It is implemented by the Ministry of Law, Justice and Human Rights. Before proceeding to discuss the human rights perspective of the AJP, it seems necessary to explain the concepts of governance and the rule of law.

Governance

There is no consensus definition of the concept of governance. According to the World Bank, governance is a broad term that refers to the exercise of power by the social, political and economic institutions of a country for efficient management of its resources.[84] In the words of the IMF: 'The term governance, as generally used, encompasses all aspects of the way a country is governed, including its economic policies and regulatory framework.'[85] The IMF claims that its assistance to countries for improving governance is aimed at promoting the rule of law, improving the efficiency and accountability of the public sector and fighting corruption.[86] The ADB defines governance as 'the manner in which power is exercised in the management of a country's economic and social resources for development . . . involving both the public and the private sectors'.[87] The ADB identifies four elements of governance, viz. accountability, participation, predictability and

82 Ibid. para. 5.106 (emphasis added).

83 See Art. 14 of the ICCPR.

84 See World Bank, 'PovertyNet, Governance'. Online. Available at: <www.worldbank.org> (accessed 30 March 2007).

85 See IMF, 'The IMF and Good Governance, A Factsheet', April 2003. Online. Available at: <http://www.imf.org/external/np/exr/facts/gov.htm> (accessed 29 March 2007).

86 Ibid.

87 ADB, 'Governance Defined', Online. Available at: <http://www.adb.org/Documents/Policies/Governance/gov200.asp?p=policies> (accessed 29 March 2007).

transparency.[88] These elements are mutually supportive and reinforcing. According to the OHCHR:

> Governance is the process whereby public institutions conduct public affairs, manage public resources and guarantee the realization of human rights. Good governance accomplishes this in a manner essentially free of abuse and corruption, and with due regard for the rule of law.[89]

The IMF and the ADB emphasize the economic aspects, while the OHCHR links the role of human rights to the concept of governance. However, from the above definitions, it is clear that there is a consensus on the main elements of governance, i.e. accountability, transparency and participation. The phrase 'regulatory framework' and the word 'predictability' both refer to the legal and judicial institutions, to ensure the rule of law.

The rule of law

In a narrow sense – the formal approach – the rule of law could be seen as the fulfilment of the formal procedures of the legal system.[90] In this sense, the rule of law includes well-defined rights and duties and efficient judicial mechanisms for enforcing them.[91] No doubt an efficient judicial system is necessary to ensure strict application of the formal rules of procedure. A broader view of the rule of law seeks to ascertain whether the laws are just, fair and equitable.[92] Involving a more behavioural approach, the answers to such a question require that the legal system should be looked at in social and political contexts. Thus the rule of law should impose 'on the government an affirmative duty to help make life better for people'[93] and thereby achieve social justice. In the contemporary world, the legitimacy of a legal order is no longer determined by judicial institutions alone.[94] Democracy, particularly participatory democracy and respect for human rights, are other notable virtues of a legal order,[95] which have sufficient influence on the rule of law. In

88 ADB, 'Elements of Governance'. Online. Available <http://www.adb.org/Governance/gov_elements.asp> (accessed 29 March 2007).

89 UNHCHR, 'Human Rights in Development'. Online. Available <http://www.unhchr.ch/development/governance.html> (accessed 29 March 2007).

90 Richard Sannerholm, 'Legal, Judicial and Administrative Reforms in Post-Conflict Societies: Beyond the Rule of Law Template', *Journal of Conflict & Security Law* 12(1), 2007), 65–94, at 74. See also M. Rosenfeld, 'The Rule of Law and Legitimacy of Constitutional Democracy', *South California Law Review* 74, 2001, 1307–52.

91 ADB, 'Elements of Governance', op. cit.

92 Sannerholm, op. cit., 74.

93 Brian Z. Tamanaha, *On the Rule of Law: History, Politics, Theory*, Cambridge, Cambridge University Press, 2004, p 113.

94 Sannerholm, op. cit., 74.

95 Ibid.

order to prevent a judicial process from being distorted, the judiciary must be independent, courts should be easily accessible to all, particularly the poor, the courts should have powers of review and the crime-police should not pervert its discretion.[96] Thus the rule of law is 'a principle of governance in which all persons, institutions and entities, public and private, including the State itself, are accountable to laws,'[97] which are implemented and applied keeping in view the principles of accountability, transparency, fairness and participation in decision-making.

While the judiciary needs to be independent and efficient to check arbitrary exercise of power by the executive, there is a growing consensus on the view that the judiciary itself should also be accountable to the people. Part of the governance structure, the judiciary's role in the promotion of the RTD, need not be emphasized. The working groups on the RTD have given due consideration to the judiciary in the realization of the RTD.

The judiciary in the RTD debate

The Global Consultation on the RTD gave importance to the role of the legal and judicial institutions in the promotion of the RTD. The Consultation thoroughly reviewed the issue of legal assistance to the poor, particularly the rural population of developing countries, and suggested that the law should be moved beyond mere legal assistance to people in criminal cases, and be used as 'an instrument for improvement of their rights'.[98] The Consultation stressed that 'the [RTD] can and should serve as a basis for the adoption of laws and procedures intended to eliminate conditions of underdevelopment or at the very least to help overcome the obstacles to development'. The Consultation also noted that the legal resources necessary for the enjoyment of the RTD should be brought within the access of the common people.[99] To this end, a three-pronged policy was suggested, viz. 'development, law and legal resources'.[100] Regarding law, it was contended that the colonial tone of the laws of most of the developing countries needs to be realigned with the requirements of the time and the interests of the ordinary people.[101] Legal resources, the Consultation added, means improvements in the legal expertise and functional competence of the institutions involved, such as courts and the police.[102]

96 See Charles Sampford, 'Reconceiving the rule of law for a globalizing world' in Spencer Zifck (ed.), *Globalization and the Rule of Law*, London/New York, Routledge, 2005, pp 9–31, at p 15.

97 UN Secretary-General Report, *Rule of Law and Transitional Justice in Conflict and Post-Conflict Societies*, UN Doc. S.2004/616, 23 Aug. 2004.

98 Global Consultation, para. 120.

99 Ibid. para. 122.

100 Ibid.

101 Ibid. para.123.

102 Ibid. para. 124.

The current working group has also, in its various sessions, underscored the need for judicial reforms for the RTD. In its first session, the working group noted that a development programme should promote an independent legal system and encourage participatory, transparent and accountable government and management.[103] The working group also observed that the role of women in development required, among other things, legal and constitutional reforms.[104] During the second session of the working group, the representative of the World Bank underlined the importance of reforms of the judicial system because such a system was an element in the implementation of the RTD.[105] One representative also noted that governance sector reforms were necessary for the RTD.[106] The third session concluded that good governance and the rule of law were necessary for the promotion of human rights.[107]

THE GUIDELINES AND JUDICIAL REFORMS

It seems pertinent to compare Pakistan's AJP, a judicial reform project, with Guideline 8 of the guidelines. The aim of this comparison is to see whether the AJP fulfils the requirements of Guideline 8. The main features of the AJP are tested on the strategies for promoting the right to access to justice, proposed by Guideline 8, to ascertain whether it can promote the RTD in Pakistan. 'Right of Equal Access to Justice' is part of Guideline 8, which deals with specific human rights standards. Each of the specific human rights standards is divided into four parts. In each case Part A spells out the importance of this right, Part B highlights its scope, Part C suggests targets/indicators, and Part D proposes key features of a strategy for its realization. These four parts are compared with the ADB policy literature, which articulates the AJP's rationale, objectives and scope, policy framework and actions. To provide a focus, selected AJP activities of the NWFP High Court will be referred to during the discussion below.

Guideline 8 and the AJP

(A) Importance of the right of equal access to justice

Guideline 13 explains the importance of the right of equal access to justice in relation to the PRSP.[108] It says that poor people in particular face human rights violations by government officials and private individuals. It proceeds

103 E/CN.4/2001/26, First session, para. 136.
104 Ibid. paras 132–4.
105 E/CN.4/2002/28/Rev.1, Second session, para. 21.
106 Ibid. para. 35.
107 Ibid. para. 104(e).
108 Guideline 8, paras 204–205.

to state that the courts provide the most effective means of human rights protection. However, income and capability poverty creates impediments to gaining access to the courts. Access to justice is one of the basic capabilities. The availability of free legal aid, for victims or accused persons, may not prove adequate because the poor have neither the necessary information nor the self-confidence to resort to court.[109] While the poor are likely to be the victims of human rights violations, it is also likely that the poor will be accused of criminal behaviour. In the latter situation, the poor need a minimum guarantee of a fair trial.[110] The guideline seeks to eliminate the vulnerability of the poor as part of a poverty-reduction strategy.

(A.1) The rationale of the AJP

According to an AJP policy document issued by the ADB, the AJP is basically a pro-poor programme. The document notes several features of poverty, ranging from income poverty to vulnerability and poor people's 'perceptions of poverty: they highlight increasing insecurity and vulnerability arising from sectarian violence, communal clashes, and declining law and order'.[111] All of these features are relevant to the AJP. However, vulnerability, a form of capability poverty, is extremely important. Vulnerability is understood as lack of access to social, political and economic assets, which renders individuals, families and communities susceptible to poverty.[112] Justice is a public good, which state institutions are to provide in a predictable, affordable and accountable manner to all citizens, particularly the poor. The justice system should be the most effective tool for the poor to secure access to social, political and economic assets.

It is clear from the above that despite the absence of a clear link with human rights, the rationale of the AJP seems to be similar to the views expressed in the guideline. Both the guideline and the AJP are pro-poor and take into consideration capability poverty. However, as observed above, the difference between the two is that the AJP is growth-oriented rather than a human rights-based programme. Perhaps the reason is that the AJP is part of Pakistan's governance reforms to strengthen the rule of law and reform key institutions. The absence of an explicit link does not mean that the programme will have no impact on human rights. Moreover, the reference to

109 Ibid. para. 204.

110 Ibid. para. 205.

111 ADB, 'Report and Recommendation of The President to The Board of Directors on Proposed Loans and Technical Assistance Grant to The Islamic Republic of Pakistan for The Access To Justice Program', November 2001. Online. Available at: <http://www.adb.org/Documents/RRPS/PAK/rrp_32023.pdf> (accessed 1 April 2007), p 3. Other features mentioned are: urban poverty because of rapid urbanization and dependency of the poor on informal sector wage labour. See p 3.

112 Ibid. p 4.

human rights is not completely missing, as is clear from the following statement: 'The AJP will tackle gender issues through creation of competent legal, judicial and police institutions through which existing basic/constitutional rights can be implemented fairly and accountably.'[113] The human rights approach adds value to reinforce the existing similarities and help create a link where the two depart from each other. The AJP policy document referred to above, observes that the present legal framework and the performance of the judicial institutions do not create an enabling environment for economic development, particularly foreign direct investment.[114] This is also true of human rights. Legal and judicial reforms are necessary for the promotion and protection of human rights, particularly those of the poor. As this study argues, the integration of human rights into the PRSP may create positive effects on the RTD in Pakistan because the RTD requires such a development policy, which may help to realize all human rights and fundamental freedoms.

(B) The scope of the right of equal access to justice (the guideline)

The guideline notes that the scope of the right of equal access to justice includes a number of procedural rights that are indispensable for the realization of the rights of equality before the law and a fair trial.[115] They are the right of equal access to an independent and impartial court or tribunal, the right to a fair and public hearing, presumption of innocence in criminal proceedings, the right not be to compelled to make a confession of guilt, the right to have access to adequate legal services, such as engagement of a lawyer, the right to examine witnesses and the right to legal assistance free of cost, such as the service of an interpreter, where necessary. In order to provide reparation to the poor for being victims of human rights violations by the state or non-state actors, it is essential that the poor should have access to courts and tribunals and other relevant institutions.

(B.1) Objectives and scope of the AJP

The main thrust of the reforms undertaken by the AJP is to promote and protect the right of equal access to justice, particularly for the poor. The scope and objectives of the AJP are as follows:

> [T]o assist the Government to improve access to justice so as to (i) provide security and ensure equal protection under the law to citizens, in particular the poor; (ii) secure and sustain entitlements and thereby

113 Ibid. p ii.
114 Ibid. p15.
115 Guideline 8, para. 206.

> reduce the poor's vulnerability; (iii) strengthen the legitimacy of state institutions; and (iv) create conditions conducive to pro-poor growth, especially by fostering investors' confidence. The reform will contribute to this aim by supporting five interrelated governance objectives: (i) providing a legal basis for judicial, policy, and administrative reforms; (ii) improving the efficiency, timeliness, and effectiveness in judicial and police services; (iii) supporting greater equity and accessibility in justice services for the vulnerable poor; (iv) improving predictability and consistency between fiscal and human resource allocation and the mandates of reformed judicial and police institutions at the federal, provincial and local government levels; and (v) ensuring greater transparency and accountability in the performance of the judiciary, the police and administrative justice institutions.[116]

The scope of the AJP includes the following three performance outcome domains: (i) policy and legal provisions, (ii) institutional performance, and (iii) budget/expenditure management.[117] The AJP also supports the enforcement of environmental laws through the establishment of environmental tribunals under the law.[118]

The objectives and scope of the AJP are directly relevant to the right of equal access to justice and other related rights. The AJP has undertaken reform in all legal and judicial institutions, such as the lower judiciary, the police, prisons and the probation service. All of these institutions are responsible for the realization of the right of equal access to justice. While human rights are constitutionally protected, some rights, particularly those related to access to justice, are also protected under the ordinary laws. It is the duty of the lower judiciary to protect human rights, which are embodied in ordinary procedural and substantive laws. As observed above, the necessity of judicial and legal reform arises because these institutions are unable to deliver efficiently the services they are obliged to provide to all, including the poor. What is needed is reiteration of the importance of human rights and to enable the lower judiciary to focus specifically on their protection. In this respect, the lower judiciary can open various windows at different stages of investigation and trial in criminal proceedings and in civil litigation. Such windows include: giving liberal interpretation to statutory provisions and exercising inherent powers at the time of granting of bail, authorizing police custody and supervising investigation.

116 ADB, 'Report and Recommendation', op. cit., p 15.
117 Ibid. p 16.
118 Ibid. p 28.

(C) Key targets and indicators

The guideline proposes some targets and indicators for the promotion of the right of equal access to justice through a PRSP.[119] Target 1 is: 'equal access to civil justice for poor people as victims'. Key indicators under this target include the number of people availing themselves of specific human rights litigation, the number of judges and courts per head of population and the level of corruption in the administration of civil justice. Target 2 relates to a fair trial for poor people accused of crime. There are two indicators under this target: firstly, the number of poor people sentenced for crimes in relation to the overall crime rate and secondly, the level of corruption in criminal justice. Target 3 aims at enhancing the ability of poor people who are victims of crime to bring perpetrators to justice. The indicator under this target is to find out how many perpetrators are brought to justice as a percentage of the number of crimes against the poor.

(C.1) The AJP

These targets and indicators require the state to collect empirical evidence through the legal and judicial institutions. The AJP in Pakistan does not propose the collection of such comprehensive data.[120] However, some targets and indicators, such as the number of judges and courts per head of population (Target 1, Indicator 5 above) are addressed by the AJP, which is discussed below.

(D) Key features of a strategy for realizing the right of equal access to justice

The guideline proposes the following key features of a strategy:

- a Introducing information campaigns, in slums and other areas where the poor live, on the right of access to justice.
- b Increasing the number of courts, tribunals and non-formal dispute-resolution mechanisms.
- c Increasing the number of judges and law-enforcement personnel, especially in poor areas.
- d Increasing the salary of judges and law-enforcement personnel.
- e Establishing law clinics for the poor.
- f Extending legal aid programmes for the poor in both civil and criminal proceedings.

119 For details of targets and their respective indicators, see Guideline 13, para. 197.

120 Personal communication with the key AJP representative in the Peshawar High Court, NWFP, dated 16 April 2007.

g Establishing training programmes for judges, lawyers and law-enforcement personnel on the right of the poor to non-discrimination.
h Improving the enforcement of judgments by the relevant authorities.
i Improving the physical access of the poor to courts, non-formal dispute-resolution mechanisms and law-enforcement officers, in particular in remote rural areas.
j Eliminating corruption in the administration of justice.
k Helping poor victims of crime to bring offenders to justice.

(D.1) The AJP policy framework

The AJP policy framework comprises the following six outcome areas:[121]

1 Improving policy-making for a more efficient and citizen-oriented judicial and legal sector that promotes access to justice.
2 Strengthening judicial independence by complete separation of the judiciary from the executive and ensuring that the mandates of the judiciary are adequately funded.
3 Ensuring efficient and inexpensive justice.
4 Legal empowerment of the poor and vulnerable.
5 Improving judicial governance.
6 Improving human resource development.

(D.2) A comparison of the two strategies

The AJP's first outcome area is not directly related to the strategy proposed by the guideline. The two strategies, however, appear to be implicitly related to each other. A national judicial policy is the starting point of the AJP for the promotion of a right of equal access to justice. An umbrella institution of judicial policy-making coordinates all the activities pertaining to the administration of justice, ranging from policy-making to the collection of empirical data necessary for performance evaluation, improving the accountability of the legal and judicial institutions, and making suggestions for reforms.[122] Moreover, such a body provides a platform for the concerned stakeholders to participate in the process of decision-making and set priorities in a PRSP for the improvement of the legal and justice system.

Pakistan has not neglected reform of its judiciary in the past. Before the current AJP reform project, as many as eight Law Reform Commissions were appointed at different times by different governments.[123] A National Judicial

121 ADB, 'Report and Recommendation', op. cit., p 16–19.
122 Ibid. p 9.
123 (1) The Law Reform Commission of 1958; (2) The Law Reform Commission of 1967–70; (3) The Hamood-ur-Rahman Commission of 1974; (4) The Law Commission for

(Policy Making) Committee (NJPMC) was established under the auspices of the AJP in 2002.[124] The NJPMC 'coordinates and harmonizes judicial policy within the court system, and in coordination with the Commission, ensures its implementation'.[125] Some functions of the NJPMC seem to promote a number of key features proposed by the guideline. The functions of the NJPMC include: to improve the capacity and performance of the administration of justice; to improve the terms and conditions of service of judicial officers and court staff; to ensure skilled and efficient judiciary. The guideline proposes similar measures for improving the working conditions of the courts and other law-enforcing agencies. Those measures include an increase in the number of judges and law-enforcement personnel, especially in the poor areas, and increasing the salary of judges and law-enforcement personnel. These proposals will be further examined below.

The second outcome area of the AJP policy framework relates to the strengthening of judicial independence by implementing the separation of the judiciary from the executive at all levels and ensuring adequate funding for the judiciary. This policy of the AJP can reinforce the strategy suggested by the guideline because the promotion of the right of equal access to justice needs an independent judiciary, with adequate funds. In Pakistan, the judiciary has for a long time, faced problems in relation to judicial independence and inadequate funds. Since colonial time, the lower judiciary has not been independent of the executive. The foremost problem of the lower judiciary in Pakistan is its bureaucratic foundation, rooted in the colonial legacy of the past.[126] After independence, the same system prevailed. The judiciary separated from the executive in 1996. The PRSP recognizes that the AJP is complementary to the Devolution Plan,[127] having a direct nexus with poverty reduction.[128] Under the Devolution Plan, another component of good governance, proposed in the PRSP, was the abolition of the powerful office of the Deputy Commissioner, the executive head of a district. An AJP policy paper

Recommending Measures for Speedy Disposal of Civil Litigation of 1978; (5) The Secretaries' Committee of 1979; (6) The Salahuddin Ahmad Committee of 1980; (7) The Committee on Islamization of Laws and Establishment of Qazi Courts of 1980; and (8) The Commission on the Reform of Civil Law of 1993. Details of Reports of Ad Hoc Law Reform Commissions online. Available at: <www.ljcp.gov.pk/menu> (accessed 9 June 2005). A Law and Justice Commission was established under Ordinance No XIV of 1979.

124 See The Government of Pakistan's Ordinance LXXI of 2002.

125 Ibid. s. 4.

126 ADB, 'Judicial Independence Overview and Country level summaries', Judicial Independence Project, RETA No. 5987, submitted by the Asia Foundation, October 2003, pp 68–72 at p 68. Online. Available at: <http://www.adb.org/Documents/Events/2003/RETA5987/Final_Overview_Report.pdf> (accessed 9 April 2007) (hereinafter ADB, Judicial Independence).

127 For details of the Devolution Plan see the PRSP, paras 5.79–5.87.

128 PRSP, para. 5.106.

notes that the allocation of the powers of the Deputy Commissioner to the lower judiciary is of historic importance.[129]

The lower judiciary is chronically under-funded in Pakistan. The lack of funds has a negative impact on the right of equal access to justice. The second outcome area addressed this issue by proposing to develop a medium-term budget and expenditure framework at the federal as well as the provincial level and to clearly specify budgetary allocations for the lower judiciary.[130] However, despite a recent budget increase of 30 per cent on average,[131] the allocation of adequate funds is still a challenge.[132]

The third outcome area of the AJP relates to the delivery of expeditious and inexpensive justice through efficiency, improved facilities, the introduction of Alternative Dispute Resolution (ADR) and more effective ombudsman services. The ADR element in the AJP policy is directly relevant to paragraphs (b) and (i) of the strategy proposed by the guideline. Paragraph (b) recommends an increase in the number of courts, tribunals and non-formal dispute-resolution mechanisms. Paragraph (i) suggests that the poor, particularly in the remote rural areas, should have improved physical access to courts, non-formal dispute-resolution mechanisms and law-enforcement officers. Under the AJP, ADR mechanisms have been widely introduced in different laws.[133] The ADR provisions facilitate involvement of the parties in the resolution of a dispute. Such involvement provides the vulnerable poor with the opportunity to participate directly in the process of dispute resolution. Thus an effective ADR system, while restoring the confidence of the vulnerable poor in the justice system, influences a rights-based approach to development.

The Family Courts law has also been amended in order to facilitate the expeditious disposal of disputes over family matters. However, no disaggregated statistical data are available to indicate whether these measures have proved helpful for the poor, and if so, to what extent. Thus while the AJP policy regarding the ADR mechanism seems to be similar to the strategy

129 ADB, 'Report and Recommendation', op. cit., p 16.

130 Ibid. p 46. The Access to Justice Development Fund (AJDF) was also established, with US$24 million, to be earmarked exclusively for the lower judiciary; ibid. Appendix 3, p 60.

131 Eveline N. Fischer, 'Lessons Learned from Judicial Reform: The ADB Experience', Speech dated 20 Oct. 2006. Online. Available at: <http://www.adb.org/Media/Articles/2006/10829-speech-Eveline-Fischer/> (accessed 11 April 2007).

132 Livingston Armytage, 'Pakistan Law and Justice Sector Reform Experience: Some Lessons Learned', *Law, Social Justice & Global Development* 2, 2003. Online. Available at: <http://www2.warwick.ac.uk/fac/soc/law/elj/lgd/2003_2/armytage/> (accessed 11 April 2007).

133 For example, the High Court Rules and the Civil Procedure Code have been amended to incorporate the ADR provisions. A specific ADR law, The Small Claims and Minor Offences Ordinance, was introduced in 2002. This law provides for amicable settlement of disputes through various modes of ADR, such as mediation, conciliation or any other lawful means mutually agreed upon by the parties.

proposed by the guideline, the extent to which the AJP policy has proved successful is not clear at this stage. In order to fully implement the strategy of the guideline, the AJP is required to collect data to find out whether and how its ADR policy has enhanced the capability of the poor to realize the right of equal access to justice. There are efforts, by the International Finance Corporation (IFC), to promote ADR in Pakistan. These efforts, which focus on commercial disputes, are made outside the AJP.[134] In the year 2000, the Lahore High Court launched a pilot ADR project in disputes over family matters.[135] The project not only proved successful at the judicial level, but also generated public awareness and interest about ADR in the legal community and academic institutions.[136]

Other elements of the AJP policy, such as efficiency, improved facilities and ombudsman's services, are not expressly covered by the guideline strategy. It follows that in this area, the AJP policy is more comprehensive than the guideline strategy. However, it is arguable that successful implementation of the said elements of the AJP policy will have positive impacts on the equal access of the poor to justice. For example, a more efficient judicial system through reducing the delay in the disposal of cases will lead the poor to have greater confidence in the judiciary. Similarly, strengthening the Ombudsman Office will also encourage the poor to have recourse to such an institution for the redress of grievances. Another example of facilitating the physical access of the poor to courts and tribunals is the conferment of the power of *habeas corpus* on the District and Sessions Judge.[137] The litigant public, particularly the poor, can now easily access the District Court.

The AJP's fourth outcome area relates to legal empowerment of the vulnerable poor through civil-society-led legal literacy, social audits, advocacy and PIL. The guideline proposes that information campaigns on the right of access to justice should be introduced in those areas where the poor people

134 In 2005, PEP-MENA (Private Enterprise Partnership-Middle East and North Africa), a technical facility of the IFC (the private-sector arm of the World Bank Group), launched the first mediation project in the city of Karachi, Pakistan's commercial centre, with the cooperation of the Sindh province's government and High Court. See James South, *The Genesis of Mediation in Pakistan, a Case Study on the New Commercial Approach to the Region*, Centre for Effective Dispute Resolution (CEDR), UK, Feb. 2007. Online. Available at: <http://www.cedr.co.uk/index.php?location=/library/articles/20070214_195.htm> (accessed 28 Aug. 2007). A pilot court-referred mediation centre is now established in Karachi.

135 Justice Tassaduq Hussain Jillani, 'The Elusive Goddess of Justice May Respond: Give ADR a Chance', Paper presented at the First South Asian Regional Judicial Colloquium on Access to Justice, New Delhi, 1–3 Nov. 2002, p 9. Online. Available at: <http://www.humanrightsinitiative.org/jc/papers/jc_2002/judges_papers/Jillani.pdf> (accessed 28 Aug. 2007).

136 Ibid. p 11.

137 Previously, the issuance of a *habeas corpus* writ was in the power of a provincial High Court and its benches, which were situated in the capital city and a few big cities of the province.

live. The AJP implemented a Citizen-Court Liaison Plan, which established information centres in the courts' premises and launched information campaigns.[138] The difference between the two strategies is that the guideline suggests information campaigns in those areas where the poor people live, for example, slums, while the AJP has launched information campaigns by establishing information kiosks in the court premises, and the publication of major laws in the Urdu language. The information campaigns of the AJP also include dissemination of information about the rights of the poor and disadvantaged, particularly women, and encourage PIL for them.[139] AJP activities such as information kiosks, the publication of laws in Urdu and financial aid for establishing legal aid clinics support paragraphs (a) and (e) of the guideline strategy.

The fifth outcome area of the AJP, which seeks to improve judicial governance, aims to achieve accountability and transparency in the judiciary. For this purpose, the AJP formulated a policy for monitoring and inspection of courts and eradication of corruption in the judiciary. The guideline strategy also includes elimination of corruption in the administration of justice. The high courts have established institutional mechanisms for implementing the AJP policy. In order to ensure transparency, the provincial high courts have published annual reports regarding the performance of the judiciary in the province since 2001.[140] The reporting system now exposes the provincial judiciary to public accountability through comments from the general public, the media, legal professionals and researchers. Thus AJP activities in this area support the guideline strategy.

The AJP's sixth outcome area and the guideline stress the training of judges and other concerned officials. It is not possible to refer to all the relevant activities of the AJP in Pakistan. However, some selected activities of the Peshawar High Court may be mentioned here. Since 2002, the Peshawar High Court has been training judges and court staff on delay reduction, case management and court administration.[141] Workshops on women's rights, refugees' law and domestic application of human rights law were also arranged.[142]

The guideline strategy proposes an increase in the number and salary of judges and other law-enforcing personnel. The AJP policy has addressed this issue and the number of judges in the lower judiciary is being increased. However, the number of judges is still far from what is required. For example, Peshawar, the capital city of NWFP, with a population of about one million, has only 33 judges. The total number of lower court judges in the NWFP has

138 See Peshawar High Court, *Newsletter* 1(IV) Oct.–Dec. 2004.

139 ADB, 'Report and Recommendation', op. cit., p 42.

140 The Peshwar High Court has also published a quarterly newsletter since 2004, which reports various activities carried out under the AJP.

141 Peshawar High Court, Annual Report, 2003, pp 59–71.

142 Ibid.

increased to 344. Similarly, the salary of judges has been increased, but not on a permanent basis.

Evaluation of the AJP

Guideline 8 aims to promote the right of the poor to equal access to justice through a PRSP. The AJP focuses on poverty reduction and justice in Pakistan. Thus the rationale of both strategies relates to poverty reduction. Despite lack of a visible link to human rights, the AJP may significantly promote such rights. Most of the AJP activities potentially support the key features of the strategy outlined by Part D of the guideline. However, the AJP has to go further by producing comprehensive data disaggregated by gender and poverty in order to implement the key targets and indicators suggested by Part C of the guideline. To make the AJP a fully rights-based policy reform project, Pakistan has the primary duty, under the Declaration, to promote the RTD through the AJP. The ADB, a donor agency, also needs to encourage human rights integration more precisely and directly as a matter of international obligation. Pakistan's AJP reform needs to extend its intervention to some other important areas, for example, legislation regarding free legal aid for poor litigants and the establishment of law clinics for the poor.

Some AJP policies face risks and challenges. Firstly, financial autonomy is the backbone of an independent judiciary. Having no control over their budget, the judiciary in Pakistan have yet to win their *de facto* judicial independence. Rather, even the AJP experts admit that 'chronic under resourcing of the judicial budget' is one of the negative aspects of the current reform project.[143]

Secondly, the encouragement of ADR is facing real difficulty because in Pakistan all informal means of dispute resolution are usually exhausted before a dispute is brought to the court. ADR, particularly in commercial disputes, is receiving considerable attention outside the AJP framework. Such activities will, however, strengthen the AJP's ADR policy. But as a mode of criminal and civil dispute resolution, ADR still has a long way to go. To date, ADR has been pursued, to a limited extent, on the basis of pilot projects. It needs to be mainstreamed in both legal education and judicial training. The encouragement of professional mediators and conciliators is also necessary to make ADR a viable option of dispute resolution. Thirdly, the AJP reform has included the police and prison departments but not the revenue department. This means that the reform agenda is significantly deficient in the area of civil justice. Delays are mostly in civil cases involving land disputes. Widespread inefficiency and corruption in the land revenue department are strong catalysts of civil litigation. While judicial management and the training of judges are addressing this issue, the failure to reform the revenue department

143 Armytage, op. cit., p 6.

still leaves much to be desired. The vital importance of immovable property rights, especially those of orphan children and women, in the land revenue records, should not be ignored. In fact, land reforms are extremely important for breaking the shackles of feudalism, which has a major determining role in the power structure at local, provincial and central level. Feudalism is the principal tool of vulnerability and the main barrier preventing the poor from having access to the productive assets of society. Fourthly, the AJP has confined judicial training to the Federal Judicial Academy only, which is insufficient particularly when these are new recruits. Judicial academies in the provinces are necessary not only to cope with the training needs of the growing number of judges, but also to provide training in certain local and specific areas of law.[144] Fifthly, the government must have a strong and long-term political commitment to improve resources for continuous reforms in the legal and judicial systems. In short, judicial and legal reform programmes must be linked 'more closely, and visibly, with higher trans-sectoral objectives'[145] with a view to pursuing economic growth in tandem with the promotion and protection of human rights. The AJP project, having a short life of three years, appears to be inadequate to face such a challenge. Critics argue that the benefits of the AJP appear to be limited because of its predominantly 'management-oriented' agenda.[146] The current judicial crisis has far-reaching implications for the whole judicial system and may have a negative impact on the holistic approach of the AJP towards revamping the judiciary.

CONCLUSION

This chapter has argued that the core principles of the PRSP framework have similarities with key features of the Declaration such as participation, international cooperation and a comprehensive concept of development. The practice of the PRSP formulation in Pakistan (and many other developing countries), however, shows strong evidence to the contrary. Two trends emerge from this practice. Firstly, the international community, particularly the multilateral as well as the bilateral donors, has to play a more constructive role to make international development cooperation a reality for the promotion and protection of human rights, including the RTD. Secondly, Pakistan also needs to specifically link human rights to its PRSP. Currently, there is a contradiction between Pakistan's PRSP-related programmes and the policies

144 Particularly in the tribal areas of Baluchistan and the NWFP.

145 Ibid. p 9.

146 Foqia Sadiq Khan, 'The Way Forward: Access and Dispensation of Justice', *SDPI (Sustainable Development Policy Institute) Research and News Bulletin* 11(2), March–October 2004) 17–21 at 18. Online. Available at: <www.sdpi.org/help/research_ and_news_bulletin/march_Oct_2004/bulletin_pdf> (accessed 21 April 2009).

of the donors. The donors have a commitment to pursue a rights-based approach, but Pakistan makes no such commitment in any of its policy documents. Neither Pakistan nor any other developing country has, so far, used the OHCHR guidelines in preparing their PRSP.

A comparison of OHCHR Guideline 8 relating to the right of equal access to justice with Pakistan's current judicial reform project shows that there are similarities between the two despite the fact that the latter has no specific link with human rights. Implemented in the wider context of poverty, the main aim of the judicial reform is to reduce the vulnerability of the poor. However, the specific incorporation of human rights will add value and reinforce the similarities because it will create an entitlement for the poor as right-holders and impose an obligation on the part of the state institutions as duty-bearers. Moreover, the promotion and protection of the right of access to justice requires that the key targets and indicators suggested by OHCHR Guideline 13 be mainstreamed in the AJP policy framework. If Pakistan follows all the OHCHR guidelines in the formulation and implementation of its PRSP, it can create enabling conditions for the promotion of the RTD.

9 Conclusion

The purpose of this book was to examine the legal status of the RTD in international law, with a focus on state practice. Pakistan's judicial experience was used as a case study to explore the implications for the RTD of the protection of the constitutionally guaranteed fundamental rights.

The key issues discussed in Part I were the history and politics, conceptual underpinnings and jurisprudence of the RTD. A discussion of these issues was necessary to examine the controversies surrounding the concept of the RTD. The results obtained in Part I were further elaborated upon in the core of the book, that is, the recognition of international cooperation in international law, with a focus on the judicial practice of Pakistan, carried out in Parts II and III, respectively.

In Part I, the following areas were analysed: the voting trends in the General Assembly and the Commission (Council) on Human Rights, the drafting history and a textual analysis of the DRD and the deliberations of the working groups, with a focus on the reports of the Independent Expert and the Task Force. The examination of the capability approach from the perspective of human rights provided sufficient insight to identify the conceptual basis of the RTD.

Part II examined the legal status of the RTD in public international law. Foreign development aid, one of the tools of international cooperation, was tested in customary international law. The legal status of international cooperation was then examined in general principles of law, soft law and 'new sources' of international law such as cooperation, consensus and interdependence. A number of factors necessary for determining the legal status of a General Assembly resolution were also applied to the Declaration.

Finally, Part III focused on an analysis of Pakistan's judicial experience. For this purpose, three sets of constitutional provisions, viz., the Objectives Resolution, the fundamental rights and the Principles of Policy were compared with the features of the Declaration. This analysis was followed by a detailed examination of the nature of the constitutional obligations and PIL, the main tool of a wider interpretation of the fundamental rights. The RTD was then reconceptualized in Islamic law from the perspective of *maslahah* as the end goal of the *Shari'ah*. The protection of human rights through an effective and efficient judicial service at the grass-roots level was examined in the context of Pakistan's policy measures as envisaged in the current PRSP.

The RTD clearly occupies a distinct position, because of its origin in the political-cum-jurisprudential tension between developed and developing countries. The distinctiveness of the RTD lies in the fact that firstly, it was rooted in the not so distant past of colonialism; secondly, it was claimed as a collective right of the people of developing countries. Politically, the RTD provided the main impetus for the demand of developing countries for an equitable global economic system. Generally, the capability approach provides a conceptual underpinning to the RTD.

This study has revealed that in positive law, the collective dimension of the RTD is still a jurisprudential challenge, for the reason that a collective right cannot be a human right. The right-holders of the RTD – either people or the state – are not specific. Similarly, the nature of obligation is also not clear. A paradigm shift, in the form of a change from individual right to social right may address this challenge. A move towards social rights may create an opportunity for targeting rights as social and economic goals. A goal-rights system may solve the issue of justiciability, particularly at the national level.

At the political level, there is an increasing willingness on the part of the international community to engage, albeit slowly, in international cooperation. There are a number of reasons for this. Firstly, a political consensus on the RTD, between developed countries (including the USA, the main opponent of the RTD) and developing countries, emerged at the 1993 Vienna Conference. While such a consensus has a strong moral force, it has no legal status. Secondly, the RTD was regularly reiterated in thematic international human rights conferences such as those concerning the environment, human rights, population, social development, women, the fiftieth anniversary of the UDHR and racism.[1] It is likely that the RTD will be brought up again in similar conferences in future. Thirdly, a pro-RTD change is discernible in the political will of the developed countries, particularly the members of the EU, which support the RTD to a limited extent, in the UN General Assembly, the Commission on Human Rights and the open-ended working group. In the eighth session of the OEWG, Germany, on behalf of the EU, 'reaffirmed the firm commitment of the EU to the realisation of the [RTD]'.[2] Given the staunch opposition of the Western countries to the notion of the RTD during the drafting of the Declaration, this change of attitude is of great significance. Fourthly, the roles of the international organizations, for

1 World Conference on environment and development (Rio de Janeiro, Brazil, 1992), Human Rights (Vienna, Austria, 1993), population and development (Cairo, Egypt, 1994), social development (Copenhagen, Denmark, 1995), women (Beijing, China, 1995) and celebration of the 50th anniversary of UDHR (1998), World Conference against Racism, Racial Discrimination, Xenophobia and Related Intolerance (2001).

2 See A/HRC/4/47, para. 20. The session was held from 26 Feb. to 2 March 2007.

example the IMF, the World Bank and the multilateral and bilateral donor agencies, in supporting a rights-based approach to development at the national level, and their supportive role in the OEWG are also positive indications for the promotion of the RTD through international cooperation. Despite these factors, there is still a resistance to the acceptance of international cooperation as a legal obligation. Developed countries actively oppose a proposal for adopting a legally binding instrument on the RTD.[3]

The principle of cooperation as a source of obligation is based mainly on international custom. The examination of foreign development aid has shown that international cooperation is not a part of customary international law. The practice of developed countries – bilateral donors – in this area is widespread, general and consistent. However, *opinio juris* – the second requirement of custom – is missing. Most developed countries consider development aid to be a moral obligation only. Most developed countries do not achieve even the development aid targets set by the General Assembly. Thus it is clear that the RTD is yet to establish itself as a right within international law.

There is growing academic support for the concept of cooperation as a good faith obligation under the UN Charter and even as a 'new source' (along with interdependence and consensus) of obligation in international law. However, the hortatory and non-obligatory nature of the Declaration demonstrates that it appears to be a soft law. Soft law has the potential to influence both the international and national dimensions of the RTD. At the international level, there is a growing call for mainstreaming the RTD in the rules and policies of IFIs and the WTO. The human rights framework, particularly the RTD, provides guidance to global institutions of trade and development in this era of globalization.[4]

This study has determined that the national dimension of the RTD is less problematic and that soft law influences national laws. In this respect, a detailed analysis of Pakistan's judicial practice has established that judicial activism may create an enabling environment for the promotion of the RTD. A number of PIL cases show that in the perspective of constitutional law the courts have adopted and applied the principles of dynamism, consistency and harmony by extending the scope of fundamental rights to the Principles of Policy. Thus a judicial intervention in social and economic matters has positive implications for the RTD. It appears that the present judicial crisis – initiated on 9 March 2007 with the suspension of Chief Justice Choudhry and further aggravated since 3 November 2007 with the imposition of emergency rule and the dismissal of Chief Justice Choudhry

3 Ibid. Annex II. Australia and Canada in their separate comments opposed the idea of a legally binding instrument on the RTD. Even the EU, which generally supports the RTD, opposed the proposal.

4 See Robert Howse, 'Mainstreaming the Right to Development into International Trade Law and Policy at the World Trade Organisation', paper submitted to the UN Sub-Commission on the Promotion and Protection of Human Rights as E/CN.4/Sub.2/2004/17.

and about sixty other superior courts judges – may have a negative impact on judicial activism in the near future. However, for a number of reasons, the negative impact, if there is any, may not last long. These reasons are: the high degree of populism attained by judicial activism, continuing political instability, economic underdevelopment and dysfunctional public institutions and the vigorous lawyers' movement.

The Islamic concept of social justice may also be a source of further strength for the RTD in a Muslim country like Pakistan. The domestic application of the RTD requires a progressive judicial interpretation of the *Shari'ah*. Notwithstanding some controversial and inconsistent rulings, the judiciary have played a constructive role by interpreting the *Shari'ah*. Through a wider interpretation of the *Shari'ah*, the judiciary have overcome some key challenges such as women's eligibility for public offices, the application of Islamic criminal punishments, women's family rights and rulers' privileges. Such an interpretation may prove a helpful tool in enabling Pakistan to fulfil its international human rights obligations. While the *Shari'ah* is generally compatible with the Declaration, where there is conflict between the *Shari'ah* and international human rights standards, the interpretive approach and the doctrine of *maslahah*, as the end goal of the *Shari'ah*, may achieve greater compatibility. *Maslahah* may also prove helpful in other Muslim countries following Sunni Islamic law in pursuing the RTD from the perspective of the *Shari'ah*.

The judicial activism of the superior court is, however, not sufficient. Improvement in the delivery of justice services by the lower judiciary has far greater implications for human rights because firstly, it has the duty to protect the human rights of citizens. Secondly, the vast majority of people have access to the lower judiciary for redress of their public as well as private grievances. Thirdly, improvement in the delivery of justice services will contribute to reducing the vulnerability of the poor. Thus the role of the lower judiciary is no less important. Pakistan's current PRSP is pursuing judicial reform under the AJP as part of a broad-based governance reform package. Indeed the success of governance reforms as part of a broader poverty-reduction strategy in Pakistan hinges on the role of an efficient and effective lower judiciary. A comparison of the AJP reform programme with Guideline 8 proposed by the OHCHR has demonstrated that they share some common features. However, the AJP still needs to be specifically aligned with a rights-based approach. OHCHR Guideline 8 can be helpful in this regard.

It seems necessary to point out some problems and limitations of the arguments advanced in this study. Firstly, the Declaration is not a treaty; it entails no legal obligation. The international community is still searching for means to implement the RTD at the international level. The true legal status of international cooperation cannot be ascertained unless there is an acceptable international standard for the implementation of the RTD.

Secondly, one may argue that judicial intervention through PIL could only be an alternative or piecemeal strategy towards social and economic justice.

The formulation and implementation of a comprehensive development policy aimed at the protection and promotion of fundamental rights is the primary duty of the executive organ of the state. However, Pakistan's frequent political instability coupled with the declining governance structure and the government's deviation from constitutional rule warrants judicial intervention. Moreover, PIL now appears to be no longer a piecemeal strategy because the Supreme Court has time and again reiterated its commitment to the protection of fundamental rights through the PIL mechanism.[5]

Thirdly, this study has suggested that the PRSP framework is a viable mechanism for implementation of the RTD at the national level. This could have led to an examination of specific poverty and human rights issues, such as bonded labour, women's role in the process of development and the provisions of basic capabilities such as the rights to education and health. These issues are beyond the scope of this study, however, because the main focus is on the experience of Pakistan's judiciary. Nevertheless a brief examination of these issues in the context of judicial case law creates scope for further research. Given Pakistan's obligations under relevant international treaties and its commitment to the MDGs, an examination of these issues may provide sufficient insights to clarify state obligations under the Declaration.

As a holistic and dynamic concept of human rights and development, the RTD should be supported and promoted both at the international and the national level to achieve basic capabilities for the world's poor. The following strategy is suggested. Firstly, multilateral and bilateral donors should not only continue their cooperation for a rights-based approach to development, but also coordinate their respective activities. This may help to eliminate the duplication of developmental activities by different donors. Secondly, at the national level, the developing countries should commit themselves to a rights-based approach to development. This will serve the purpose of the Declaration, which makes the RTD primarily the duty of the state. Thirdly, in the Muslim world generally, but particularly in Pakistan, a wider interpretation of the *Shari'ah* aimed at *maslahah* should be linked to social and economic policies.

5 See, for example, Report of the Supreme Court's Golden Jubilee Edition, 2006, p 2. See also Address by Mr Justice Iftikhar Muhammad Chaudhry, Chief Justice of Pakistan, at the opening ceremony of the Judicial Year 2007–2008, 10 Sept. 2007. Online. Available at: <http://www.supremecourt.gov.pk/> (accessed 26 Sept. 2007).

Glossary of Islamic words

Amanah	Trust.
Daruriyyah	Essential; five rights/interests which are indispensable: life, religion, property, family and reason.
Diyat	Blood money; monetary compensation for murder or bodily injury.
Fiqh	Islamic jurisprudence.
Fuqaha	Plural of *faqih*: Jurist.
Hajiyyah	Necessary; a category of rights/interest, which is of lesser importance than essentials.
Haraba	Highway robbery.
Hisba	Accountability.
Hudood	Plural of *hadd*; limit; punishments for certain crimes fixed in the Qur'an.
Ibadat	Plural of *ibadah*; worship.
Ibahah	Permissibility.
Ijma	Consensus of opinion of jurists on a legal issue at a certain time.
Ijtihad	Independent human reasoning of a jurist to expound the law by means of interpretation.
Illah	Effective cause; the underlying cause of a rule on the basis of which the rule is extended to other situations.
Imam	Ruler; leader.
Istihsan	Juristic preference.
Khul	Dissolution of marriage at the demand of wife.
Madhabs	Schools of Islamic jurisprudence.
Majlis-e-Shoora	Council of Consultation.
Maqasid al-Shari'ah	Objectives of the Islamic law.
Maslahah	Interest; benefit; welfare.
Maslahah mu'tabarah	A kind of *maslahah* validated by primary sources of Islamic law.
Maslahah mursala	Independent *maslahah* neither supported nor opposed by primary sources.

Mu'amalat	Transaction; social relations.
Mudaraba	A kind of partnership in which one party provides funds, the other party – *mudarib* – provides expertise and management. The latter party does not share the loss.
Nazim	Head of district government.
Nisab	The basic minimum scale necessary for creating an obligation or liability, for example, *zakat* and theft.
Qazf	False imputation of adultery or fornication.
Qawwam	Maintainer; protector.
Qisas	Retribution.
Qiyas	Analogy; extension of the text of the law to a matter, which is not governed by the language of the text, but by the reason of the text.
Riba	Usury; interest.
Shari'ah	Islamic law.
Shura	Process of democratic deliberation.
Siyasah Shar'iyah	*Shari'ah*-based policy of a government.
Sura	Chapter in the Qur'an.
Tahsinyyah	Embellishments; the third category of rights/interest, which is of lesser importance than *hajiyyah*.
Tazir	A kind of punishment other than *Hadd.*
Ulama	Islamic law scholars.
Urf	Custom.
Ushr	A 10 per cent obligatory tax payable on agricultural produce.
Wali	Parents or guardian.
Zakat	Poor rate.
Zina	Adultery; fornication.

Bibliography

PRIMARY SOURCES

Books

Ali, Abdullah Yousaf, *The Meaning of the Holy Qur'an*, Markfield/Leicester, the Islamic Foundation, 2002.

SECONDARY SOURCES

Books, journal articles, papers

Abdelkader, Deina, *Social Justice in Islam*, Herndon, Virginia, USA, International Institute of Islamic Thought, 2000.

Abi-Saab, George, 'The Legal Formulation of a Right to Development' in R.-J. Dupuy (ed.), *The Right to Development at the International Level*, Hague Academy of International Law Workshop, The Hague, Sijhoff & Noordhoff, 1980, pp 159–75.

Action Aid, *Inclusive Circles Lost in Exclusive Cycles*, 2002. Online. Available at: <www.imf.org/external/np/prspgn/review/2002/comm/v2.pdf> (accessed 27 April 2007)

ADB, 'Elements of governance'. Online. Available at: <http://www.adb.org/Governance/gov_elements.asp> (accessed 9 March 2009).

—— 'Governance Defined'. Online. Available at: http://www.adb.org/Documents/Policies/Governance/gov200.asp?p=policies> (accessed 29 March 2007).

—— 'Report And Recommendation of The President to The Board of Directors on Proposed Loans and Technical Assistance Grant to The Islamic Republic of Pakistan for The Access To Justice Program', November 2001. Online. Available at: <http://www.adb.org/Documents/RRPS/PAK/rrp_32023.pdf> (Accessed 1 April 2007).

—— 'Judicial Independence Overview and Country level summaries', Judicial Independence Project, RETA No. 5987, submitted by the Asia Foundation, Oct. 2003. Online. Available at: <http://www.adb.org/Documents/Events/2003/RETA5987/Final_Overview_Report.pdf> (accessed 9 April 2007).

Ahmed, Akbar S., *Jinnah, Pakistan and Islamic Identity: The Search for Saladin*, London/New York, Routledge, 1997.

Akehurst, Michael, 'Custom as a Source of International Law', *British Year Book of International Law* XLVII, 1974–75, 1–53.

—— *A Modern Introduction to International Law*, London/New York, Routledge, 6th Edition, 1987, Reprinted, 1993.

A-Khavari, Afshin and Rothwell, Donald R., 'The ICJ and the Danube Case: A Missed Opportunity for Environmental Law', *Melbourne University Law Review* 22(3), 1998, 507–36.

Ali, Syed Mohammad, 'Infusing Participation into Development Planning: A CSO Review of the PRSP'. Online. Available at: <http://www.policy.hu/ali/SAP%20review%20of%20PRSP.pdf> (accessed 24 March 2007).

—— 'Participation as the means to assess effectiveness of the Poverty Reduction Strategy Paper for Pakistan', IPF Research Paper, 2005–6. Online. Available at: <http://www.policy.hu/ali/IPF%20research%20paper.pdf> (accessed 24 April 2007).

Al-Raysuni, Ahmad, *Imam Al-Shatibi's Theory of the Higher Objectives and Intents of Islamic Law* (translated by Nancy Robert), London/Washington, The International Institute of Islamic Thought, 2005.

Al-Sayyid, Ridwan, 'Contemporary Muslim Thought and Human Rights', *Islamochristiana* 21, 1995, 27–41.

Alston, Philip, 'A Third Generation of Solidarity Rights', *Netherlands International Law Review* 29, 1982, 307–22.

—— 'The Universal Declaration at 35: Western and Passé or Alive and Universal', *Review of the International Commission of Jurists* 31, 1983, 60–70.

—— 'Conjuring Up New Human Rights: A Proposal for Quality Control', *American Journal of International Law* 78, 1984, 607–21.

—— 'The Shortcomings of a "Garfield the Cat" Approach to the Right to Development', *California Western International Law Journal* 15, 1985, 510–18.

—— 'The Right to Development at the International Level', in F.E. Snyder and S. Sathirathai (eds), *Third World Attitudes Towards International Law*, Dordrecht/Lancaster, Martinus Nijhoff Publishers, 1987, pp 812–13. Also published in R.-J. Dupuy (ed.), *The Right to Development at the International Level*, The Hague Academy of International Law Workshop, The Hague, Sijhoff & Noordhoff, 1980.

—— 'Making Space for New Human Rights: The Case of the Right to Development', *Harvard Human Rights Year Book of International Law* 1, 1988, 3–40.

—— 'Revitalising United Nations Work on Human Rights and Development', *Melbourne University Law Review* 18, 1991, 216–57.

—— 'Peoples' Rights: Their Rise and Fall' in Philip Alston (ed.) *The Rights of Peoples*, Oxford, Oxford University Press, 2001, pp 259–93.

Alvi, Hamza, 'Ethnicity, Muslim Society, and the Pakistan Ideology' in Anita M. Weiss (ed.), *Islamic Reassertion in Pakistan: An Application of Islamic Laws in a Modern State*, New York, Syracuse University Press, 1986, pp 21–47.

Anderson, J.N.D., 'Pakistan: An Islamic State?' in R.H. Holland and G. Schwarzenberger (eds), *Law, Justice and Equity*, London, Sir Isaac Pitman and Sons Ltd., 1967, pp 127–36.

Andreassen. B.-A., 'Article 22' in Asbjorn Eide et al. (ed.), *The Universal Declaration of Human Rights: A Commentary*, Oslo, Scandinavian Universities Press, 1992, p 352.

Ansah, J.M.M., 'The Right to Development and the Malawian Law: A Critical Study', PhD Dissertation, University of Nottingham, 2002.

Armytage, Livingston, 'Pakistan Law and Justice Sector Reform Experience: Some Lessons Learned', *Law, Social Justice & Global Development* 2, 2003. Online. Available at: <http://www2.warwick.ac.uk/fac/soc/law/elj/lgd/2003_2/armytage/> (accessed 11 April 2007).

Asamoah, Obed, 'The Legal Effect of Resolutions of the General Assembly', *Columbia Journal of Transnational Law* 3(2), 1965, 210–30.

Asnbach, Tatjana, 'Peoples and individuals as subjects of the right to development' in Subrata Roy Chowdhury et al. (eds), *The Right to Development in International Law*, Dordrecht/London, Martinus Nijhoff Publishers, 1992, pp 155–65.

Australia, Commonwealth of, 'Australia's Aid Program'. Online. Available at: <http://www.ausaid.gov.au/makediff/whatis.cfm> (accessed 6 Julyl 2007).

Baderin, Mashood A., *International Human Rights and Islamic Law*, Oxford, Oxford University Press, 2003.

Barsh, R.L., 'The Right to Development as a Human Right: Results of the Global Consultation', *Human Rights Quarterly* 13, 1991, 322–38.

Baxi, Upendra, 'The New International Economic Order, Basic Needs and Rights: Noted Towards Development of the Right of Development', *Indian Journal of International Law* 23, 1983, 225–45.

Beckerman, Wilfred and Clark, S., *Poverty and Social Security in Britain Since 1961*, Oxford, Oxford University Press, 1982.

Bedjaoui, Mohammed, *Towards a New International Economic Order*, Paris, UNESCO, 1979.

—— 'The Right to Development' in Mohammed Bedjaoui (ed.), *International Law: Achievements and Prospects*, Paris, UNESCO, 1991.

Behr, Thomas, 'Luigi Taparelli and Social Justice: Rediscovering the Origin of a "Hallowed" Concept', *Social Justice in Context* 1, 2005, 3–16, at <http://www.ecu.edu/che/cfbi/socialjustice2005vol1.pdf> (accessed 27 February 2009).

Berlin, Isaiah, *Four Essays on Liberty*, Oxford, Oxford University Press, 1969.

Berween, Mohammed, 'Fundamental Human Rights: An Islamic Perspective', *International Journal of Human Rights* 6(1), Spring 2002), 61–78.

Bhagwati, P.N., 'Judicial Activism and Public Interest Litigation', *Columbia Journal of Transnational Law* 23(3), 1985, 561–575.

Bhutto, Zulfikar Ali, 'Is Aid Charity?' in Hamid Jalal and Khalid Hasan, (eds) *Reshaping Foreign Policy: A collection of articles, statements and speeches by Zulfikar Ali Bhutto*, Politics of the People, Lahore, Classic, Politics of the People Volume One, 1948–1966, p 151.

Bilder, Richard, 'Rethinking International Human Rights Law: Some Basic Questions', *Wisconsin Law Review* 1969, 171–217.

Bossuyt, M.J., *Guide to the 'Trauvax Preparatoires' of the International Covenant on Civil and Political Rights*, Dordrecht/Lancaster, Martinus Nijhoff Publishers, 1987, pp 19–48.

Boutros-Ghali, Boutros, *An Agenda for Development*, New York, United Nations, 1995.

Boven, Theo C. van, 'The Right to Development and Human Rights', *Review of the International Commission of Jurists* 28, 1982, 49–56.

Boyle, Alan, 'Soft Law in International Law-making' in Malcolm D. Evans (ed.) *International Law*, Oxford, Oxford University Press, 2nd Edition, 2006, pp 141–58.

Brierly, J.L., *The Basis of Obligation in International Law*, Oxford, Clarendon Press, 1958, pp 51–65.

—— *The Law of Nations*, Oxford, Clarendon Press, 1963.

Brownlie, Ian, *The Human Right to Development* (Study prepared for the Commonwealth Secretariat), London, Commonwealth Secretariat, 1989.

—— *Principles of Public International Law*, Oxford, Clarendon Press, 6th Edition, 2003.

Bulajic, Milan, 'Principles of International Development Law' in S.R. Chowdhury et al. (eds) *International Law and Development*, Dordrecht, London, Martinus Nijhoff Publishers, 1988, pp 359–69.

Bunn, Isabella D., 'The Right to Development: Implications for International Economic Law', *American University Journal of International Law Review* 15, 1999–2000, 1425–68.

—— 'Legal and Moral Implications of the Right to Development: Implications for International Economic Law', PhD Dissertation, University of Bristol, 2002.

Canadian Council for International Cooperation. Online. Available at: <http://www.ccic.ca/e/docs/002_aid_roa_2004.pdf> (accessed 29 July 2007).

Canadian Society of Muslims, 'USHR' [Definition]. Online. Available at: <http://muslim-canada.org/fiqhch4.html> (accessed 27 June 2007).

Cassese, Antonio, *International Law in a Divided World*, Oxford, Clarendon Press, 1986, para. 68.

—— *International Law*, Oxford, Oxford University Press, 2001.

Catholic Relief Services, *Review of the Poverty Reduction Strategy Paper Initiative*, 2001. Online. Available at: <http://www.imf.org/external/np/prspgen/review/2002/comm/v2.pdf> (accessed 27 April 2007).

Centre for Development and Human Rights, *The Right to Development: A Primer*, New Delhi/London, Sage, 2005.

Charlesworth, Hilary, 'The Public/Private Distinction and the Right to Development in International Law', *Australian Year Book of International Law* 1999, 190–204.

—— *The Boundaries of International Law: The Feminist Analysis*, Manchester, Manchester University Press, 2000.

Charney, Jonathan I., 'The Persistent Objector Rule and the Development of Customary International Law', *British Year Book of International Law* LVI, 1985, 1–24.

Chaudry, Mr Justice Iftikhar Muhammed, Chief Justice of Pakistan, Address at Opening Ceremony of Judicial Year 2007–8, 10 Sept. 2007. Online. Available at: <http://www.supremecourt.gov.pk> (accessed 26 Sept. 2007).

Cheng, Ben, 'United Nations Resolution on Outer Space: "Instant" International Customary Law?', *Indian Journal of International Law* 5, 1965, 23–48.

Chinkin, C.M., 'The Challenge of Soft Law: Development and Change in International Law', *International and Comparative Law Quarterly* 38, 1989, 850–66.

Choudhury, Masudul Alam and Malik, ʿUzir Abdul, *The Foundations of Islamic Political Economy*, London, Macmillan, 1992.

Christian Aid, *Ignoring the Experts: Poor Peoples' Exclusion from Poverty Reduction Strategies*. Online. Available at: <http://www.imf.org/external/np/prspgen/review/2002/comm.pdf> (accessed 27 April 2007).

—— *The Politics of Poverty: Aid in the New Cold War*, May 2004. Online. Available at <http://www.un-ngls.org/orf/politics%20of%20poverty.pdf> (accessed 15 March 2009).

Clark, Grace, 'Pakistan's Zakat and Ushr as a Welfare System' in Anita M. Weiss (ed.), *Islamic Reassertion in Pakistan: The Application of Islamic Laws in a Modern State*, New York, Syracuse University Press, 1986, pp79–95.

Commission on Human Rights, Reports of the Fifty-Fourth session (16 March–24 April 1998), ECOSOC, Chapter VI, pp 116–28.

—— Reports of the Fifty-Fifth session (22 March–30 April 1999), Chapter VII, pp 103–10.

—— Reports of the Fifty-Sixth session, (20 March–28 April 2000), Official Record 2000, Supplement No. 3, Chapter VII, p 99.

Cornelius, A.R., 'Fundamental Rights under Shari'at', *PLD Journal* 1970, 144–5.

Coulson, N.J., *A History of Islamic Law*, Edinburgh, Edinburgh University Press, 1964.

Cranston, Maurice, *What are Human Rights?*, London, The Bodley Head, 1973.

Crawford, James, (ed.) *The Rights of Peoples*, Oxford, Oxford University Press, 1988, p 58–9.

Curzon, L.B., *Dictionary of Law*, London, Pitman Publishing, 4th edition, 1993.

D'Amato, Anthony, 'On Consensus', *Canadian Year Book of International Law* 8, 1970, 104–22.

D'Souza, Radha, 'The "Third World" and Socio-Legal Studies: Neo-Liberalism and Lessons from India's Legal Innovations', *Social & Legal Studies* 14(4) 2005, 487–513.

Dixon, M., *Text Book on International Law*, Oxford, Oxford University Press, 5th Edition, 2005.

Donnelly, Jack, 'Human Rights as Natural Rights', *Human Rights Quarterly* 4, 1982, 341–405.

—— 'Cultural Relativism and Universal Human Rights', *Human Rights Quarterly* 6(4), 1984, 400–20.

—— 'Human Rights and Human Dignity: An Analytic Critique of Non-Western Conceptions of Human Rights', *American Political Science Review* 76, 1985, 303–16.

—— 'In Search of a Unicorn: the Jurisprudence and Politics of the Right to Development', *California Western International Law Journal* 15, 1985, 473–509.

—— *Universal Human Rights in Theory and Practice*, Ithaca, New York/London, Cornell University Press, 2003.

Drydyk, Jay, 'When is Development More Democratic?', *Journal of Human Development* 6(2), 2005, 247–67.

Dupuy, Rene Jean, 'Declaratory Law and Programmatory Law: From Revolutionary Custom to "Soft Law" ' in R.K. Akkerman et al. (eds) *Declarations on Principles, A Quest for Universal Peace*, Leyden, A.W. Sijthoff, pp 247–57.

Dworkin, Ronald, *Taking Rights Seriously*, London, Duckworth, First Edition, 1977, (2005 Impression, with reply to critics).

Dyke, Vernon Van, *Human Rights, Ethnicity and Discrimination*, 10 Contributions in Ethnic Studies, Westport, Connecticut, Greenwood Press, 1985.

Easterly, William, 'The Political Economy of Growth Without Development: A Case Study of Pakistan', Paper for the Analytical Narratives of Growth Project, Kennedy School of Government, Harvard University, Development Research Group, World Bank, June 2001. Online. Available at: <http://ksghome.harvard.edu/~drodrik/Growth%20volume/Easterly-Pakistan.pdf> (accessed 29 Aug. 2007).

E/CN.4/2004/15, ODI, 'The right to development: study on existing bilateral and multilateral programmes and policies for development partnership', Independent Study by ODI, p 12 (hereinafter ODI Study).

Eide, Asbjorn, 'Maldevelopment and the "Right to Development": A Critical Note with a Constructive Intent' in R.-J. Dupuy (ed.), *The Right to Development at the International Level*, The Hague Academy of International Law Workshop, The Hague, Sijhoff & Noordhoff, 1980, pp 397–416.

—— 'Article 28' in Asbjorn Eide, et al. (ed.), *The Universal Declaration of Human Rights: A Commentary*, Oslo, Scandinavian Universities Press, 1992, pp 433–47.

Espiel, Hector Gros, 'The Right to Development as a Human Right', *Texas International Law Journal* 16, 1981, 189–205.

Esposito, John L., 'Perspectives on Islamic Law Reform: The Case of Pakistan', *New York University Journal of International Law and Politics* 13(1), 1980, 217–45.

—— (ed.), *The Oxford Dictionary of Islam*, Oxford, Oxford University Press 1999, 2nd edition 2003. Oxford University Press. Online. Available at: <http://www.oxfordreference.com/views/ENTRY.html?subview=Main&entry=t125.e1107> (accessed 11 Jan. 2007).

—— and Voll, John O., *Islam and Democracy*, Oxford, Oxford University Press, 1996, pp 102–23.

European Union, EU Presidency Statement, 'Commission on Human Rights – Right to Development', 2002. Online. Available at: <http://www.europa-eu-un.org/articles/en/article_1296_en.htm> (accessed 28 Feb. 2009).

—— EU Presidency Statement: 'Commission on Human Right – Right to Development', 2005. Online. Available at: <http://www.europa-eu-un.org/articles/en/article_5414_en.htm> (accessed 25 Jan. 2007).

Falk, Richard A., 'On Quasi-Legislative Competence of the General Assembly', *American Journal of International Law* 60, 1966, 782–91.

Farouki, Kamal F., 'Pakistan Islamic Government and Society' in John L. Esposito (ed.), *Islam in Asia: Religion, Politics and Society*, Oxford, Oxford University Press, 1987, pp 53–78.

Fenwick, Charles G., 'International Law: Old and New', *American Journal of International Law* 60, 1966, 475–83.

Fischer, Eveline N., 'Lessons Learned from Judicial Reform: The ADB Experience', Speech, 20 Oct. 2006. Online. Available at: <http://www.adb.org/Media/Articles/2006/10829-speech-Eveline-Fischer/> (accessed 11 April 2007).

Fitzgerald, P.J., *Salmond on Jurisprudence*, London, Sweet & Maxwell, Twelfth Edition, 1966.

Franck, Thomas M. and Munansangu, Mark M., *The New International Economic Order: International Law in the Making?*, Geneva, United Nations Institute for Training and Research (UNITAR), 1982.

Freeman, Michael, 'Human Rights and Real Cultures: Towards a Dialogue on "Asian Values" ', *Netherlands Quarterly of Human Rights* 16(1), 1998, 25–39.

—— 'The Problem of Secularism in Human Rights Theory', *Human Rights Quarterly* 26, 2004, 375–400.

Friedmann, Wolfgang, 'The Changing Dimensions of International Law', *Columbia Law Review* 62, 1962, 1147–65.

—— 'The Uses of "General Principles" in the Development of International Law', *American Journal of International Law* 57, 1963, 279–99.

Fung, Archon and Wright, Erik Olin, 'Deepening Democracy: Innovations in Empowered Participatory Governance', *Politics and Society* 29(1), March 2001, 5–41.

Ghai, Yash, *Whose Right to Development?*, Human Rights Unit Occasional Paper,

Human Rights in Development Series, London, Commonwealth Secretariat, 1989, p 3.

—— 'Human Rights and Governance: The Asia Debate', *Australian Year Book of International Law* 15, 1994, 1–34.

—— 'Redesigning the State for "Right Development" ' in B.A. Andreassen and Stephen Marks (ed.), *Development as a Human Right, Legal, Political and Economic Dimensions*, Harvard School of Public Health, Cambridge, Massachusetts, Harvard University Press, 2006, pp 141–66.

Ghazzali, Abdus Sattar, *Islamic Pakistan: Illusion or Reality*, Islamabad, National Book Club, 1997.

Ginther, Konrad, 'Participation and Accountability: Two Aspects of the Internal and International Dimension of the Right to Development', *Third World Legal Studies*, 1992, 55–77.

—— 'The domestic policy function of a right of peoples to development: popular participation a new hope for development and a challenge for the discipline', in S.R. Chowdhury et al. (eds), *The Right to Development in International Law*, The Hague, Kluwer Law International, 1992, pp 35–41.

Hakro, Ahmad Nawaz and Talpur, Mustafa, 'A Civil Society Perspective on the Millennium Development Goals and the Poverty Reduction Strategy Paper: The Case of Pakistan', Commonwealth Foundation, 2005. Online. Available at: <http://www.commonwealthfoundation.com/uploads/documents/mdg_pakistan.pdf> (accessed 24 March 2007).

Haleem, Muhammad, 'Law, Justice and Society', *PLD Journal* 1986 205–12.

Hallaq, Wael B., *A History of Islamic Legal Theories, An Introduction to Sunni Usul al-Fiqh*, Cambridge, Cambridge University Press, 1997.

Hamm, Brigitte I., 'A Human Rights Approach to Development', *Human Rights Quarterly* 23(4), 2001, 1005–31.

Harel, Alon, 'Theories of Rights' in Martin P. Golding and William A. Edmundson (eds), *Philosophy of Law and Legal Theory*, Oxford, Blackwell Publishing, 2005, pp 191–206.

Hayek, Friedrich, *Law, Legislation and Liberty, A new statement of the liberal principles of justice and political economy: Volume 2 The Mirage of Social Justice*, London and Henley, Routledge & Kegan Paul, 1976.

Higgins, Roslyn, *The Development of International Law through the Political Organs of the United Nations*, Oxford, Oxford University Press, 1963.

Hohfeld, Wesley Newcomb, *Fundamental Legal Conceptions, As Applied in Judicial Reasoning* (edited by Walter Wheeler Cook, with a new foreword by Arthur L. Corbin), New Haven, Yale University Press, 1919.

Holland, T.E., *The Elements of Jurisprudence*, Oxford, Clarendon Press, 13th Edition, Impression of 1928.

Howard, Marilyn et al., *Poverty: the Facts*, London, CPAG, 4th Edition, 2001.

Howse. Robert, 'Mainstreaming the Right to Development into International Trade Law and Policy at the World Trade Organisation', paper submitted to the UN Sub-Commission on the Promotion and Protection of Human Rights as E/CN.4/Sub.2/2004/17.

Human Rights Commission of Pakistan (HRCP), *The State of Human Rights, 2006*. Online. Available at: <http://www.hrcp-web.org/ar_home_05.cfm> (Accessed 29 June 2007).

Hunt, Paul, Nowak Manfred and Osmani, S.R., *Guidelines: A Human Rights Approach to Poverty Reduction Strategies*. Online. Available at: <http://www.unhchr.ch/development/povertyfinal.html> (accessed 9 July 2007).

Hussain, Faqir, 'Public Interest Litigation in Pakistan', *PLD Journal* 1993 72–83.

Hussain, Ishrat, 'Economic Reforms and Macroeconomic Management in Pakistan, 1999–2001'. Online. Available at: <http://www.spb.org.pk>.

Hussain, Sheikh Showkat, 'Human Right in Islam: Principles and Precedents', *Islamic and Comparative Law Quarterly* 3(2), 1983, 103–28.

Ibhawoh, Bony, 'Between Culture and Constitution: Evaluating the Cultural Legitimacy of Human Rights in the African States', *Human Rights Quarterly* 22, 2000, 838–60.

International Commission of Jurists, Rijksuniversiteit Limburg, Centre of Human Rights and Urban Morgan Institute for Human Rights, 'The Maastricht Guidelines on Violation of Economic, Social and Cultural Rights', *Human Rights Quarterly* 20, 1998, 691–704.

International Monetary Fund (IMF) Independent Evaluation Office Report on Pakistan. Online. Available at: <http://www.imf.org/external/np/ieo/2002/pu/file12.pdf> (accessed 24 March 2007).

—— 'IMF and Good Governance, A Factsheet', April 2003. Online. Available at: <http://www.imf.org/external/np/exr/facts/gov.htm> (accessed 29 March 2007).

—— Poverty Reduction Strategy Papers (PRSPs). Online. Available at: <http://www.imf.org/external/np/exr/facts/prsp.htm> (accessed 27 April 2007).

Iqbal, Muhammad, *The Reconstruction of Religious Thought in Islam*, London, Oxford University Press, 1934.

Ismail, Faizel, 'Mainstreaming Development in the World Trade Organization', *Journal of World Trade* 39(1), 2005, 11–21.

Jenks, C. Wilfred, *Law, Freedom and Welfare*, London, Stevens & Sons, 1968.

Jennings, Sir Robert, 'Recent Developments in the International Law Commission: Its Relation to the Sources of International Law', *International and Comparative Law Quarterly* 13, 1964, 385–97.

—— 'What is International Law and how do we tell it when we see it?', *The Cambridge-Tilburg Law Lectures*, 3rd series, 1980, London, Deventer, Kluwer, 1983.

Jillani, Justice Tassaduq, 'The Elusive Goddess of Justice May Respond: Give ADR a Chance', Paper presented at the First South Asian Regional Judicial Colloquium on Access to Justice, New Delhi, 1–3 Nov. 2002. Online. Available at: <http://www.humanrightsinitiative.org/jc/papers/jc_2002/judges_papers/Jillani.pdf> (accessed 28 Aug. 2007).

Jing-Bao, Nie, 'Cultural Values Embodying Universal Norms: A Critique of a Popular Assumption about Cultures and Human Rights', *Developing World Bioethics* 5(3), 2005, 251–7.

Johnson, D.H.N., 'The Effect of Resolutions of the General Assembly of the United Nations', *British Year Book of International Law* XXXII, 1955–6, 97–122.

Johnston, David L., 'The Human Khilafa: A Growing Overlap of Reformism and Islamism on Human Rights Discourse', *Islamochristiana* 28, 2002, 35–53.

Joyner, Christopher C., 'U.N. General Assembly Resolutions and International Law: Rethinking the Contemporary Dynamics of Norm-Creation', *California Western International Law Journal* 11, 1981, 445–78.

Kamali, M. Hashim, 'Have we Neglected the Shari̒ah-Law Doctrine of Maslahah?', *Islamic Studies* 27(4), 1988, 287–303.

—— 'Siyasah Shar'iyah or the Policies of Islamic Government', *American Journal of Islamic Social Sciences* 6(1), 1989, 59–80.

—— 'Sources, Nature and Objective of Shari'ah', *Islamic Quarterly* 33, 1989, 215–35.

—— 'Fundamental Rights of the Individual: An Analysis of Haqq (Rights) in Islamic Law', *American Journal of Islamic Social Sciences* 10(3), 1993, 340–66.

—— 'Maqasid al-Shariah: The Objectives of Islamic Law', *Association of Muslim Lawyers Newsletter* 3, 1998, 1–7.

—— 'Law and Society, the Interplay of Revelation and Reason in the Shariah' in John L. Esposito (ed.), *The Oxford History of Islam*, Oxford, Oxford University Press, 1999, pp 107–53.

—— *Principles of Islamic Jurisprudence*, Cambridge, The Islamic Text Society, 2000.

—— *Freedom, Equality and Justice in Islam*, Cambridge, The Islamic Text Society, 2002.

—— *The Dignity of Man: An Islamic Perspective*, Cambridge, The Islamic Text Society, 2002, first published by Ilmiah Publishers, Kuala Lumpur, Malaysia, 1999.

—— *Equity and Fairness in Islam*, Cambridge, The Islamic Text Society, 2005.

Kelsen, Hans, *The Law of the United Nations*, London, Steven & Sons Limited, 1950.

Kenig-Witkowska, Maria Magdalena, 'The UN Declaration on the Right to Development in the light of its Travaux Preparatoires' in S.R. Chowdhury et al. (eds) *International Law and Development*, Dordrecht; London, Martinus Nijhoff Publishers, 1988, pp 381–7.

—— 'Development ideology in international law' in S.R. Chowdhury et al. (eds), *The Right to Development in International Law*, The Hague, Kluwer Law International, 1992, pp 35–41.

Kennedy, Charles H., 'Repugnancy to Islam – Who Decides? Islam and Legal Reform in Pakistan', *International and Comparative Law Quarterly* 41, Oct. 1992, 769–87.

Khan, Foqia Sadiq, 'The Way Forward: Access and Dispensation of Justice', *SDPI (Sustainable Development Policy Institute) Research and News Bulletin* 11 (2), March–October (2004) 17–21 at 18. Online. Available <www.sdpi.org/help/research_and_news_bulletin/march_Oct_2004/bulletin_pdf> (accessed 21 April 2009).

Khan, Kabir-Ur-Rahman, 'The International Right to Development and the Law of G.A.T.T.', *Third World Legal Studies*, 1984, 160–74.

Khan, Mansoor Hassan, 'The Concept of Public Interest Litigation and its Meaning in Pakistan', *PLD Journal*, 1992.

—— *The Concept of Public Interest Litigation and its Meaning in Pakistan*, Karachi, Pakistan Law House, 1993.

Khan, Tariq Amin, 'Economy, Society and the State in Pakistan', *Contemporary South Asia* 9(2), 2000, 181–95.

Khor, Martin, 'Paradigm Clash', *Our Planet* Feb. 2007. Online. Available at: <http://www.unep.org/pdf/Ourplanet/2007/february/en/OP-2007-02-en-ARTICLE8.pdf> (accessed 19 June 2007).

Khosa, Asif Saeed Khan, 'Judiciary's Role towards Promotion of Social Justice: The Pakistan Experience', *PLD Journal* 1995, SC Section, 79–102.

Kiwanuka, R.N., 'Developing Rights: The UN Declaration on the Right to Development', *Netherlands International Law Review* 35, 1988, 257–72.

Knoke, Irene and Morazan, Pedro, 'PRSP: Beyond the Theory. Practical Experiences and Positions of Involved Civil Society Organisations', 2002. Online. Available at: <http://www.eurodad.org/uploadstore/cms/docs/suedwind_prsp_review.pdf> (accessed 12 March 2007).

Kopelmans, Lazare, 'Custom as a Means of the Creation of International Law', *British Year Book of International Law* XVIII, 1937, 127–51.

Laszalo, Ervin et al., *The Obstacles to the New International Economic Order*, Oxford, Pergamon Press, 1980.

Lau, Martin, *The Role of Islam in the Legal System of Pakistan*,' Leiden/Boston, Martinus Nijhoff Publishers, 2006.

Lauterpacht, H., *International Law and Human Rights*, New York, Frederick A. Praeger, Inc., 1950, pp 27–45.

Lewis, A.W., *The Evolution of the International Economic Order*, Princeton, NJ, Princeton University Press, 1978.

Lin, Brian Chi-ang, 'A New Vision of the Knowledge Economy', *Journal of Economic Surveys* 21(3), 2007, 553–84.

Lindroos, Anja, *The Right to Development*, Helsinki, The Erik Carsten Institute of International Law and Human Rights Research Report 2/1999.

M'Baye, Keba, 'Le droit de développement comme un droit de l'homme', *Revue des Droits de l'homme* 5, 1972, 505–34.

—— 'Human Rights and Peoples' Rights' in Mohammed Bedjaoui (ed.), *International Law: Achievements and Prospects*, Paris, UNESCO, 1991, pp 1041–58.

McGee, Rosemary with Josh Levine and Alexandra Hughes, 'Assessing Participation in Poverty Reduction Strategy Papers: A Desk-based Synthesis of Experience in sub-Saharan Africa', Brighton, Institute of Development Studies, Research Report 52, Feb. 2002 Online. Available at: <http://www.ids.ac.uk/ids/bookshop/rr/rr52.pdf>.

MacGibbon, I.C., 'Customary International Law and Acquiescence', *British Year Book of International Law* XXXIII, 1957, 114–45.

McNair, Q.C., Lord, 'The General Principles of Law Recognized by Civilized Nations', *British Year Book of International Law* XXXIII, 1957, 1–19.

Malanczuk, Peter, *Akehurt's Modern Introduction to International Law*, London/New York, Routledge, 7th Edition, 1997.

Malhotra, Rajeev, 'Right to Development: Where Are We Today?' in Arjun Sengupta, et al. (eds), *Reflections of the Right to Development*, New Delhi, Sage, 2006, pp 127–52.

Mangu, Andre Mbata B., 'The Changing Human Rights Landscape in Africa: Organisation of African Unity, African Union, New Partnership for Africa's Development and the African Court', *Netherlands Quarterly of Human Rights* 23(3), 2005, 379–408.

Mansell, Wade and Scott, Joanne, 'Why Bother About the Right to Development?', *Journal of Law and Society* 21(4), 1994, 171–92.

Marks, Stephen, 'Emerging Human Rights: A New Generation for the 1980s?', *Rutgers Law Review* 33, 1981, 435–52.

—— 'The Human Right to Development: Between Rhetoric and Reality', *Harvard Human Rights Law Journal* 17, 2004, 137–68.

—— 'The Human Rights Framework for Development: Seven Approaches' in Arjun Sengupta, et al. (eds), *Reflections on the Right to Development*, London, New Delhi, Sage, 2005, pp 23–60.

—— 'Obstacles to the Right to Development'. Abstract online. Available at: <http://harvardfxbcenter.org/resources/working-papers/FXBC-WP17_Marks.pdf> (accessed 14 March 2009).

Martin, J. Paul, 'The Three Monotheistic World Religions and International Human Rights', *Journal of Social Issues* 61(4), 2005, 827–45.

Masud, M. Khalid, *Shatibi Philosophy of Islamic Law*, Islamabad, Islamic Research Institute, International Islamic University, 1995, p 151.

Mayer, Ann Elizabeth, 'Islamization and Taxation in Pakistan' in Anita M. Weiss (ed.), *Islamic Reassertion in Pakistan: An Application of Islamic Laws in a Modern State*, New York, Syracuse University Press, 1986, pp 59–77.

Mehdi, Rubya, *The Islamization of the Law in Pakistan*, Richmond, Surrey, Nordic Institute of Asian Studies, Curzon Press, 1994.

Mehmood, Tahir, 'The Islamic Law of Human Rights', *Islamic and Comparative Law Quarterly* 4(1/2), 1984, 32–44.

Mendelson, Maurice, 'The Subjective Element in Customary International Law', *British Year Book of International Law* LXVI, 1995, 177–208.

Menegat, Rualdo, 'Participatory democracy and sustainable development: integrated urban environment management in Porto Alegre, Brazil', *Environment and Urbanization* 14, 2002, 181–206.

Menski, Werner Alam, Rafay, Ahmad and Kasuri, Mehreen Raza, *Public Interest Litigation in Pakistan*, Karachi, Pakistan Law House/Platinum Publishing, 2000.

Mestdagh, Karel de Vey, 'The Right to Development', *Netherlands International Law Review* 3, 1981, 30–53.

Miller, S.M. and Roby, P., 'Poverty: Changing Social Stratification' in Peter Townsend (ed.), *The Concept of Poverty, Working Papers on Methods of Investigation and Life-Styles of the Poor in Different Countries*, London, Heinemann, 1971, pp 124–45.

Moosa, Ebrahim, 'The Dilemma of Islamic Rights Scheme', *Journal of Law and Religion* 15(1/2), 2000–1, 185–215.

Moose, George, Ambassador US Delegation and US Permanent Representative to the UN Offices in Geneva, Remarks to the 57th Session of the UN Commission on Human Rights, Geneva, Switzerland, 27 March 2001. Online. Available at: <http://www.usmission.ch/humanrights/2002/statements/0327development.html> (accessed 28 Feb. 2009).

Morsink, John, 'The Philosophy of the Universal Declaration', *Human Rights Quarterly* 6(3), 1984, 309–34.

Mullally, Siobhan, ' "As Nearly as May Be": Debating Women's Human Rights in Pakistan', *Social & Legal Studies* 14(3), 2005, 341–58.

Nankani, Gobind et al., 'Human Rights and Poverty Reduction Strategies: Moving Towards Convergence?' in Philip Alston and Mary Robinson (eds), *Human Rights and Development: Towards Mutual Reinforcement*, Oxford, Oxford University Press, 2005, pp 475–97.

NEPAD, *The African Peer Review Mechanism (APRM)*. Online. Available at: <http://www.nepad.org/2005/files/documents/49.pdf> (accessed 21 June 2007).

Newberg, Paula R., *Judging the State: Courts and Constitutional Politics in Pakistan*, Cambridge, Cambridge University Press, 1995.

North-South: A Programme for Survival, Report of the Independent Commission on International Development Issues, Cambridge, Mass., MIT Press, 1980, Eighth Printing, 1986.

Nozick, Robert, *Anarchy, State and Utopia*, Oxford, Basil Blackwell, 1974.

Nussbaum, Martha, 'Capabilities and Human Rights', *Fordham Law Review* 66, 1997, 273–300

Nyazee, Imran Ahsan Khan, *Islamic Jurisprudence*, Islamabad, International Institute of Islamic Thought and Islamic Research Institute, 2000.

Obiora, L. Amede, 'Beyond the Rhetoric of a Right to Development', *Law & Policy* 18, 1996, 355–418.

ODI, 'Experience with Poverty Reduction Strategy Papers in Latin America and the Caribbean', PRSP Synthesis Note No. 5, Feb. 2003. Online. Available at: <www.prspsythensis.org> (accessed 12 March 2007).

—— DAC, *Development Co-operation Report, 2006*. Online. Available at: <http://caliban.sourceoecd.org/pdf/dac06/01.pdf> (accessed 27 June 2007).

OECD, Report dated 3 April 2007. Online. Available at: <http://www.oecd.org/document/17/0,3343,en_2649_201185_38341265_1_1_1_1,00.html> (accessed 27 June 2007).

—— Development Directorate, *Doing Aid Better*. Online. Available at: <www.oecd.org> (Accessed 28 June 2007).

OHCHR, 'Human Rights and Poverty Reduction: A Conceptual Framework', New York/Geneva, United Nations, 2004, p 2

Onuf, N.G., 'Professor Falk on Quasi-legislative Competence of the General Assembly', *American Journal of International Law* 64, 1970, 349–55.

Orford, Anne, 'Globalization and the Right to Development' in Philip Alston (ed.), *The Rights of Peoples*, Oxford, Oxford University Press, 2001, pp 127–84.

Osmani, S.R., 'Some Thoughts on the Right to Development', in *The Right to Development Book, Reflections on the First Four Reports of the Independent Expert on the Right to Development*, Geneva, Franciscans International, 2004, pp 34–45.

—— 'Poverty and Human Rights: Building on the Capability Approach', *Journal of Human Development* 6(2), 2005, 205–19.

—— 'An Essay on the Human Rights Approach to Development' in Arjun Sengupta et al. (eds), *Reflections on the Right to Development*, New Delhi, Sage, 2006, pp 110–26.

—— 'Participatory Governance and Poverty Reduction' in Alejandro Grinspun et al. (eds), *Choices for the Poor: Lessons from national poverty strategies*, UNDP, pp 121–43. Online. Available at: <http://www.undp.org/dpa/publications/choicesforpoor/ENGLISH/CHAP05.PDF> (accessed 24 June 2007).

—— NWFP EIROP. Online. Available at: <http://www.eirop.org/> (accessed 24 March 2007).

—— 'Plan of Action to Implement the SAARC Social Charter'. Online. Available at: <http://www.pakistan.gov.pk/ministries/planninganddevelopment-ministry/usefull%20links/Economics/SAARC%SOCIAL%20CHARTER.pdf> (accessed 27 Feb. 2009).

—— 'Poverty Reduction Strategy Paper of the NWFP'. Online. Available at: <http:/ /nwfp.gov.pk/AISdownload_file.php?Distld=22&Langld=filed=305> (accessed 8 May 2007).

—— PRSP, 'Accelerating Economic Growth and Reducing Poverty: The Road Ahead'. Online. Available at: <www.moe.gov.pk/prsps_03.pdf> (accessed 24 March 2007).

—— Supreme Court, Report of the Supreme Court's Golden Jubilee Edition, p 2. Online. Available at: <http://www.supremecourt.gov.pk> (accessed 26 Sept. 2007).

—— Foreign Minister's statement on the RTD in the UN, 1996. Online. Available at: <http://www.scienceblog.com/community/older/archives/L/1996/A/un960574.html> (accessed 29 Nov. 2006).

Pakistan, *Economic Survey of Pakistan, 1999–2000*, p 1. Online. Available at: <http://www.paksearch.com/Government/STATISTICS/Survey00/OVERVIEW.html> (accessed 23 July 2007).

—— Foreign Minister's statement on the RTD in the UN, 2000. Online. Available at: <http://www.un.org/ga/webcast/statements/pakistanE.htm> (accessed 29 Nov. 2006).

—— SDPI, Letter sent by a coalition of CSOs led by SDPI, Islamabad to Pakistan's Ministry of Finance, 20 Dec. 2002. Online. Available at: <http://www.eurodad.org/uploadstore/cms/docs/LetterCSOsPakistan.doc> (accessed 24 March 2007).

—— State Bank of, *Annual Report, FY02*. Online. Available at: <http://www.sbp.org.pk/reports/annual/arFY02/chap10.pdf> (accessed 16 July 2007).

—— Supreme Court, *Hisba* bill judgment, 2005. Online. Available at: <www.supremecourt.gov.pk//judgment.htm> (accessed 29 Aug. 2007).

—— Statement of the Deputy Permanent Representative on the RTD in the UN, 2005. Online. Available at: <http://missions.itu.int/~pakistan/2005_Statements/CHR/CHR_Item_7_Statement_22_March_2005.htm> (accessed 29 Nov. 2006).

—— Supreme Court, Review judgment on *Riba*, 2002. Online. Available at: <http://www.supremecourt.gov.pk//judgment.htm> (accessed 28 Aug. 2007).

—— *Economic Survey of Pakistan, 2006–07*. Online. Available at: <www.finance.gov.pk/survey/survey.htm> (accessed 19 Nov. 2007).

—— *Federal Budget, 2006–07*, highlights. Online. Available at: <http://www.finance.gov.pk/budget/2006_07/highlights_2006_07.pdf> (accessed 19 Nov. 2006).

Palacio, Ana, 'The Way Forward: Human Rights and the World Bank', The World Bank Development Outreach, Jan. 2007. Online. Available at: <http://www1.worldbank.org/devoutreach/article.asp?id=388> (accessed 28 Feb. 2009).

Piedra, Lino J., 'Statement by Lino J. Piedra, Public Member of the US delegation before the Commission on 22 March 2005'. Online. Available at: <http://geneva.usmission.gov/humanrights/2005/0322Item7.htm> (accessed 28 Feb. 2009).

Piron, Laure-Helene, 'Are "Development Compacts" Required to Realise the Right to Development?' in *The Right to Development Book, Reflections on the First Four Reports of the Independent Expert on the Right to Development*, Geneva, Franciscans International, 2004, pp 46–61.

—— 'Integrating Human Rights into Development, A Synthesis of Donor Approaches and Experiences', Prepared for the OECD DAC Network on Governance (GOVNET), Sept. 2005. Online. Available at: <http://www.odi.org.uk/rights/Publications/humanrights_into_development_execsumm.pdf> (accessed 28 Feb. 2009).

—— with Alison Evans, 'Politics and the PRSP Approach: A Synthesis Paper', *Working Paper* 137. London, ODI, March 2004, 5.

Piscatori, James P., *Islam in a World of Nation-States*, Cambridge, Cambridge University Press, 1986.

Pogge, Thomas, *World Poverty and Human Rights*, Cambridge, Polity Press, 2002.

Pronk, J.P., 'Human Rights and Development Aid', *International Commission of Jurists Review* 18, 1977, 33–9.

Raghavan, Chakravarthy, *Recolonization: GATT, the Uruguay Round and the Third World*, London, Zed Books, 1990.

Rahim, Abdur, *The Principles of Muhammadan Jurisprudence*, Lahore, PLD Publishers (first published 1911), p 17.

Rawls, John, *A Theory of Justice*, Oxford, Oxford University Press, 1972.

—— 'The Idea of an Overlapping Consensus', *Oxford Journal of Legal Studies* 7, 1987, 1.

Ray, Arun, *Public Interest Litigation and Human Rights in India*, New Delhi, Radha Publications, 2003, p 70.

Rein, Martin, 'Problems in the Definition and Measurement of Poverty' in Peter Townsend (ed.), *The Concept of Poverty, Working Papers on Methods of Investigation and Life-Styles of the Poor in Different Countries*, London, Heinemann, 1971, pp 46–63.

Rich, Roland Y., 'The Right to Development an Emerging Human Right', *Virginia Journal of International Law*, 23(2), 1983, 287–327.

—— 'The Right to Development: A Right of Peoples?' in James Crawford (ed.), *The Rights of Peoples*, Oxford, Clarendon Press, 1988, pp 39–54.

Robinson, Mary, 'What Rights Can Add to Good Development Practice' in Philip Alston and Mary Robinson (ed.), *Human Rights and Development: Towards Mutual Reinforcement*, Oxford, Oxford University Press, 2005, pp 25–41.

Rosas, Allan, 'The Right of Self-determination' in Asbjorn Eide, Catarina Kraus and Allan Rosas (eds), *Economic, Social and Cultural Rights, A Text Book*, The Hague, Martinus Nijhoff Publishers, 1995, pp 79–86.

Rosenfeld, M., 'The Rule of Law and Legitimacy of Constitutional Democracy', *South California Law Review* 74, 2001, 1307–52.

Rowntree, B. Seebohm and Lavers, G.R., *Poverty and the Welfare State, A third study of York dealing only with economic questions*, London, Longman, 1951.

SAARC, Social Charter. Online. Available at: <http://saarc-sdmc.nic.in/pdf/social_charter.pdf> (accessed 14 March 2009).

Salomon, Margot E., 'Globalization of Responsibility: Interdependence and Cooperation in the Protection of Human Rights in International Law', PhD Dissertation, London School of Economics, 2003.

—— 'Towards a Just International Order: A Commentary on the First Session of the UN Task Force on the Right to Development', *Netherlands Quarterly of Human Rights* 23(3), 2005, 409–38.

—— with Sengupta, Arjun, *The Right to Development: Obligations of States and the Rights of Minorities and Indigenous Peoples*, London, Minority Group International, 2003.

Sampford, Charles, 'Reconceiving the rule of law for a globalizing world' in Spencer Zifck (ed.), *Globalization and the Rule of Law*, London/New York, Routledge, 2005, pp 9–31.

Sannerholm, Richard, 'Legal, Judicial and Administrative Reforms in Post-Conflict Societies: Beyond the Rule of Law Template', *Journal of Conflict & Security Law* 12(1), 2007, 65–94.

Sarkar, Amin U., 'Sustainable development and technology', *The Environmentalist* 17, 1997, 97–102.

Schachter, Oscar, 'The Evolving International Law of Development', *Columbia Journal of Transnational Law* 15, 1976, 1–16.

—— *International Law in Theory and Practice*, Dordrecht, London, Martinus Nijhoff, 1991.

Schwebel, Stephen M., 'The Effect of Resolutions of the U.N. General Assembly on

Customary International Law', *Proceedings of the American Society of International Law* 1979, pp 301–309.

SDPI (Sustainable Development Policy Institute), *Research and News Bulletin* 11(2), March–Oct. 2004. Online. Available at: <www.sdpi.org/help/research_and_news_bulletin/march_Oct_2004/bulletin_pdf> (accessed 16 July 2007).

Seil-Hohenveldern, Ignaz, 'International Economic "Soft Law" ', *Recuiel Des Cours* 163(2), 1979, 165–246.

Sen, Amartya, 'Equality of What?' in Amartya Sen, *Choice, Welfare and Measurement*, Oxford, Basil Blackwell, 1982, pp 353–69, p 355.

—— 'Rights and Agency', *Philosophy and Public Affairs* 11(1), 1982, 11–39.

—— *Poor, Relatively Speaking*, Dublin, Economic and Social Research Institute, Fifteenth Geary Lecture, 1983.

—— 'Rights and Capabilities' in Ted Honderich (ed.), *Morality and Objectivity – A Tribute to J.L. Mackie*, London, Routledge & Kegan Paul, 1985, pp 130–48.

—— 'Rights as Goals' in S. Guest and A. Milne (eds), *Equality and Discrimination: Essays in Freedom and Justice*, Stuttgart, Franz Steiner, 1985, pp 11–25.

—— *Commodities and Capabilities*, London, North-Holland, 1985.

—— 'Concepts and Critiques' in Geoffrey Hawthorn (ed.), *The Standard of Living*, Cambridge, Cambridge University Press, 1987, pp 1–19.

—— 'Lives and Capabilities', in Geoffrey Hawthorn (ed.), *The Standard of Living*, Cambridge, Cambridge University Press, 1987, pp 20–38.

—— *Inequality Re-examined*, Oxford, Clarendon Press, 1992.

—— *Development as Freedom*, Oxford, Oxford University Press, 1999.

—— 'Consequential Evaluation and Practical Reason', *The Journal of Philosophy* 97(9), 2000, 477–502.

—— 'Human Rights and Capabilities', *Journal of Human Development* 6(2), 2005, 151–66.

Sengupta, Arjun, 'Realizing the Right to Development', *Development and Change* 31, 2000, 553–78.

—— 'On the Theory and Practice of the Right to Development', *Human Rights Quarterly* 24, 2002, 837–89.

—— 'The Right to Development and Human Rights: A Social Choice Approach to Implementation and Measurement', in Arjun Sengupta, et al. (ed.), *Reflections on the Right to Development*, New Delhi, Sage, 2006, pp 321–49.

—— 'The Right to Development as a Human Right', pp 1–16. Online. Available at: <www.hsph.harvard.edu/fxbcenter/FXBC_wp—Sengupta.pdf> (accessed 11 July 2006).

Sepulveda, Magdalena, 'Obligations of "International Assistance and Co-operation" in an optional protocol to the International Covenant on Economic, Social and Cultural Rights', *Netherlands Quarterly of Human Rights* 24(2), 2006, 271–303.

Sfeir-Younis, Alfredo, 'The Right to Development: The Political Economy of Implementation' in *The Right to Development Book, Reflections on the First Four Reports of the Independent Expert on the Right to Development*, Geneva, Franciscans International, 2004, pp 46–61 at p 56.

Shah, Nasim Hassan, 'Public Interest Litigation as a means of social justice', *PLD Journal* 1993, 31–4 at 34.

Shah, Niaz A., *Women, the Koran and International Human Rights Law: the Experience of Pakistan*, Leiden, Martinus Nijhoff Publishers, 2006.

Shaw, Malcolm N., *International Law*, Cambridge, Cambridge University Press, Fifth Edition, 2003.

Shestack, Jerome J., 'Philosophic Foundations of Human Right', *Human Rights Quarterly* 20, 1998, 201–34.

Sloan, Blaine, 'The Binding Force of a "Recommendation" of the General Assembly', *British Year Book of International Law* XXV, 1948, 1–33.

—— 'General Assembly Resolutions Revisited (Forty Years Later)', *British Year Book of International Law* LVIII, 1987, 39–150.

South, James, *The Genesis of Mediation in Pakistan, a Case Study on the New Commercial Approach to the Region*, Centre for Effective Dispute Resolution (CEDR), UK, Feb. 2007. Online. Available at: <http://www.cedr.co.uk/index.php?location=/library/articles/20070214_195.htm> (accessed 28 Aug 2007).

Steiner, Henry and Alston, Philip, *International Human Rights in Context: Texts and Materials: Law, Politics and Morals*, Oxford, Oxford University Press, 2000.

Stewart, Francis and Wang, Michael, 'Do PRSPs Empower Poor Countries and Disempower the World Bank or is it the Other Way Round?', *Queen Elizabeth House Working Paper No. 108.* Online. Available at: <http://www3.qeh.ox.ac.uk/RePEc/qeh/qehwps/qehwps108.pdf> (accessed 24 March 2007).

—— 'Poverty Reduction Strategy Papers within the Human Rights Perspective' in Philip Alston and Mary Robinson (eds), *Human Rights and Development: Towards Mutual Reinforcement*, Oxford, Oxford University Press, 2005, pp 447–74.

Svensson, Jakob, 'Aid, Growth and Democracy', *Economics and Politics* 11(3), Nov. 1999, 275–97.

Swiss Agency for Development and Cooperation. Online. Available at: <http://web.mit.edu/urbanupgrading/upgrading/resources/organizations/sdc.html> (accessed 28 June 2008).

Talbot, Ian, *Pakistan: A Modern History*, London, C. Hurst, 1998.

Tamanaha, Brian Z., *On the Rule of Law: History, Politics, Theory*, Cambridge, Cambridge University Press, 2004.

Terror Free Tomorrow, 'Pakistan, Results of a New Nationwide Survey by Terror Free Tomorrow'. Online. Available at: <http://www.terrorfreetomorrow.org/upimagestft/Pakistan%20Poll%20Report.pdf> (accessed 14 Sept. 2007).

Teson, Fernando R., 'International Human Rights and Cultural Relativism', *Virginia Journal of International Law* 25(4), 1985, 869–98.

Thirlway, Hugh, 'The Sources of International Law' in Malcolm D. Evans (ed.), *International Law*, Oxford, Oxford University Press, 2003, pp 117–44.

Thirwall, A.P., *Growth & Development*, New York, Palgrave Macmillan, Seventh Edition, 2003.

Thompson, Janna, *Justice and World Order A Philosophical Inquiry*, London, Routledge, 1992.

Todaro, Michael P. and Smith, Stephen C., *Economic Development*, Harlow, Addison Wesley, Ninth Edition, 2006.

Townsend, Peter (ed.), *The Concept of Poverty, Working Papers on Methods of Investigation and Life-Styles of the Poor in Different Countries*, London, Heinemann, 1971.

Turk, Danilo, 'Participation of Developing Countries in Decision-Making Process' in S.R. Chowdhury et al. (eds), *International Law and Development*, Dordrecht, London, Martinus Nijhoff Publishers, 1988, pp 341–57.

UK, Department for International Development, 'Eliminating World Poverty: A Challenge for the 21st Century', White Paper on International Development

Strategy, 1997. Online. Available at: <http://www.dfid.gov.uk/Pubs/files/whitepaper1997.pdf> (accessed 6 July 2007).

—— 'Eliminating World Poverty: Making Globalisation Work for the Poor', White Paper on International Development Strategy, 2000. Online. Available at: <http://www.dfid.gov.uk/Pubs/files/whitepaper2000.pdf> (accessed 6 July 2007).

United Nations (UN), *Year Book of the United Nations*, Leiden, Martinus Nijhoff Publishers, vol. 36, 1982.

—— *Year Book of the United Nations*, Leiden, Martinus Nijhoff Publishers, vol. 37, 1983.

—— *Year Book of the United Nations*, Leiden, Martinus Nijhoff Publishers, vol. 38, 1984.

—— *Year Book of the United Nations*, Leiden, Martinus Nijhoff Publishers, vol. 39, 1985.

—— *Year Book of the United Nations*, Leiden, Martinus Nijhoff Publishers, vol. 40, 1986.

—— *Human Development Report*, New York/Oxford, Oxford University Press, 1990.

—— *Human Development Report*, New York/Oxford, Oxford University Press, 1993.

—— *Human Development Report*, New York/Oxford, Oxford University Press, 1996.

—— *Human Development Report*, New York/Oxford University Press, 2007–8.

—— 'Access to Justice Through Integrated Legal Aid Services', Project Document. Online. Available at: <http://www.un.org.pk/undp/governance/prodoc-a2j.doc> (accessed 14 Sept. 2007).

—— 'Human Development'. Online. Available at: <http://hdr.undp.org/hd/> (accessed 26 Feb 2009).

—— 'Integrating human rights with sustainable development', UNDP Policy Document, Jan. 1998. Online. Available at: <www.undp.org> (accessed 9 July 2007).

—— Official Records of the GA 54th Session, 83rd Plenary Meeting, 17 Dec. 1999, A/54//PV.83. Online. Available at: <http://daccessdds.un.org/doc/UNDOC/GEN/N00/277/29/PDF/N0027729.pdf?OpenElement> (accessed 28 Feb. 2009).

—— 'Report of the World Summit for Social Development', Copenhagen, Denmark, 6–12 March 1995, Annex II. Online. Available at: <http://daccessdds.un.org/doc/UNDOC/GEN/N95/116/51/PDF/N9511651.pdf?OpenElement> (accessed 10 April 2007).

—— 'United Nations Development Assistance Framework (UNDAF)'. Online. Available at: <http://www.un.org/special-rep/ohrlls/cca_undaf_prsp.htm> (accessed 28 Feb. 2009).

UNEP (United Nations Environment Programme), 'Declaration on Environment and Development'. Online. Available at: <http://www.unep.org/Documents.Multilingual/Default.asp?DocumentID=78&ArticleID=1163> (accessed 27 April 2007).

UNESCO, *Education for All, Global Monitoring Report*, New York, UNESCO, 2006.

UNGA resolutions. Online. Available at <http://www.un.org/documents/resga.htm> (accessed 28 Oct. 2006).

UNHCHR, 'Human Rights in Development'. Online. Available at: <http://www.unhchr.ch/development/governance.html> (accessed 29 March 2007).

—— 'Principles and Guidelines for a Human Rights Approach to Poverty Reduction Strategies'. Online. Available at: <www.ohchr.org/Documents/publications/povertyStrategiesen.pdf> (accessed 11 Nov. 2008).

—— 'Vienna Declaration and Programme of Action', 1993. Online. Available at: <http://www.unhchr.ch/huridocda/huridoca.nsf/(Symbol)/A.CONF.157.23.En?OpenDocument> (accessed 27 Feb. 2009).

—— 'Pakistan, Conclusions of the eleventh Workshop on regional co-operation for the promotion of human rights in the Asia-Pacific region', 2003. Online. Available at: <http://www.unhchr.ch/html/menu6/islamabad.htm> (accessed 29 Nov. 2006).

UN Secretary-General Report, *Rule of Law and Transitional Justice in Conflict and Post-Conflict Societies*, UN Doc. S.2004/616, 23 Aug. 2004.

USA, 'Millennium Challenge Account'. Online. Available at: <http://www.whitehouse.gov/infocus/developingnations/millennium.html> (accessed 6 July 2007).

Uvin, Peter, *Human Rights and Development*, Bloomfield, Connecticut, Kumarian Press, Inc., 2004.

Vasak, Karel, 'A 30-year struggle, the sustained efforts to give force of law to the Universal Declaration of Human Rights', *UNESCO Courier* 1977, 29.

Verwey, Wil D., 'The New International Economic Order and the Realisation of the Right to Development and Welfare – A Legal Survey' in Frederick E. Snyder and Surakiart Sathirathai (eds), *Third World Attitudes Towards International Law*, Dordrecht, London, Martinus Nijhoff Publishers, 1987, pp 825–49 at p 833.

Walker, David, *Oxford Companion to Law*, Oxford, Clarendon Press, 1980.

Watson, J. Shand, *Theory & Reality in the International Protection of Human Rights*, New York, Transnational Publishers, Inc., 1999, chapter V: 'General Assembly Resolutions as a Source of Human Rights', pp 107–38.

Weeramantry, C.G. Clayton, 'Fundamental Perspective on Equality and Freedom: some Third World Aspects' in Carl Wellman, Saint Louis (ed.), *Equality And Freedom: Past, Present and Future*, Wiesbaden, Germany, Franz Steiner Verlag, 1977.

—— *Universalising International Law*, Leiden, Martinus Nijhoff Publishers, 2004

Wolfensohn, James D., 'Some Reflections on Human Rights and Development' in Philip Alston and Mary Robinson (eds), *Human Rights and Development: Towards Mutual Reinforcement*, Oxford, Oxford University Press, 2005, pp 19–24.

World Bank, *Development and Human Rights: The Role of the World Bank*, Washington, 1998. Online. Available at: <www.worldbank.org/html/extdr/rights/hrtext.pdf> (accessed 8 Feb 2009).

—— 'Pages from World Bank History: the Pearson Commission'. Online. Available at: <www.worldbank.org> (accessed 28 Feb. 2009).

—— 'Poverty Reduction Strategies'. Online. Available at: <www.worldbank.org> (accessed 9 March 2007).

—— 'PovertyNet, Governance'. Online. Available at: <www.worldbank.org> (accessed 30 March 2007).

—— *Attacking Poverty, World Development Report, 2000/2001*, Oxford, Oxford University Press, 2000.

World Commission on Environment and Development, *Our Common Future* (known as the Brundtland Report), Oxford, Oxford University Press, 1987.

World Summit on Sustainable Development. Online. Available at: <www.worldsummit2002.org/> (accessed 16 July 2007).

Yamani, Ahmad Zaki, 'The Eternal Sharia', *New York University Journal of International Law and Politics* 12, 1979, 205–12.

Yusuf, Abdulqawi A., 'Differential Treatment as a Dimension of the Right to

Development' in R.-J. Dupuy (ed.), *The Right to Development at the International Level*, Hague Academy of International Law Workshop, The Hague, Sijhoff & Noordhoff, 1980, 1980, pp 233–45.

Zaman, Mishka, 'Are We Getting Lost in Exclusive Anti-poor, Adjustment Lending Policy Cycles?', *Action Aid Policy Briefs on PRSPs*, January 2002. Online. Available at: <http://www.esrftz.org/ppa/documents/aa_1.pdf> (accessed 12 March 2007).

Newspapers

Ahmad, Noman, 'What our Courts cannot do', *The Dawn* (daily newspaper), 27 Aug. 2007.

News International (daily newspaper), Islamabad, 16 Aug. 2006; 12 Sept. 2006.

Rehman, I.A., 'A Tale of Two Bills', *The Dawn* (daily newspaper), 30 Nov. 2006.

Index

Abi-Saab, George 47, 66
abstention 121–2
Access to Justice Programme (AJP) 204, 216–17, 220–31, 236
accountability of state institutions 85
adultery 192
Afghanistan 150
African Charter 24, 137
African Court on Human and Peoples' Rights 137
aid programmes 2, 12, 99, 123–6, 128
Akehurst, Michael 120
al-Qardawi, Yusuf 179
Alston, Philip 47, 52, 66, 70, 80
analytical jurisprudence 64–6
Anderson, J.N.D. 187–8
Ansah, J.M.M. 14
apartheid 122
Asian Development Bank (ADB) 217, 218
atonement 74
Australia: aid programmes 125; right to development (RTD) and 31, 33
Austria 31; right to development (RTD) and 33

Baderin, Mashood A 184, 185
Bangladesh 148
Bedjaoui, Muhammad 45, 47, 49, 50, 58, 86–7, 88
behaviouralism 67
Belgium 31; right to development (RTD) and 33
Benin: right to development (RTD) in 25
Bhutto, Benazir 158
Bhutto, Zulfikar Ali 149
bonded labour: prohibition of 159–61
Brierly, J.L. 116, 134
Brownlie, Ian 47
Brundtland Report 90
Bulgaria: right to development (RTD) in 25
Bunn, I.D. 14
Burundi: right to development (RTD) in 25
Bush, George W. 128

Canada: right to development (RTD) and 31, 33
capability approach 35–7, 41; human rights and 37–9; Islamic perspective 40; list of capabilities 39; realizing capabilities through the RTD 39–40
Cassese, Antonio 46
Central African Republic: right to development (RTD) in 25
Charlesworth, Hilary 95, 181
Chinkin, C.N. 131
Choudhry, Iftikhar 149, 150, 151, 157, 167, 168
Choudhry, Masudul Alam 190
Cold War 6, 8
collective rights 44–5; RTD as 58–9, 234
Congo, Democratic Republic of: right to development (RTD) in 25
consultation on the RTD 54, 78, 96–8, 152, 219
content of the RTD 56; collective right 58–9; individual right 57–8; right to process of development 59–62
cooperation principle 49–50, 86–7, 92, 235
Cranston, Maurice 67
Crawford, James 46
culture: cultural relativism 181–4; right to development (RTD) and 95–6
custom: *Sharia'ah* law and 176
customary international law 115–16, 140; General Assembly recommendations 116–19; *opinio juris* 116, 119–22; state practice 116, 122–6; USA as persistent objector 126–8

Declaration on Right to Development 1–2, 4, 22, 108, 109; as compromise document 93–4; concept of development 87–90; determination of value 135–40; drafting of 81–3; international cooperation 86–7; legal status in international law 113–14, 140–1; national dimension of the RTD 152–3; New International Economic Order (NIEO) and 94–5; participation 84–6; as soft law 130–2; unity of human rights and 83–4; vagueness and imprecision 92–3; women's rights and 95–6
decolonization 19–20
Denmark 31; aid programmes 125–6; drafting of Declaration and 83
developing countries 20, 25, 26–7, 41; sustainable development and 91
development: aid programmes 2, 12, 99, 123–6, 128; concept of 87–90; human rights and 8–11, 34, 124; right to *see* right to development (RTD); sustainable 90–2
Development Compact 101–3, 108–9, 203; critical appraisal 104–5; debate in the working group 103–4
Donnelly, Jack 45–6, 48, 50, 52, 66, 70
Dupuy, Rene Jean 131, 132
Dworkin, Ronald 67, 68

economic development *see* development
Eide, Asbjorn 89
enforceability *see* justiciability of the RTD
environmental issues 163–5; sustainable development 90–2
equality of citizens 162; access to justice and 220–1
Eritrea: right to development (RTD) in 25
Espiel, H.G. 47
Esposito, John L. 172
ethical jurisprudence 66–8
Ethiopia: right to development (RTD) in 25
European Union (EU): right to development (RTD) and 2, 31, 32, 33, 234
evidence 192

Falk, Richard 132–3
Falkland Islands 46
federalism 151–2
feminism: right to development (RTD) and 95
Fenwick, Charles G. 134
Finland: drafting of Declaration and 83
Food and Agricultural Organization (FAO) 26
forced labour: prohibition of 159–61
foreign development aid programmes 2, 12, 99, 123–6, 128
France 31; drafting of Declaration and 82; right to development (RTD) and 33
fraternity: principle of 49
freedom: development and 89
Friedmann, Wolfgang 134

General Agreement on Tariffs and Trade (GATT) 27
General Assembly of the UN: competency 135; international law and 116–19, 133; voting trends 29–32, 137
general principles of international law 128–30
Germany 31; drafting of Declaration and 82, 83; right to development (RTD) and 33, 234
Ghai, Yash 53
Global Consultation on the RTD 54, 78, 96–8, 152, 219
goals: rights as 66–8

Hague Academy of International Law 21
Higgins, Roslyn 116
high-level task force 105–7; evaluation of reports 107–8
Hobbes, Thomas 70
Hohfeld, Wesley Newcomb 64–6, 67
human rights 41; capability approach and 37–9; development and 8–11, 34, 124; Islam and 5, 40, 71, 96, 179–80, 181–6, 198; pluralistic foundations of human rights 70–1; poverty and 38–9; poverty-reduction programmes and 205–7; unity of 83–4; *see also* right to development (RTD)

Iceland: drafting of Declaration and 83
ijma (consensus of opinion) 174–5
Independent Expert on the RTD 10, 23, 24, 35, 59–61, 89, 100–1, 102, 103, 105, 109, 124, 203
India: public interest litigation (PIL) 156, 166, 167
individuals: as subjects of the RTD 55–6
International Commission of Jurists 34
International Labour Organization (ILO) 26, 99
international law: custom 115–28, 140; Declaration as soft law 130–2; general principles 128–30; justiciability of the RTD 73; legal status of the RTD in

113–14; RTD and new sources 132–5, 141; sources 114–15
International Monetary Fund (IMF) 99, 204, 208–9, 218, 235; Poverty Reduction Strategy 8
international solidarity 49–50
Iqbal, Muhammad 187
Islam 13; as basis for state of Pakistan 4–5, 147, 150, 171, 186–96, 201–2; capability approach and 40; human rights and 5, 40, 71, 96, 179–80, 181–6, 198; right to development (RTD) and 5, 200–1; rights and duties in Islamic jurisprudence 74; *Sharia'ah see Sharia'ah* law; social justice and 190–1, 236; women's rights and 162
Ivory Coast (Côte d'Ivoire): right to development (RTD) in 25

Japan: drafting of Declaration and 83; right to development (RTD) and 31, 33
Jennings, Robert 132
Jinnah, Muhammad Ali 186–8
justice 71
justiciability of the RTD 43, 62–3, 75; ethical jurisprudence 66–8; international level 73; Maastricht Guidelines 68–9; national level 71–3, 102; pluralistic foundations of human rights 70–1; rights and duties in analytical jurisprudence 64–6; rights and duties in Islamic jurisprudence 74

Kelsen, Hans 116
Key Donor Countries (KDC) 29, 31
Khan, Ayub 148
Khan, Ghulam Ishaq 192
Kiwanuka, R.N. 94

Lauterpacht, Hersch 116
legal positivism 67
lex ferenda 119, 121
life: right to 84, 158–9
Like-Minded Group (LMG) 27–8, 29
Locke, John 70
locus standi 157–8

Malawi: right to development (RTD) in 25
Malaysia 29, 108
Malik, 'Uzir Abdul 190
Marks, Stephen 25
Marxism 71
maslahah (public interest) 3, 5, 13, 40
M'Baye, Keba 20, 45, 47, 49, 71, 84, 88
Mendelson, Maurice 119, 120
Mestagh, Karel de Vey 49
Millennium Challenge Account (MCA) 127–8
Millennium Development Goals (MDGs) 24, 106, 107, 128
Muhammad, Prophet 174, 183
Musharraf, General 149–50, 151, 192, 193

nation states *see* states
natural law 71
Netherlands: drafting of Declaration and 82
New International Economic Order (NIEO) 20–1, 26, 50, 80, 86; Declaration on Right to Development and 94–5
New Partnership for Africa's Development (NEPAD) 102–3
Non-Aligned Movement (NAM) 27, 29
Norway 31; aid programmes 125–6; drafting of Declaration and 83
Nozick, Robert 37, 66, 67, 70
Nussbaum, Martha 40

Open-Ended Working Group (OEWG) 23, 24, 78, 100–1, 104, 234, 235
opinio juris 116, 119–22
Orford, Anne 26–7
Organization for Economic Co-operation and Development (OECD) 128; Development Assistance Committee (DAC) 101, 102, 122–4
Osmani, S.R. 9, 60–1

Pakistan 2–3, 145–6, 233; Access to Justice Programme (AJP) 204, 216–17, 220–31, 236; constitution 4–5, 147–52, 154–6, 156–7, 169, 171, 189; drafting of Declaration and 82; economy 72, 146–7, 193–4; environmental protection 163–5; equality of citizens 162; federalism 151–2; governance 217–18; implications of Pakistan's experience for other Muslim countries 200–1; institutions 6–7, 12; Islam as basis of state 4–5, 147, 150, 171, 186–96, 201–2; Jinnah's vision for 186–8; judicial system 167–9, 191–3, 197–200, 219–20, 226–7, 235; political participation 161; poverty-reduction programmes 25, 86, 92, 194–5, 212–31; Principles of Policy 165–6; prohibition of forced labour 159–61; public interest litigation (PIL) 3, 5, 156–69, 237; reasons for choice as case study 4–8; right to life 158–9; role in mainstream RTD debate 153–4; rule of law 218–19; towards a

Pakistan – *Contd.*
rights-based approach to development 12; women in 152, 162–3, 184, 192, 194, 198–9; *zakat* (poor rate) 193–4, 213
participation: in development 84–6; political 161; poverty-reduction programmes 209–10, 212–16
peoples: as subject of the RTD 54–5
Piron, Laure-Helene 104
pluralistic foundations of human rights 70–1
political participation 161
Portugal: right to development (RTD) in 25
poverty 89, 124; definition 11, 204–5; human rights and 38–9
poverty-reduction programmes 8, 11, 25, 102, 203–4, 231–2; background 204–5; comprehensive 211; country ownership of 207–9, 212–16; governance and 217–18; human rights approach 205–7; long-term 211–12; OHCHR guidelines 205–7; Pakistan 25, 86, 92, 194–5, 212–31; participation 209–10, 212–16; partnership in 211; right to development (RTD) and 207–20
precautionary principle 164
public interest *(maslahah)* 3, 5, 13, 40, 171, 236; implications of Pakistan's experience for other Muslim countries 200–1; as purpose of *Sharia'ah* law 176–8; relevance to the RTD 178–80
public interest litigation (PIL) 3, 5, 156, 169, 237; analysis of case law 157–8; conceptual basis 156–7; environmental protection 163–5; equality of citizens 162; impact of current judicial crisis 167–9; political participation 161; Principles of Policy 165–6; problems and prospects 166–7; right to life 158–9; women's rights 162–3

Qur'an 13, 173–4, 182, 185, 190

Rawls, John 70
realization of the RTD 96; current status 100–8; global consultation 54, 78, 96–8, 152, 219
regionalism 115
relativism: cultural 181–4
right to development (RTD) 8–11, 12, 41, 233–7; background 1–3; current status 23–4, 100–8; from economic sovereignty to the RTD 19–22; international dimension 3–4; North-South divide 26–7; political positions of states and groups of states 27–9; realizing capabilities through 39–40; reasons for choice of Pakistan as case study 4–8; regional and national perspectives 24–6; Vienna Declaration (1993) 22–3; *see also* individual topics
right to life 84, 158–9
Rivero, J. 47
Rubin, Nancy 127
rule of law 218–19

Salomon, M.E. 14
Schachter, Oscar 122, 125
self-determination right 44–9
Sen, Amartya 7, 11, 35–9, 41, 66, 67, 68, 71, 74, 89, 182
Senegal: right to development (RTD) in 25
Shah, Niaz A. 184, 185
Sharia'ah law 3, 5, 13–14, 40, 171, 236; human rights and 181–6; juristic techniques 175–6; meaning 171–3; purpose 176–8; social justice and 190–1, 236; sources 173–5
Sharif, Nawaz 161
Shatibi 177
Shia Islam 172–3
Sloan, Blaine 117, 119, 133, 135
Smith, Stephan C. 87
social justice: Islam and 190–1, 236
social progress 51
soft law: Declaration on Right to Development as 130–2
solidarity: international 49–50
sources of international law 114–15; RTD and new sources 132–5, 141
sources of *Sharia'ah* law 173–5
sources of the RTD 44, 74; other international instruments 51–2; right to self-determination 44–9; UDHR Art 28 48–9; UN Charter Arts 55 and 56 49–50
South Africa 122
South Asian Association for Regional Cooperation (SAARC) 24, 137–8
states: accountability 85; concept of development and 89–90; country ownership of poverty-reduction programmes 207–9, 212–16; customary international law and state practice 116, 122–6; as duty-holders 53–4; justiciability of the RTD at national level 71–3, 102; national dimension of the RTD 152–6; participation in development and 85; as subjects of the RTD 52–4
structural adjustment policies 27

subjects of the RTD 52, 74–5; individuals 55–6; peoples 54–5; states 52–4
Sunnah 174
Sunni Islam 172–3
suo motu jurisdiction 157
sustainable development 90–2
Sweden 31; drafting of Declaration and 83
Switzerland: aid programmes 125

Tehran Conference on Human Rights (1968) 20
terrorism 6, 149, 150
theft 192
Thirlwall, A.P. 87
Thirlway, Hugh 114
tithes 74
Todaro, Michael P. 87
Townsend, Peter 11
treaties 114–15

Uganda: right to development (RTD) in 25
'Umar ibn al-Khattab 177
underdevelopment: causes of 2, 20
United Kingdom 31; aid programmes 126; drafting of Declaration and 83; right to development (RTD) and 33
United Nations: Conference on Trade and Development (UNCTAD) 26; Development Assistance Framework (UNDAF) 34; Development Group (UNDG) 34; Development Programme (UNDP) 39, 41, 138, 205; Economic and Social Council 23, 26; Economic Commission for Europe 99; Education, Scientific and Cultural Organization (UNESCO) 34; First Decade for Eradication of Poverty 11; General Assembly *see* General Assembly; High Commissioner for Human Rights 8, 100, 138, 203–4, 218; human rights and 70; Human Rights Committee 47; Human Rights Council (*formerly* Commission) 12, 24, 32–3, 78; Independent Expert on the RTD 10, 23, 24, 35, 59–61, 89; Open-Ended Working Group (OEWG) 23, 24; right to development (RTD) and 2, 20–7, 29–32, 34, 41, 77–8, 97, 99; self-determination right and 44; World Summit for Social Development 11
United States of America: aid programmes 123; drafting of Declaration and 82–3; human rights in 70; Millennium Challenge Account (MCA) 127–8; as persistent objector 126–8; public interest litigation (PIL) 156; right to development (RTD) and 2, 26–7, 28–9, 31, 80, 94, 96, 122, 126–8; war on terrorism 6, 149, 150
urban development planning 91–2
utilitarianism 36

values 138–9
Van Dyke, Vernon 70
Vienna Conference on Human Rights (1993) 2, 8, 11, 22–3, 28, 41, 84, 122, 127, 234

Weeramantry, C.G. 134
women 184, 185; in Pakistan 152, 162–3, 184, 192, 194, 198–9; participation in development by 85; poverty-reduction programmes and 209–10; right to development (RTD) and 95–6
working groups on RTD 78; debate on Development Compact 103–4; drafting of Declaration 81–3; evaluation of reports 107–8; first working group 79–83; high-level task force 105–7; Open-Ended Working Group (OEWG) 23, 24, 78, 100–1, 104, 234, 235; second 98–100; third 98–100
World Bank 11, 204, 208–9, 217, 220, 235; human rights and 34; Poverty Reduction Strategy 8; structural adjustment policies 27
World Health Organization (WHO) 26
World Trade Organization (WTO) 27, 47, 115, 138

Yamani, Ahmad Zaki 171
Yemen: right to development (RTD) in 25
Yugoslavia: drafting of Declaration and 81–2

zakat (poor rate) 74, 193–4, 213
Zia-ul-Haq, General 149, 171, 189, 191, 192, 199